A·N·N·U·A·L E·D·I·T·I·O·N·S

# The Family 05/06

*Thirty-First Edition*

**EDITOR**

**Kathleen R. Gilbert**

*Indiana University*

Kathleen Gilbert is an associate professor in the Department of Applied Health Science at Indiana University. She received a B.A. in Sociology and an M.S. in Marriage and Family Relations from Northern Illinois University. Her Ph.D. in Family Studies is from Purdue University. Dr. Gilbert's primary areas of interest are loss and grief in a family context, trauma and the family, family process, and minority families. She has published several books and articles in these areas.

*McGraw-Hill/Dushkin*
2460 Kerper Blvd., Dubuque, IA 52001

Visit us on the Internet
***http://www.dushkin.com***

# Credits

1. **Varied Perspectives on the Family**
   Unit photo—© CORBIS/Royalty-Free
2. **Exploring and Establishing Relationships**
   Unit photo—© CORBIS/Royalty-Free
3. **Finding a Balance: Maintaining Relationships**
   Unit photo—© Getty Image/Ryan McVay
4. **Crises—Challenges and Opportunities**
   Unit photo—© Getty Images/Mel Curtis
5. **Families, Now and Into the Future**
   Unit photo—© Getty Images/Bronwyn Kidd

# Copyright

Cataloging in Publication Data
Main entry under title: Annual Editions: The Family. 2005/2006.
1. The Family—Periodicals. I. Gilbert, Kathleen R., *comp.* II. Title: The Family.
ISBN 0–07–310198–2 658'.05 ISSN 0272–7897



Thirty-First Edition

Cover image © Ryan McVay/Getty Images and Photos.com
Printed in the United States of America 1234567890QPDQPD987654 Printed on Recycled Paper

# Editors/Advisory Board

Members of the Advisory Board are instrumental in the final selection of articles for each edition of ANNUAL EDITIONS. Their review of articles for content, level, currentness, and appropriateness provides critical direction to the editor and staff. We think that you will find their careful consideration well reflected in this volume.



# Staff

# Preface

In publishing ANNUAL EDITIONS we recognize the enormous role played by the magazines, newspapers, and journals of the public press in providing current, first-rate educational information in a broad spectrum of interest areas. Many of these articles are appropriate for students, researchers, and professionals seeking accurate, current material to help bridge the gap between principles and theories and the real world. These articles, however, become more useful for study when those of lasting value are carefully collected, organized, and reproduced in a low-cost format, which provides easy and permanent access when the material is needed. That is the role played by ANNUAL EDITIONS.

The purpose of *Annual Editions: The Family 05/06* is to bring to the reader the latest thoughts and trends in our understanding of the family, to identify current concerns as well as problems and potential solutions, and to present alternative views of the family process. The intent of this anthology is to explore intimate relationships as they are played out within the family and, in doing this, to reflect the family's evolving function and importance.

The articles in this volume are taken from professional journals as well as semi-professional publications and popular lay publications aimed at both special populations and a general readership. The selections are carefully reviewed for their currency and accuracy. In some cases, contrasting viewpoints are presented; in others, articles are paired in such a way as to personalize the more impersonal scholarly information. In the current edition, a number of new articles have been added to reflect reviewers' comments. As the reader, you will note the tremendous range in tone and focus of these articles, from first-person accounts to reports of scientific discoveries as well as philosophical and theoretical writings. Some are more practical and applications-oriented, while others are more conceptual and research-oriented.

This anthology is organized to cover many of the important aspects of family and family relationships. The first unit looks at varied perspectives on the family. The second unit examines the beginning steps of relationship building as individuals go through the process of exploring and establishing connections. In the third unit, means of finding and maintaining a relationship balance, for romantic as well as for other intimate relationships, are examined. Unit 4 is concerned with crises and ways in which these can act as challenges and opportunities for families and their members. Finally, unit 5 takes an affirming tone as it looks at family strengths and ways of empowering families.

Instructors can use *Annual Editions: The Family 05/06* as a primary text for lower-level, introductory marriage and family classes, particularly when they tie the content of the readings to basic information on marriage and family. This book can also be used as a supplement to update or emphasize certain aspects of standard marriage and family textbooks. Because of the provocative nature of many of the essays in this anthology, it works well as a basis for class discussion about various aspects of marriage and family relationships.

This edition of *Annual Editions: The Family* contains *World Wide Web* sites that can be used to further explore topics addressed in the articles.

I would like to thank everyone involved in the development of this volume. My appreciation goes to those who sent in *article rating forms* and comments on the previous edition as well as those who suggested articles to consider for inclusion in this edition. To all of the students in my Marriage and Family Interaction class who have contributed critiques of articles, I would like to say thanks.

Anyone interested in providing input for future editions of *Annual Editions: The Family* should complete and return the postage-paid *article rating form* at the end of this book. Your suggestions are much appreciated and contribute to the continuing quality of this anthology.

Kathleen R Gilbert

Kathleen R. Gilbert
*Editor*

# Contents

## UNIT 1
## Varied Perspectives on the Family

Two articles explore different views on how our image of family is influenced by our life experiences as well as societal and cultural constraints.

## UNIT 2
## Exploring and Establishing Relationships

Sixteen articles address factors that influence the formation of close relationships, both romantic and generative.



The concepts in bold italics are developed in the article. For further expansion, please refer to the Topic Guide.

The concepts in bold italics are developed in the article. For further expansion, please refer to the Topic Guide.

The concepts in bold italics are developed in the article. For further expansion, please refer to the Topic Guide.

# UNIT 3
## Finding a Balance: Maintaining Relationships

Twelve articles consider the complex issues relating to relationships. From marriage to parent/child relationships, maintaining relationships requires thought and commitment from members.



The concepts in bold italics are developed in the article. For further expansion, please refer to the Topic Guide.

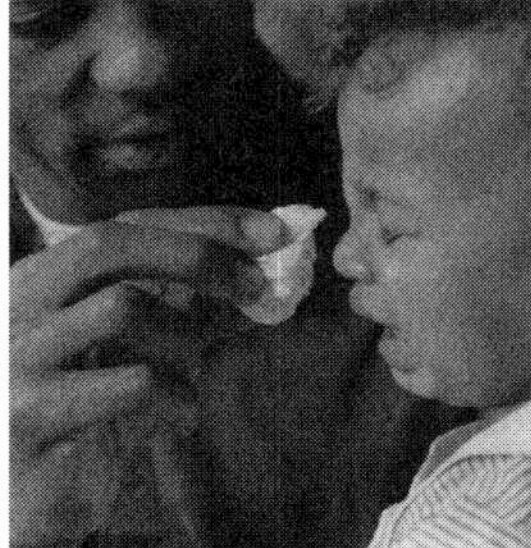

## UNIT 4
## Crises—Challenges and Opportunities

A wide variety of crises, normative and catastrophic, are detailed in thirteen articles. From family violence, stress, and chaos to the intimate crises of infidelity, divorce, and death, these articles provide accounts of devastation and hope.



The concepts in bold italics are developed in the article. For further expansion, please refer to the Topic Guide.

The concepts in bold italics are developed in the article. For further expansion, please refer to the Topic Guide.

## UNIT 5
## Families, Now and Into the Future

Five articles look at means of establishing and/or maintaining health and healthy relationships.



The concepts in bold italics are developed in the article. For further expansion, please refer to the Topic Guide.

The concepts in bold italics are developed in the article. For further expansion, please refer to the Topic Guide.

# Topic Guide

**This topic guide suggests how the selections in this book relate to the subjects covered in your course. You may want to use the topics listed on these pages to search the Web more easily.**

**On the following pages a number of Web sites have been gathered specifically for this book. They are arranged to reflect the units of this *Annual Edition*. You can link to these sites by going to the DUSHKIN ONLINE support site at *http://www.dushkin.com/online/*.**

**ALL THE ARTICLES THAT RELATE TO EACH TOPIC ARE LISTED BELOW THE BOLD-FACED TERM.**

### Abortion

13. The Abortion Wars: 30 Years After Roe v. Wade

### Abuse

2. American Families Are Drifting Apart
22. New Evidence for the Benefits of Never Spanking
31. Hitting Home
32. The Myths and Truths of Family Abduction

### Adoption

25. Adoption by Lesbian Couples

### Aging

11. Sex for Grown-Ups
12. What Turns You On? (Hint: It's Not Work!)
15. Making Time for a Baby
27. The Perma Parent Trap
29. Why We Break Up With Our Siblings
30. The Grandparent as Parent

### Bereavement

16. Barren
39. Terrorism, Trauma, and Children: What Can We Do?

### Biology

3. Are Boys the Weaker Sex?
4. Sexual Stereotypes
6. Can Men and Women Be Friends?
8. Go Ahead, Kiss Your Cousin: Heck, Marry Her if You Want To
14. Brave New Babies
15. Making Time for a Baby
16. Barren
17. Inside the Womb
23. Father Nature: The Making of a Modern Dad

### Birth defects

8. Go Ahead, Kiss Your Cousin: Heck, Marry Her if You Want To
17. Inside the Womb

### Brain development

17. Inside the Womb
18. Who's Raising Baby?
21. The War Over Gay Marriage

### Child care

23. Father Nature: The Making of a Modern Dad
30. The Grandparent as Parent
34. What Kids (Really) Need

### Children

14. Brave New Babies
15. Making Time for a Baby
18. Who's Raising Baby?
22. New Evidence for the Benefits of Never Spanking
23. Father Nature: The Making of a Modern Dad
24. What About Black Fathers?
25. Adoption by Lesbian Couples
26. Are Married Parents Really Better for Children?
28. Oldest, Youngest, or In Between
32. The Myths and Truths of Family Abduction
34. What Kids (Really) Need
39. Terrorism, Trauma, and Children: What Can We Do?

### Communication

6. Can Men and Women Be Friends?
10. Sexual Satisfaction in Premarital Relationships: Associations With Satisfaction, Love, Commitment, and Stability
29. Why We Break Up With Our Siblings
35. For Better or Worse: Couples Confront Unemployment
45. Getting the Word

### Dating

6. Can Men and Women Be Friends?
8. Go Ahead, Kiss Your Cousin: Heck, Marry Her if You Want To
9. Interracial Intimacy
41. Dating After Divorce

### Divorce

32. The Myths and Truths of Family Abduction
40. Marriage and Divorce American Style
41. Dating After Divorce
42. Divorced? Don't Even Think of Remarrying Until You Read This
43. Managing a Blended Family

### Emotions

3. Are Boys the Weaker Sex?
18. Who's Raising Baby?
46. Happiness Explained

### Family and marriage

1. The American Family
16. Barren
19. No Wedding? No Ring? No Problem
20. Marriage at First Sight
21. The War Over Gay Marriage
26. Are Married Parents Really Better for Children?
43. Managing a Blended Family
46. Happiness Explained

### Family interaction

27. The Perma Parent Trap
30. The Grandparent as Parent
45. Getting the Word
46. Happiness Explained
47. Examining Family Rituals
48. Reconnect With Your Family

### Fathers

23. Father Nature: The Making of a Modern Dad
24. What About Black Fathers?

### Finances, family

8. Go Ahead, Kiss Your Cousin: Heck, Marry Her if You Want To
27. The Perma Parent Trap
30. The Grandparent as Parent
38. Home Alone

# World Wide Web Sites

**The following World Wide Web sites have been carefully researched and selected to support the articles found in this reader. The easiest way to access these selected sites is to go to our DUSHKIN ONLINE support site at *http://www.dushkin.com/online/*.**

# AE: The Family 05/06

**The following sites were available at the time of publication. Visit our Web site—we update DUSHKIN ONLINE regularly to reflect any changes.**

## General Sources

### AARP (American Association of Retired Persons)

*http://www.aarp.org*

This major advocacy group for older people includes among its many resources suggested readings and Internet links to organizations that deal with social issues that may affect people and their families as they age.

### Encyclopedia Britannica

*http://www.britannica.com*

This huge "Britannica Internet Guide" leads to a cornucopia of informational sites and reference sources on such topics as family structure,the family cycle, forms of family organization, and other social issues.

### Planned Parenthood

*http://www.plannedparenthood.org*

Visit this well-known organization's home page for links to information on the various kinds of contraceptives (including outercourse and abstinence) and to discussions of other topics related to sexual and reproductive health.

### Social Science Information Gateway

*http://sosig.esrc.bris.ac.uk/*

This is an online catalog of Internet resources relevant to social science education and research. Sites are selected and described by a librarian or subject specialist.

### Sympatico: HealthyWay: Health Links

*http://www1.sympatico.ca/Contents/health/*

This Canadian site, which is meant for consumers, will lead you to many links that are related to sexual orientation. *Sympatico* also addresses aspects of human sexuality as well as reproductive health over the life span.

## UNIT 1: Varied Perspectives on the Family

### American Studies Web

*http://www.georgetown.edu/crossroads/asw/*

This site provides links to a wealth of resources on the Internet related to American studies, from gender to race and ethnicity to demography and population studies.

### Anthropology Resources Page

*http://www.usd.edu/anth/*

Many cultural topics can be accessed from this site from the University of South Dakota. Click on the links to find comparisons of values and lifestyles among the world's peoples.

### Women's Studies Resources

*http://www.inform.umd.edu/EdRes/Topic/WomensStudies/*

This site provides a wealth of resources related to women and their concerns. You can find links to such topics as body image, comfort (or discomfort) with sexuality, personal relationships, pornography, and more.

## UNIT 2: Exploring and Establishing Relationships

### Ask NOAH About Pregnancy: Fertility & Infertility

*http://www.noah-health.org/english/pregnancy/fertility.html*

NOAH (New York Online Access to Health) seeks to provide relevant, timely, and unbiased health information for consumers. At this site, the organization presents extensive links to a variety of resources about infertility treatments and many other issues of pregnancy and possible infertility.

### Bonobo Sex and Society

*http://songweaver.com/info/bonobos.html*

This site, accessed through Carnegie Mellon University, contains an article explaining how a primate's behavior challenges traditional assumptions about male supremacy in human evolution. This interesting site is guaranteed to generate much spirited debate.

### Go Ask Alice!

*http://www.goaskalice.columbia.edu/index.html*

This interactive site of the Columbia University Health Services provides discussion and insight into a number of personal issues of interest to college-age people—and those younger and older.

### The Kinsey Institute for Research in Sex, Gender, and Reproduction

*http://www.indiana.edu/~kinsey/*

The purpose of this Kinsey Institute Web site is to support interdisciplinary research in the study of human sexuality.

### Mysteries of Odor in Human Sexuality

*http://www.pheromones.com*

This is a commercial site with the goal of selling a book by James Kohl. Look here to find topics of interest to nonscientists about pheromones. Check out the diagram of "Mammalian Olfactory-Genetic-Neuronal-Hormonal-Behavioral Reciprocity and Human Sexuality" for a sense of the myriad biological influences that play a part in sexual behavior.

### The Society for the Scientific Study of Sexuality

*http://www.sexscience.org*

The Society for the Scientific Study of Sexuality is an international organization dedicated to the advancement of knowledge about sexuality.

## UNIT 3: Finding a Balance: Maintaining Relationships

### Child Welfare League of America

*http://www.cwla.org*

The CWLA is the largest U.S. organization devoted entirely to the well-being of vulnerable children and their families. This site provides links to information about such issues as teaching morality and values.

### Coalition for Marriage, Family, and Couples Education

*http://www.smartmarriages.com*

CMFCE is dedicated to bringing information about and directories of skill-based marriage education courses to the public. It hopes to lower the rate of family breakdown through couple-empowering preventive education.

**The National Academy for Child Development**

*http://www.nacd.org*

The NACD, dedicated to helping children and adults reach their full potential, presents links to various programs, research, and resources into a variety of family topics.

**National Council on Family Relations**

*http://www.ncfr.com*

This NCFR home page leads to valuable links to articles, research, and other resources on issues in family relations, such as stepfamilies, couples, and children of divorce.

**Positive Parenting**

*http://www.positiveparenting.com*

Positive Parenting is an organization dedicated to providing resources and information to make parenting rewarding, effective, and fun.

**SocioSite**

*http://www.pscw.uva.nl/sociosite/TOPICS/Women.html*

Open this site to gain insights into a number of issues that affect family relationships. It provides wide-ranging issues of women and men, of family and children, and more.

## UNIT 4: Crises—Challenges and Opportunities

**Alzheimer's Association**

*http://www.alz.org*

The Alzheimer's Association, dedicated to the prevention, cure, and treatment of Alzheimer's and related disorders, provides support to afflicted patients and their families.

**Caregiver's Handbook**

*http://www.acsu.buffalo.edu/~drstall/hndbk0.html*

This site is an online handbook for caregivers. Topics include medical aspects and liabilities of caregiving.

**Children & Divorce**

*http://www.hec.ohio-state.edu/famlife/divorce/*

Open this site to find links to articles and discussions of divorce and its effects on the family. Many bibliographical references are provided by the Ohio State University Department of Human Development & Family Science.

**National Crime Prevention Council**

*http://www.ncpc.org*

NCPC's mission is to enable people to create safer and more caring communities by addressing the causes of crime and violence and reducing the opportunities for crime to occur.

**Widow Net**

*http://www.fortnet.org/WidowNet/*

Widow Net is an information and self-help resource for and by widows and widowers. The information is helpful to people of all ages, religious backgrounds, and sexual orientation who have experienced a loss.

## UNIT 5: Families, Now and Into the Future

**National Institute on Aging**

*http://www.nih.gov/nia/*

The NIA presents this home page that will take you to a variety of resources on health and lifestyle issues that are of interest to people as they grow older.

**The North-South Institute**

*http://www.nsi-ins.ca/ensi/about_nsi/research.html*

Searching this site of the North-South Institute—which works to strengthen international development cooperation and enhance gender and social equity—will lead to a variety of issues related to the family and social transitions.

**We highly recommend that you review our Web site for expanded information and our other product lines. We are continually updating and adding links to our Web site in order to offer you the most usable and useful information that will support and expand the value of your Annual Editions. You can reach us at: *http://www.dushkin.com/annualeditions/*.**

# UNIT 1

# Varied Perspectives on the Family

## Unit Selections

1. **The American Family**, Stephanie Coontz
2. **American Families Are Drifting Apart**, Barbara LeBey

## Key Points to Consider

- Why, in the face of strong evidence that the "good old days" weren't all that good, do we cling to the view that life in the past was superior to the present? What are some of the common beliefs about the past in contrast with the present? What is the truth about the quality of life in earlier times?
- What are your expectations for the family, as an institution? How do personally held views of family influence policy? What might be the effects of this?
- What are your views on the changing nature of the American family? Does the change indicate that the family is "drifting apart"? Is there an alternative interpretation?

**Links: www.dushkin.com/online/**
These sites are annotated in the World Wide Web pages.

**American Studies Web**
*http://www.georgetown.edu/crossroads/asw/*

**Anthropology Resources Page**
*http://www.usd.edu/anth/*

**Women's Studies Resources**
*http://www.inform.umd.edu/EdRes/Topic/WomensStudies/*

Our image of what family is and what it should be is a powerful combination of personal experience, family forms we encounter or observe, and attitudes we hold. Once formed, this image informs decision making and interpersonal interaction throughout our lives. It has far-reaching effects: On an intimate level, it influences individual and family development as well as relationships both inside and outside the family. On a broader level, it affects legislation as well as social policy and programming.

In many ways, this image can be positive. It can act to clarify our thinking and facilitate interaction with like-minded individuals. It can also be negative, because it can narrow our thinking and limit our ability to see that other ways of carrying out the functions of family have value. Their very differences can make them seem "bad." In this case, interaction with others can be impeded because of contrasting views.

This unit is intended to meet several goals with regard to perspectives on the family: (1) to sensitize the reader to sources of beliefs about the "shoulds" of the family—what the family should be and the ways in which family roles should be carried out, (2) to show how different views of the family can influence attitudes toward community responsibility and family policy, and (3) to show how views that dominate one's culture can influence awareness of ways of structuring family life.

In the first reading, "The American Family," Stephanie Coontz takes a historical perspective to examine the contrast between common beliefs about the past and the reality of that time. The final reading, "American Families Are Drifting Apart" posits that the American family is drifting apart in that various forces in current American life are destroying the traditional family structure.

# THE AMERICAN FAMILY

**New research about an old institution challenges the conventional wisdom that the family today is worse off than in the past. Essay by Stephanie Coontz**

As the century comes to an end, many observers fear for the future of America's families. Our divorce rate is the highest in the world, and the percentage of unmarried women is significantly higher than in 1960. Educated women are having fewer babies, while immigrant children flood the schools, demanding to be taught in their native language. Harvard University reports that only 4 percent of its applicants can write a proper sentence.

**Things were worse at the turn of the last century than they are today. Most workers labored 10 hours a day, six days a week, leaving little time for family life.**

There's an epidemic of sexually transmitted diseases among men. Many streets in urban neighborhoods are littered with cocaine vials. Youths call heroin "happy dust." Even in small towns, people have easy access to addictive drugs, and drug abuse by middle-class wives is skyrocketing. Police see 16-year-old killers, 12-year-old prostitutes, and gang members as young as 11.

America at the end of the 1990s? No, America at the end of the 1890s.

The litany of complaints may sound familiar, but the truth is that many things were worse at the start of this century than they are today. Then, thousands of children worked full-time in mines, mills and sweatshops. Most workers labored 10 hours a day, often six days a week, which left them little time or energy for family life. Race riots were more frequent and more deadly than those experienced by recent generations. Women couldn't vote, and their wages were so low that many turned to prostitution.

Photograph courtesy of Thomas L. Gavin.

© 1900 A Couple and their eight children sit for a family portrait. Wth smaller families today, mothers are able to spend twice as much time with each child.

In 1900 a white child had one chance in three of losing a brother or sister before age 15, and a black child had a fifty-fifty chance of seeing a sibling die. Children's-aid groups reported widespread abuse and neglect by parents. Men who deserted or divorced their wives rarely paid child support. And only 6 percent of the children graduated from high school, compared with 88 percent today.

Photograph courtesy of Kathryn M. Gavin.

On the 1940s family farm, fathers out working the fields had less time to spend with their families.

Why do so many people think American families are facing worse problems now than in the past? Partly it's because we compare the complex and diverse families of the 1990s with the seemingly more standard-issue ones of the 1950s, a unique decade when every long-term trend of the 20th century was temporarily reversed. In the 1950s, for the first time in 100 years, the divorce rate fell while marriage and fertility rates soared, crating a boom in nuclear-family living. The percentage of foreign-born individuals in the country decreased. And the debates over social and cultural issues that had divided Americans for 150 years were silenced, suggesting a national consensus on family values and norms.

Some nostalgia for the 1950s is understandable: Life looked pretty good in comparison with the hardship of the Great Depression and World War II. The GI Bill gave a generation of young fathers a college education and a subsidized mortgage on a new house. For the first time, a majority of men could support a family and buy a home without pooling their earnings with those of other family members. Many Americans built a stable family life on these foundations.

But much nostalgia for the 1950s is a result of selective amnesia—the same process that makes childhood memories of summer vacations grow sunnier with each passing year. The superficial sameness of 1950s family life was achieved through censorship, coercion and discrimination. People with unconventional beliefs faced governmental investigation and arbitrary firings. African Americans and Mexican Americans were prevented from voting in some states by literacy tests that were not administered to whites. Individuals who didn't follow the rigid gender and sexual rules of the day were ostracized.

*Leave It to Beaver* did not reflect the real-life experience of most American families. While many moved into the middle class during the 1950s, poverty remained more widespread than in the worst of our last three recessions. More children went hungry, and poverty rates for the elderly were more than twice as high as today's.

Even in the white middle class, not every woman was as serenely happy with her lot as June Cleaver was on TV. Housewives of the 1950s may have been less rushed than today's working mothers, but they were more likely to suffer anxiety and depression. In many states, women couldn't serve on juries or get loans or credit cards in their own names.

And not every kid was as wholesome as Beaver Cleaver, whose mischievous antics could be handled by Dad at the dinner table. In 1955 alone, Congress discussed 200 bills aimed at curbing juvenile delinquency. Three years later, LIFE reported that urban teachers were being terrorized by their students. The drugs that were so freely available in 1900 had been outlawed, but many children grew up in families ravaged by alcohol and barbiturate abuse.

Rates of unwed childbearing tripled between 1940 and 1958, but most Americans didn't notice because unwed mothers generally left town, gave their babies up for adoption and returned home as if nothing had happened. Troubled youths were encouraged to drop out of high school. Mentally handicapped children were warehoused in institutions like the Home for Idiotic and Imbecilic Children in Kansas, where a woman whose sister had lived there for most of the 1950s once took me. Wives routinely told pollsters that being disparaged or ignored by their husbands was a normal part of a happier than-average marriage.

**Many of our worries today reflect how much better we want to be, not how much better we used to be.**

Denial extended to other areas of life as well. In the early 1900s, doctors refused to believe that the cases of gonorrhea and syphilis they saw in young girls could have been caused by sexual abuse. Instead, they reasoned, girls could get these diseases from toilet seats, a myth that terrified generations of mothers and daughters. In the 1950s, psychiatrists dismissed incest reports as Oedipal fantasies on the part of children.

Spousal rape was legal throughout the period and wife beating was not taken seriously by authorities. Much of what we now label child abuse was accepted as a normal part of parental discipline. Physicians saw no reason to question parents who claimed that their child's broken bones had been caused by a fall from a tree.

## American Mirror

Muncie, Ind. (pop. 67,476), calls itself America's Hometown. But to generations of sociologists it is better known as America's Middletown—the most studied place in the 20th century American landscape. "Muncie has nothing extraordinary about it," says University of Virginia professor Theodore Caplow, which is why, for the past 75 years, researchers have gone there to observe the typical American family. Muncie's averageness first drew sociologists Robert and Helen Lynd in 1924. They returned in 1935 (their follow-up study was featured in a LIFE photo essay by Margaret Bourke-White). And in 1976, armed with the Lynds' original questionnaires, Caplow launched yet another survey of the town's citizens.

Caplow discovered that family life in Muncie was much healthier in the 1970s than in the 1920s. No only were husbands and wives communicating more, but unlike married couples in the 1920s, they were also shopping, eating out, exercising and going to movies and concerts together. More than 90 percent of Muncie's couples characterized their marriages as "happy" or "very happy." In 1929 the Lynds had described partnerships of a drearier kind, "marked by sober accommodation of each partner to his share in the joint undertaking of children, paying off the mortgage and generally 'getting on.' "

Caplow's five-year study, which inspired a six-part PBS series, found that even though more moms were working outside the home, two thirds of them spent at least two hours a day with their children; in 1924 fewer than half did. In 1924 most children expected their mothers to be good cooks and housekeepers, and wanted their fathers to spend time with them and respect their opinions. Fifty years later, expectations of fathers were unchanged, but children wanted the same—time and respect—from their mothers.

This year, Caplow went back to survey the town again. The results (and another TV documentary) won't be released until December 2000.

—*Sora Song*

There are plenty of stresses in modern family life, but one reason they seem worse is that we no longer sweep them under the rug. Another is that we have higher expectations of parenting and marriage. That's a good thing. We're right to be concerned about inattentive parents, conflicted marriages, antisocial values, teen violence and child abuse. But we need to realize that many of our worries reflect how much better we *want* to be, not how much better we *used* to be.

Fathers in intact families are spending more time with their children than at any other point in the past 100 years. Although the number of hours the average woman spends at home with her children has declined since the early 1900s, there has been a decrease in the number of children per family and an increase in individual attention to each child. As a result, mothers today, including working moms, spend almost twice as much time with each child as mothers did in the 1920s. People who raised children in the 1940s and 1950s typically report that their own adult children and grandchildren communicate far better with their kids and spend more time helping with homework than they did—even as they complain that other parents today are doing a worse job than in the past.

Despite the rise in youth violence from the 1960s to the early 1990s, America's children are also safer now than they've ever been. An infant was four times more likely to die in the 1950s than today. A parent then was three times more likely than a modern one to preside at the funeral of a child under the age of 15, and 27 percent more likely to lose an older teen to death.

If we look back over the last millennium, we can see that families have always been diverse and in flux. In each period, families have solved one set of problems only to face a new array of challenges. What works for a family in one economic and cultural setting doesn't work for a family in another. What's helpful at one stage of a family's life may be destructive at the next stage. If there is one lesson to be drawn from the last millennium of family history, it's that families are always having to play catch-up with a changing world.

Take the issue of working mothers. Families in which mothers spend as much time earning a living as they do raising children are nothing new. They were the norm throughout most of the last two millennia. In the 19th century, married women in the United States began a withdrawal from the workforce, but for most families this was made possible only by sending their children out to work instead. When child labor was abolished, married women began reentering the workforce in ever large numbers.

For a few decades, the decline in child labor was greater than the growth of women's employment. The result was an aberration: the male-breadwinner family. In the 1920s, for the first time, a bare majority of American children grew up in families where the husband provided all the income, the wife stayed home full-time, and they and their siblings went to school instead of work. During the 1950s, almost two thirds of children grew up in such families, an all-time high. Yet that same decade saw an acceleration of workforce participation by wives and mothers that soon made the dual-earner family the norm, a trend not likely to be reversed in the next century.

What's new is not that women make half their families' living, but that for the first time they have substantial control over their own income, along with the social freedom

© Getty Images/Index Stock

In the 1950s, life looked pretty good in comparison with the hardships of the Great Depression and World War II.

to remain single or to leave an unsatisfactory marriage. Also new is the declining proportion of their lives that people devote to rearing children, both because they have fewer kids and because they are living longer. Until about 1940, the typical marriage was broken by the death of one partner within a few years after the last child left home. Today, couples can look forward to spending more than two decades together after the children leave.

The growing length of time partners spend with only each other for company has made many individuals less willing to put up with an unhappy marriage, while women's economic independence makes it less essential for them to do so. It is no wonder that divorce has risen steadily since 1900. Disregarding a spurt in 1946, a dip in the 1950s and another peak around 1980, the divorce rate is just where you'd expect to find it, based on the rate of increase from 1900 to 1950. Today, 40 percent of all marriages will end in divorce before a couple's 40th anniversary. Yet despite this high divorce rate, expanded life expectancies mean that more couples are reaching that anniversary than ever before.

Families and individuals in contemporary America have more life choices than in the past. That makes it easier for some to consider dangerous or unpopular options. But it also makes success easier for many families that never would have had a chance before—interracial, gay or lesbian, and single-mother families, for example. And it expands horizons for most families.

Women's new options are good not just for themselves but for their children. While some people say that women who choose to work are selfish, it turns out that maternal self-sacrifice is not good for children. Kids do better when their mothers are happy with their lives, whether their satisfaction comes from being a full-time homemaker or from having a job.

Largely because of women's new roles at work, men are doing more at home. Although most men still do less housework than their wives, the gap has been halved since the 1960s. Today, 49 percent of couples say they share childcare equally, compared with 25 percent of 1985.

Men's greater involvement at home is good for their relationships with their parents, and also good for their children. Hands-on fathers make better parents than men who let their wives do all the nurturing and childcare: They raise sons who are more expressive and daughters who are more likely to do well in school, especially in math and science.

**The biggest problem is not that our families have changed too much but that our institutions have changed too little.**

In 1900, life expectancy was 47 years, and only 4 percent of the population was 65 or older. Today, life expectancy is 76 years, and by 2025, about 20 percent of Americans will be 65 or older. For the first time, a generation of adults must plan for the needs of both their parents and their children. Most Americans are responding with remarkable grace. One in four households gives the equivalent of a full day a week or more in unpaid care to an aging relative, and more than half say they expect to do so in the next 10 years. Older people are less likely to be impoverished or incapacitated by illness than in the past, and they have more opportunity to develop a relationship with their grandchildren.

Even some of the choices that worry us the most are turning out to be manageable. Divorce rates are likely to remain high, but more non-custodial parents are staying in touch with their children. Child-support receipts are up. And a lower proportion of kids from divorced families are exhibiting problems than in earlier decades. Stepfamilies are learning to maximize children's access to supportive adults rather than cutting them off from one side of the family.

Out-of-wedlock births are also high, however, and this will probably continue because the age of first marriage for women has risen to an all-time high of 25, almost five years above what it was in the 1950s. Women who marry at an older age are less likely to divorce, but they have more years when they are at risk—or at choice—for a nonmarital birth.

Nevertheless, births to teenagers have fallen from 50 percent of all nonmarital births in the late 1970s to just 30 percent today. A growing proportion of women who have a nonmarital birth are in their twenties and thirties and usually have more economic and educational resources than unwed mothers of the past. While two involved parents are generally better than one, a mother's personal maturity, along with her educational and economic status, is a better predictor of how well her child will turn out than her marital status. We should no longer assume that children raised by single parents face debilitating disadvantages.

As we begin to understand the range of sizes, shapes and colors that today's families come in, we find that the differences *within* family types are more important than the differences *between* them. No particular family form guarantees success, and no particular form is doomed to fail. How a family functions on the inside is more important than how it looks from the outside.

The biggest problem facing most families as this century draws to a close is not that our families have changed too much but that our institutions have changed too little. America's work policies are 50 years out of date, designed for a time when most moms weren't in the workforce and most dads didn't understand the joys of being involved in childcare. Our school schedules are 150 years out of date, designed for a time when kids needed to be home to help with the milking and haying. And many political leaders feel they have to decide whether to help parents stay home longer with their kids or invest in better childcare, preschool and afterschool programs, when most industrialized nations have long since learned it's possible to do both.

So America's social institutions have some Y2K bugs to iron out. But for the most part, our families are ready for the next millennium.

---

LIFE IN AMERICA

# AMERICAN FAMILIES
## Are Drifting Apart

*The sexual revolution, women's liberation, relaxation of divorce laws, and greater mobility are fracturing the traditional family structure.*

BY BARBARA LEBEY

A VARIETY OF REASONS—from petty grievances to deep-seated prejudices, misunderstandings to all-out conflicts, jealousies, sibling rivalry, inheritance feuds, family business disputes, and homosexual outings—are cause for families to grow apart. Family estrangements are becoming more numerous, more intense, and more hurtful. When I speak to groups on the subject, I always ask: Who has or had an estrangement or knows someone who does? Almost every hand in the room goes up. Sisters aren't speaking to each other since one of them took the silver when Mom died. Two brothers rarely visit because their wives don't like each other.

A son alienates himself from his family when he marries a woman who wants to believe that he sprung from the earth. Because Mom is the travel agent for guilt trips, her daughter avoids contact with her. A family banishes a daughter for marrying outside her race or religion. A son eradicates a divorced father when he reveals his homosexuality. And so it goes.

The nation is facing a rapidly changing family relationship landscape. Every assumption made about the family structure has been challenged, from the outer boundaries of single mothers raising out-of-wedlock children to gay couples having or adopting children to grandparents raising their grandchildren. If the so-called traditional family is having trouble maintaining harmony, imagine what problems can and do arise in less-conventional situations. Fault lines in Americans' family structure were widening throughout the last 40 years of the 20th century. The cracks became evident in the mid 1970s when the divorce rate doubled. According to a 1999 Rutgers University study, divorce has risen 30% since 1970; the marriage rate has fallen faster; and just 38% of Americans consider themselves happy in their married state, a drop from 53% 25 years ago. Today, 51% of all marriages end in divorce.

How Americans managed to alter their concept of marriage and family so profoundly during those four decades is the subject of much scholarly investigation and academic debate. In a May, 2000, *New York Times Magazine* article titled "The Pursuit of Autonomy," the writer maintains that "the family is no longer a haven; all too often a center of dysfunction, it has become one with the heartless world that surrounds it." Unlike the past, the job that fits you in your 20s is not the job or career you'll likely have in your 40s. This is now true of marriage as well—the spouse you had in your 20s may not be the one you will have after you've gone through your midlife crisis.

In the 1960s, four main societal changes occurred that have had an enormous impact on the traditional family structure. The sexual revolution, women's liberation movement, states' relaxation of divorce laws, and mobility of American families have converged to foster family alienation, exacerbate old family rifts, and create new ones. It must be emphasized, however, that many of these changes had positive outcomes. The nation experienced a strengthened social conscience, women's rights, constraints on going to war, and a growing tolerance for diversity, but society also paid a price.

The 1960s perpetuated the notion that we are first and foremost *entitled* to happiness and fulfillment. It's positively un-American *not* to seek it! This idea goes back to that early period of our history when Thomas Jefferson dropped the final term from British philosopher John Locke's definition of human rights—"life, liberty, and... property"—and replaced it with what would become the slogan of our new nation: "the pursuit of happiness." In the words of author Gail Sheehy, the 1960s generation "expressed their collective personality as idealistic, narcissistic, anti-establishment, hairy, horny and preferably high."

Any relationship that was failing to deliver happiness was being tossed out like an empty beer can, including spousal ones. For at least 20 years, the pharmaceutical industry has learned how to cash in on the American obsession with feeling good by hyping mood drugs to rewire the brain circuitry for happiness through the elimination of sadness and depression.

Young people fled from the confines of family, whose members were frantic, worrying about exactly where their adult children were and what they were doing. There were probably more estrangements between parents and adult children during the 1960s and early 1970s than ever before.

In the wake of the civil rights movement and Pres. Lyndon Johnson's Great Society came the women's liberation movement, and what a flashy role it played in changing perceptions about the family structure. Women who graduated from college in the late 1960s and early 1970s were living in a time when they could establish and assert their independent identities. In Atlanta, Emory Law School's 1968 graduating class had six women in it, the largest number ever to that point, and all six were in the top 10%, including the number-one graduate. In that same period, many all-male colleges opened their doors to women for the first time. No one could doubt the message singer Helen Reddy proclaimed: "I am woman, hear me roar." For all the self-indulgence of the "hippie" generation, there was an intense awakening in young people of a recognition that civil rights must mean equal rights for everyone in our society, and that has to include women.

Full equality was the battle cry of every minority, a status that women claimed despite their majority position. As they had once marched for the right to vote, women began marching for sexual equality and the same broad range of career and job opportunities that were always available to men. Financial independence gave women the freedom to walk away from unhappy marriages. This was a dramatic departure from the puritanical sense of duty that had been woven into the American fabric since the birth of this nation.

For all the good that came out of this movement, though, it also changed forever traditional notions of marriage, motherhood, and family unity, as well as that overwhelming sense of children first. Even in the most-conservative young families, wives were letting their husbands know that they were going back to work or back to school. Many women had to return to work either because there was a need for two incomes to maintain a moderate standard of living or because they were divorced and forced to support their offspring on their own. "Don't ask, don't tell" day-care centers proliferated where overworked, undertrained staff, and two-income yuppie parents, ignored the children's emotional needs—all in the name of equality and to enable women to reclaim their identifies. Some might say these were the parents who ran away from home.

Many states began to approve legislation that allowed no-fault divorce, eliminating the need to lay blame on spouses or stage adulterous scenes in sleazy motels to provide evidence for states that demanded such evidence for divorces. The legal system established procedures for easily dissolving marriages, dividing property, and sharing responsibility for the children. There were even do-it-yourself divorce manuals on bookstore shelves. Marriage had become a choice rather than a necessity, a one-dimensional status sustained almost exclusively by emotional satisfaction and not worth maintaining in its absence. Attitudes about divorce were becoming more lenient, so much so that the nation finally elected its first divorced president in 1980—Ronald Reagan.

With divorced fathers always running the risk of estrangement from their children, this growing divorce statistic has had the predictable impact of increasing the number of those estrangements. Grandparents also experienced undeserved fallout from divorce, since, almost invariably, they are alienated from their grandchildren.

The fourth change, and certainly one of the most pivotal, was the increased mobility of families that occurred during those four decades. Family members were no longer living in close proximity to one another. The organization man moved to wherever he could advance more quickly up the corporate ladder. College graduates took the best job offer, even if it was 3,000 miles away from where they grew up and where their family still lived.

Some were getting out of small towns for new vistas, new adventures, and new job opportunities. Others were fleeing the overcrowded dirty cities in search of cleaner air, a more reasonable cost of living, and retirement communities in snow-free, warmer, more-scenic locations. Moving from company to company had begun, reaching what is now a crescendo of job-hopping. Many young people chose to marry someone who lived in a different location, so family ties were geographically severed for indeterminate periods of time, sometimes forever.

According to Lynn H. Dennis' *Corporate Relocation Takes Its Toll on Society*, during the 10 years from 1989 to 1999, more than 5,000,000 families were relocated one or more times by their employers. In addition to employer-directed moves, one out of five Americans relocated at least once, not for exciting adventure, but for economic advancement and/or a safer place to raise children. From March, 1996, to March, 1997, 42,000,000 Americans, or 16% of the population, packed up and moved from where they were living to another location. That is a striking statistic. Six million of these people moved from one region of the country to another, and young adults aged 20 to 29 were the most mobile, making up 32% of the moves during that year. This disbursement of nuclear families throughout the country disconnected them from parents, brothers, sisters, grandparents, aunts, uncles, and cousins—the extended family and all its adhesive qualities.

Today, with cell phones, computers, faxes, and the Internet, the office can be anywhere, including in the home. Therefore, we can *live* anywhere we want to. If that is the case, why aren't more people choosing to live in the cities or towns where they grew up? There's no definitive answer. Except for the praise heaped on "family values," staying close to family no longer plays a meaningful role in choosing where we reside.

These relocations require individuals to invest an enormous amount of time to reestablish their lives without help from family or old friends. Although nothing can compare to the experience of immigrants who left their countries knowing they probably would never see their families again, the phenomenon of Americans continually relocating makes family relationships difficult to sustain.

Our culture tends to focus on the individual, or, at most, on the nuclear family, downplaying the benefits of extended families, though their role is vital in shaping our lives. The notion of "moving on" whenever problems arise has been a time-honored American concept. Too many people would rather cast aside some family member than iron out the situation and keep the relationship alive. If we don't get along with our father or if our mother doesn't like our choice of mate or our way of life, we just move away and see the family once or twice a year. After we're married, with children in school, and with both parents working, visits become even more difficult. If the family visits are that infrequent, why bother at all? Some children grow up barely knowing any of their relatives. Contact ceases; rifts don't resolve; and divisiveness often germinates into a full-blown estrangement.

In an odd sort of way, the more financially independent people become, the more families scatter and grow apart. It's not a cause, but it is a facilitator. Tolerance levels decrease as financial means increase. Just think how much more we tolerate from our families when they are providing financial support. Look at the divorced wife who depends on her family for money to supplement alimony and child support, the student whose parents are paying all college expenses, or the brother who borrows family money to save his business.

Recently, a well-known actress being interviewed in a popular magazine was asked, if there was one thing she could change in her family, what would it be? Her answer was simple: "That we could all live in the same city." She understood the importance of being near loved ones and how, even in a harmonious family, geographical distance often leads to emotional disconnectedness. When relatives are regularly in each other's company, they will usually make a greater effort to get along. Even when there is dissension among family members, they are more likely to work it out, either on their own or because another relative has intervened to calm the troubled waters. When rifts occur, relatives often need a real jolt to perform an act of forgiveness. Forgiving a family member can be the hardest thing to do, probably because the emotional bonds are so much deeper and usually go all the way back to childhood. Could it be that blood is a thicker medium in which to hold a grudge?

With today's families scattered all over the country, the matriarch or patriarch of the extended family is far less able to keep his or her kin united, caring, and supportive of one another. In these disconnected nuclear families, certain trends—workaholism, alcoholism, depression, severe stress, isolation, escapism, and a push toward continuous supervised activity for children—are routinely observed. What happened to that family day of rest and togetherness? We should mourn its absence.

For the widely dispersed baby boomers with more financial means than any prior generation, commitment, intimacy, and family togetherness have never been high on their list of priorities. How many times have you heard of family members trying to maintain a relationship with a relative via e-mail and answering machines? One young man now sends his Mother's Day greeting by leaving a message for his mom on *his* answering machine. When she calls to scold him for forgetting to call her, she'll get a few sweet words wishing her a happy Mother's Day and his apology for being too busy to call or send a card! His sister can expect the same kind of greeting for her birthday, but only if she bothers to call to find out why her brother hadn't contacted her.

Right now, and probably for the foreseeable future, we will be searching for answers to the burgeoning problems we unwittingly created by these societal changes, but don't be unduly pessimistic. Those who have studied and understood the American psyche are far more optimistic. The 19th-century French historian and philosopher Alexis de Tocqueville once said of Americans, "No natural boundary seems to be set to the effort of Americans, and in their eyes what is not yet done, is only what they have not yet attempted to do." Some day, I hope this mindset will apply not to political rhetoric on family values, but to bringing families back together again.

---

***Barbara LeBey****, an Atlanta, Ga.-based attorney and former judge, is the author of* Family Estrangements—How They Begin, How to Mend Them, How to Cope with Them.

# UNIT 2

# Exploring and Establishing Relationships

## Unit Selections



## Key Points to Consider

- Is it possible for men and women to be friends without their relationship becoming a sexual one? Is sexual tension between men and women inevitable? Defend your answer.
- What are your attitudes about abortion? What do you think of the current state of the abortion debate? How do you see it being resolved?
- Do you see children as a part of your life? Why or why not? At what age do you think one should stop considering having a child? What should be the determining factor? How would you respond if you learned you could not have children? Would you consider adoption?

## Links: www.dushkin.com/online/

These sites are annotated in the World Wide Web pages.

**Ask NOAH About Pregnancy: Fertility & Infertility**
*http://www.noah-health.org/english/pregnancy/fertility.html*

**Bonobo Sex and Society**
*http://songweaver.com/info/bonobos.html*

**Go Ask Alice!**
*http://www.goaskalice.columbia.edu/index.html*

**The Kinsey Institute for Research in Sex, Gender, and Reproduction**
*http://www.indiana.edu/~kinsey/*

**Mysteries of Odor in Human Sexuality**
*http://www.pheromones.com*

**The Society for the Scientific Study of Sexuality**
*http://www.sexscience.org*

By and large, humans are social animals, and as such, we seek out meaningful connections with other humans. John Bowlby, Mary Ainsworth, and others have proposed that this drive toward connection is biologically based and is at the core of what it means to be human. However it plays out in childhood and adulthood—the need for connection, to love and be loved, is a powerful force moving us to establish and maintain close relationships. At the same time, our biology influences the way in which we relate to each other and the way in which we create and maintain relationships.

As we explore various possibilities, we engage in the complex business of relationship building. In this business, many processes occur simultaneously: Messages are sent and received; differences are negotiated; assumptions and expectations are or are not met. The ultimate goals are closeness and continuity.

How we feel about others and what we see as essential to these relationships play an important role in our establishing and maintaining relationships. In this unit, we look at factors that underlie the establishment of relationships as well as the beginning stages of relationships.

The first subsection explores gender differences and their influences in relationships and on how we relate to the world. The first article, "Are Boys the Weaker Sex?" responds to the question with a strong affirmative, and complements that with a presentation of ways in which society can compensate for boys' weaknesses. "Sexual Stereotypes" questions Bateman's principle that says men are promiscuous and females are choosey. "In Praise of Nurturing Men" confronts the conflict in our culture, between a positive view of women who take on traditional men's roles and a negative one of men who do the same with traditional women's roles.

The second subsection takes a broad look at factors that influence the building of meaningful connections and at the beginning stages of adult relationships. The first essay, "Can Men and Women Be Friends?" explores the nature of male-female friendship relationships and questions the assumption that these relationships are inherently sexualized. For all its power, love is not the only requirement for a satisfying, long-lasting relationship. The second article in this section, "Love is *Not* All You Need," describes six components of a successful relationship.

In the third subsection, mate selection is examined. "Go Ahead, Kiss Your Cousin: Heck, Marry Her if You Want To" may surprise some readers. In it, the authors discuss one of the more common forms of marriage across the globe—marriage between cousins. The next article, "Interracial Intimacy," discusses an increasingly common phenomenon, dating and marriage of couples who are of different racial and ethnic backgrounds.

The next section addresses an important aspect of adult relationships: sexuality. "Sexual Satisfaction in Premarital Relationships" looks at the relationship of sexual satisfaction in premarital relationships and such relationship factors as satisfaction, love, commitment, and stability and finds that it is significantly associated with all of these factors. "What Turns You On? (Hint: It's Not Work!)" looks at the results of a large-scale study of adults in midlife and finds that, at this age, adults are more comfortable in their sexuality.

The fifth subsection looks at conception and pregnancy. "The Abortion Wars," the first article, examines the current state of things 30 years after Roe v. Wade. Both sides continue to battle, as no middle ground has (or perhaps can be) found. "Brave New Babies" explores new fertility technologies and the ethical question of how these technologies should be used. The question of using these technologies to select children who will not suffer from known genetic illness, but should they be used to "balance" families? Is gender an appropriate selection criteria for implantation? "Making Time for a Baby" presents a controversial position that waiting to have children puts women at risk of never being able to have a child.

In the final subsection, two articles focus on the idea of the next generation. "Inside the Womb" discusses the prenatal world of developing babies. Much has been learned in the past few years that has enriched our understanding of what this world is like. Finally, "Who's Raising Baby?" questions the role of caregivers for babies as they develop their sense of self as well as their first relationships as they begin to interact with the world around them.

# Are Boys the Weaker Sex?

## *Science says yes. But society is trying to deal with male handicaps*

BY ANNA MULRINE

Sandy Descourouez worries about her sons. The eldest, 18-year-old Greg, was never the chatty type, but he became positively withdrawn following his parents' nasty divorce a decade ago. Last year, Greg's problems erupted into the open: He was arrested for stealing a golf cart and caught smoking marijuana. David, 13—loving, messy, and disorganized—struggles with borderline grades and attention deficit disorder. Sandy's baby, 2 1/2-year-old Luke, is a one-boy demolition derby. But his reckless energy isn't her main cause of concern. While the toddler strings together sound effects with reasonably good results, he rarely utters a word.

Sandy initially took Greg's silence for male reserve—that is, until she happened on his journal. The teenager's diary roiled with frustration and pain. Perhaps to positive effect: Greg wrote a letter to his absent father and reached out for help. "I don't know how to talk about these things," he wrote, "and I know you don't either, so maybe we can help each other."

**Boys earn 70 percent of the D's and F's doled out by teachers.**

Sandy's "boys will be boys" sighs gave way to bewilderment—and fear. The Aurora, Ill., real-estate broker realized that all three sons had problems very distinct from those she had encountered in her daughter, a champion speller; problems that needed attention.

The travails of the Descourouez family mirror America's struggle with its sons. "We are experiencing a crisis of the boy next door," says William Pollack, a clinical psychologist at Harvard University and author of *Real Boys*. Across the country, boys have never been in more trouble: They earn 70 percent of the D's and F's that teachers dole out. They make up two thirds of students labeled "learning disabled." They are the culprits in a whopping 9 of 10 alcohol and drug violations and the suspected perpetrators in 4 out of 5 crimes that end up in juvenile court. They account for 80 percent of high school dropouts and attention deficit disorder diagnoses. And they are less likely to go to college than ever before. By 2007, universities are projected to enroll 9.2 million women to 6.9 million men.

**Truth to power**. That's not what America expects from its boys. "Maybe because men enjoy so much power and prestige in society, there is a tendency to see boys as shoo-ins for success," says child psychologist Michael Thompson, coauthor of *Raising Cain*. "So people see in boys signs of strength where there are none, and they ignore all of the evidence that they are in trouble."

But that evidence is getting tougher than ever to overlook. Today, scientists are discovering very real biological differences that can make boys more impulsive, more vulnerable to benign neglect, less efficient classroom learners—in sum, the weaker sex. "The notion of male vulnerability is so novel, but the biological facts support it," says Sebastian Kraemer, a child psychiatrist in London and author of a recent *British Medical Journal* article on male fragility. "We're only just now beginning to understand the underlying weakness of men, for so many centuries almost universally projected onto women."

What's more, social pressure often compounds biological vulnerability. "Boys today are growing up with tremendous expectations but without adequate emotional fuel or the tools they need to succeed in school or sustain deep relationships," says Eli Newberger, a pediatrician at Boston Children's Hospital and author of *The Men They Will Become*. Girls now outnumber boys in student government, honor societies, school newspapers, and debating clubs. A recent study found girls ahead of boys in almost every measure of well-being: Girls feel closer to their families, have higher aspirations, and even boast better assertiveness skills. "I regularly see girls who are both valedictorian and captain of the soccer team, but I almost never see that in boys," says Leonard Sax, a family physician and psychologist in Poolesville, Md.

Schools are taking note, too—and they are beginning to act. Early childhood specialists, concerned with ever accelerating curriculum demands, are advocating delayed entrance of boys into kindergarten, to give them time to catch up with girls developmentally. Other districts are experimenting with single-sex classrooms within coed schools, in the hopes that all-boy classes will allow boys to improve standardized test scores in reading and writing, much the way girls have narrowed the gap in math and science. (Currently, the average 11th-grade boy writes with the proficiency of the average eighth-grade girl.) In response to charges of the "feminization" of the classroom—including, critics argue, female teachers with too little tolerance for the physicality of boys—schools are beginning to re-examine their attitudes toward male activity levels and even revamp disciplinary techniques.

## Boys make up two thirds of learning-disabled students.

The measures aren't without skeptics. "Isn't it ironic that it's only been in the last two decades that we've really considered making schools equitable for girls," says David Sadker, an American University professor and pioneer in research on girls' treatment in the classroom. "And now people are already saying, 'Whoa, too much time on girls. Let's get back to boys.'"

**Pole position**. Yet the latest research not only documents boys' unexpected vulnerabilities but indicates that they can be traced back to the womb. While more boys than girls are conceived (the speculation is that sperm carrying the male's Y chromosomes swim faster than those carrying the larger X), this biological pole position doesn't last long, says Kraemer. Perhaps to offset the speed advantage, when mothers experience stress, male embryos are more likely to perish. The male fetus is at greater risk of peril from almost all obstetric complications, including brain damage, cerebral palsy, and premature birth. By the time a baby boy enters the world, he is trailing the average girl, developmentally, by six weeks.

Male newborns are also more emotionally demonstrative than females—a fact that has been shown experimentally despite the cultural stereotype to the contrary. When asked to rate photos for expressiveness, adults who had not been told the children's sex were far more likely to dub boys "more intensely expressive" than girls. And when researchers intentionally misidentified the boys as girls, adults gave the boys presumed to be girls the highest expressiveness marks. In other words, their actual perceptions trumped the stereotypes.

What's particularly interesting, says Thompson, is that while there is evidence that boys may feel more stress in emotional situations, they routinely show less. When placed within earshot of a crying baby, boys have higher increases in heart rate and sweatier palms than girls. But their behavior belies their biological reaction: Their typical response is to turn off the speaker broadcasting the crying.

Judy Chu, a researcher at Harvard University, has also noted how boys' behavior often masks emotional inclinations. "Boys are a lot more attuned and a lot more sensitive than people give them credit for," she says. Chu spent two years having conversations with a group of boys in a preschool classroom outside Boston. At age 4, the boys candidly discussed their feelings about subjects that ranged from sharing toys to hurt feelings. "They were insightful in ways I hadn't expected—so articulate and attentive," says Chu. Over time, however, as the expectations of parents, teachers, and peers compounded, the boys' behavior changed. "They became inattentive, indirect, and inarticulate," says Chu, "and self-conscious about what other boys thought." Chu recalls one child who was friends with a preschool group of kids who had dubbed themselves "the mean team." "I'm friends with all of the girls," he told Chu. "But if Bill [the unofficial leader of the team] finds that out, he'll fire me from the team." As the result of these observations, Chu firmly believes that boys lose their voice, much as girls do in adolescence, and begin to camouflage feelings and behaviors that might put them in conflict with other boys.

## Girls outnumber boys in student councils and debate clubs.

Their friendships also begin to change. "We associate girls with the sharing of secrets, the emotional intimacy, and boys with the sports and activity-oriented friendships," says Niobe Way, a professor of psychology at New York University. "But what's interesting is that these very tough boys talk about wanting friends to share their secrets with, to confide in."

She recalls Malcolm, great in sports, admired by the other boys. One day, Malcolm learned that one of his closest friends had been talking about him and began to cry. "The conventional wisdom is that gossip and arguments with friends don't affect boys or that they'll just 'fight it out,' then let it roll off their backs," says Way. But that's often a misconception. In Malcolm's case, he announced that he was giving up on his friends ("They won't keep your secrets, and they'll stab you in the back")—an attitude he maintained throughout high school.

When boys get emotional, parents and other adults often encourage them to tone it down. "People come to me time and time again saying, 'My son, he's so sensitive,'" says Thompson. "What they don't realize is that it's not the exception. It's the norm." And so, parents react differently to upset daughters and sons. "The actions can be as subtle as asking a girl what's wrong when she's crying but patting a boy on the head and saying, 'You're OK; now get back out there.'" The result can be emotional isolation that starts in boyhood and plagues men in middle age, often with emotional, and even physical, consequences. "Every now and then I catch myself saying things to my sons that I wouldn't say to my daughter—like 'Be tough, don't cry,'" worries Descourouez. "Now I'm trying not to say anything to them that I wouldn't say to my daughter. They can decide what they want to cry about."

**Action figures**. But despite the evidence of boys' sensitivity, not all of the old stereotypes are unfounded. As much as day care provider Marcy Shrage encourages sensitivity in her boys, she has noticed how they crave action. At her home in Lawrenceville, N.J., she cares for five boys under the age of 4. She piles them all into her minivan and takes them on drives. She'll stop for senior citizens in crosswalks to model good behavior and take them on long walks through the woods. But, the karate black belt admits, the boys do get most excited when she teaches them martial-arts moves. And though she doesn't allow toy weapons in the house, "There are plenty of days when they'll bite their sandwiches into the shape of guns and start firing away at each other."

It is the unexpected combination of physical aggressiveness and emotional vulnerability that now fascinates scientists at the University of Pennsylvania's Brain Behavior Laboratory, who are looking for explanations in the neurons. According to center director Ruben Gur, they have found some intriguing differences in brain structure—anatomical disparities that make it harder for boys to process information and even read faces but easier for them to excel at gross motor skills and visualize objects in three dimensions.

Women's brains are, on average, 11 percent smaller than men's, says Gur. And while there appears to be a subtle correlation between brain volume and IQ, he adds, there is no difference in the IQs of males and females. "So we have to ask how women manage to have the same IQ in a proportionally smaller brain." The answer is that female brains are not simply a smaller version of male brains. From a strictly evolutionary standpoint, the female brain is a bit more finely developed, says Gur. Brains are composed of gray matter (where information processing is done), white matter (long fibers covered in fat that, much like rubber-coated wire, transmit electrical impulses from brain to body), and spinal fluid (which acts as a buffer from the skull). The most recent research shows that males have less gray matter and more white matter than do females. And the right and left hemispheres of the brain are linked by a bundle of nerves that helps the two sides of the brain communicate. In women, this bundle—the corpus callosum—is thicker. It's the difference, researchers explain, between a narrow path in the woods and a two-lane highway.

As a result, says Gur, female brains tend to be more facile when it comes to verbal skills. This may explain why girls utter their first words earlier, string together complete sentences first, and generally surpass boys in tests that involve verbal fluency. "The female brain is an easier brain to teach," says Michael Gurian, a family therapist and author of *Boys and Girls Learn Differently*. "It's harder for the male brain to learn." It may also explain why, when Sandy Descourouez subscribed to a "developmental milestones" E-mail update from a babyfood site, she learned her son Luke was, like many boys, a "late talker."

Males do have more white matter, however—with longer, more complex nerve networks from their brains to the tips of their toes—allowing boys like Luke to excel at gross motor skills. And their greater volume of spinal fluid, says Gur, also means that male brains are built to sustain blows. "Thank goodness for that," says Descourouez, recalling Luke's penchant for spinning in circles near the fireplace.

**Reptilian feelings?** There appear to be brain-related differences in male and female emotions as well. The latest research suggests that the emotional brain is "more primitive" in men. Women make use of an emotional processing center adjacent to the speech areas of the brain, which makes it easier for them to link emotions to speech. The female brain is also "architecturally finer—a later arrival in evolution," says Gur. Men make use of an older limbic system "present in more primitive creatures," often known as the reptilian brain. Which means that male emotion is often more closely linked with action.

These are just the sort of details that the "Raising Sons" seminar participants at the Parenting Center in Fort Worth are gathering to learn. Moms and dads circle their chairs and share their fears, trying to come to some sort of agreement on what constitutes "normal" boy behavior: Why is their son struggling in school? Why won't he listen? Is he too sensitive? Too taken with guns and violent video games?

## Boys are the culprits in 9 of 10 alcohol and drug violations.

Pam Young debates with fellow "Raising Sons" classmate Brian Rice about her sons' penchant for wrestling. "They seem to know what drives me crazy," she says, conceding that it's also their way of bonding with dad. Rice, by contrast, worries that *his* son doesn't wrestle enough.

Another parent wonders aloud where his son's high spiritedness ends and brattiness begins. "I'm curious about the back talk," he inquires. "I want my son to be an independent thinker, but I also want him to have respect." Young leans in, nodding in agreement. "Yes," she says. "My son is very independent, then very dependent for approval."

In class, parents learn about the selective "pruning" of brain cells that scientists believe can lead to impulsivity—and that is thought to occur more rigorously in adolescent boys than girls. "It would explain why my son acts like a windshield wiper sometimes," says Young. "He's on, then he's off. He gets it, then he doesn't."

Later, a facilitator asks, "What's the only emotion that it's OK for boys to have?" The class pauses for a moment, then answers virtually in unison: "anger." Maybe that's why we have so many angry boys, the facilitator suggests. And so the parents learn how to teach their sons to match words with feelings, to build a vocabulary for the emotions that they often have trouble expressing.

## Boys are twice as likely as girls to be held back a grade in school.

**Let's get physical**. The teachers at Thomas Edison Elementary School in St. Joseph, Mo., have begun to put some of the brain science to the test. Three years ago, when third-grade teacher Denise Young asked the boys in her class a question, she would get frustrated if they didn't respond, and simply move on. Today, she gives them at least 60 seconds to "process" the question. "They need more time to stop, switch gears, and respond," says Young. "But they didn't have it, and I think that's why a lot of boys have gotten into trouble in the past." She also gives them "stress balls" to squeeze while they're reading or working out a problem. "It seems to help them engage when they're also doing something physical," she says.

### For more information

- **Real Boys Workbook** by William Pollack. Outlines "Some Do's and Don'ts With Boys." Also specific tips for talking to sensitive sons.
- **Speaking of Boys** by Michael Thompson. *Raising Cain* coauthor answers "the most asked questions about raising sons," delving into topics such as male puberty and underage drinking.
- **The Men They Will Become** by Eli Newberger. A thoughtful look at the emotional tug-of-war within boys.
- **Boys and Girls Learn Differently!** by Michael Gurian. The latest on boys' and girls' thinking styles.

On a typical day, her children stand by their desks as they complete work sheets and work on projects. That's because there is now a greater understanding, says principal Debbie Murphy, of the activity level and physicality of their school's boys. "There was a child who just couldn't sit still in music class, and we decided, well, if it's not going to bother anyone, it's fine if he stands at the back of the room."

Murphy also tried something new during her disciplinary chats with the boys. "I will not make the children talk when they're angry, for starters. Boys, in particular, just have trouble verbalizing when they're upset." Once they've cooled down, Murphy takes them for a stroll. "I find boys have an easier time talking if they're walking, too—it seems to tap into something in their brains," she says. In three years, Edison Elementary has watched its test scores skyrocket from what Murphy calls "ghetto statistics" to among the top 10 percent in the state. Incidents of in-school suspension have decreased from 300 to 22 this year.

The controversial drugging of boys also appears related to fundamental temperamental differences. Family physician Sax became alarmed when, increasingly, he was asked to prescribe Ritalin to otherwise healthy boys who simply couldn't sit still through long lessons. But the fact that boys are prescribed medicines and still fail at twice the rate of girls has given him pause. One of his patients, Andrew Yost, was a bright 8-year-old but uninspired by school and constantly getting into spats with his teachers. Sax suspected ADD and suggested Andrew's family consult with a child psychiatrist from the National Institutes of Health. The specialist confirmed the diagnosis and prescribed Ritalin.

When Sax encountered Andrew again several years later, he had indeed shown dramatic improvement. But it was not the result of the drugs. The difference, according to Andrew's parents, was that they had enrolled him in an all-boys school. "The teachers just seem to understand boy behaviors," says his father, David. "We tried so much before that, but now, I think he's where he should be." Andrew no longer takes any medications and, he adds, "I don't worry as much about what girls think."

**By 2007, girls may outnumber boys in college nearly 3 to 2.**

Other school districts are experimenting with voluntary single-sex classrooms within coed schools. "Parents are showing up in droves to sign up for the classes," says Anthony Basanese, middle school principal in Pellston, Mich. This fall, fully half of the sixth-grade class will be enrolled in single-sex classes, meeting throughout the day for coed lunch periods and extracurricular activities. "Parents like it because they see their kids doing better in school."

While American University's Sadker worries about the declining presence of male teachers—"down from 20 percent when I was a boy to 15 percent of all elementary school teachers now"—he is also wary of single-sex education. "Why aren't we fixing coed classes instead of running away from them? If we want a democracy that lives and works together, don't we also want one that learns together?"

**Too much too soon**. But many boys may need a substantial boost in schooling, say Sax and other specialists advocating a later start in kindergarten for boys. "The early curriculum is more accelerated than ever before," says Sax. "Boys are expected to do too much too soon—their brains aren't ready for it." The result, he adds, is too often a lifelong struggle with school. "They begin their school careers in 'the dumb group.' They're frustrated with their lack of ability, they start disliking school, and they begin to avoid it. We're seeing that more than ever now."

The extra year before kindergarten would allow boys to catch up. "Not all girls are precocious, and not all boys are delayed," says Sax. "But I've come to the conclusion that later enrollment would solve 80 percent of the problems we see with boys and school today."

Descourouez is considering holding Luke back from kindergarten. "His speech isn't up to speed," she worries, "and I don't want school to be a miserable experience for him." School is no pleasure for her son David, but she's determined to nurture the tenderness she sees in him. "He designs computer screens that say, 'I love you.' I can't remember the last time Greg said that to me." And she vows not to disregard the silence of her sons. "When they can't find the words for their emotions, I try to help them," she says. As they find the words, she hopes they will break the old patterns—and become husbands and fathers who talk.

# Sexual stereotypes

Males are promiscuous and females are choosy, according to evolutionary dogma embodied in a theory called Bateman's principle. Only recently have researchers begun to test the theory's limits, says Jonathan Knight.

*"The female, with the rarest exceptions, is less eager than the male... she is coy, and may often be seen endeavouring for a long time to escape."*[1]

With these words, Charles Darwin cast the die for evolutionary studies of male and female sexual roles. Darwin realized that the peacock's tail and the lion's mane owe their existence to aeons of fierce competition between their male ancestors for mates. Competitive males, Darwin assumed, will attempt to mate at every opportunity; females, he reasoned, are inherently choosy, reserving their favours for the strongest or gaudiest suitor.

These ideas were later crystallized in a theory known as Bateman's principle. In 1948, the British biologist Angus John Bateman concluded from experiments with fruitflies that promiscuity is more valuable to the reproductive success of males than to that of females. Males, he concluded, have therefore evolved an "undiscriminating eagerness" to mate, whereas females display "discriminating passivity"[2]—a fundamental dichotomy that Bateman suggested even applies, to an extent, to our own species.

The explanation, Bateman argued, is that sperm are small and cost next to nothing to produce—so the wider a male can spread them, the better off he will be. A female, on the other hand, produces many fewer eggs, and invests a relatively large amount of energy in each one. All she really needs is one good male to fertilize them to reach her maximum reproductive output. It all seemed to make sense, and Bateman's principle soon became one of the grounding truisms of behavioural biology.

But several researchers have since taken exception to this characterization of male and female sexual roles. Objections were first heard, but largely ignored, in the 1970s. Today, behavioural biologists are finding evidence that the world of sex is more complicated than Bateman thought. It's not that his principle is invalid, they say, but rather that it has been used to extend dated preconceptions about human sexual behaviour to the entire animal kingdom, sometimes to the detriment of scientific knowledge.

Despite the Victorians' reputation for prudishness, nineteenth-century natural philosophers spent lots of time watching animals mate. At the height of the British Empire, there were few places in the world where courting animals could escape the note-taking naturalist, and Darwin relied heavily on these descriptions in developing his theory of sexual selection[1], with its underlying assumptions of eager males and reluctant females.

## Counting on success

Bateman, who worked at the John Innes Horticultural Institution near London, was one of the first biologists to furnish the theory with experimental evidence. In a series of genetic experiments[2], Bateman combined groups of male and female fruitflies (*Drosophila melanogaster*) in vials. Each fruitfly carried a different dominant genetic marker, so Bateman could score the breeding success of each individual by counting the number of times the marker showed up in the next generation.

His conclusion was that, for males, promiscuity pays off. Males that mated with several females produced three to four times as many offspring as their monogamous peers. But females gained little by playing the field—on average, their reproductive output less than doubled when their progeny were sired by more than one male.

Bateman couched his explanation in terms of the relative energetic costs of producing sperm and eggs, but today the principle that bears his name includes an important modification made in 1972 by Robert Trivers of Harvard University, one of the founders of the discipline of sociobiology[3]. He expanded Bateman's concept beyond gametes to include a parent's entire investment in its offspring—including gestation, feeding and protection. The sex that invests more, Trivers argued, should be more passive and discriminating, whereas that with the smaller investment should court more mates and be ready to fight over them. This competition in turn drives Darwin's sexual selection by favouring traits such as showy colours and aggressiveness.

As evidence, Trivers cited well-known examples of sexual role reversal, such as seahorses and pipefish, and birds such as the greater painted snipe (*Rostratula benghalensis*). In this species, males incubate the eggs and rear the young. As the Bateman principle predicts, female painted snipes have brighter coloration and aggressively court males.

But over the next few years, a handful of primatologists began to notice behaviour in apes and monkeys that did not fit the Bateman mould. When doing field research in India on Hanuman langur monkeys (*Presbytis entellus*), Sarah Hrdy, then a graduate student at Harvard University, observed that, around the time of ovulation, females would aggressively seek copulations with multiple males. And when a new male rose to power in a group of langurs, even pregnant females would copulate with him.

Although female langurs are promiscuous, this is not a classic case of sexual role reversal—the females still take on most of the burden of parental care. Hrdy, who is now an emeritus professor at the University of California, Davis, proposed an alternative explanation[4]. In langurs, as in several other primate species, males sometimes kill the unweaned young of females with which they mate, presumably so that more attention will be lavished on their own offspring when they are born. As a defence against infanticide, Hrdy argued, females may confuse the issue of paternity through flagrant promiscuity.

Hrdy's idea that promiscuity might have an adaptive value for females met with a great deal of criticism at the time[5]. Hrdy and her supporters became characterized as'feminist' behavioural ecologists, and were seen by many researchers as a marginal group. But over the years, the number of cases of female promiscuity described in the animal-behaviour literature has mushroomed, particularly since the advent a decade ago of techniques for determining paternity by DNA analysis.

A degree of female promiscuity now seems to be the rule rather than the exception[6]. It has been documented in animals as diverse as whales[7], rodents[8] and bees[9]. In some animals, such as pseudoscorpions—arthropods that are related to scorpions and spiders—females prefer to switch partners much more often than males[10].

Bateman would not have predicted that what is good for the gander is good for the goose. And behavioural biologists are now striving to understand what females gain from promiscuity. According to Hrdy's 'confused paternity' argument, a promiscuous female stands to get more help, or at least less interference, with raising her young. In certain insect species, where males often make nuptial gifts of food items, the benefits may be primarily nutritional[11].

But several recent studies have suggested that there may also be a benefit to the health of the offspring. John Hoogland of the University of Maryland's Center for Environmental Science in Frostburg has found that female prairie dogs (*Cynomys gunnisoni*) that mate with multiple males end up with larger litters, and that their pups are more healthy[8]. Female sand lizards (*Lacerta agilis*) and adders (*Vipera berus*) also do better with multiple mates[12].

## Fishing for genes

Why should this be? Evolutionary biologists Jeanne and David Zeh of the University of Nevada in Reno argue that promiscuous females gain a genetic benefit: they improve their chance of finding a genetically compatible male. In 1999, the Zehs published an experiment[13] that confirmed this principle in the pseudoscorpion *Cordylochernes scorpioides*. They allowed females to mate either twice with one male or once each with two males. Even though all females received the same amount of sperm, females that mated with multiple males had a higher percentage of offspring mature to adulthood. The Zehs argued that promiscuity can help a female by reducing problems with low offspring viability that can result from mating with a partner whose genes don't happen to complement her own. In essence, promiscuity means that a female does not have to put all her eggs in one basket.

Earlier this month, Tom Tregenza and Nina Wedell of the University of Leeds, UK, reported that female field crickets (*Gryllus bimaculatus*) may use promiscuity to avoid the cost of inbreeding[14]. In their experiment, females were allowed to mate with two brothers, with a brother and an unrelated male, or with two unrelated males. The second and third groups had similar reproductive success, but eggs laid by females in the first group were less likely to hatch. By some unknown mechanism, females that mate with multiple males seem able to fertilize their eggs selectively with the sperm of unrelated males, and so avoid the problems of poor embryo viability that are a consequence of inbreeding.

## Multiple orgasms

The flip side of the Bateman equation—that males are boundlessly eager to mate because of their almost inexhaustible sperm supply—has also come under scrutiny. Although it may take very little energy to make a single sperm, males never deliver just one at a time. And in certain circumstances, the energetic costs of fertilizing a single female's eggs can be high.

Again, dissenting voices were first raised against this facet of the Bateman principle in the 1970s. Donald Dewsbury, a comparative psychologist at the University of Florida in Gainesville, noticed that male deer mice, hamsters and other rodents tended to copulate several times with the same female. It turned out that females are more likely to release the hormones needed for pregnancy if they are stimulated by multiple ejaculations, regardless of the amount of sperm they receive[15].

As a result, Dewsbury pointed out in a 1982 review[16] that a hit-and-run mating strategy might not always be the best option for males. If a male mates once and takes off, leaving the female in question open to the attentions of rival males, his sperm may not fertilize her eggs, and he also has to spend time and energy searching for another mate. Particularly when the number of receptive females is relatively low, a male may be better off sticking to one mate, and guarding her against rival suitors. This is a complexity that Bateman failed to recognize, Dewsbury argued. Under such conditions, he concluded, males might well be the choosy sex.

Bateman didn't actually report on the choosiness of his fruitflies, nor on any other aspect of their behaviour, notes Patricia Gowaty, an evolutionary biologist at the University of Georgia in Athens. "I think the reason Bateman's observation became 'Bateman's principle' is that it appealed to people's intuition about the behaviour of individuals," she says. "Very few people actually questioned the basic statement about the ubiquity of coy females and competitive males."

But if the layers of behavioural complexity are removed, how well does Bateman's basic theory about the relative benefits of promiscuity for the two sexes hold up? To find out, several groups are now putting Bateman's principle to more rigorous tests.

Species that exhibit sexual role reversal are particularly useful for this purpose. In the pipefish *Syngnathus typhle*, for example, the males carry the young, whereas the females compete with one another for mates. In 2000, researchers at the University of Georgia and at Uppsala University in Sweden showed that the relationship between the number of mates taken and the number of offspring produced, which they termed the Bateman gradient, was also reversed. Taking multiple mates was of greater value to the fertility of females than to that of males[17].

These experiments were done with captive fish. But the study's lead author, Adam Jones, who is now at Oregon State University in Corvallis, is attempting for the first time to measure Bateman's gradient in a natural setting—this time in a species with conventional male and female roles. He is gathering data from a local population of Oregon newts (*Taricha granulosa*), which conveniently breed in large aggregations so that every parent and offspring can be counted. The results are preliminary, but Jones says that so far they fit the Bateman model.

## Cricket supporter

Leigh Simmons, of the University of Western Australia near Perth, meanwhile, has found empirical support for Bateman's principle in the bushcricket *Requena verticalis*. In this species, the male donates a droplet of nutrients to his mate. This is no problem when there is lots of food around. But under starvation conditions, males become reluctant to mate and females must compete for them. Simmons has shown in the laboratory that, when sexual roles are reversed in this way, the Bateman gradient is also reversed[18]. This, he argues, indicates that the basic Bateman principle is sound, despite the overlying layers of complexity. "Bateman was naively simplistic, but then it was 1948," Simmons says.

"The basic principle is right," agrees Tim Clutton-Brock, a behavioural ecologist at the University of Cambridge, UK. Females can gain from promiscuity, but the fact that they more often get left holding the baby means that males can usually take more mates in a given time period[19].

Although the principle remains valid, recent experiments have revealed intriguing complexities—even among Bateman's own experimental subjects. In 1999, researchers at University College London and Cornell University in Ithaca, New York, described proteins in fruitfly seminal fluid that increase the time that a female waits before allowing another male to copulate with her[20].

Gowaty likens the proteins to a chemical chastity belt. "Everybody assumes Bateman was about coy females and ardent males," she says. "Now here's a modern discovery that suggests maybe the reason females were holding back from mating is that they were being manipulated by a male protein."

This theory has yet to be tested. But if Gowaty is correct, Bateman's experimental observations may have had much less to do with inherent female coyness than he assumed—another example, perhaps, of the truth being obscured by nineteenth-century sexual stereotypes.

## Notes

1. Darwin, C. *The Descent of Man, and Selection in Relation to Sex* (John Murray, London, 1871).
2. Bateman, A. J. *Heredity* **2**, 349–368 (1948).
3. Trivers, R. L. in *Sexual Selection and the Descent of Man* (ed. Campbell, B.) 136–177 (Aldine, Chicago, 1972).
4. Hrdy, S. B. *The Woman that Never Evolved* (Harvard Univ. Press, Cambridge, Massachusetts, 1981).
5. Symons, D. *Q. Rev. Biol.* **57**, 297–298 (1982).
6. Birkhead, T. R. & Møller, A. P. (eds) *Sperm Competition and Sexual Selection* (Academic, New York, 1998).
7. Clapham, P. J. & Palsboll, P. J. *Proc. R. Soc. Lond. B* **264**, 95–98 (1997).
8. Hoogland, J. *Anim. Behav.* **55**, 351–359 (1998).
9. Moritz, R. F. A. *et al. Behav. Ecol. Sociobiol.* **37**, 357–363 (1995).
10. Zeh, J. A., Newcomer, S. D. & Zeh, D. W. *Proc. Natl Acad. Sci. USA* **95**, 13732–13736 (1998).
11. Simmons, L. W. & Parker, G. A. *Ethology* **81**, 332–343 (1989).
12. Olsson, M. & Madsen, T. J. *Hered.* **92**, 190–197 (2001).
13. Newcomer, S. D., Zeh, J. A. & Zeh, D. W. *Proc. Natl Acad. Sci. USA* **96**, 10236–10241 (1999).
14. Tregenza, T. & Wedell, N. *Nature* **415**, 71–73 (2002).
15. Dewsbury, D. A. *J. Comp. Physiol. Psychol.* **93**, 178–188 (1979).
16. Dewsbury, D. A. *Am. Nat.* **119**, 601–610 (1982).
17. Jones, A. G., Rosenqvist, G., Berglund, A., Arnold, S. J. & Avise, J. C. *Proc. R. Soc. Lond. B* **267**, 677–680 (2000).
18. Kvarnemo, C. & Simmons, L. W. *Anim. Behav.* **55**, 1499–1506 (1998).
19. Clutton-Brock, T. H. & Vincent, A. C. J. *Nature* **351**, 58–60 (1991).
20. Neubaum, D. M. & Wolfner, M. F. *Genetics* **153**, 845–857 (1999).

**Jonathan Knight writes for *Nature* from San Francisco.**

# In Praise of Nurturing Men

We celebrate that women can be doctors, firefighters, and engineers, but we still make fun of men who work at traditionally female jobs. It's time to make equity a two-way street.

By Andrea Warren

Several years ago, weary of housework, I responded to a newspaper ad placed by a local cleaning person. To my surprise, the voice on the telephone was male. I immediately felt conflicted. Would a man be able to polish furniture, clean windows, and dust nooks and crannies with the finesse of a female?

Fortunately, I ignored my doubts and hired him. You can guess the rest. Our house sparkled; never had it received such attention to detail. Which only confirmed what I already knew from personal experience: Just as women can be fighter pilots and professional wrestlers, men can be housekeepers, nurses, and kindergarten teachers. Woman can wrestle alligators, and men can do needlepoint. Women can play basketball and fix leaky toilets, while men can study ballet and arrange flowers.

Still, our society tends to denigrate men who gravitate toward traditionally female pursuits; we question their motives and their masculinity. Stay-at-home dads who have breadwinner wives are still referred to as "Mr. Mom"—as if to remind them that they're doing women's work. Male elementary-school teachers, who are sorely needed as role models for kids, are often viewed with suspicion and mistrust. The same goes for male nurses. (Remember the movie *Meet the Parents,* in which Ben Stiller plays a nurse? His choice of career elicits endless ridicule.) Instead of celebrating a man who chooses a hands-on role in caregiving, society views him as an anomaly.

Even I have fallen victim to old stereotypes on occasion, and I of all people should know better: My husband, Jay, is director of a child-care center. Mostly he is an administrator, his day jammed with meetings, paperwork, and personnel issues. But occasionally he's been needed to fill in for a classroom teacher, and then he puts everything aside to assume the task of nurturing and caring for infants and toddlers. This is the part of the job he loves best, and if you see him on these occasions, you immediately sense magic in the air.

Let's **cheer on men** who break down the **walls** of **gender** bias.

The price he pays for his chosen career, apart from its low salary, is having to deal with suspicion from some parents—and occasionally even outright hostility. It takes a man who's very secure in his masculinity to wade into the sea of skepticism that will engulf him if he decides to work with young children. Ask any male preschool teacher—if you can find one. The prevailing attitude: Surely something must be wrong with a man who's not clawing his way up the corporate ladder, not doing something more manly, like trading bonds or laying construction pipe.

### Still a **Woman's** World

Women have made great progress in what were once considered male fields: In 1971, 5.4 percent of law-school graduates were female, but by the end of the 1990s, that figure had risen to 44 percent. Similarly, the number of women graduating from medical school rose from 8.4 percent in 1970 to 41 percent by the end of the 1990s. Men, however, have not fared so well in traditionally female fields. Only 13 percent of elementary-school teachers are men, and despite aggressive recruitment efforts, only 5.4 percent of registered nurses are male.

When I tell people my husband works at a child-care center, I usually get a blank stare. I could say, defensively, that he's also a psychologist with a part-time private practice. I could say that he's a black belt in tae kwon do, that he loves sailing, in-line skating, motorcycles, and golf. Or I might choose to rant about the bias in this country against male caregivers and about how it's keeping many good men from entering such careers. Job satisfaction just doesn't seem reward enough for the affront to their masculinity; as a result, all of us ultimately lose out.

I know just how extraordinary men like my husband are. I've watched Jay stoop to greet a small child and seen that child's eyes light up. I've watched toddlers wrap themselves around him as he's leaving the classroom because they don't want him to go. I've walked into his office to find a baby cooing happily in an infant seat on his desk, keeping him company while he works.

Last Halloween, Jay's child-care center hosted its annual fund-raiser, complete with a haunted house. Jay was taking his turn on the dunking stool, which was especially popular with the 3- and 4-year-olds, who loved hitting the bell with a ball and watching Jay splash into the water. Two other men were helping out: a dad who's a nurse and a college student planning a career in art. These three guys were having a great time with the kids, holding up the toddlers so they could toss their balls at the bell, encouraging hesitant children, celebrating victories, and making certain every child felt like a winner.

Another woman and I stood to one side, taking all this in. "There's nothing more attractive than a man who truly enjoys children," she mused. I wholeheartedly agreed. I'm privileged that my life partner is man enough to follow his heart. Many children have benefited as a result. Would most high-level corporate executives say the same about their work? I wonder how many mid-level managers stuck in jobs they hate would come alive if they followed their inner desires and became teachers, nurses—even housekeepers.

Just as we celebrate women who shatter the "glass ceiling," we should cheer on men who are struggling to break down the wall of gender bias. None of us will achieve true equity until those barriers are gone.

---

From *Parents*, March 2002, pp. 29-31. 

OVERCOMING SEX

# CAN MEN AND WOMEN BE FRIENDS?

By Camille Chatterjee

**If men are from Mars and women are from Venus, it may explain at least one of their shared beliefs: Men and women can't be real friends. Blame the sexual tension that almost inevitably exists between any red-blooded, heterosexual man and woman. Point to the jealousy that plagues many rational people when a significant other befriends someone of the opposite sex. Boil it down to the inherent differences between the sexes. It just can't be done. Right?**

WRONG, SAY RELATIONSHIP EXPERTS. "THE BELIEF that men and women can't be friends comes from another era in which women were at home and men were in the workplace, and the only way they could get together was for romance," explains Linda Sapadin, Ph.D., a psychologist in private practice in Valley Stream, New York. "Now they work together and have sports interests together and socialize together." This cultural shift is encouraging psychologists, sociologists and communications experts to put forth a new message: Though it may be tricky, men and women can successfully become close friends. What's more, there are good reasons for them to do so.

Society has long singled out romance as the prototypical male-female relationship because it spawns babies and keeps the life cycle going; cross-sex friendship, as researchers call it, has been either ignored or trivialized. We have rules for how to act in romantic relationships (flirt, date, get married, have kids) and even same-sex friendships (boys relate by doing activities together, girls by talking and sharing). But there are so few platonic male-female friendships on display in our culture that we're at a loss to even define these relationships.

**Peggy and Phil**

**Is there sexual tension between you?**

**Phil:** No, but there are times that I swear she is jealous of my girlfriends. It could just be my head.

**Peggy:** No, not really. But at times I feel weird about bringing my boyfriends around; I don't want Phil to get jealous.

**Do you fight?**

**Phil:** We only argue when we disagree about which rides to go on at Coney Island.

**Peggy:** There were actually a few times we got into arguements that ended in physical fights. But no one got hurt.

**How is your friendship rewarding?**

**Phil:** We could see each other naked and talk dirty without having to worry about sleeping over or whether or not our breath stinks.

**Peggy:** We just have so much fun together. I feel like I can tell him anything. There is no pressure.

Part of this confusion stems from the media. A certain 1989 film starring Meg Ryan and Billy Crystal convinced a nation of moviegoers that sex always comes between men and women, making true friendship impossible. "*When Harry Met Sally* set the potential for male-female friendship back about 25 years," says Michael Monsour, Ph.D., assistant professor of communications at the University of Colorado at Denver and author of *Women and Men as Friends: Relationships Across the Life Span in the 21st Century* (Lawrence Erldbaum, 2001). Television hasn't helped either. "Almost every time you see a male-female friendship, it winds up turning into romance," Monsour notes. Think Sam and Diane or Chandler and Monica. These cultural images are hard to overcome, he says. It's no wonder that we expect that men and women are always on the road to romance.

**Jenni and Mike**

**Is there any sexual tension between you?**

**Jenni:** No, I have never experienced any sexual tension between us. We only recently renewed our friendship after many years of living in separate countries, and our focus is on building up a friendship. I trust Mike a lot and could call him in the middle of the night if I needed him—but not to relieve any sexual tension, of course.

**Mike:** No. None at all. We grew up in Scotland together. I've known her since she was eight years old. I used to babysit her, and that's not really grounds for good sexual tension.

**Do you ever fight?**

**Jenni:** No, we don't fight. I don't tend to fight with friends. I wouldn't let it get that far. I am pretty outspoken, and so is Mike. We always find more constructive ways of communicating our differences than by fighting. We both rely on humor too much to move too far into the dark side of friendship.

**How is your friendship rewarding?**

**Jenni:** Mike has amazing energy and a positive outlook, and I always get a good vibe when I hang out with him. We share similar passions, such as dance, theatre, cycling and human rights and so we will always find it easy to do stuff together. However, it is just as easy to sit in a cafe with him and laugh, tell stories and chat for hours. I am excited at the prospect of deepening our friendship even further and amazed at the ease with which our lives have connected in New York in such a short time. It is a rare and special thing to click with someone in that way.

**Mike:** We have a lot of common interests and mutual concerns. We're from the same place. She works for the UN—it's rewarding to hear about the things she does with her life. She's inspiring.

But that's only one of the major barriers. In 1989, Don O'Meara, Ph.D., a sociology professor at the University of Cincinnati-Raymond Walters College, published a landmark study in the journal *Sex Roles* on the top impediments to cross-sex friendship. "I started my research because one of my best friends is a woman," says O'Meara. "She said, 'Do you think anyone else has the incredible friendship we do?'" He decided to find out, and after reviewing the scant existing research dating back to only 1974, O'Meara identified the following four challenges to male-female friendship: defining it, dealing with sexual attraction, seeing each other as equals and facing people's responses to the relationship. A few years later, he added a fifth: meeting in the first place.

## CHALLENGE #1
## Defining the relationship: Friends or lovers?

Platonic, friendly love does exist, O'Meara asserts, and a study of 20 pairs of friends published last year in the *Journal of Social and Personal Relationships* lends credence to the notion. In it, Heidi Reeder, Ph.D., an assistant professor in Boise State University's communication department, confirms that "friendship attraction" or a connection devoid of lust or longing, is a bona fide type of bond that people experience. Distinguishing between romantic, sexual and friendly feelings, however, can be exceedingly difficult.

"People don't know what feelings are appropriate toward the opposite sex, unless they're what our culture defines as appropriate," says O'Meara. "You know you love someone and enjoy them as a person, but not enough to date or marry them. What does this mean?"

## CHALLENGE #2
## Overcoming Attraction: Let's talk about sex

The reality that sexual attraction could suddenly enter the equation of a cross-sex friendship uninvited is always lurking in the background. A simple, platonic hug could instantaneously take on a more amorous meaning. "You're trying to do a friend-friend thing," says O'Meara, "but the male-female parts of you get in the way." Unwelcome or not, the attraction is difficult to ignore.

In a major 1988 study published in the *Journal of Social and Personal Relationships*, Sapadin asked over 150 professional men and women what they liked and disliked about their cross-sex friendships. Topping women's list of dislikes: sexual tension. Men, on the other hand, more frequently replied that sexual attraction was a prime reason for initiating a friendship, and that it could even deepen a friendship. Either way, 62% of all subjects reported that sexual tension was present in their cross-sex friendships.

## CHALLENGE #3
## Establishing Equality: The Power Play

Friendship should be a pairing of equals. But, O'Meara says, "in a culture where men have always been more equal than women, male dominance, prestige and power is baggage that both men and women are likely to bring to a relationship." Women are at risk of subconsciously adopting a more submissive role in cross-sex friendships, he says, although that is slowly changing as society begins to treat both genders more equally.

## CHALLENGE #4
## The Public Eye: Dealing with doubters

Society may not be entirely ready for friendships between men and women that have no sexual subtext. People with close friends of the opposite sex are often barraged with nudging, winking and skepticism: "Are you really *just* friends?" This is especially true, says O'Meara, of older adults, who grew up when men and women were off-limits to each other until marriage.

**Philou and Patou**

**Do you ever fight?**

**Patou:** Yes, we do have arguments. Generally our favorite topic relates to our own sexual experiences. He likes to push his frustrations, I think, to reevaluate the intimacy of female and male mysteries. I adore these hot moments, because we always challenge our emotions and mutual fantasies. Overall, I think that a man and woman, lovers or friends, is the best duet.

**Philou:** I don't really think we fight. We argue, yes. We often meet for dinner and engage in passionate discussions. But I feel we view life in the same way and that's why we are friends. Sometimes she gets mad at my jokes, sometimes I joke at her madness.

## CHALLENGE #5
## The Meeting Place: Finding friends

As the workplace and other social arenas become increasingly open to women, the sexes are mingling more and more. Still, men and women continue to have surprisingly few opportunities to interact.

"Boys and girls form their own gender groups in elementary school," explains Monsour. "They learn their own ways of relating to each other. So when they do get together, inspired by puberty, they see each other as dating partners because they've never really known each other as friends." A surprisingly major factor in this phenomenon is the kids' own innate interest in children who act like they do. Called "voluntary gender segregation," it continues into adulthood. "You see it at cocktail parties," says Monsour. "Men go off to one corner, and women go to another."

These obstacles may seem numerous and formidable, but male-female friendship is becoming not only a possibility, but also a necessity. If men and women are to work, play and co-exist in modern society, researchers believe they must learn to understand and communicate with each other. To that end, social scientists like Monsour, Sapadin and O'Meara have begun studying how to do just that. The field of research is still in its infancy, but they are now beginning to understand some basic truths about male-female friendship:

## TRUTH #1
## Friendship is not equal opportunity

Not until high school does puberty really draw boys and girls together, which then continues into college. But as people develop serious romantic relationships or get married, making and maintaining cross-sex friendships becomes harder. "Even the most secure people in a strong marriage probably don't want a spouse to be establishing a new friendship, especially with someone who's very attractive," says Monsour.

**Luis and Tiffany**

**Any sexual tension?**

**Luis:** No, not at all. I'm gay.

**Do you fight?**

**Luis:** We don't usually fight because we are mature enough to talk things over. However, when we do, it is usually due to miscommunication.

**Tiffany:** We have only had one or two arguements, both while working together in very stressful situations. I hate to fight and try to resolve things very quickly. We usually laugh about it afterward.

**Rewarding aspects?**

**Luis:** We laugh a lot when we are together.

**Tiffany:** He makes me smile and we are always laughing together. Luis was also really supportive when I moved from London to Manhattan; he is a friend I will always remember.

The number of cross-sex friendships continues to decline with age—not surprising, since most older adults grew up in an age where consorting with the opposite sex outside of wedlock was taboo. According to Rosemary Blieszner, Ph.D., a family studies professor at Virginia Tech and author of *Adult Friendship* (Sage, 1993), elderly people rarely form new friendships with members of the opposite sex. Her research shows that only about 2% of the friendships elderly women have are with men.

## TRUTH #2
## Men get more out of cross-sex friendship than women

There are proven—and apparent—distinct differences between female friendship and male friendship. Women spend the majority of their time together discussing their thoughts and feelings, while men tend to be far more group-oriented. Males gather to play sports or travel or talk stock quotes; rarely do they share feelings or personal

**Zucco and Deborah**

**Any sexual tension?**

**Zucco:** Sometimes, without falling in love with Deborah, I wish to be part of eternity with her. Imagining our two bodies connected to each other and becoming one, it's calling me.

**Do you fight?**

**Zucco:** Yes, if Deborah's crossing the line, I'll be here to remind her of reality. Isn't that what friends are for? Rewarding aspects?

**Zucco:** It's like having a wife without the inconvenience.

reflections. This may explain why they seem to get far more out of cross-sex friendship than their female counterparts.

In Sapadin's study, men rated cross-sex friendships as being much higher in overall quality, enjoyment and nurturance than their same-sex friendships. What they reported liking most was talking and relating to women-something they can't do with their buddies. Meanwhile, women rated their same-sex friendships higher on all these counts. They expect more emotional rewards from friendship than men do, explains Sapadin, so they're easily disappointed when they don't receive them. "Women confide in women," notes Blieszner. "Men confide in women."

**Eric and Pam**

**Any sexual tension?**

**Pam:** We've known each other for nearly 15 years. For the first few years we were very flirtatious, but we've moved past that.

**Eric:** No. We're both involved with people we love, and it's just not an issue.

**Do you fight?**

**Pam:** We used to have some ridiculous fights, but that was when we were young. "Did you tell so and so that I said such and such?" Very juvenille. I can't imagine what we would fight about now.

## TRUTH #3
## ...but women benefit too

All that sharing and discussing in female-female friendship can become exhausting, as any woman who's stayed up all night comforting a brokenhearted girlfriend can attest. With men, women can joke and banter without any emotional baggage. "Friendships with men are lighter, more fun," says Sapadin. "Men aren't so sensitive about things." Some women in his study also liked the protective, familial and casual warmth they got from men, viewing them as surrogate big brothers. What they liked most of all, however, was getting some insight into what guys really think.

## TRUTH #4
## Cross-sex friendships are emotionally rewarding

Although women dig men's lighthearted attitude, most male-female friendships resemble women's emotionally-involving friendships more than they do men's activity-oriented relationships, according to Kathy Werking, Ph.D., an assistant professor of communications at Eastern Kentucky University and author of *We're Just Good Friends* (Guilford, 1997). Her work has shown that the number one thing male and female friends do together is talk one-on-one. Other activities they prefer—like dining out and going for drives—simply facilitate that communication. In fact, Werking found, close male-female friends are extremely emotionally supportive if they continuously examine their feelings, opinions and ideas. "Males appreciate this because it tends not to be a part of their same-sex friendships," she says. "Females appreciate garnering the male perspective on their lives."

## TRUTH #5
## It's not all about sex

"In reality, sex isn't always on the agenda," says Werking. "That could be due to sexual orientation, lack of physical attraction or involvement in another romantic relationship." After all, even friends who are attracted to each other may also recognize that qualities they tolerate in a friendship wouldn't necessarily work in a serious romantic relationship. And after years of considering someone as a friend, it often becomes difficult to see a cross-sex pal as a romantic possibility.

Of pairs that do face the question of lust, those that decide early on to bypass an uncertain romantic relationship are more likely to have an enduring friendship, says Werking. One study published last year in the *Journal of Social and Personal Relationships* by Walid Afifi, Ph.D., of Penn State University, showed that of over 300 college students surveyed, 67% reported having had sex with a friend. Interestingly, 56% of those subjects did not transition the friendship into a romantic relationship, suggesting that they preferred friendship over sex.

## TRUTH #6
## Male-female friendships are political

Men and women have increasingly similar rights, opportunities and interests, which can make cross-sex friendship very political, notes Werking. "It upsets the agreed-upon social order," she explains. "Women and men

**Lea and Jean-Christian**

**Any sexual tension?**

**Lea:** Yes, maybe when I was single. But for as long as we've known each other, he's been a married man.

**Jean-Christian:** All the time. But she is also my friend's girlfriend, and he would kill me—or go after my wife.

**Rewarding aspects?**

**Lea:** I always seem to discover something new about myself, something male and creative that he brings out in me, that I would not otherwise think about. He taught me how to play the harmonica the way an old black man plays the blues.

**Jean-Christian:** Each time I see her it's like the first time. I always discover new and surprising aspects of her personality.

engage in an equal relationship, or they aren't friends." For one thing, new generations of kids grow up believing that boys can play with dolls and girls can take kickboxing, and they're crossing paths more as a result.

Men and women are also becoming more androgynous as their societal roles become more similar. "Men are more willing to have feminine characteristics, and women are a lot more willing to admit to traditionally masculine characteristics, like assertiveness," says Monsour. His dissertation showed that women and men categorized as androgynous had twice the number of cross-sex friends.

Whatever the challenges of male-female friendship, researchers agree that to succeed as friends, both genders have to openly and honestly negotiate exactly what their relationship will mean-whether sexual attraction is a factor and how they'll deal with it-and establish boundaries. In Afifi's and Reeder's studies, the friendships that survived-and even thrived-after sex or attraction came into play were those in which the friends extensively discussed the meaning of the sexual activity and felt confident and positive about each other's feelings. Once they got past that, they were home free.

"If sex is part of the dynamic, addressing it explicitly is the best strategy" for making sure the friendship survives, says Werking. "The issue will fester if friends try to ignore it." So in the end, male-female friendship does have something in common with romantic relationships: To work, communication is key.

**RESEARCHERS tell us that men and women can be friends. But do we really believe them? A survey of more than 1,450 members of the match.com dating site revealed that we're an optimistic bunch:**

**1.** Do you believe men and women can be platonic friends?

**Yes: 83%**
**No: 11%**
**Unsure: 6%**

**2.** Have you had a platonic friendship that crossed the line and became romantic or sexual?

**Yes: 62%**
**No: 36%**
**Unsure: 2%**

**3.** Who is more likely to misinterpret the intimacy of friendship for sexual desire?

**Men: 64%**
**Women: 25%**
**Unsure: 11%**

**4.** It is possible to fall in love with someone who first enters your life as a friend?

**Yes: 94%**
**No: 4%**
**Unsure: 2%**

**5.** Do you hope that when you do fall in love, your partner will have started out as your friend?

**Yes: 71%**
**No: 9%**
**Unsure 20%**

**6.** Who is better at keeping sex out of a platonic relationship?

**Men: 13%**
**Women: 67%**
**Unsure: 20%**

## READ MORE ABOUT IT:

***Men and Women as Friends,*** *Michael Monsour, Ph.D. (Lawrence Erlbaum, 2001)*

***Adult Friendship,*** *Rosemary Blieszner (Sage, 1993)*

---

*Camille Chatterjee is an associate editor at* More *magazine.*

# Love is *not* all you need

By Pepper Schwartz, Ph.D.

The experience of love is unique for every person, and using that feeling to measure the potential success of a relationship is even more subjective. Nonetheless, at some point most of us face the timeless question of what makes a relationship work. Though we can't quantify love, we can look at variables that help us choose the right partner. Research shows that a few crucial compatibilities make the difference between making up and breaking up.

WE ARE A LOVE CULTURE. UNLIKE SOME SOCIETIES that think of passionate love as a nuisance that can undermine sound reasoning about whom and when to marry, we think passion is our truest guide. When we say, "He did it all for love," we mean it as a compliment. In many cultures it would be said with pity or contempt. But not us—we sigh with happiness when witnessing lovers who barely know each other connect as powerfully as lightning striking the Earth.

This approach is romantic, but it's also a little daft. Sure, being passionately attracted to someone is a great elixir, but making a commitment based on hormone-addled logic is a recipe for disappointment, if not disaster. We shouldn't be misled by fleeting moments of bliss. Love is not all you need, and you will not know—across a crowded room or even on a first date—that this person absolutely is the One. While some hunches work out (and, of course, those are the Cinderella stories), most do not. There is a real danger when you think that fate has delivered the One: You may stop looking for disconfirming evidence, even if there are big problems (like his tendency to drink too much or her occasional disappearances).

Theories about love that are based on fate are not only untrue, they aren't even in the best interest of love. Of course, Cupid forbid, if the One does not work out, you might think you've lost your true love and forego giving other people a chance. Choosing the right partner is arguably the most important decision you will make. In the last 10 years, a multitude of studies have shown how bad relationships can negatively affect job performance, physical and mental health, financial security and even life span. Certainly, such an important decision requires more than the adrenaline rush of infatuation.

When considering what it takes to make love work, it is useful to look at those who have tried and succeeded as well as those who have tried and failed. Besides observations from my own work, I have included data from The Enrich Couple Inventory, 195 questions developed by David Olson, Ph.D., David Fournier, Ph.D., and Joan Druckman, Ph.D., that were administered to 21,501 couples throughout the country. The researchers compared the answers of the happiest couples to those of the most unhappy and found that the differences between their answers to a few key questions tell a lot about what makes love work. If we are willing to be rational about love, we can learn from others' experiences—and perhaps find and maintain a true love even after the initial chemistry fades.

**"I DIDN'T KNOW YOU FELT THAT WAY...."**

| **My partner is a very good listener** | |
|---|---|
| Percentage of unhappy couples who agree: | **18%** |
| Percentage of happy couples who agree: | **83%** |
| **My partner does not understand how I feel** | |
| Unhappy couples: | **79%** |
| Happy couples: | **13%** |

If you want to feel alone in a relationship, be with someone who hasn't a clue about what you are going through. Or worse, someone who does have a clue but cannot understand why your pain is a big deal. The two of you can be totally different people

| *On Flexibility* | *On Sexual Compatibility* |
|---|---|
| **Joel and Gaby**<br>Married four years<br><br>Joel, 34, composer: "A lot of people imagine that when you're in a relationship you're facing opposite your partner. I like to think of a relationship as your partner standing next to you, and you're both facing the same direction, which means that the relationship doesn't block your view of the world. And your partner is actually and metaphorically by and on your side. That's going to demand some flexibility, because at times, you're going to have to go against yourself to be on your partner's side."<br><br>Gaby, 36, administrative assistant: "It doesn't work if things are too patterned and strict; every day is different. If you are flexible, then surprises don't catch you off guard and it's easier to get along." | **Kiera and Matt**<br>Together one year, three months<br><br>Kiera, 28, marketing consultant: "It doesn't determine the success of a relationship, but it is important. Everyone is looking for something different—if we weren't, we'd all want to date the same person and be in the same relationship. However, if there's no sexual compatibility, there would be very little distinguishing this person from any other close friend."<br><br>Matt, 27, art director: "It is an important piece, but only one of many that make up a relationship. Just because you have sexual compatibility does not mean you have a relationship. At least not one that is going to last." |
| *On Empathy*<br>**Zucco and Barbara**<br>Together one year<br><br>Zucco, 48, bartender: "Empathy is very important. Our relationship is based on mutual understanding. It permits us to progress together toward a better life. Barbara moved from France to the U.S. to be with me, and I know it's not easy for her—she's learning a new language and hasn't made many friends yet. I feel for her, and sometimes I embrace her tightly to give her my energy and receive hers. Couples who don't see each other's point of view are destined to fail. When two beings get together, there is some kind of electric reaction. First there is passion, then in the aftermath they feel for each other, protect one another, respect the other's mind. then finally—through understanding, learning from each other, apologizing, laughing, crying, talking, experiencing day-to-day reality—they become a couple, whereas before they were just lovers." | *On Intelligence*<br>**Melissa and Will**<br>Together one year, six months<br><br>Melissa, 20, college student: "I think it's good if you challenge your partner intellectually, because otherwise there's not enough substance to the relationship. If you can't do it on the same abstract level—if you can't sit down to dinner and have a conversation about what's going on in the world—then there's a lot missing. You need someone who can push you and make you think in a different way. It's good to have similar interests, but I think it's also good to have different points of view and be able to talk candidly about things, just so you grow as people. If you're too similar, it's no fun." |
| *On Communication*<br>**Brisco and Ann**<br>Together one year, one month<br><br>Brisco, 34, photographer: "If there's a problem, you should speak up immediately so the other person will know where you are coming from, instead of not communicating or waiting until the last minute to reveal your feelings. When you first start dating, you don't voice everything you feel out of fear of what the other person might think. But after a certain period of time, the communication comes. Trust and communication go hand in hand; you become comfortable enough to trust that you're not going to be judged. Right now we live in different cities, and I think good communication is even more important if you are in a long-distance relationship. We talk every day on the phone, if only for a short time. The communication we have is good enough that we don't have to see each other to reinforce the comfort level or security. I am sure that when we are living in the same place we will have to continue to let each other know when we need space." | *On Time Together*<br>**Pat and George**<br>Together 10 years<br><br>George, 52, salesman: "I rate spending time together as the most important thing in a relationship. You always need some time alone, but time with the other person is more fun. They become your partner, your soul mate, your best friend, the person you confide in. Spending time with that person is sheer pleasure. We like to go out to dinner and then dancing, but just sitting and talking is probably the most meaningful thing we spend time doing. From that we get support, companionship, friendship, love and obviously, passion." |

in a number of ways, but if a partner is sensitive to how you see the world and experience life, then those differences are unimportant.

Ruth, who has been married to Alex for 31 years, puts it this way, "When we got married, nobody thought it would last because we are so different. Alex is from a working-class family; I am Jewish, he is Lutheran—everyone thought it was a nonstarter from the wedding day on. But what they didn't know, and what has been the most important thing in our relationship, is that Alex knows how to listen. Really listen. No matter what, he can see how I'm feeling and he can feel for me. Trust me, that solves a lot of problems."

### "WE NEVER SEE EACH OTHER ANYMORE...."

**We have a good balance of leisure time spent together and separately**

| | |
|---|---|
| Unhappy couples: | 17% |
| Happy couples: | 71% |

**We find it easy to think of things to do together**

| | |
|---|---|
| Unhappy couples: | 28% |
| Happy couples: | 86% |

Although it sometimes works if people have different priorities, most often, being out of sync is damaging in the long run. Allotting time in your day, your week and your life for your partner is an important ingredient in a relationship. If one person wants to spend every Saturday and Sunday relaxing in front of the television when the other wants to hike, bike and explore, both will feel deprived. This may not show up in the busy early years of child raising, but over time it can become a real problem. As Marty, an executive for a shipping company, says, "The best thing my second wife and I do together is hang out, just be friends sharing the same space. My first marriage was all about seeing things, doing things, as if just being together wasn't enough. Well, maybe it wasn't with her, but it is one of the greatest joys I have with Ellen."

### "DO YOU SEE WHAT I'M SAYING?"

**I am very satisfied with how we talk to each other**

| | |
|---|---|
| Unhappy couples: | 15% |
| Happy couples: | 90% |

**We are creative in how we handle our differences**

| | |
|---|---|
| Unhappy couples: | 15% |
| Happy couples: | 78% |

Marriage exists in a constantly changing world. Couples need to be able to talk about these changes, how they feel about them and what they want to do in response. They need to have a sense of teamwork, one arrived at by discussion and joint action. If one person refuses to discuss things, one or both persons will feel the relationship is not intimate and perhaps unfair. And if no one's talking, there is no way to fix a problem and keep it from getting worse. Life is not static, it's messy, and it requires communication.

### "WHY ARE YOU SO AMBITIOUS?"

**Making financial decisions is not difficult**

| | |
|---|---|
| Unhappy couples: | 32% |
| Happy couples: | 80% |

If one person is ambitious, and the other person wants a lifestyle that doesn't support that ambition, there will be growing resentment. Lisa, a young woman who has a small home-based mail-order business, became increasingly unhappy with her husband, Rob. Both wanted a higher standard of living, but he had also promised that he would be "a good father to our children." Instead, he was around less and less as he became more and more entangled in his work. He wanted to spend more time making money; she wanted him to be home more often. Neither she nor Rob had given serious thought to how incompatible their personalities might be. As life went on, she felt more deprived, and he felt more resentful. Ultimately, they separated.

### "SINCE WE'RE ALONE...."

**Our sexual relationship is satisfying and fulfilling**

| | |
|---|---|
| Unhappy couples: | 29% |
| Happy couples: | 85% |

Sexual incompatibilities can be fixed, right? And sexual disappointment isn't the worst problem when so much else is good about the relationship, right? Wrong and double wrong. First, while it is true that sex therapy can help many problems (especially mechanical ones such as erectile failure or pain during intercourse), it has a woeful track record when it comes to creating or resurrecting sexual desire. Second, while therapists can improve a lover's skill, either you have compatibility in bed or you don't. You can put someone on skates and they can learn to make it around the rink, but triple lutzes? No. Sex isn't important if it isn't important to both of you. But, if one partner is interested and the other is not, the interested party will rarely be content to just forget about it.

### "IF IT MAKES YOU HAPPY...."

**We are both equally willing to make adjustments in the relationship**

| | |
|---|---|
| Unhappy couples: | 46% |
| Happy couples: | 87% |

**I can share feelings and ideas with my partner during disagreements**

| | |
|---|---|
| Unhappy couples | 22% |
| Happy couples | 85% |

Although it may be mistaken for strength, rigidity is not a good personal or marital quality. If someone doesn't like to admit they are wrong or show some flexibility in how they view problems, the partnership will be either fragile or full of anger and loneliness. Rachel, a woman who describes herself as a "giver," believed she could change her husband's inflexibility. "I thought I could bring him out, make him less rigid by doing so much for him, by always being ready to see his point of view. But he just took and took. When I backed down, he would see it as weakness, not flexibility. Finally, I just couldn't take being so unloved, so I left." There is no marriage in which the ability to apologize and be flexible isn't necessary.

### "YOU JUST DON'T GET IT"

**My partner understands my opinions and ideas**

| | |
|---|---|
| Unhappy couples: | 19% |
| Happy couples: | 87% |

## READ MORE ABOUT IT:

***Everything You Know About Love and Sex Is Wrong*** by Pepper Schwartz, Ph.D. (G.P. Putnam's Sons, 2000)

***Empowering Couples, Building on Your Strengths*** by David Olson, Ph.D., and Amy Olson, Ph.D. (Life Innovations, 2000)

***Schopenhauer's Porcupines: Intimacy and Its Dilemmas*** by Deborah Anna Luepnitz, Ph.D. (Basic Books, 2001)

***Loving Him Without Losing You: Seven Empowering Strategies for Better Relationships*** by Beverly Engel, M.S. (John Wiley & Sons, 2000)

In the beginning of a relationship, conversation is mostly self-revelation, which is interesting at first. But over time there are many circumstances that allow you to see the quality of a person's mind. It's OK to be awed by your partner's intelligence, but beware if you think she is less than overwhelmed by the way you solve problems, come to conclusions and think about life. The bedrock of mutual respect is comfort and admiration for each other's opinions. If that isn't present, contempt is just around the corner.

---

*Pepper Schwartz, Ph.D., is professor of sociology at the University of Washington and author of 14 books, including* Ten Talks Parents Must Have With Children About Sex and Character (Hyperion, 2000) *and* The Great Sex Weekend (Putnam, 1998).

# GO AHEAD, *KISS* YOUR COUSIN

## HECK, *MARRY* HER IF YOU WANT TO

*By Richard Conniff*

**In Paris in 1876** a 31-year-old banker named Albert took an 18-year-old named Bettina as his wife. Both were Rothschilds, and they were cousins. According to conventional notions about inbreeding, their marriage ought to have been a prescription for infertility and enfeeblement.

In fact, Albert and Bettina went on to produce seven children, and six of them lived to be adults. Moreover, for generations the Rothschild family had been inbreeding almost as intensively as European royalty, without apparent ill effect. Despite his own limited gene pool, Albert, for instance, was an outdoorsman and the seventh person ever to climb the Matterhorn. The American du Ponts practiced the same strategy of cousin marriage for a century. Charles Darwin, the grandchild of first cousins, married a first cousin. So did Albert Einstein.

In our lore, cousin marriages are unnatural, the province of hillbillies and swamp rats, not Rothschilds and Darwins. In the United States they are deemed such a threat to mental health that 31 states have outlawed first-cousin marriages. This phobia is distinctly American, a heritage of early evolutionists with misguided notions about the upward march of human societies. Their fear was that cousin marriages would cause us to breed our way back to frontier savagery—or worse. "You can't marry your first cousin," a character declares in the 1982 play *Brighton Beach Memoirs.* "You get babies with nine heads."

So when a team of scientists led by Robin L. Bennett, a genetic counselor at the University of Washington and the president of the National Society of Genetic Counselors, announced that cousin marriages are not significantly riskier than any other marriage, it made the front page of *The New York Times.* The study, published in the *Journal of Genetic Counseling* last year, determined that children of first cousins face about a 2 to 3 percent higher risk of birth defects than the population at large. To put it another way, first-cousin marriages entail roughly the same increased risk of abnormality that a woman undertakes when she gives birth at 41 rather than at 30. Banning cousin marriages makes about as much sense, critics argue, as trying to ban childbearing by older women.

THE MARRIAGE OF ALBERT ROTHSCHILD AND BETTINA ROTHSCHILD WAS THE RESULT OF FOUR GENERATIONS OF INBREEDING IN THE BANKING DYNASTY—A PRACTICE ADVOCATED BY THE FAMILY FOUNDER MAYER AMSCHEL ROTHSCHILD. HIS INTENTION WAS CERTAINLY A FRUITFUL ONE IF THE DARWINIAN MEASURE OF CAPITALISTIC SUCCESS IS THE PRESERVATION OF WEALTH.

But the nature of cousin marriage is far more surprising than recent publicity has suggested. A closer look reveals that moderate inbreeding has always been the rule, not the exception, for humans. Inbreeding is also commonplace in the natural world, and contrary to our expectations, some biologists argue that this can be a very good thing. It depends in part on the degree of inbreeding.

The idea that inbreeding might sometimes be beneficial is clearly contrarian. So it's important to acknowledge first that inbreeding can sometimes also go horribly wrong—and in ways that, at first glance, make our stereotypes about cousin marriage seem completely correct.

## A CLOSER LOOK REVEALS THAT MODERATE INBREEDING HAS ALWAYS BEEN THE RULE, NOT THE EXCEPTION, FOR HUMANS

In the Yorkshire city of Bradford, in England, for instance, a majority of the large Pakistani community can trace their origins to the village of Mirpur in Kashmir, which was inundated by a new dam in the 1960s. Cousin marriages have been customary in Kashmir for generations, and more than 85 percent of Bradford's Pakistanis marry their cousins. Local doctors are seeing sharp spikes in the number of children with serious genetic disabilities, and each case is its own poignant tragedy. One couple was recently raising two apparently healthy children. Then, when they were 5 and 7, both were diagnosed with neural degenerative disease in the same week. The children are now slowly dying. Neural degenerative diseases are eight times more common in Bradford than in the rest of the United Kingdom.

The great hazard of inbreeding is that it can result in the unmasking of deleterious recessives, to use the clinical language of geneticists. Each of us carries an unknown number of genes—an individual typically has between five and seven—capable of killing our children or grandchildren. These so-called lethal recessives are associated with diseases like cystic fibrosis and sickle-cell anemia.

Most lethal genes never get expressed unless we inherit the recessive form of the gene from both our mother and father. But when both parents come from the same gene pool, their children are more likely to inherit two recessives.

So how do scientists reconcile the experience in Bradford with the relatively moderate level of risk reported in the *Journal of Genetic Counseling?* How did Rothschilds or Darwins manage to marry their cousins with apparent impunity? Above all, how could any such marriages ever possibly be beneficial?

The traditional view of human inbreeding was that we did it, in essence, because we could not get the car on Saturday night. Until the past century, families tended to remain in the same area for generations, and men typically went courting no more than about five miles from home—the distance they could walk out and back on their day off from work. As a result, according to Robin Fox, a professor of anthropology at Rutgers University, it's likely that 80 percent of all marriages in history have been between second cousins or closer.

Factors other than mere proximity can make inbreeding attractive. Pierre-Samuel du Pont, founder of an American dynasty that believed in inbreeding, hinted at these factors when he told his family: "The marriages that I should prefer for our colony would be between the cousins. In that way we should be sure of honesty of soul and purity of blood." He got his wish, with seven cousin marriages in the family during the 19th century. Mayer Amschel Rothschild, founder of the banking family, likewise arranged his affairs so that cousin marriages among his descendants were inevitable. His will barred female descendants from any direct inheritance. Without an inheritance, female Rothschilds had few possible marriage partners of the same religion and suitable economic and social stature—except other Rothschilds. Rothschild brides bound the family together. Four of Mayer's granddaughters married grandsons, and one married her uncle. These were hardly people whose mate choice was limited by the distance they could walk on their day off.

Some families have traditionally chosen inbreeding as the best strategy for success because it offers at least three highly practical benefits. First, such marriages make it likelier that a shared set of cultural values will pass down intact to the children.

Second, cousin marriages make it more likely that spouses will be compatible, particularly in an alien environment. Such marriages may be even more attractive for Pakistanis in Bradford, England, than back home in Kashmir. Intermarriage decreases the divorce rate and enhances the independence of wives, who retain the support of familiar friends and relatives. Among the 19th-century du Ponts, for instance, women had an equal vote with men in family meetings.

Finally, marrying cousins minimizes the need to break up family wealth from one generation to the next. The rich have frequently chosen inbreeding as a means to keep estates intact and consolidate power.

Moderate inbreeding may also produce biological benefits. Contrary to lore, cousin marriages may do even better than ordinary marriages by the standard Darwinian measure of success, which is reproduction. A 1960 study of first-cousin marriages in 19th-century England done by C. D. Darlington, a geneticist at Oxford University, found that inbred couples produced twice as many great-grandchildren as did their outbred counterparts.

Consider, for example, the marriage of Albert and Bettina Rothschild. Their children were descended from a genetic pool of just 24 people (beginning with family founders Mayer Amschel and Gutle Rothschild), and more than three-fifths of them were born Rothschilds. In a family that had not inbred, the same children would have 38 ancestors. Because of inbreeding, they were directly descended no fewer than six times each from Mayer and Gutle Rothschild. If our subconscious Darwinian agenda is to get as much of our genome as possible into future generations, then inbreeding clearly provided a genetic benefit for Mayer and Gutle.

And for their descendants? How could the remarkably untroubled reproductive experience of intermarried Rothschilds differ so strikingly from that of intermarried families in Bradford?

The consequences of inbreeding are unpredictable and depend largely on what biologists call the founder effect: If the founding couple pass on a large number of lethal recessives, as appears to have happened in Bradford, these recessives will spread and double up through intermarriage. If, however,

Mayer and Gutle Rothschild handed down a comparatively healthy genone, their descendants could safely intermarry for generations—at least until small deleterious effects inevitably began to pile up and produce inbreeding depression, a long-term decline in the well-being of a family or a species.

A founding couple can also pass on advantageous genes. Among animal populations, generations of inbreeding frequently lead to the development of coadapted gene complexes, suites of genetic traits that tend to be inherited together. These traits may confer special adaptations to a local environment, like resistance to disease.

The evidence for such benefits in humans is slim, perhaps in part because any genetic advantages conferred by inbreeding may be too small or too gradual to detect. Alan Bittles, a professor of human biology at Edith Cowan University in Australia, points out that there's a dearth of data on the subject of genetic disadvantages too. Not until some rare disorder crops up in a place like Bradford do doctors even notice intermarriage.

Something disturbingly eugenic about the idea of better-families-through-inbreeding also causes researchers to look away. Oxford historian Niall Ferguson, author of *The House of Rothschild,* speculates that that there may have been "a Rothschild 'gene for financial acumen,' which intermarriage somehow helped to perpetuate. Perhaps it was that which made the Rothschilds truly exceptional." But he quickly dismisses this as "unlikely."

At the same time, humans are perfectly comfortable with the idea that inbreeding can produce genetic benefits for domesticated animals. When we want a dog with the points to take Best in Show at Madison Square Garden, we often get it by taking individuals displaying the desired traits and "breeding them back" with their close kin.

Researchers have observed that animals in the wild may also attain genetic benefits from inbreeding. Ten mouse colonies may set up housekeeping in a field but remain separate. The dominant male in each colony typically inbreeds with his kin. His genes rapidly spread through the colony—the founder effect again—and each colony thus becomes a little different from the others, with double recessives proliferating for both good and ill effects. When the weather changes or some deadly virus blows through, one colony may end up better adapted to the new circumstances than the other nine, which die out.

Inbreeding may help explain why insects can develop resistance almost overnight to pesticides like DDT: The resistance first shows up as a recessive trait in one obscure family line. Inbreeding, with its cascade of double recessives, causes the trait to be expressed in every generation of this family—and under the intense selective pressure of DDT, this family of resistant insects survives and proliferates.

THE OBVIOUS PROBLEM WITH THIS CONTRARIAN argument is that so many animals seem to go out of their way to avoid inbreeding. Field biologists have often observed that animals reared together from an early age become imprinted on one another and lack mutual sexual interest as adults; they have an innate aversion to homegrown romance.

But what they are avoiding, according to William Shields, a biologist at the State University of New York College of Environmental Science and Forestry at Syracuse, is merely incest, the most extreme form of inbreeding, not inbreeding itself. He argues that normal patterns of dispersal actually encourage inbreeding. When young birds leave the nest, for instance, they typically move four or five home ranges away, not 10 or 100; that is, they stay within breeding distance of their cousins. Intense loyalty to a home territory helps keep a population healthy, according to Shields, because it encourages "optimal inbreeding." This elusive ideal is the point at which a population gets the benefit of adaptations to local habitat—the coadapted gene complexes—without the hazardous unmasking of recessive disorders.

## GENETIC AND METABOLIC TESTS CAN NOW SCREEN FOR ABOUT 100 RECESSIVE DISORDERS

In some cases, outbreeding can be the real hazard. A study conducted by E. L. Brannon, an ecologist at the University of Idaho, looked at two separate populations of sockeye salmon, one breeding where a river entered a lake, the other where it exited. Salmon fry at the inlet evolved to swim downstream to the lake. The ones at the outlet evolved to swim upstream. When researchers crossed the populations, they ended up with salmon young too confused to know which way to go. In the wild, such a hybrid population might lose half or more of its fry and soon vanish.

It is, of course, a long way from sockeye salmon and inbred insects to human mating behavior. But Patrick Bateson, a professor of ethology at Cambridge University, argues that outbreeding has at times been hazardous for humans too. For instance, the size and shape of our teeth is a strongly inherited trait. So is jaw size and shape. But the two traits aren't inherited together. If a woman with small jaws and small teeth marries a man with big jaws and big teeth, their grandchildren may end up with a mouthful of gnashers in a Tinkertoy jaw. Before dentistry was commonplace, Bateson adds, "ill-fitting teeth were probably a serious cause of mortality because it increased the likelihood of abscesses in the mouth." Marrying a cousin was one way to avoid a potentially lethal mismatch.

Bateson suggests that while youngsters imprinting on their siblings lose sexual interest in one another they may also gain a search image for a mate—someone who's not a sibling but *like* a sibling. Studies have shown that people overwhelmingly choose spouses similar to themselves, a phenomenon called assortative mating. The similarities are social, psychological, and physical, even down to traits like earlobe length. Cousins, Bateson says, perfectly fit this human preference for "slight novelty."

So where does this leave us? No scientist is advocating intermarriage, but the evidence indicates that we should at least moderate our automatic disdain for it. One unlucky woman, whom Robin Bennett encountered in the course of her research, recalled the reaction when she became pregnant after living with her first cousin for two years. Her gynecologist professed horror, told her the baby "would be sick all the time," and advised her to have an abortion. Her boyfriend's mother, who was also her aunt, "went nuts, saying that our baby would be retarded." The woman had an abortion, which she now calls "the worst mistake of my life."

Science is increasingly able to help such people look at their own choices more objectively. Genetic and metabolic tests can now screen for about 10 recessive disorders. In the past, families in Bradford rarely recognized genetic origins of causes of death or patterns of abnormality. The likelihood of stigma within the community or racism from without also made people reluctant to discuss such problems. But new tests have helped change that. Last year two siblings in Bradford were hoping to intermarry their children despite a family history of thalassemia, a recessive blood disorder that is frequently fatal before the age of 30. After testing determined which of the children carried the thalassemia gene, the families were able to arrange a pair of carrier-to-noncarrier first-cousin marriages.

Such planning may seem complicated. It may even be the sort of thing that causes Americans, with their entrenched dread of inbreeding, to shudder. But the needs of both culture and medicine were satisfied, and an observer could only conclude that the urge to marry cousins must be more powerful, and more deeply rooted, than we yet understand.

---

# INTERRACIAL INTIMACY

*White-black dating, marriage, and adoption are on the rise. This development, however, is being met with resistance—more vocally by blacks than by whites*

BY RANDALL KENNEDY

Americans are already what racial purists have long feared: a people characterized by a great deal of racial admixture, or what many in the past referred to distastefully as "mongrelization." In pigmentation, width of noses, breadth of lips, texture of hair, and other telltale signs, the faces and bodies of millions of Americans bear witness to interracial sexual encounters. Some were joyful, passionate, loving affairs. Many were rapes. Others contained elements of both choice and coercion. These different kinds of interracial intimacy and sexual depredation all reached their peak in the United States during the age of slavery, and following the Civil War they decreased markedly. Since the end of the civil-rights revolution interracial dating, interracial sex, and interracial marriage have steadily increased, as has the number of children born of interracial unions. This development has prompted commentators to speak of the "creolization" or "browning" or "beiging" of America.

Over the years legions of white-supremacist legislators, judges, prosecutors, police officers, and other officials have attempted to prohibit open romantic interracial attachments, particularly those between black men and white women. From the 1660s to the 1960s, forty-one territories, colonies, or states enacted laws—anti-miscegenation statutes—barring sex or marriage between blacks and whites, and many states ultimately made marriage across the color line a felony. Such laws crystallized attitudes about interracial intimacy that remain influential today, but all were invalidated by the U.S. Supreme Court in 1967, in the most aptly named case in all of American constitutional history: *Loving* v. *Commonwealth of Virginia*. Although white and black Americans are far more likely to date and marry within their own race than outside it, the cultural environment has changed considerably since *Loving*. Recall what happened in the spring of 2000, when George W. Bush, at a crucial moment in his primary campaign, paid a highly publicized visit to Bob Jones University, in South Carolina. During that visit he offered no criticism of the university's then existing prohibition against interracial dating. In the controversy that ensued, no nationally prominent figures defended Bob Jones's policy. Public opinion not only forced Bush to distance himself from Bob Jones but also prompted the notoriously stubborn and reactionary administration of that institution to drop its ban.

The de-stigmatization in this country of interracial intimacy is profoundly encouraging. Against the tragic backdrop of American history, it is a sign that Frederick Douglass may have been right when he prophesied, even before the abolition of slavery, that eventually "the white and colored people of this country [can] be blended into a common nationality, and enjoy together... the inestimable blessings of life, liberty and the pursuit of happiness."

The great but altogether predictable irony is that just as white opposition to white-black intimacy finally lessened, during the last third of the twentieth century, black opposition became vocal and aggressive. In college classrooms today, when discussions about the ethics of interracial dating and marriage arise, black students are frequently the ones most likely to voice disapproval.

## MARITAL INTEGRATION

Despite some ongoing resistance (a subject to which I will return), the situation for people involved in interracial intimacy has never been better. For the most part, the law prohibits officials from taking race into account in licensing marriages, making child-custody decisions, and arranging adoptions. Moreover, the American public accepts interracial intimacy as it never has before. This trend will almost certainly continue; polling data and common observation indicate that young people tend to be more liberal on these matters than their elders.

In 1960 there were about 51,000 black-white married couples in the United States; in 1970 there were 65,000, in 1980 there were 121,000, in 1990 there were 213,000, and by 1998 the number had reached 330,000. In other words, in the past four decades black-white marriages increased more than sixfold. And black-white marriages are not only becoming more numerous. Previously, the new couples in mixed marriages tended to be older than other brides and grooms. They were frequently veterans of divorce, embarking on second or third marriages. In recent years, however, couples in mixed marriages seem to be marrying younger than their pioneering predecessors and seem more inclined to have children and to pursue all the other "normal" activities that married life offers.

It should be stressed that black-white marriages remain remarkably rare—fewer than one percent of the total. In 1998, when 330,000 black-white couples were married, 55,305,000 couples were married overall. Moreover, the racial isolation of blacks on the marriage market appears to be greater than that of other people of color: much larger percentages of Native Americans and Asian-Americans marry whites. According to 1990 Census data, in the age cohort twenty-five to thirty-four, 36 percent of U.S.-born Asian-American husbands and 45 percent of U.S.-born Asian-American wives had white spouses; 53 percent of Native American husbands and 54 percent of Native American wives had white spouses. Only eight percent of African-American husbands and only four percent of African-American wives had white spouses. The sociologist Nathan Glazer was correct in stating, in *The Public Interest* (September 1995), that "blacks stand out uniquely among the array of American ethnic and racial groups in the degree to which marriage remains within the group." Of course, the Native American and Asian-American populations are so much smaller than the African-American population that relatively few intermarriages make a big difference in percentage terms. But the disparity is real: it has to do not only with demographics but also with generations' worth of subjective judgments about marriageability, beauty, personality, comfort, compatibility, and prestige. Even now a wide array of social pressures continue to make white-black marriages more difficult and thus less frequent than other interethnic or interracial marriages.

Nevertheless, the trend toward more interracial marriage is clear, as is a growing acceptance of the phenomenon. Successful, high-profile interracial couples include the white William Cohen (a former senator from Maine and the Secretary of Defense under Bill Clinton) and the black Janet Langhart; and the white Wendy Raines and the black Franklin Raines (he is a former director of the Office of Management and Budget and the CEO of Fannie Mae). Some African-Americans whose positions make them directly dependent on black public opinion have nonetheless married whites without losing their footing. A good example is Julian Bond, the chairman of the board of directors of the National Association for the Advancement of Colored People. Though married to a white woman, Bond ascended to the chairmanship of the oldest and most influential black-advancement organization in the country in 1998, and as of this writing continues to enjoy widespread support within the NAACP.

There are other signs that black-white romance has become more widely accepted; indeed, it is quite fashionable in some contexts. One is advertising. When advertisers addressing general audiences use romance to deliver their messages, they most often depict couples of the same race. But now at least occasionally one sees interracial couples deployed as enticements to shop at Diesel or Club Monaco, or to buy furniture from Ikea, jeans from Guess, sweaters from Tommy Hilfiger, cologne from Calvin Klein, or water from Perrier.

Scores of interracial support groups have emerged across the country, among them Kaleidoscope, at the University of Virginia; Students of Mixed Heritage at Amherst College; Interracial Family Club, in Washington, D.C.; Half and Half, at Bryn Mawr; and Mixed Plate, at Grinnell. Although most of these organizations lack deep roots, many display a vigor and resourcefulness that suggest they will survive into the foreseeable future. They stem from and represent a community in the making. It is a community united by a demand that the larger society respect and be attentive to people who by descent or by choice fall outside conventional racial groupings: interracial couples, parents of children of a different race, and children of parents of a different race. Those within this community want it known that they are not products or agents of an alarming mongrelization, as white racists still believe; nor are they inauthentic and unstable in-betweeners, as some people of color would have it. They want security amid the established communities from which they have migrated. They want to emerge from what the writer Lise Funderburg has identified as the "racial netherworld," and they want to enjoy interaction with others without regret or fear, defensiveness or embarrassment.

## "Sleeping White"

African-Americans largely fall into three camps with respect to white-black marriage. One camp, relatively small, openly champions it as a good. Its members argue that increasing rates of interracial marriage will decrease social segregation, encourage racial open-mindedness, enhance blacks' access to enriching social networks, elevate their status, and empower black women in their interactions with black men by subjecting the latter to greater competition in the marketplace for companionship.

A second camp sees interracial marriage merely as a choice that individuals should have the right to make. For example, while noting in *Race Matters* (1993) that "more and more white Americans are willing to interact sexually with black Americans *on an equal basis*," Cornel West maintains that he views this as "neither cause for celebration nor reason for lament." This is probably the predominant view among blacks. It allows a person simultaneously to oppose anti-miscegenation laws and to disclaim any desire to marry across racial lines. Many African-Americans are attracted to this position, because, among other things, it helps to refute a deeply annoying assumption on the part of many whites: that blacks would like nothing more than to be intimate with whites and even, if possible, to become white.

A third camp opposes interracial marriage, on the grounds that it expresses racial disloyalty, suggests disapproval of fellow blacks, undermines black culture, weakens the African-American marriage market, and feeds racist mythologies, particularly the canard that blacks lack pride of race.

Such opposition has always been a powerful undercurrent. When Walter White, the executive secretary of the NAACP, divorced his black wife (the mother of their two children) and married a white woman from South Africa, in 1949, the Norfolk (Virginia) *Journal and Guide* spoke for many blacks when it asserted, "A prompt and official announcement that [White] will not return to his post… is in order." Part of the anger stemmed from apprehension that segregationists would seize upon White's marriage to substantiate the charge that what black male civil-rights activists were really after was sex with white women. Part stemmed from a widespread sense that perhaps White thought no black woman was good enough for him.

By the late 1960s, with the repudiation of anti-miscegenation and Jim Crow laws, increasing numbers of blacks felt emboldened to openly oppose mixed marriages. "We Shall Overcome" was giving way to "Black Power": improving the image of blacks in the minds of whites seemed less important than cultivating a deeper allegiance to racial solidarity. To blacks, interracial intimacy compromised that allegiance. The African-American social reformer George Wiley dedicated himself to struggles for racial justice as a leading figure in the Congress for Racial Equality (CORE) and the founder of the National Welfare Rights Organization. Yet many black activists denounced him for marrying and remaining married to a white woman. When he addressed a rally in Washington, D.C., on African Liberation Day in April of 1972, a group of black women heckled him by chanting, "Where's your white wife? Where's your white wife?" When he attempted to focus his remarks on the situation of black women, the hecklers merely took up a different chant: "Talking black and sleeping white."

Other politically active blacks married to whites—James Farmer, a founder of CORE, and Julius Hobson, a tenacious activist in Washington—faced similar pressure. Julius Lester, a longtime member of the Student Nonviolent Coordinating Committee, wrote a book with one of the most arresting titles of that flamboyant era: *Look Out, Whitey! Black Power's Gon' Get Your Mama!* (1968). But to many black activists, Lester's writings and ideas were decidedly less significant than his choice of a white wife. To them, his selection bespoke hypocrisy. Ridiculing Lester, one black woman wrote a letter to the editor of *Ebony* in which she suggested that it was foolish to regard him as a trustworthy leader. After all, she cautioned, he couldn't even "crawl out of bed" with whites.

The "sleeping white" critique embarrassed a wide variety of people as distinctions between the personal and the political evaporated. At many colleges and universities black students ostracized other blacks who dated (much less married) whites. A black student who wanted to walk around "with a blonde draped on his arm" could certainly do so, a black student leader at the University of Washington told St. Clair Drake, a leading African-American sociologist. "All we say," the student continued, "is don't try to join the black studies association." Drake himself became the target of this critique. When he visited his old high school in 1968, he says, the Black Student Union refused to have anything to do with him, because he was involved in an interracial relationship. Drake's classmate Charles V. Hamilton, a co-author, with Stokely Carmichael, of *Black Power: The Politics of Liberation in America* (1967), was shunned for the same reason.

In some instances black opposition to interracial intimacy played a part in destroying a marriage. A dramatic example is the breakup of Everett LeRoi Jones (now known as Amiri Baraka) and Hettie Jones. LeRoi Jones was born of middle-class black parents in Newark, New Jersey, in 1934. For two years he attended Howard University, which he detested. He served in the Air Force for a short time, and in 1957 he moved to Greenwich Village. He worked for the magazine *Record Changer* and was a co-editor, with Hettie Cohen, of *Yugen*, an avant-garde magazine that published writings by William Burroughs, Gregory Corso, Allen Ginsberg, Jack Kerouac, Charles Olson, and Jones himself. Hettie Cohen was a woman of Jewish parentage who had grown up in suburban New York and attended Mary Washington, the women's college of the University of Virginia. Jones and Cohen married in 1958. Although his parents accepted the marriage easily, her parents totally opposed it.

For a while LeRoi and Hettie Jones lived together in what she remembers as a loving relationship. But then the pressure of bohemian penury, the demands of two children, and mutual infidelities (including one in which LeRoi fathered a baby by another woman who also happened to be white) caused their marriage to falter. Other forces also emerged to doom the union: LeRoi's deep internal tensions, his ambition to become a black leader, and the growing sense in many black communities that no purported leader could be trusted who "talked black but slept white."

As the black protest movement gathered steam in the early sixties, Jones aimed at becoming an important figure in it. At the same time, his career as a writer blossomed. He wrote well-regarded poetry, social and political essays, and a significant book, *Blues People* (1963), on the history of African-American music. What made LeRoi Jones a celebrity, however, and what ensures him a niche in American literary history, is his two-act play *Dutchman*, which opened in New York City in March of 1964. In *Dutchman* a reticent, bookish middle-class black man named Clay meets a white temptress named Lula in a New York subway car. The play consists mainly of their verbal combat. Angered by Clay's refusal to dance with her, Lula shouts, "Come on, Clay. Let's rub bellies on the train… Forget your social-working mother for a few seconds and let's knock stomachs. Clay, you liver-lipped white man. You would-be Christian. You ain't no nigger, you're just a dirty white man." Clay responds in kind.

> "Tallulah Bankhead!… Don't you tell me anything! If I'm a middle-class fake white man… let me be… Let me be who I feel like being. Uncle Tom. Thomas. Whoever. It's none of your business… I sit here, in this buttoned-up suit, to keep myself from cutting all your throats… You great liberated whore! You fuck some black man, and right away you're an expert on black people. What a lotta shit that is."

But Lula has the last word, so to speak: she suddenly stabs Clay to death. Other passengers throw his body out of the subway car and depart. Alone, Lula re-occupies her seat. When another black man enters the car, she begins her lethal routine anew.

Though living in a predominantly white, bohemian environment when he wrote *Dutchman*, Jones had begun to believe that it was blacks to whom he should be addressing his art. Increasingly successful, he was also becoming increasingly radical in his condemnation of white American society. Asked by a white woman what white people could do to help the race problem, Jones replied, "You can help by dying. You are a cancer. You can help the world's people with your death." An outrageous statement coming from anyone, this comment was even more arresting coming from a man who was married to a white woman. Jones was by no means alone in living within this particular contradiction. He noted in his autobiography that at one point he and some other black intellectuals objected to the presence of white radicals on a committee they were in the process of establishing. "What was so wild," he recalled, "was that some of us were talking about how we didn't want white people on the committee but we were all hooked up to white women… Such were the contradictions of that period of political organization."

The more prominent Jones became, however, the more critics, both black and white, charged him with being hypocritical. The critic Stanley Kauffmann, for example, asserted that Jones constituted an exemplary figure in "the Tradition of the Fake." Stung by such charges, infatuated with black-nationalist rhetoric, inspired by the prospect of re-creating himself, and bored with a disappointing marriage, LeRoi Jones divorced Hettie Jones in 1965.

Throughout the black-power era substantial numbers of African-Americans loudly condemned black participation in interracial relationships (especially with whites), deeming it to be racial betrayal. A reader named Joyce Blake searingly articulated this sentiment in a letter to the editor of the *Village Voice*.

> It really hurts and baffles me and many other black sisters to see our black brothers (?) coming down the streets in their African garbs with a white woman on their arms. It is fast becoming a standard joke among the white girls that they can get our men still—African styles and all…
>
> It certainly seems to many black sisters that the Movement is just another subterfuge to aid the Negro male in procuring a white woman. If this be so, then the black sisters don't need it, for surely we have suffered enough humiliation from both white and black men in America.

## A Demographic Betrayal?

Although racial solidarity has been the principal reason for black opposition to intermarriage over the years, another reason is the perception that intermarriage by black men weakens black women in the marriage market. A reader named Lula Miles asserted this view in an August 1969 letter to the editor of *Ebony*. Responding to a white woman who had expressed bewilderment at black women's anger, Miles wrote, "Non-sister wonders why the sight of a black man with a white woman is revolting to a black woman… The name of the game is 'competition.' Non-sister, you are trespassing!"

Another letter writer, named Miraonda J. Stevens, reinforced this point: "In the near future there aren't going to be enough nice black men around for us [black women] to marry." This "market" critique of interracial marriage has a long history. In 1929 Palestine Wells, a black columnist for the Baltimore *Afro-American*, wrote,

> I have a sneaking suspicion that national intermarriage will make it harder to get husbands. A girl has a hard time enough getting a husband, but methinks 'twill be worse. Think how

> awful it would be if all the ofay girls with a secret hankering for brown skin men, could openly compete with us.

Forty-five years later an *Ebony* reader named Katrina Williams echoed Wells. "The white man is marrying the white woman," she wrote. "The black man is marrying the white woman. Who's gonna marry me?"

Behind her anxious question resides more than demographics: there is also the perception that large numbers of African-American men believe not only that white women are relatively more desirable but that black women are positively unattractive. Again the pages of *Ebony* offer vivid testimony. A reader named Mary A. Dowdell wrote in 1969,

> Let's just lay all phony excuses aside and get down to the true nitty, nitty, NITTY- GRITTY and tell it like it really is. Black males hate black women just because they are black. The whole so-called Civil Rights Act was really this: "I want a white woman because she's white and I not only hate but don't want a black woman because she's black."... The whole world knows this.

Decades later African-American hostility to interracial intimacy remained widespread and influential. Three examples are revealing. The first is the movie *Jungle Fever* (1991), which portrays an interracial affair set in New York City in the early 1990s. The director, Spike Lee, made sure the relationship was unhappy. Flipper Purify is an ambitious, college-educated black architect who lives in Harlem with his black wife and their young daughter. Angie Tucci, a young white woman, works for Purify as a secretary. Educated only through high school, she lives in Bensonhurst, Brooklyn, with her father and brothers, all of whom are outspoken racists. One evening when Flipper and Angie stay late at his office, work is superseded by erotic longing tinged with racial curiosity. He has never been sexually intimate with a white woman, and she has never been sexually intimate with a black man. They close that gap in their experience, and then stupidly confide in indiscreet friends, who carelessly reveal their secret. Angie's father throws her out of the family home after viciously beating her for "fucking a black nigger." Flipper's wife, Drew, throws him out as well. Flipper and Angie move into an apartment together, but that arrangement falls apart rather quickly under the pressure of their own guilt and uncertainty and the strong disapproval they encounter among blacks and whites alike.

The second example is Lawrence Otis Graham's 1995 essay "I Never Dated a White Girl." Educated at Princeton University and Harvard Law School, Graham sought to explain why "black middle-class kids... [who are] raised in integrated or mostly white neighborhoods, [and] told to befriend white neighbors, socialize and study with white classmates, join white social and professional organizations, and go to work for mostly white employers" are also told by their relatives, "Oh, and by the way, don't ever forget that you are black, and that you should never get so close to whites that you happen to fall in love with them." Graham did more than explain, however; he justified this advice in a candid polemic that might well have been titled "Why I Am *Proud* That I Never Dated a White Girl."

The third example is "Black Men, White Women: A Sister Relinquishes Her Anger," a 1993 essay by the novelist Bebe Moore Campbell. Describing a scene in which she and her girlfriends spied a handsome black celebrity escorting a white woman at a trendy Beverly Hills restaurant, Campbell wrote,

> In unison, we moaned, we groaned, we rolled our eyes heavenward. We gnashed our teeth in harmony and made ugly faces. We sang "Umph! Umph! Umph!" a cappella-style, then shook our heads as we lamented for the ten thousandth time the perfidy of black men and cursed trespassing white women who dared to "take our men."... Before lunch was over I had a headache, indigestion, and probably elevated blood pressure.

Only a small percentage of black men marry interracially; one report, published in 1999, estimated that seven percent of married black men have non-black wives. But with poverty, imprisonment, sexual orientation, and other factors limiting the number of marriageable black men, a substantial number of black women feel this loss of potential mates acutely. In 1992 researchers found that for every three unmarried black women in their twenties there was only one unmarried black man with earnings above the poverty level. Given these realities, black women's disparagement of interracial marriage should come as no surprise. "In a drought," Campbell wrote, "even one drop of water is missed."

Compiling a roster of prominent blacks—Clarence Thomas, Henry Louis Gates Jr., Quincy Jones, Franklin A. Thomas, John Edgar Wideman—married to or otherwise romantically involved with whites, Graham voiced disappointment. When a prominent black role model "turns out to be married to a white mate," he wrote, "our children say, 'Well, if it's so good to be black, why do all my role models date and marry whites?'... As a child growing up in the 'black is beautiful' 1970s, I remember asking these questions."

Anticipating the objection that his views amount to "reverse racism," no less an evil than anti-black bigotry, Graham wrote that his aim was neither keeping the races separate nor assigning superiority to one over the other. Rather, he wanted to develop "solutions for the loss of black mentors and role models at a time when the black community is overrun with crime, drug use, a high dropout rate, and a sense that any black who hopes to find... career success must necessarily disassociate himself from his people with the assistance of a white spouse." He maintained,

> It's not the discrete decision of any one of these individuals that makes black America stand up and take notice. It is the cumulative effect of each of these personal decisions that bespeaks a frightening pattern for an increasingly impoverished and wayward black community. The cumulative effect is that the very blacks who are potential mentors and supporters of a financially and psychologically depressed black community are increasingly deserting the black community en masse, both physically and emotionally.

## THE CASE FOR AMALGAMATION

Although Graham's view is widespread, there are blacks who not only tolerate but applaud increasing rates of interracial intimacy. The most outspoken and distinguished African-American proponent of free trade in the marital marketplace is the Harvard sociologist Orlando Patterson. Patterson makes three main claims. First, he maintains that interracial marriage typically gives people access to valuable new advice, know-how, and social networks. "When we marry," he writes in *Rituals of Blood: Consequences of Slavery in Two American Centuries*, "we engage in an exchange of social and cultural dowries potentially far more valuable than gold-rimmed china. The cultural capital exchanged in ethnic intermarriage is considerably greater than that within ethnic groups."

Patterson's second claim is that removing the informal racial boundaries within the marriage market would especially benefit black women—because large numbers of white men are and will increasingly become open to marrying black women, if given a chance. He notes that if only one in five nonblack men were to court black women, the pool of potential spouses available to those women would immediately double. According to Patterson, this would be good not only because it would make marriage more accessible to black women but also because larger numbers of white (and other) suitors might well fortify black women in their dealings with black men. As Patterson sees it, by forswearing nonblack suitors, many black women have senselessly put themselves at the mercy of black men, who have declined to be as accommodating as they might be in the face of greater competition.

Patterson's third claim is that widespread intermarriage is necessary to the integration of blacks into American society. He agrees with the writer Calvin Hernton that intermarriage is "the crucial test in determining when a people have completely won their way into the mainstream of any given society." In *Ordeals of Integration* he therefore urges blacks, particularly women, to renounce their objections to interracial intimacy. Higher rates of intermarriage "will complete the process of total integration as [blacks] become to other Americans not only full members of the political and moral community, but also people whom 'we' marry," he counsels. "When that happens, the goal of integration will have been fully achieved."

Some may question whether higher rates of interracial marriage will do as much or signify as much as Patterson contends. The history of racially divided societies elsewhere suggests that it will not. Addressing "the uncertain legacy of miscegenation," Professor Anthony W. Marx, of Columbia University, writes that despite considerable race mixing in Brazil, and that country's formal repudiation of racism, Brazil nonetheless retains "an informal racial order that [discriminates] against 'blacks and browns.'" Contrary to optimistic projections, Brazil's multiracialism did not so much produce upward mobility for dark Brazilians as reinforce a myth of mobility. That myth has undergirded a pigmentocracy that continues to privilege whiteness. A similar outcome is possible in the United States. Various peoples of color—Latinos, Asian-Americans, Native Americans, and light-skinned African-Americans—could well intermarry with whites in increasingly large numbers and join with them in a de facto alliance against darker-skinned blacks, who might remain racial outcasts even in a more racially mixed society.

Historically, though, at least in the United States, openness to interracial marriage has been a good barometer of racial enlightenment in thought and practice. As a general rule, those persons most welcoming of interracial marriage (and other intimate interracial associations) are also those who have most determinedly embraced racial justice, a healthy respect for individualistic pluralism, and a belief in the essential oneness of humanity.

---

*Randall Kennedy is a professor at Harvard Law School. He is the author of* Nigger *(2002) and* Interracial Intimacies: Sex, Marriage, Identity, and Adoption, *published by Pentheon Books, January 7,2003.*

# Sexual Satisfaction in Premarital Relationships: Associations With Satisfaction, Love, Commitment, and Stability

*This investigation focused on how sexual satisfaction is associated with relationship quality and stability in premarital couples. With data collected at multiple times over several years from a sample of heterosexual couples (who were all dating at Time 1), I examined how sexual satisfaction was associated with relationship satisfaction, love, commitment, and stability. At each wave of the study, sexual satisfaction was associated positively with relationship satisfaction, love, and commitment for both men and women. In addition, change in sexual satisfaction between Time 1 and Time 2 was associated with change over the same period in relationship sexual satisfaction, love, and commitment. Furthermore, some evidence was found that sexual satisfaction was associated with relationship stability. Overall, sexual satisfaction had stronger links with relationship quality for men than for women.*

**Susan Sprecher**
**Illinois State University**

American culture gives emphasis to sexual expression in marriage. For example, people are expected to base their choice of a marriage partner on sexual attraction. In addition, sexual satisfaction is considered to be a barometer for the quality of marriage. Indeed, research shows that how married individuals feel about the sex in their relationship is related to how they feel about their entire relationship (e.g., Henderson-King & Veroff, 1994). Less is known, however, about the connection between sexual satisfaction and relationship quality in premarital relationships, despite the fact that most couples who eventually marry begin their sexual activity prior to marriage. In addition, there is little information about how change in sexual satisfaction is associated with change in relationship quality, in either marital or premarital relationships. The purpose of this investigation was to examine how sexual satisfaction, including its change over time, is associated with the relationship quality and stability of premarital relationships.

### *Social Exchange Theory and Sexuality*

The social exchange perspective provides a lens through which we can examine why sexual satisfaction might be associated positively with general relationship quality (for a discussion of exchange theory applications to sexuality, see Sprecher, 1998). To some degree, sexual satisfaction represents a favorable balance of rewards and costs in the sexual aspect of the relationship. For example, according to Lawrance and Byers' (1992, 1995) Interpersonal Model of Sexual Satisfaction, sexual satisfaction is increased to the degree that within the sexual relationship, rewards are high, costs are low, the difference between rewards and costs compares favorably with a comparison level, and there is equality between partners in the exchange of rewards and costs (see also Byers, Demmons, & Lawrance, 1998). A rewarding sexual relationship can then lead to overall relationship quality (satisfaction, love, and commitment). In general, the more rewards in an important area of the relationship (e.g., the sexual relationship), the more the overall relationship quality. In addition, the more equitable the exchange in the relationship, including in sexual behaviors and feelings, the more likely the partners are to be satisfied with the relationship (e.g., Hatfield, Greenberger, Traupmann, & Lambert, 1982; Hatfield, Utne, & Traupmann, 1979).

### *The Association Between Sexual Satisfaction and Relationship Quality*

Several studies have shown an association between sexual satisfaction and overall relationship satisfaction in marriage. More specifically, husbands and wives who say they are sexually satisfied in their marriage are also likely to report high levels of overall satisfaction with their relationship (e.g., Blumstein & Schwartz, 1983; Cupach & Comstock, 1990; Edwards & Booth, 1994; Henderson-King & Veroff, 1994). The few studies that have examined this association in dating relationships have also found a link between sexual satisfaction and relationship satisfaction (Byers et al., 1998; Davies, Katz, & Jackson, 1999). Sexual satisfaction and related subjective measures of sexuality (e.g., sexual intimacy) also have been found to be associated positively with other indicators of relationship quality, including love (Aron & Henkemeyer, 1995; Grote & Frieze, 1998; Sprecher & Regan, 1998; Yela, 2000) and commitment or the likelihood that the relationship will last (Pinney, Gerrard, & Denney, 1987; Sprecher,

Metts, Burleson, Hatfield, & Thompson, 1995; Waite & Joyner, 2001). For a more thorough review of this literature, see Christopher and Sprecher 2000) and Sprecher and Regan (2000).

Most of the research demonstrating the association between sexual satisfaction and relationship quality has been cross-sectional. In one exception, Henderson-King and Veroff (1994) analyzed data from the Early Years of Marriage Project (see Veroff, Douvan, & Hatchett, 1995, for more detail), and found positive associations between sexual satisfaction (joy and excitement during sex, absence of upset with sex) and measures of relationship quality during both the first and third years of the couples' marriage. They also conducted cross-lagged correlations, which indicated no significant differences in strength between the correlations of measures of sexual feelings at Year 1 with measures of sexual feelings at Year 3. Another longitudinal study that included measures of both sexual satisfaction and marital satisfaction at multiple times is the Longitudinal Study of Martial Instability. With their data, Edwards and Booth (1994) examined the association between change in sexual happiness and change in marital well-being by correlating change scores; in other words, they correlated scores created from the difference between Wave 1 (1980) and Wave 3 (1988) sexual satisfaction with scores created from the difference between Wave 1 and Wave 3 marital satisfaction. These correlations were positive and significant, leading the researchers to conclude, "Although we cannot sort out the causal direction of these changes, it is clear that changes in sexual behavior are generally related to changes in psychological well-being and marital quality" (Edwards & Booth, 1994, p. 247). Overall, though, almost no longitudinal studies have been conducted that include measures of both sexual satisfaction and relationship quality at two or more times, and to my knowledge, no such longitudinal research has been conducted with premarital couples.

### *Sexual Satisfaction as a Predictor of Relationship Stability vs. Instability*

A related issue to address is whether sexual satisfaction contributes to relationship longevity. Does satisfying sex help sustain a relationship? Two of the above longitudinal studies have relevant data. Oggins, Leber, and Veroff (1993), using data from the Early Years of Marriage project, reported that measures of sexual satisfaction at Year 1 predicted (negatively) marital dissolution by the fourth year of marriage (also see Veroff et al., 1995). Furthermore, Edwards and Booth (1994) reported that a decline in sexual satisfaction between 1980 and 1983 was associated with the probability of divorce by 1988. White and Keith (1990), using a national sample of married individuals first interviewed in 1980 and again in 1983, reported that a measure of sexual problems (dissatisfaction) at Time 1 was associated positively with the likelihood of divorce by Time 2.

Although no longitudinal study has been conducted that examines whether sexual satisfaction predicts premarital relationship breakups, the associations of more objective aspects of sexuality and premarital relationship stability have been studied. In the Boston Dating Couples Study, Hill, Rubin, and Peplau (1976) found that whether or not the dating couple was sexually intimate at the time of the initial contact had no effect on the status of the relationship two years later. Furthermore, no difference was found in relationship stability between the couples who had sex early in their relationship and couples who had sex later (Peplau, Rubin, & Hill, 1977). However, in a 3-month longitudinal study of dating individuals, Simpson (1987) found that whether or not the couple had engaged in sexual intercourse had a significant and positive effect on relationship stability. The significant effect for sexual involvement was found even when other variables (e.g., satisfaction, closeness, length of relationship) were controlled. Furthermore, Felmlee, Sprecher, and Bassin (1990) found that an index representing sexual intimacy was a positive predictor of the stability of premarital relationships, although it was not significant when included in a model with several other predictors. Additional longitudinal research is needed with premarital couples to examine whether sexual satisfaction is predictive of relationship stability.

### *Purposes of This Investigation*

This study combines cross-sectional analyses with longitudinal analyses conducted with a sample of romantic couples (all dating at Time 1), who were surveyed multiple times, for the purpose of extending our understanding of the role of sexual satisfaction in contributing to the quality and stability of the relationship. I present two research hypotheses and two research questions:

1. Research Hypothesis 1 (RH1): Sexual satisfaction is associated positively with relationship satisfaction, love, and commitment.
2. Research Hypothesis 2 (RH2): Changes in sexual satisfaction are associated with changes in relationship satisfaction, love, and commitment.
3. Research Question 1 (RQ1): Does sexual satisfaction at Time 1 predict an increase in relationship quality (satisfaction, love, and commitment) by Time 2; and/or does relationship quality (satisfaction, love, and commitment) at Time 1 predict an increase in sexual satisfaction by Time 2?
4. Research Question 2 (RQ2): Is sexual satisfaction a predictor of later relationship stability?

I examine the above associations for men and women separately because considerable prior research (e.g., Baumeister, Catanese, & Vohs, 2001) suggests that sex may be more important or at least have different meanings to men than to women.

## Method

### Overview of the Data

The data are from a longitudinal study conducted at a Midwestern university with a sample of romantic couples. The original sample consisted of both partners of 101 dating couples who completed a self-administered questionnaire in the Fall of 1988. Follow-ups were conducted in the Spring and Summer of 1989, 1990, 1991, and 1992. The sample size decreased with each wave primarily because couples who experienced their relationship terminate ended their participation in the study. By Wave 5, 59% ($n$ = 60) of the couples had ended their relationship.

### Participants

The sample at Time 1 consisted of 101 dating couples (202 individuals), most of whom were students at a large Midwestern university. The participants were volunteers who were recruited through announcements in classes, advertisements in the student newspaper, and posters placed around campus. The average age of the participants at Time 1 was approximately 20 years (20.3 [*SD* = 2.51] for men and 19.75 [*SD* = 1.37] for women). Most of the sample was White (97.5%) and of the middle or upper-middle class (86.6%). The mean number of months the couples had been dating at Time 1 was 18.6 [*SD* = 13.73]; the range was 1 month to 55 months.

### Procedure

At Time 1, participants who responded to the announcement of the study completed a self-administered questionnaire in a university office. The partners completed the questionnaire at the same time but independently of each other.

At each of the four follow-ups (Times 2–5), participants who were still attending the university or living in the vicinity came to the researcher's office to complete another questionnaire (partners from couples who broke up arrived at different times). Participants who had moved away were mailed the questionnaire, with a stamped self-addressed return envelope. Among the couples whose relationship remained intact over the entire study ($n$ = 41), there was very little nonresponse.[1]

### Measurement

All participants at Time 1 and all participants in the follow-ups whose relationships were intact completed a lengthy questionnaire about various aspects of their relationship. The variables analyzed in this study were measured in the following ways (each scale of index was represented by the mean of the items).

*Sexual satisfaction.* A two-item index was formed to measure *sexual satisfaction.* One item was the global question, "How sexually satisfying is the relationship to you?" (1 = *not at all* to 7 = *very*). A similar global question has been used in several other studies on sex (e.g., Blumstein & Schwartz, 1983; Edwards & Booth, 1994; Greeley, 1991). The second item, which appeared in a different section of the questionnaire, asked how unrewarding or rewarding the partner's contributions were in the area of sex (meeting needs and preferences) on a 1 (*very unrewarding*) to 7 (*very rewarding*) response scale. Cronbach's alpha was relatively high for a 2-item measure (.82 for men and .70 for women at Time 1, and ranged from .77 to .93 at the follow-ups).

*Relationship quality measures.* The Hendrick Relationship Assessment Scale (RAS; 1988) was used to assess *satisfaction* in the relationship. Example items of this 7-item scale are "In general, how satisfied are you with your relationship?" and "To what extent has your relationship met your original expectations?" A 5-point response scale followed each item (anchors varied depending on the item, but a higher score always indicated greater satisfaction). Cronbach's alpha at Time 1 was .81 for men and .75 for women, and ranged from .65 to .87 at the follow-ups.

The Braiker and Kelley (1979) love scale was used to measure *love.* The original version consisted of 10 items that assessed feelings of belonging, closeness, and attachment (examples; "To what extent to you love ____ at this stage?" and "To what extent do you feel that your relationship is special compared with others you have been in?"). However, a sexual intimacy item was deleted from this scale because of possible measurement overlap with the sexual satisfaction item. The responses to the items ranged from 1 (*not at all*) to 7 (*a great deal*). Cronbach's alpha for the 9-item version of the love scale at Time 1 was .88 for men and .82 for women, and ranged from .71 to .93 at the follow-ups.

Five items were included to measure relationship *commitment.* Four of these items were from the commitment scale developed by Lund (1985) and included "How likely is it that your relationship will be permanent?" and "How likely are you to pursue another relationship or single life in the future?" Each of these items was followed by a 7-point response scale, ranging from 1 (*very unlikely*) to 7 (*very likely*). The final item was the general question, "How committed are you to your partner?" (1 = *not at all committed* to 7 = *very committed*). Cronbach's Alpha at Time 1 was .89 for men and .78 for women, and ranged from .52 to .97 at the follow-ups.

## Results

### Descriptive Information on the Sexual Satisfaction Index

Overall, the participants reported being sexually satisfied in their relationship. For example, the mean to the 2-item sexual satisfaction index was 6.06 (*SD* = 1.16) for men and 6.34 (*SD* = .79) for women (on a 7-point scale) at Time 1. At each wave of the study, women's sexual satisfaction was higher than men's, and this difference was significant ($p < .05$) at every wave except Wave 3. A trend was found

**Table 1. Associations of Sexual Satisfaction With Relationship Satisfaction, Love, and Commitment at Five Waves of Longitudinal Study**

| | Men | | | Women | | |
|---|---|---|---|---|---|---|
| | Satisfaction | Love | Commitment | Satisfaction | Love | Commitment |
| Time 1 | .54*** | .52*** | .46*** | .24* | .31** | .22* |
| Time 2 | .64*** | .64*** | .57*** | .30** | .33** | .27* |
| Time 3 | .54*** | .34** | .28* | .38** | .26* | .34** |
| Time 4 | .66*** | .60*** | .50*** | .63*** | .56*** | .54*** |
| Time 5 | .68*** | .53** | .55*** | .30 | .45** | .35* |

* $p < .05$. ** $p < .01$. *** $p < .001$.

**Table 2. Associations of Change in Sexual Satisfaction With Change in Relationship Satisfaction, Love, and Commitment Over Five Waves of Longitudinal Study**

| | Men | | | Women | | |
|---|---|---|---|---|---|---|
| | Satisfaction | Love | Commitment | Satisfaction | Love | Commitment |
| Change from Time 1 to Time 2 | .46*** | .50*** | .43*** | .42*** | .27* | .30** |
| Change from Time 2 to Time 3 | .33* | .24* | .26* | -.06 | .05 | .08 |
| Change from Time 3 to Time 4 | .45** | .52*** | .43** | .20 | .12 | .12 |
| Change from Time 4 to Time 5 | .05 | .09 | .16 | .39* | .06 | .01 |

* $p < .05$. ** $p < .01$. *** $p < .001$.

for sexual satisfaction to decrease over the five waves of the study. A repeated measures MANOVA conducted with the respondents ($n$ = 35 men and 36 women) who stayed in their relationship throughout the study and participated at every wave indicated a linear decrease in sexual satisfaction scores over the waves of the study; this decrease was significant ($p < .05$) for men and borderline significant ($p = .06$) for women.

The partners' sexual satisfaction scores were moderately correlated ($r$ was .37 [$p < .001$] at Time 1 and ranged from .30 to .46 [all $p < .01$] at the follow-ups).[2]

### *Association of Sexual Satisfaction with Relationship Quality*

I had hypothesized (RH1) that sexual satisfaction would be associated positively with relationship satisfaction, love, and commitment. As the results in Table 1 indicate, the participants' sexual satisfaction was correlated positively and significantly with their relationship satisfaction, love for partner, and commitment to the relationship, at each wave of the study (the only nonsignificant correlation was between sexual satisfaction and relationship satisfaction for women at Time 5, and this correlation was borderline significant; $p < .10$). Overall, the correlations were moderate to strong in strength (the mean $r$ was = .45), although the correlations were generally stronger for men than for women (mean $r$ was .54 for men and .37 for women). The men's correlations were compared to women's correlations by means of the $z$ test. The correlations were significantly different between the genders at both Time 1 and Time 2 (and for satisfaction at Time 5). In sum, the results indicate that sexual satisfaction is associated with variables referring to the general quality of the relationship, the associations exist for all three indicators of relationship quality (satisfaction, love, and commitment), the associations remain quite consistent over time, and the associations are stronger for men than for women.[3]

### *Association of Change in Sexual Satisfaction With Change in Relationship Quality*

Next, I tested RH2, which states that change in sexual satisfaction over time is associated with change in relationship satisfaction, love, and commitment. Similar to the analyses conducted by Edwards and Booth (1994), the difference score between Wave 1 and Wave 2 sexual satisfaction scores was correlated with the difference scores between these two waves for relationship satisfaction, love, and commitment. These correlations of difference scores are presented in the first row of Table 2. For both men and women, these correlations were positive and significant, indicating that increases in sexual satisfaction between Time 1 and Time 2 are associated with increases in relationship satisfaction, love, and commitment between the same waves. Although the sample size diminished over time, similar change scores were calculated for the periods from Time 2 to Time 3, Time 3 to Time 4, and Time 4 to Time 5. Changes in sexual satisfaction were generally not related to changes in the relationship quality variables at the follow-ups for women, but for men, these correlations were significant with the exception of those between Time 4 and Time 5.

### *Does Sexual Satisfaction Contribute to a Change in Relationship Quality?*

Next, I examined whether there was any evidence for a causal relationship, of either direction, between sexual satisfaction and each relationship quality variable (RQ1). More specifically, regressions (for men and women separately) were first conducted in which the Time 2 score of relationship satisfaction, love, or commitment, one at a time, was regressed on the Time 1 score of sexual satisfaction, controlling for the Time 1 score of relationship satisfaction, love, or commitment, respectively. In these regressions, relationship satisfaction at Time 1 was a significant predictor of relationship satisfaction at Time 2 (6 months later), commitment at Time 1 was a significant predictor of commitment at Time 2, and love at Time 1 was a significant predictor of love at Time 2 (βs ranged from .45 to .66, all $p < .001$). However, sexual satisfaction at Time 1 did not explain unique variance in any of the relationship quality variables at Time 2, controlling for the respective relationship quality measure at Time 1 (βs ranged from -.07 to .10, all *ns*). The percent of variance accounted for by the variables in these analyses ranged from 24% to 42%.

In a second set of regressions conducted to examine the reverse causal direction, sexual satisfaction at Time 1 was found to be a significant predictor of sexual satisfaction at Time 2 for both men and women (βs ranged from .39 to .58, $p < .01$). However, the relationship quality measure (relationship satisfaction, love, commitment) at Time 1 did not explain unique variance in sexual satisfaction at Time 2, controlling for sexual satisfaction at Time 1 (βs ranged from .00 to .15). The percent of variance accounted for by the variables in these analyses ranged from 29% to 34%. Thus, no evidence was found to indicate that sexual satisfaction leads to change in relationship quality, or, conversely, that relationship quality leads to change in sexual satisfaction.

### *Does Sexual Satisfaction Predict Later Relationship Breakups?*

The next issue examined with the longitudinal data is whether sexual satisfaction was associated with relationship stability versus termination over time. I first compared the couples who broke up by Time 2 ($n = 17$) with those couples who stayed together ($n = 84$) on sexual satisfaction measured at Time 1. Both the male partner's sexual satisfaction score and the female partner's sexual satisfaction score (at Time 1) were significantly higher in the couples who remained together over the 6 month period than in the couples who broke up (male satisfaction: 6.17 [$SD$ = 1.01] vs. 5.44 [$SD$ = 1.59], $t$ (98) = 2.43, $p < .05$; female satisfaction: 6.43 [$SD$ = .74], vs. 5.97 [$SD$ = .93], $t$ (97) = 2.22, $p <$ .05). A follow-up one-way ANOVA was conducted to determine the amount of variance in relationship status at Time 2 accounted for by sexual satisfaction at Time 1. For men, the $\eta^2$ was .06; for women, it was .05.

To determine the robustness of these findings, I next compared the couples who broke up between Time 2 and Time 3 ($n = 22$) with those couples who stayed together ($n$ = 62) on sexual satisfaction measured at Time 2. Male sexual satisfaction was higher among the couples who stayed together than among those who broke up (6.03 [$SD$ = 1.16] vs. 5.33 [$SD$ = 1.98], $t$ (78) = 1.96, $p = .05$; $\eta^2$ was .05). Female sexual satisfaction was also higher among those who stayed together than among those who broke up, although the difference was only marginally significant (6.31 [$SD$ = .80] vs. 5.88 [$SD$ = 1.06], $t$ (78) = 1.94, $p = .06$; $\eta^2$ was .05).[4]

I also examined whether sexual satisfaction explained any unique variance in dissolution beyond what might be explained by a general measure of relationship quality. To explore this, logistic regression was conducted for each gender, in which Time 2 relationship status (together vs. broken-up) was regressed on Time 1 sexual satisfaction and Time 1 relationship satisfaction. For men, relationship satisfaction at Time 1 had no effect on the likelihood of breaking up by Time 2 (the odds ratio, or exp(B) was 1.20; Wald test was not significant); however, sexual satisfaction had a negative effect on dissolution (the odds ratio, or exp(B) was .60; Wald test was significant, $p < .05$). For women, just the opposite results were found: General relationship satisfaction had a negative effect on dissolution by Time 2 (the odds ratio, or exp(B) was .15; Wald test was significant, $p < .01$); however, sexual satisfaction had no effect (the odds ratio, or exp(B) was .64; Wald test was not significant).

## Discussion

The results of this study indicate that sexual satisfaction is linked to relationship satisfaction, love, and commitment, for both men and women. Those participants who were most sexually satisfied were those who tended to report high levels of relationship satisfaction, love, and commitment. In addition, change in sexual satisfaction was associated with change, in the same direction, in relationship satisfaction, love, and commitment, although especially between Waves 1 and 2. While prior research had documented an association between sexual satisfaction and relationship quality (e.g., relationship satisfaction) primarily in married and other committed couples (e.g., Blumstein & Schwartz, 1983), this study demonstrated that sexual satisfaction is also linked to satisfaction, love, and commitment in dating couples, including at different times in the development of their relationship. Furthermore, the associations did not reduce in strength over time. While it may not seem surprising that satisfaction in a specific area of the relationship (sex) is associated with overall relationship satisfaction, the associations found between sexual satisfaction and love and commitment indicate that sexual satisfaction also has implications for how partners feel about each other and how committed they are to staying in the relationship. These results are consistent with the exchange perspective (e.g., Rusbult, 1983; Sprecher, 1998), which argues that positive and balanced sexual exchanges are associated with love, satisfaction, and the desire to stay committed to the relationship.

However, no evidence was found that sexual satisfaction scores at one time predicted change in relationship satisfaction, love, and commitment over time (i.e., between Times 1 and 2), or that relationship satisfaction, love, and commitment at one time predicted change over time (i.e., between Times 1 and 2) in sexual satisfaction. Thus, it cannot be stated, unequivocally, that people increase their love, satisfaction, or commitment in the relationship because they first experience sexual satisfaction, or vice versa. However, sexual satisfaction and relationship quality may influence each other almost simultaneously, which cannot be determined from these data. As noted many years ago by Henderson-King and Veroff (1994), "The relationship between sex and affection, in particular, would seem so reciprocal that the question of causation appears futile" (p. 521). In addition, and as noted elsewhere (see Sprecher, 1999), the scale scores of satisfaction, love, and commitment in this longitudinal study reached ceiling effects early in the study (at Time 1), which limits the amount of change over time in these variables that can be explained by another variable.

Another issue examined with the longitudinal data was whether sexual satisfaction predicted the likelihood of relationship dissolution over time. The partners in couples who stayed together between Times 1 and 2 had higher sexual satisfaction scores (at Time 1) than partners in couples who broke up. Although the difference between the two groups on sexual satisfaction was significant, it was not large in magnitude, probably because most of the couples (including those who eventually broke up) experienced relatively high levels of sexual satisfaction. These results extend previous studies on sexuality in premarital relationships (Felmlee et al., 1990; Simpson, 1987), which found that level of sexual involvement was a positive predictor of relationship stability.

Although sexual satisfaction was associated with relationship satisfaction, love, and commitment in the contemporaneous analyses for both genders, the associations were generally stronger for men than for women. I would speculate that men are more likely than women to use the quality of their sexual relationship as a barometer for the quality of the entire relationship. The logistic regression results in which sexual satisfaction and relationship satisfaction (at Time 1) were compared in their relative ability to predict breakup status by Time 2 also demonstrated the greater importance of sex to men than to women. Sexual satisfaction (but not relationship satisfaction) was negatively associated with the likelihood of a breakup for men, whereas relationship satisfaction was the significant predictor for women.

There were several strengths to this study, including data collected over time and from both members of couples. Very little prior research has examined sexual satisfaction and other subjective measures of sexuality at multiple times in the relationship, particularly in premarital relationships. A limitation was the homogeneous sample, which consisted primarily of college-educated young adults. Further longitudinal research, including with daily diaries, is needed to examine how daily and weekly changes in sexual satisfaction are associated with overall relationship quality.

## Notes

1. Six participants from five different relationships could not participate in one of the waves and one couple (2 participants) were missing at two waves.
2. As a comparison, the inter-partner correlations were .26 ($p = .01$) for relationship satisfaction, .47 ($p < .001$) for love, and .54 ($p < .001$) for commitment.
3. Because data were collected from both partners, it was also possible to examine how one's sexual satisfaction was associated with partner's relationship satisfaction, love, and commitment. This was explored with Time 1 data. Men's sexual satisfaction was modestly associated with their partner's love ($r = .22, p < .05$), satisfaction ($r = .17, p < .10$), and commitment ($r = .25, p < .05$). Women's sexual satisfaction was positively correlated with their partners' love ($r = .20, p < .05$), although unrelated to their satisfaction ($r = .09$, *ns*), and commitment ($r = .16$, *ns*).
4. However, when I compared those who broke up at any point during the study ($n = 60$) with those who remained together throughout the study ($n = 41$) on sexual satisfaction and sexual desire at Time 1, no significant differences were found between the two groups. However, it would be unlikely that relationship variables would predict relationship outcomes almost 5 years later.

## References


Aron, A., & Henkemeyer, L. (1995). Marital satisfaction and passionate love. *Journal of Social and Personal Relationships, 12,* 139–146.

Baumeister, R. F., Catanese, K. R., & Vohs, K. D. (2001). Is there a gender difference in strength of sex drive? Theoretical views, conceptual distinctions, and a review of relevant evidence. *Personality and Social Psychology Review, 5,* 242–273.

Blumstein, P., & Schwartz, P. (1983). *American couples.* New York: William Morrow.

Braiker, H. B., & Kelley, H. H. (1979). Conflict in the development of close relationships. In R. L. Burgess & T. L. Huston (Eds.), *Social exchange in developing relationships* (pp. 135–168). New York: Academic Press.

Byers, E. S., Demmons, S., & Lawrance, K. (1998). Sexual satisfaction within dating relationships: A test of the interpersonal exchange model of sexual satisfaction. *Journal of Social and Personal Relationships, 15,* 257–267.

Christopher, F. S., & Sprecher, S. (2000). Sexuality in marriage, dating, and other relationships: A decade review. *Journal of Marriage and the Family, 62,* 999–1017.

Cupach, W. R., & Comstock, J. (1990). Satisfaction with sexual communication in marriage. Links to sexual satisfaction and dyadic adjustment. *Journal of Social and Personal Relationships, 7,* 179–186.

Davies, S., Katz, J., & Jackson, J. L. (1999). Sexual desire discrepancies: Effects on sexual and relationship satisfaction in heterosexual dating couples. *Archives of Sexual Behavior, 28,* 553–567.

Edwards, J. N., & Booth, A. (1994). Sexuality, marriage, and well-being: The middle years. In A. S. Rossi (Ed.), *Sexuality across the life course* (pp. 233–259). Chicago: The University of Chicago Press.

Felmlee, D., Sprecher, S., & Bassin, E. (1990). The dissolution of intimate relationships: A hazard model. *Social Psychology Quarterly, 53,* 13–30.

Greeley, A. M. (1991). *Faithful attraction: Discovering intimacy, love, and fidelity in American marriage.* New York: Doherty.

Grote, N. K., & Frieze, I. H. (1998). Remembrance of things past: Perceptions of marital love from its beginnings to the present. *Journal of Social and Personal Relationships, 15,* 91–109.

Hatfield, E., Greenberger, D., Traupmann, J., & Lambert, P. (1982). Equity and sexual satisfaction in recently married couples. *The Journal of Sex Research, 17,* 18–32.

Hatfield, E., Utne, M. K., & Traupmann, J. (1979). Equity theory and intimate relationships. In R. L. Burgess & T. L. Huston (Eds.), *Social exchange in developing relationships* (pp. 91–171). New York: Springer-Verlag.

Henderson-King, D. H., & Veroff, J. (1994). Sexual satisfaction and marital well-being in the first years of marriages. *Journal of Social and Personal Relationships, 11,* 509–534.

Hendrick, S. S. (1988). A generic measure of relationship satisfaction. *Journal of Marriage and the Family, 50,* 93–98.

Hill, C. T., Rubin, Z., & Peplau, L. A. (1976). Breakups before marriage: The end of 103 affairs. *Journal of Social Issues, 32,* 147–168.

Lawrance, K., & Byers, E. S. (1992). Development of the interpersonal exchange model of sexual satisfaction in long-term relationships. *The Canadian Journal of Human Sexuality, 1,* 123–128.

Lawrance, K., & Byers, E. S. (1995). Sexual satisfaction in long-term heterosexual relationships: The interpersonal exchange model of sexual satisfaction. *Personal Relationships, 2,* 267–285.

Lund, M. (1985). The development of investment and commitment scales for predicting continuity of personal relationships. *Journal of Social Psychology, 22,* 101–112.

Oggins, J., Leber, D., & Veroff, J. (1993). Race and gender differences in Black and White newlyweds' perceptions of sexual and marital relationships. *The Journal of Sex Research, 30,* 152–160.

Peplau, L. A., Rubin, Z., & Hill, C. T. (1997). Sexual intimacy in dating relationships. *Journal of Social Issues, 33,* 86–109.

Pinney, E. M., Gerrard, M., & Denney, N. W. (1987). The Pinney sexual satisfaction inventory. *The Journal of Sex Research, 23,* 233–251.

Rusbult, C. E. (1983). A longitudinal test of the investment model: The development (and deterioration) of satisfaction and commitment in heterosexual involvements. *Journal of Personality and Social Psychology, 45,* 101–117.

Simpson, J. A. (1987). The dissolution of romantic relationships: Favors involved in relationship stability and emotional distress. *Journal of Personality and Social Psychology, 53,* 683–692.

Sprecher, S. (1998). Social exchange theories and sexuality. *The Journal of Sex Research, 35,* 32–43.

Sprecher, S. (1999). "I love you more today than yesterday": Romantic partners' perceptions of changes in love and related affect over time. *Journal of Personality and Social Psychology, 76,* 46–53.

Sprecher, S., Metts, S., Burleson, B., Hatfield, E., & Thompson, A. (1995). Domains of expressive interaction in intimate relationships: Associations with satisfaction and commitment. *Family Relations, 44,* 203–210.

Sprecher, S., & Regan, P. C. (1998). Passionate and companionate love in courting and young married couples. *Sociological Inquiry, 68,* 163–185.

Sprecher, S., & Regan, P. C. (2000). Sexuality in a relational context. In C. Hendrick & S. S. Hendrick (Eds.), *Close relationships: A sourcebook* (pp. 217

Veroff, J., Douvan, E., & Hatchett, S. J. (1995). *Marital instability: A social and behavioral study of the early years.* Westport, CT: Praeger.

Waite, L. J., & Joyner, K. (2001). Emotional satisfaction and physical pleasure in sexual unions: Time horizon, sexual behavior, and sexual exclusivity. *Journal of Marriage and Family, 63,* 247–264.

White, L., & Keith, B. (1990). The effect of shift work on the quality and stability of martial relations. *Journal of Marriage and the Family, 52,* 453–462.

Yela, C. (2000). Predictors of and factors related to loving and sexual satisfaction for men and women. *European Review of Applied Psychology, 50,* 235–243.

Manuscript accepted February 18, 2002

---

An earlier version of this paper was presented at the 62nd Annual Conference for the National Council on Family Relations, Nov. 10–13, 2000, Minneapolis, MN. The author would like to thank Scott Christopher and two anonymous reviewers for comments on an earlier version of this paper. The data collection for this longitudinal study was funded by several small grants from Illinois State University and the paper was written during a research sabbatical granted the author from Illinois State University.

Address correspondence to Susan Sprecher, Department of Sociology and Anthropology, Illinois State University, Normal, IL 61790-4660; e-mail: Sprecher@ilstu.edu.

# SEX for Grown-ups

## Sorry, all you teenage heartthrobs. Some things get better with age, and making love is one of them

By Carol Lynn Mithers

If you look at advertising, go to movies or watch TV, you're forgiven for thinking that passion is the sole province of the young, the thin and the single. In love scenes, there's nary a sag, wrinkle or wedding ring in sight. The message: Sexually speaking, grown-up means washed up. Right?

Wrong. Here's the startling discovery that a lot of us mature married folks have made: Not only are we having nearly as much sex as the kids, we're—how to put this politely?—having more fun.

And it's probably no coincidence that a growing number of researchers, psychologists and sex therapists are beginning to look at what really happens to hot young lovers after a decade or more of sharing a bed, a mortgage and a couple of kids. It turns out that the old advertising slogan had it right: "You're not getting older, you're getting better." Here's why:

**Biology is on our side.** Studies over the years—not to mention anecdotes from our friends—have demonstrated again and again that women become more sexually responsive with time, until we reach a peak in our thirties or forties. (After that, we plateau.)

An important confirmation came in 1992, when social scientists Robert T. Michael, John H. Gagnon, Edward O. Laumann and Gina Kolata, working through the National Opinion Research Center at the University of Chicago, embarked on a landmark survey of America's sex life. Among their results, catalogued in the book *Sex in America: A Definitive Survey* (Warner Books, 1995): While 61 percent of women between ages eighteen and twenty-four said that they always or usually reached orgasm with their primary partner, by age forty it was a whopping 78 percent.

No one has definitively proved that a particular physiological change in women's bodies makes them more orgasmic. However, some researchers, notably Helen E. Fisher, Ph.D., the author of *Anatomy of Love* (Fawcett, 1995), and Theresa L. Crenshaw, M.D., a San Diego-based sex therapist and author of *The Alchemy of Love and Lust* (Pocket Books, 1997), speculate that the gradual dropping of our estrogen levels allows the small amount of testosterone in our bodies to exert more influence.

Researchers do agree, though, that men's testosterone levels fall during these same years, causing their sex drives to quiet down. Their lovemaking becomes much more leisurely and touch-oriented, and that translates into more pleasure for their wives.

Terry, forty, married for sixteen years, agrees: "When we were first married, Jack specialized in quickies. These days, he likes to take his time. He says his greatest pleasure is in driving me wild."

Nature also seems to help bind us to those we know best, says Fisher. She points out that levels of oxytocin, a hormone secreted by the hypothalamus gland and associated with mother-infant (and in some cases, male-female) attachment in animals, rise each time we climax. (In men, orgasm stimulates a spike in a similar hormone, vasopressin.)

"I don't think it's much of a leap to say that the feeling of deep attachment that comes after orgasm is associated with those hormone levels," Fisher, who originated this theory, asserts. "And that the more you have orgasms with someone, the more attached you feel. We get addicted to those we love."

**Practice makes perfect.** Regardless of the role physiology plays, the experience grown-ups bring to their sexual encounters is even more important. "By the time they're in their twenties, most men have had much more sex—most of it through masturbation—than women have," notes James W. Maddock, Ph.D., professor of family social science at the University of Minnesota, St. Paul. At that age, however, sex may be less than mind-blowing for women, who are still learning what pleases them and their partners.

By the time we reach our thirties, though, most of us have honed our skills. "I hate to sound clinical," says Judith, thirty-eight, married for eight years, "but only seventeen years of having sex could have taught me how men like to be touched, how I like it, what positions work."

Experience that teaches what women like—especially when combined with the physical slowdown that comes naturally over the years—makes men better lovers, too. "With time, men learn a greater appreciation of activities like kissing, petting and hugging—things that women have wanted all along," says Alvin Baraff, Ph.D., a therapist and director of Men Center Counseling in Washington, D.C., who has treated and surveyed hundreds of men.

**Love me, love my body.** One of the great ironies of female aging is that even as we grow more genuinely sexual, society tells us that we're less physically desirable. Happily, grown-up women today are far more likely to tell society to go stuff it.

Pepper Schwartz, Ph.D., professor of sociology at the University of Washington, in Seattle, and co-author of *The Great Sex Weekend* (Putnam, 1998), observes, "With time, you realize that it's not having perfect legs or breasts that makes you attractive. It's all of you—your experience, your mind, your personality, your sense of humor. And you learn to say, 'This body may not look like Cindy Crawford's, but I like it.'"

"I can't tell you how many hours I used to spend in front of the mirror hating my big butt and thighs," says Anne, forty-two. "I finally realized that they have nothing to do with the things that are important to me—being a good mother, a good worker, a good wife."

Anne gets no complaints from her husband of eighteen years. "It's clear that he wants me as much as he ever has," she says.

That's the other good news: When it comes to accepting physical imperfections, men are forgiving. In 1996, when Baraff surveyed one hundred men about what they most longed for in marriage, they never mentioned specifics about their spouses' appearance. And the National Opinion Research Center survey found that 67 percent of men over forty-five said they still got great enjoyment from watching their mates undress.

**Love can set you free.** The sensuality, experience and confidence that define the sexual grown-up would be striking in any intimate relationship, but they reach full flower in a long, happy marriage. Evidence suggests that long-married couples do have sex less often than new lovers, but we also seem to get more out of the encounters we have. The National Opinion Research Center survey found married couples to be the most physically satisfied with their sex lives, while single people—especially those who had more than one partner—were the least satisfied.

These findings are no fluke, asserts Maddock. "The trend is clear: The longer, more steady in all respects of the relationship, the more likely the incidence and consistency of orgasm."

A happy marriage isn't magic; it just makes good sex easier. When lovemaking isn't about proving anything, when it's part of a larger, shared life, it's "less fraught with anxiety," says Amanda, forty, married twelve years. "If sex one night isn't so great, you have faith that tomorrow it will be."

Feeling safe in a relationship also gives us the confidence to make our needs known—or to know what we don't want. Even the most liberated young woman can get hung up by worry "about how her partner perceives her," says Shirley Glass, Ph.D., a psychologist and marital therapist in private practice in Owings Mills, Maryland. "A history of emotional intimacy, vulnerability and acceptance lets a woman expose herself without fear of judgment."

Says Katie, thirty-nine, married for fifteen years, "Because I know my husband does respect me and takes me seriously, I've felt free to do things I never would have dared before. I recently bought my first vibrator—not for me, for us."

**Intimacy is the best aphrodisiac.** The kids would have us think that nothing is duller than making love to the same person year in and year out. Guess again. A long-term relationship, where you've weathered storms together, laughed at the same jokes—in short, have a history—fosters a kind of intimacy that gives lovemaking an intensity, complexity and richness that isn't available to us earlier in our lives.

In fact, peak sexual experiences are available *only* to grown-ups, suggests David Schnarch, Ph.D., director of the Marriage and Family Health Center in Evergreen, Colorado, and author of *Passionate Marriage* (W. W. Norton & Co., 1997). Why? Because the ability to be intimate—to reveal who we are and what turns us on—is what really makes sex great. And that requires a strong sense of identity and security.

When a couple makes the leap from hormone-driven passion to desire specifically for each other, their sexual connection can really bloom. "It's the difference," Schnarch says, "between having sex like kids and having sex like a woman and a man."

"If you had told me at twenty that my sex life would get better the older I got, I never would have believed you," says Mary, forty-two, married for seventeen years. "But that's exactly what's happened. Maybe it's because my husband and I have gone through so much together, and I feel connected to him in a really deep way. Maybe it's all these things. But something happened just before I turned forty: I fell more deeply in love with him than ever. And I started feeling explosively feminine, explosively sexual. After all these years together, we're having the time of our lives."

*Carol Lynn Mithers is a contributing editor to* Ladies' Home Journal.

First appeared *Ladies' Home Journal*, March 1999, pp. 69, 73–74. 

# what turns you on? (*hint:* it's not work!)

By Carin Rubenstein

HERE IS THE GOOD NEWS: WE ARE NOT HAVING A MIDLIFE CRIsis (our gen-x kids may be). We are the people we set out to be, and we love to have sex and spend time with our families. In our exploration of how baby boomers see themselves and what really makes them feel alive, in the summer of 2001, *My Generation* and AARP conducted a major national telephone survey of 2,118 Americans age 18 and older. After September 11, we followed up with another survey of 1,071 Americans to gauge the shifts, if any, in sentiment.*

The results of our surveys should surprise and encourage boomers everywhere. Even before September 11, boomers weren't nearly as self-centered as some suspected; after the acts of terrorism, they aren't nearly as traumatized as many expected. The evidence: In the summer of 2001, the majority of boomers, men and women, said that they wished they could do more good deeds for others and that their lives were more meaningful. A year later, these wishes still hold.

In both 2001 and 2002, boomers were enthralled by love and focused on their sexuality—just what we would have hoped for ourselves when we were young.

## what *midlife* crisis?

THE BEST NEWS OF ALL IS THAT THERE SEEMS TO BE NO MIDLIFE crisis. Despite the dread with which many of us approach our 50th birthday, the roughest emotional times of our lives are usually behind us. Midlife can be a time of relative personal tranquility, happiness and self-confidence, a time when boomers begin taking stock of their lives and feeling grateful for what they have.

"There is no 'midlife crisis,'" agrees Alice Rossi, Ph.D., an expert on midlife and editor of the book *Caring and Doing for Others: Social Responsibility in the Domains of Family, Work and Community*. "Much more critical and traumatic events occur in early adulthood than in midlife," she says. It's during their 20s and 30s that Americans are searching for the right partner, a suitable career and a sense of identity. So, she says, "the peak in depression and anxiety occurs in early adulthood, not in midlife."

In our surveys, we, too, found that Americans under the age of 35 experience negative feelings more often than older Americans. A majority of boomers often feel happy, capable and competent, truly alive and peaceful. (See charts)

## no more *pretending*

FOR MANY BOOMERS, MIDLIFE IS THE FIRST TIME WHEN THEY can rid themselves of what they don't like, embrace what they do like and learn to be comfortable with who they are. By the age of 40 or 50, Americans no longer have to pretend. "I don't do anything anymore that I don't want to do," explains a 54-year-old beautician in Ohio. "I spend all day talking with women, so on the weekends I don't socialize."

"The degree of freedom we have to do what we want increases with middle age, but just isn't there for a younger person," explains Rossi. Young adults may feel obliged to attend social events, but midlifers—who are much more secure about their social status—are more likely either to enjoy such shindigs or to skip them altogether, Rossi believes.

## midlife *dreamin'*

MIDLIFERS ARE LESS LIKELY THAN YOUNGER AMERICANS TO harbor hidden fantasies and pipe dreams. For young Americans, crazy dreams "are motivators," says Margie Lachman, Ph.D., a psychologist at Brandeis University who researches adult development.

Those of us further on in life, however, "realize that there are limitations, and that we can't achieve everything or be everybody," Lachman adds. Boomers still dream, of course, but their fantasies become less whimsical and more civic-minded

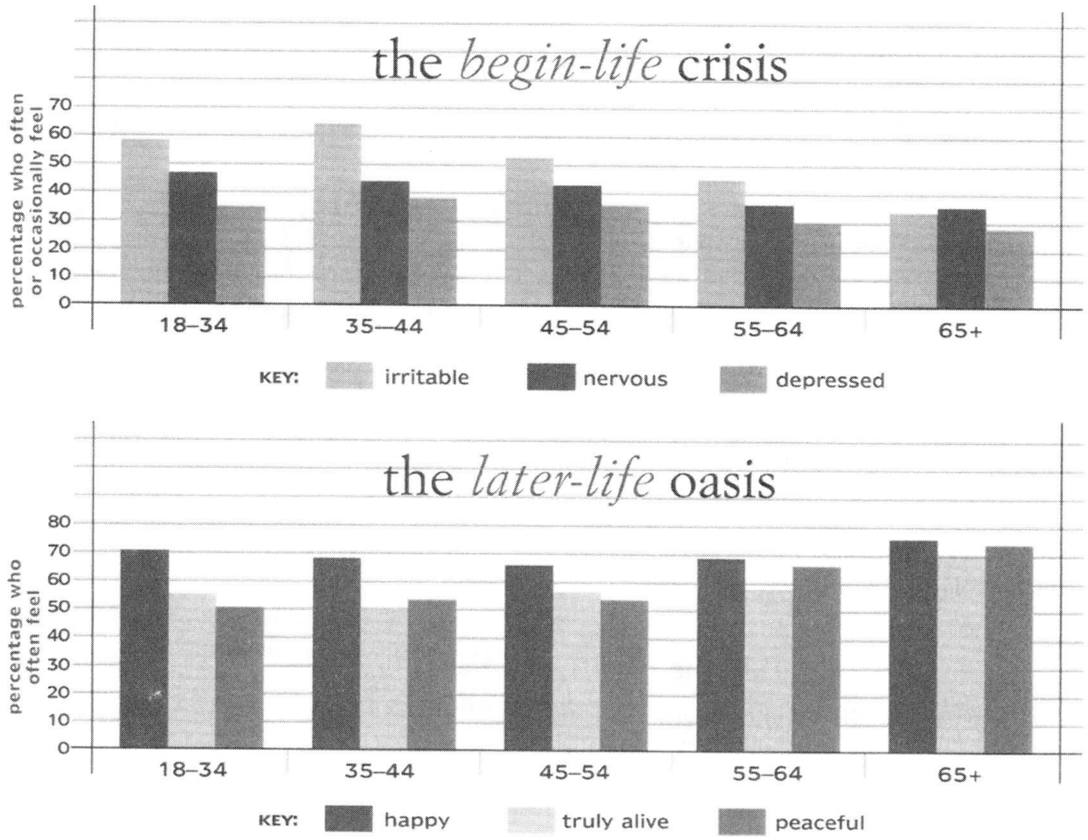


(trading in the goal of wanting to be a rock star for organizing a fund-raising concert to benefit a local charity).

## *giving* back

MIDLIFE IS THE TIME WHEN WE BEGIN TO SEARCH FOR A WAY TO make a meaningful contribution to the world, regardless of national events. Both before and after September 11, six in 10 boomers wished they had a more socially meaningful life. Financially stable and having reached a comfortable level of well-being, "we realize we have a responsibility that goes beyond our own life and our own family, and we seek meaning by helping other people," says Lachman.

Last summer, eight in 10 Americans between 45 and 54 said they wished they could do good deeds for other people; slightly more say that this year. This is how we felt when we were younger, and we haven't lost our commitment to social responsibility. That's why one 49-year-old man we surveyed volunteers to help the local high school football team by videotaping every game and making a highlight tape for the players to watch. Another boomer admits that he's started to think "more about what we as Americans can do to help each other."

## a little *romance*

BOOMERS ARE PASSIONATELY SEXUAL BEINGS. AMERICANS IN midlife were flourishing sexually before last September, and they still are now.

Our 2001 survey reveals that nearly six in 10 boomers really love to make love, and almost as many love to spend romantic evenings with their partners.

"Unless you've let yourself go to the dogs, why shouldn't you love sex?" says a 48-year-old real estate agent and devoted husband from Arizona. It's clear that boomers with partners are even more likely than single boomers to be enamored of love-making; 60 percent of married boomers love to make love, compared to 48 percent of those without a partner.

## what *we* want

WHEN WE BREAK DOWN THESE FIGURES, WE FIND THAT IN MID-life men have more sexual enthusiasm than women. Two-thirds of men (66 percent) between 45 and 54 love to make love, compared to 51 percent of women in that age group. This striking gender difference exists among younger Americans, as well, so it is not just a side effect of menopause.

Both boomer men and women love to spend romantic evenings with their mates, although they may be interpreting "romance" in very different ways. For a 54-year-old woman from Ohio, romance means eating at a restaurant with "white linen tablecloths and a bucket for the wine," a place where she can talk to her husband. But a 48-year-old man in Tucson confesses that he's only willing to get dressed up and go out for dinner as long as he knows he'll be able to "spice it up a bit" when he gets home.

## more *sex,* better sex

BOOMERS HAVEN'T YET ACHIEVED A STATE OF PERFECT SEXUAL union. In fact, many of them often fantasize about having better sex. About half, 58 percent of men and 48 percent of women, say that they secretly dream of having a more satisfying sex life, because as one man puts it, "it's just human nature" to want better sex.

What do so many mid-lifers think they're missing sex-wise? When men talk about having better sex, they usually mean more frequent lovemaking and especially more oral sex, says sex researcher Dr. Robert Kolodny, a co-author of 14 books on sexuality. The more often men have oral sex, research shows, the happier they say they are with their marriage.

Being desired is what women need at this age, according to Susan M. Seidman, Ph.D., a psychologist who counsels couples and families in New York City. Women in midlife need to know that their husbands accept their changing physical appearance and think they're aging well, "and they get this from physical closeness and sexual intimacy," Seidman says.

## all in the *family*

BOOMERS LOVE SPENDING TIME WITH THEIR FAMILIES. ABOUT four in 10, we found, think of themselves as nurturers above all, dedicated to spending time with, and taking care of, their children, as well as their spouses and a larger group of family and friends.

Since September 11, Americans are more focused on family. A 51-year-old woman tells us that her loved ones have become much more important, and "material things" less so.

## t.g.i.*f.*

NINE OUT OF 10 BOOMERS, BOTH MEN AND WOMEN, DID NOT name work as a major passion; six in 10 don't love their jobs.

"People fall in and out of love with their careers," explains Seidman. And for boomers especially, "who had expectations of making big, big bucks and being big, big happy," the midlife reality of the work grind can be exhausting, she says. That's why many baby boomers look beyond work for personal fulfillment and a sense of self-worth.

A 53-year-old man who used to be consumed with his job as a quality assurance manager says he no longer finds it as challenging or inspiring. Now his passion is competitive swimming. "I'm in better shape than I ever was, and I'm happier about what I achieve in the pool than what I achieve at my desk," he explains.

## does money buy *happiness?*

THE MORE MONEY AMERICANS EARN THE MORE LIKELY THEY ARE to be positive about their work, we found. On average, boomers earned the highest salaries of those in our survey. Among workers who earn more than $50,000 a year, many of whom are boomers, 45 percent really love their work; but only 34 percent of those who earn less than $30,000 a year are as enthusiastic. Plus, more of the highest earners often feel happy, capable and competent than those who earn the least.

## a *boomer* profile

**7 in 10** boomers feel sexually attractive (often or occasionally)

**6 in 10** boomers love to make love

**55%** of boomers love to spend romantic evenings with their partner

**54%** secretly dream of having a better sex life

**6 in 10** boomers wish their lives were more meaningful

**5 in 10** boomers are always trying to learn new things

**83%** of boomers say they wish they could do good deeds for other people

**6 in 10** boomers don't really love their jobs

## how we have *fun*

BOOMERS LOVE BEING ACTIVE AND DOING THINGS OUTSIDE; GOLF, camping, gardening, waterskiing and hiking are just a few of our interests. Being active is a primary passion of 62 percent of boomer men, and it's second only to nurturing for boomer women, 46 percent of whom love being active.

Creative activities—crafts, writing, drawing and cooking—are also popular. A 50-year-old man is passionate about the computer programs he writes; a woman in her 50s pens historical romances for her own enjoyment.

## the *learning* curve

CONSTANTLY CHALLENGING THEMSELVES WITH NEW EXPERIences and ideas, a majority of midlifers—about six in 10—say they're always trying to learn new things. A 49-year-old man tells us he's going back to school to learn how to make guitars, and a 52-year-old woman just joined a Bible-study organization.

## *spirituality*

ONLY A FEW BOOMERS, ABOUT ONE IN 10, ARE PASSIONATE about worship. Spiritual pursuits divide along gender lines. While six in 10 boomer women often engage in spiritual and religious activities, only 39 percent of boomer men do. More boomer women than men really love this kind of religious involvement: 37 percent of women compared to 26 percent of men.

This gap is not surprising, says Diana Kirschner, Ph.D., a psychologist who regularly addresses spirituality. "Women tend to be more connected with other people and that lends itself to being more spiritual. Men are more instrumental, into doing rather than being," she says.

## who has the most *fun?*

PASSION IS WHAT ENGAGES AND EXCITES US IN THE LONG TERM, but fun is what we do for quick pleasure. Men and women regard having fun very differently, we found. In fact, men are much more focused on fun than women are. Our evidence:

- 55 percent of men deliberately take time to have fun, either every day or every few days, compared to 43 percent of women.
- Men spend more time than women having fun: On average, men have 22 hours of fun each week, compared to 17 hours a week for women.

"Women are called on much more to be caregivers, and it's difficult to mix fun and changing diapers or disciplining children," explains John Robinson, Ph.D., a sociologist at the University of Maryland and director of the Americans' Use of Time Project. Fathers usually spend time with their kids doing things like playing baseball. Both mothers and fathers love being with their children, but fathers tend to have the most fun doing it.

An almost-50-year-old Iowa man sheepishly agrees that "in lots of families, like mine, the men are more free to have fun." He is certainly up for it: He rides horses and argues about anything from "politics to cosmology."

A woman in her mid-40s says that although she spends less time having fun as she has grown older, "I enjoy the fun more, because I'm doing things I like, not just doing anything. In my late 20s, I'd go clubbing and dancing," she says, "but I was trying to please other people. Now, I only do the things I want to do." These things, she says, include going to dinner and a movie with her boyfriend and shopping.

FOR BOOMERS, MIDLIFE IS STILL YOUTHFUL LIFE, OUR "FINALLY Doing What I Want" years. Instead of wallowing in a 50th-year crisis, we're living out our sexual and romantic dreams, as we de-emphasize the fantasies we once had about careers and money. And we cautiously but firmly pursue our ideals of community through service and family responsibility.

Midlife: A pretty great place to be, after all.

* *Our special focus was on baby boomers, specifically women and men between the ages of 45 and 54. Both surveys were conducted for AARP/*My Generation *by RoperASW and included data weighted to census norms to correct for sampling errors. The word "boomer" here means "leading edge" boomers, those ages 45 to 54 years old.*

*George Sharrard provided assistance with computer analysis*

*Let us know what turns you on.*
*Take the poll at* www.mygeneration.org.

# THE Abortion WARS

## 30 years after Roe v. Wade

**By Linda Feldmann**
Staff writer of The Christian Science Monitor

WASHINGTON

AUDREY DIEHL will never forget the time her mother took her to an abortion-rights rally in downtown San Antonio.

Ms. Diehl was 9 years old, and antiabortion protesters shoved posters of aborted fetuses in her face. But it wasn't the images that upset the girl. It was "the act," she says, "all that yelling."

"That crystallized for me the zealotry of the antichoice movement," says Diehl, now a 25-year-old living in Los Angeles. "It made me more understanding of why people need to continue to voice prochoice ideas."

Yet until recently, Diehl says, she took the right to abortion for granted. Like many women who have no memory of life before the Supreme Court legalized abortion in its historic Roe v. Wade ruling—30 years ago today—she wasn't active in the abortion-rights movement.

Now, since the election of the second President Bush, who is pursuing antiabortion policies on many fronts, and has the potential to name enough Supreme Court justices to overturn Roe, Diehl is scared. And she's just started volunteering at her local Planned Parenthood.

Across the country, at the American Life League in Stafford, Va., Sara McKalips is hard at work at the Rock for Life project, trying to get young people to join the fight against abortion. She says she has always opposed abortion, but didn't become active until she was 18 and saw pictures of aborted fetuses on the Internet. She knows, she says, that "from the moment of fertilization, a unique human being exists who deserves to be protected."

While at Messiah College in Grantham, Pa., she supposed most of her fellow students were also against abortion. "But most students didn't really do anything with their prolife beliefs," says Ms. McKalips, who graduated last May. "The prolife movement needs people to take more of a stand on the issue and be less compromising."

These two young women, members of a generation who have lived their entire lives under Roe, are in a way atypical for their activism. Since 1973, nearly 38 million abortions have been performed in the US—yet a majority of Americans are conflicted on the issue, and avoid it.

But those with firmly held beliefs, like Diehl and McKalips, still number in the millions. And they reflect what author Lawrence Tribe has called an enduring "clash of absolutes" that's made Roe v. Wade one of the most contentious Supreme Court rulings ever handed down—one that has had a profound

## Regional abortion rates – and availability

| | NORTHEAST | WEST | SOUTH | MIDWEST |
|---|---|---|---|---|
| Abortions per 1,000 women aged 15-44 in 2000 | 28.0 | 24.9 | 19.0 | 15.9 |
| Counties without abortion clinics in 2000 | 50% | 78% | 91% | 94% |

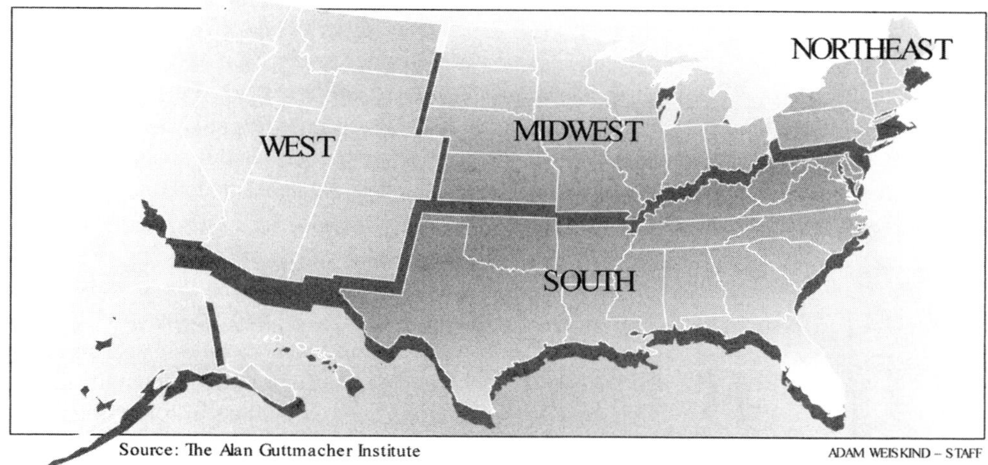


Source: The Alan Guttmacher Institute

ADAM WEISKIND – STAFF

impact on American culture and politics, and, in the eyes of some scholars and activists, could one day be overturned.

## Jan. 22, 1973

Frances Kissling was the director of an abortion clinic in New York City on the day that Roe v. Wade was handed down. She remembers arriving at work at 8 a.m. and "having kids in their dirty cars sitting in the parking lot, having driven from Kentucky and Connecticut and wherever, being afraid, dealing with the fact that they've just come from someplace where abortion was illegal to a place where it was legal."

Then the legal and cultural earthquake struck. In two 7–2 decisions—Roe v. Wade and Doe v. Bolton—abortion was declared a constitutionally protected right, under a right to privacy not explicitly stated in the Constitution, but developed through Supreme Court precedent. Though the justices ruled that states could regulate and ultimately ban abortion as pregnancies progressed, there was no mistaking the fundamental shift.

"It was a shock," says Ms. Kissling, now president of Catholics for Free Choice. "No one expected it."

In his dissent, Justice Byron White castigated the majority for holding that "the Constitution of the United States values the convenience, whim or caprice of the putative mother more than the life or potential life of the fetus."

Justice William Rehnquist decried the trimester system laid out by the majority as "judicial legislation."

At the time, abortion was legal in only four states—New York, Hawaii, Alaska, and Washington. Suddenly, it was legal everywhere. But for abortion-rights forces, the celebration didn't last long. The antiabortion movement, centered at first in the Catholic Church, galvanized and fought abortion on many levels—at the clinics, in state legislatures and courts, in the US Congress, and back in the Supreme Court itself. Abortion-rights forces have played defense ever since.

Since 1973, attitudes toward abortion, as charted by Gallup and the General Social Survey, have held remarkably stable even as the public has become more liberal on other social issues, such as gay rights and women's equality.

"There has been some movement in a prolife direction, but you'd have to get out a magnifying glass" to see it, says Ted Jelen, a political scientist at the University of Nevada at Las Vegas and an author on the subject. "Fifteen percent are prolife, about a quarter to a third are prochoice, and the balance, it depends."

Opinion experts suggest that the effectiveness of the antiabortion movement has bumped up against other trends—such as higher education levels and less affiliation with organized religion—that might otherwise have liberalized opinion toward abortion. When framed around the question of whose choice an abortion decision should be, the public clearly favors the woman. Two-thirds of the public also consistently oppose overturning Roe.

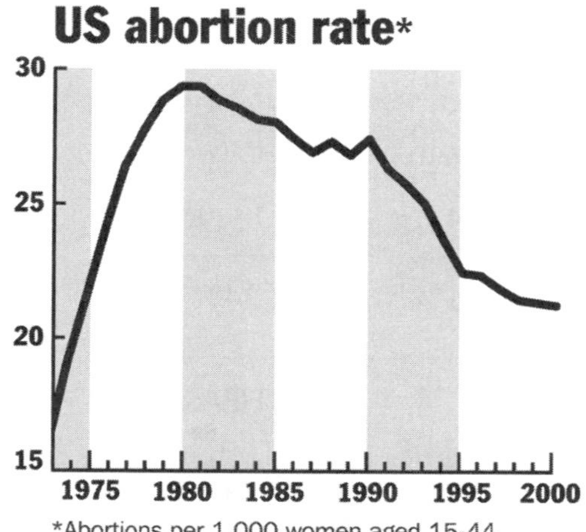

*Abortions per 1,000 women aged 15-44

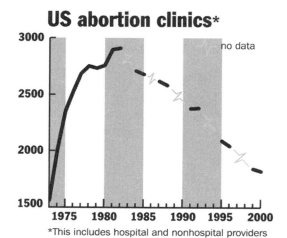

US abortion clinics*

3000
2500
2000
1500
no data
1975 1980 1985 1990 1995 2000

*This includes hospital and nonhospital providers

Source for above: The Alan Guttmacher Institute

ADAM WEISKIND – STAFF

Still, the way abortion is perceived has evolved since 1973. At the time of Roe, discussion centered on the woman's rights. But the rise of technology has altered that.

"All the remarkable developments in fetology and the images we now have of an embryo—how quickly you start to get all those characteristics that we call human, measurable brain activity, and so on—have made it impossible for anyone to make a coherent argument that it's just a blob that isn't human yet," says Jean Bethke Elshtain, a professor at the University of Chicago divinity school. "Clearly, it's a nascent human being. It's not going to be a giraffe."

What makes America's abortion wars so remarkable is how public and political they've been. Part of that speaks to the larger US cultural mosaic—the conflicts of a country that is both deeply religious and committed to secularism, a nation that invented modern feminism but remains ambivalent about women's roles. America's highly legalistic culture has also made it inevitable that a matter as private as reproduction would wind up in the courts.

Has 30 years of legalized abortion made Americans more cavalier on issues of human life, as some antiabortion advocates had warned?

Not necessarily: On physician-assisted suicide and euthanasia, Americans remain queasy, ethicists say. Public discomfort over the use of embryonic stem cells and human cloning has also shown that "there is still a moral seriousness in the American people that is quite uplifting," says Professor Elshtain.

Looked at another way, it's not necessarily true that banning abortion would enhance respect for life. Consider Romania under former President Nicolae Ceaucescu, says Ms. Kissling of Catholics for Free Choice: Abortion was strictly illegal—and unwanted children packed orphanages.

But abortion critics also say that, in fact, women facing unwanted pregnancies in this country don't have as much "choice" as the abortion-rights side claims.

"As a woman, my concern with 30 years of Roe is that it has created an abortion mentality," says Carrie Gordon Earll, a bioethics analyst at Focus on the Family, a conservative organization based in Colorado Springs.

"Even though most Americans don't like abortion," she says, "it has become the cultural default—almost an automatic assumption that a woman in a less-than-ideal pregnancy will at least consider it."

Since Roe, support systems that existed to help women with unwanted pregnancies—such as homes for unwed mothers—have shrunk. A classic cry among abortion-rights forces has been that abortion critics care more about the unborn than the born.

But in recent years, the antiabortion movement has built up a network of crisis-pregnancy centers—clinics where pregnant women can go for help with prenatal and postnatal care. Care Net, an umbrella organization for these centers in Sterling, Va., estimates that there are now about 2,500 in the US; in 1980, there were less than 500.

## A declining abortion rate

Amid all the fierce debate and violence surrounding abortion clinics and doctors, the number and rate of abortions in America has steadily declined. The reasons are hotly debated. Prochoice advocates credit the growth of emergency contraception, a high-dose birth-control pill a woman can take after unprotected sex to prevent pregnancy. In general, a wider range of contraceptive choices means women are doing a better job of using contraception, they say.

Both abstinence and the use of contraceptives are on the rise among teenagers, in particular, so fewer are getting pregnant to begin with. Among girls aged 15 to 19, the abortion rate has been dropping since the late 1980s—and fell another 27 percent between 1994 and 2000.

Another factor that may be contributing to the overall decline in abortions is the availability of ultrasound technology, showing the earliest fetal development—which, some observers suggest, leads some women to think twice about ending pregnancies.

## By the numbers...

**Worldwide, about 46 million abortions** occur each year. Twenty million are illegally obtained.
**Among American women**, almost half of pregnancies are unintended. About half of those end in abortion—1.3 million annually.
**Between 1994 and 2000**, the US abortion rate fell more than 10 percent, in part because of the growing availability of emergency contraception.
**Abortion rates are at their lowest** levels since 1974. They peaked in 1980–1981.
**Of American women obtaining abortions**, 52 percent are under 25. Women aged 20 to 24 account for 33 percent of abortions, and women under 20 obtain 19 percent of abortions.
**In 2000, 87 percent of US counties** had no abortion clinic, and 34 percent of women of childbearing age lived in those counties. In addition, 31 percent of US metropolitan areas had no abortion facilities.
**Between 1996 and 2000**, the number of abortion providers declined 11 percent. It's been dropping since 1982.
**In 1997, 57 percent** of obstetrician/gynecologists performing abortions were aged 50 or older.
**Eighty-two percent** of large, nonhospital abortion facilities were harassed in 2000; most clinics are picketed at least 20 times a year. From 1985 to 2000, the proportion of large providers reporting bomb threats dropped from 48 percent to 15 percent.
**The 1996–2000 abortion rate** was highest in Washington, D.C.—68.1 abortions per 1,000 women—and lowest in Wyoming, where 1 in 1,000 women had an abortion.

Source: The Alan Guttmacher Institute

But the bottom line is that the US still has one of the highest abortion rates in the industrialized West. And the abortion war is only intensifying.

Now that Republicans control both the White House and Congress, abortion opponents are readying a major push for new restrictions, starting with a ban on so-called "partial birth abortions." Another bill would ban transporting a minor across state lines for an abortion so that she can avoid parental-notification laws; a third would criminalize harming a fetus during an attack on a pregnant woman.

Laws protecting clinic entrances have helped reduce clinic violence, and litigants have successfully used racketeering laws to thwart some of the most extreme antiabortion activists. Since 2000, US government approval of medical abortion through the use of mifepristone (RU486) has given women an alternative to surgical abortion.

Yet abortion-rights leaders still feel they are losing ground, and acknowledge that their opponents have gotten savvier about shaping public opinion and "chipping away" at abortion rights. Since 1982, the number of abortion providers has been declining.

But there are still young people eager to join the shrinking ranks, inspired by stories of risky, sometimes deadly, abortions before legalization.

Angel Foster, a medical student at Harvard University, is training for a career in women's reproductive health—including providing abortions. As a young adolescent, she learned of her mother's illegal, pre-Roe abortion.

"That experience was extremely traumatic for her—not the abortion itself, but what she had to do to get it," says Ms. Foster, who, as president-elect of Medical Students for Choice, is working to beef up medical-school curricula on abortion and other issues of women's reproductive health.

Foster has also worked in countries where abortion is illegal, such as Egypt, and seen firsthand what she calls the "psychological and physical consequences of a shortage of reproductive services." But is she really willing to risk her life, working in a clinic in this country? "Even when I have kids, I can imagine doing this," she says. "My husband and I have discussed this."

## Could Roe be overturned?

To some abortion-rights advocates, the Supreme Court is only one vote away from undoing 30 years of nationwide legalized abortion. But more likely, say legal scholars, there would need to be a larger shift in the court's composition for such an earthshaking ruling. And even if the court eventually had a solid majority of justices who believed Roe v. Wade was improperly decided, it's unclear that it would undo what many analysts, including antiabortion conservatives, call "settled law."

"What's hard for people who lack an acquaintance with the Supreme Court to understand is what a tremendously negative institutional, historical impact there would be on the stature of the court if they were to overturn it," says David Garrow, a historian at Emory Law School in Atlanta. "That's why I think it could never happen."

But if that day were to come, the legality of abortion would once again vary state by state. According to NARAL Pro-Choice America, 17 states currently have greater protection for reproductive choice than the federal Constitution; 17 other states "could face sweeping criminal bans on abortion" if Roe were reversed.

Conservative writer Marvin Olasky prefers to look at the movement through a cultural lens. The culture that accepts abortion is changing, he says, and the current view that Roe is acceptable will eventually seem untenable. That, he suggests, could eventually lead to a legal shift. "How long did it take the court to overturn Plessy v. Ferguson?" he asks, referring to the 1896 case that endorsed racial segregation. "That took 60 years. We're halfway there."

# Brave New Babies

**Parents now have the power to choose the sex of their children. But as technology answers prayers, it also raises some troubling questions.**

**BY CLAUDIA KALB**

SHARLA MILLER OF GILLETTE, WYO., ALWAYS wanted a baby girl, but the odds seemed stacked against her. Her husband, Shane, is one of three brothers, and Sharla and her five siblings (four girls, two boys) have produced twice as many males as females. After the Millers' first son, Anthony, was born in 1991, along came Ashton, now 8, and Alec, 4. Each one was a gift, says Sharla, but the desire for a girl never waned. "I'm best friends with my mother;' she says. "I couldn't get it out of my mind that I wanted a daughter." Two years ago Sharla, who had her fallopian tubes tied after Alec's birth, began looking into adopting a baby girl. In the course of her Internet research, she stumbled upon a Web site for the Fertility Institutes in Los Angeles, headed by Dr. Jeffrey Steinberg, where she learned about an in vitro fertilization technique called preimplantation genetic diagnosis. By creating embryos outside the womb, then testing them for gender, PGD could guarantee with almost 100 percent certainty—the sex of her baby. Price tag: $18,480, plus travel. Last November Sharla's eggs and Shane's sperm were mixed in a lab dish, producing 14 healthy embryos, seven male and seven female. Steinberg transferred three of the females into Sharla's uterus, where two implanted successfully. If all goes well, the run of Miller boys will end in July with the arrival of twin baby girls. "I have three wonderful boys," says Sharla, "but since there was a chance I could have a daughter, why not?"

The brave new world is definitely here. After 25 years of staggering advances in reproductive medicine—first test-tube babies, then donor eggs and surrogate mothers—technology is changing babymaking in a whole new way. No longer can science simply help couples have babies, it can help them have the kind of babies they want. Choosing gender may obliterate one of the fundamental mysteries of procreation, but for people who have grown accustomed to taking 3-D ultrasounds of fetuses, learning a baby's sex within weeks of conception and scheduling convenient delivery dates, it's simply the next logical step. That gleeful exclamation, "It's a boy!" or "It's a girl!" may soon just be a quaint reminder of how random births used to be.

Throughout history, humans have wished for a child of one sex or the other and have been willing to do just about anything to get it. Now that gender selection is scientifically feasible, interest in the controversial practice (banned, except for medical reasons, in the United Kingdom) is exploding. Despite considerable moral murkiness, Americans are talking to their doctors and visiting catchy Web sites like www.choosethesexofyourbaby.com and myboyorgirl.com—many of them offering money-back guarantees. In just the last six months, Steinberg's site has had 85,000 hits. At the Genetics and IVF Institute (GIVF) in Fairfax, Va., an FDA clinical trial of a sophisticated sperm-sorting technology called MicroSort is more than halfway to completion. Through radio, newspaper and magazine ads ("Do you want to choose the gender of your next baby?"), the clinic has recruited hundreds of eager couples, and more than 400 babies out of 750 needed for the trial have been born. Other couples continue to flock to older, more low-tech and questionable sperm-sorting techniques like the Ericsson method, which is offered at about two dozen clinics nationwide. By far, the most provocative gender-selection technique is PGD. Some clinics offer the procedure as a bonus for couples already going through fertility treatments, but a small number are beginning to provide the option for otherwise healthy couples. Once Steinberg decided to offer PGD gender selection to all comers, he says, "word spread like wildfire."

The ability to create baby Jack or baby Jill opens a high-tech can of worms. While the advances have received kudos from grateful families, they also raise loaded ethical questions about whether science is finally crossing a line that shouldn't be crossed. Even fertility specialists are divided over whether choosing a male or female embryo is acceptable. If couples can request a baby boy or girl, what's next on the slippery slope of modern reproductive medicine? Eye color? Height? Intelligence? Could picking one gender over the other become the 21st century's form of sex discrimination? Or, as in China, upset the ratio of males to females? Many European countries already forbid sex selection; should there be similar regulations in the United States? These explosive issues are being debated in medical journals, on university ethics boards and at the highest levels in Washington. Just last week the President's Council on Bioethics discussed proposals for possible legislation that would ban the buying and selling of human embryos and far-out reproductive experimentation, like creating human-animal hybrids. While the recommendations—part of a report due out this spring—do not suggest limiting IVF or gender selection, the goals are clear: the government should clamp down before technology goes too far. "Even though people have strong differences of opinion on some issues," says council chair and leading bioethieist Leon Kass, "all of us have a stake in keeping human reproduction human."

After their first son, Jesse, was born in 1988, Mary and Sam Toedtman tried all sorts of folksy remedies to boost their chances of having a girl. When Jesse was followed by Jacob, now 10, and Lucas, 7, it seemed clear that boys would be boys in the Toedtman family. Sam has two brothers and comes from a line of boys 70 years long. So, after a lot of serious thinking, the Toedtmans decided to enroll in GIVF's clinical trial of MicroSort for "family balancing." That's the popular new term for gender selection by couples who already have at least one child and want to control their family mix. Since MicroSort's family balance trial began in 1995, more than 1,300 couples have signed on—almost 10 times more than joined a companion trial aimed at avoiding genetic illnesses that strike boys. GIVF is actively recruiting new candidates for both trials. In 2003 a second MicroSort clinic was opened near Los Angeles, and a third is planned for Florida this year. GIVF hopes MicroSort will become the first sperm-sorting device to receive the FDA's stamp of approval for safety and effectiveness. "This will completely change reproductive choices for women, and that's very exciting," says MicroSort's medical director, Dr. Keith Blauer. "We hope to make it available to as many couples as possible."

The MicroSort technology—created originally by the Department of Agriculture to sort livestock sperm—works by mixing sperm with a DNA-specific dye that helps separate X's from Y's (graphic).The majority of couples who use MicroSort for gender selection have no fertility problems and use standard artificial insemination to conceive. The technique is far from perfect: most participants have to make more than one attempt, each costing at least $2,500, to get pregnant. And not all end up with the gender of choice. At last count, 91 percent of couples who requested an "X sort" gave birth to a baby girl and 76 percent who chose a "Y sort" produced a boy. It worked for the Stock family. Six-month-old Amberlyn was spared the debilitating neuromuscular disorder that plagues her brother, Chancellor, 7. The Toedtmans were lucky, too. Though it took three tries to get pregnant, Mary finally delivered a girl, Natalie, last April. "She's a total joy," she says.

Determined as she was, Toedtman says she would not have felt comfortable creating embryos to ensure that Natalie was Natalie and not Nathaniel. But a small number of others, knowing that their chance of success with PGD is exponentially better, are becoming pioneers in the newest form of family planning. Available at a limited number of clinics nationwide, PGD was designed and originally intended to diagnose serious genetic diseases in embryos, like Tay-Sachs and cystic fibrosis, before implantation. Over the last decade the technology has allowed hundreds of couples, many of whom have endured the death of sick children, to have healthy babies. Today, some doctors are using PGD to increase the odds of successful IVF pregnancies by screening out chromosomally abnormal embryos. Some of those patients are asking about gender—and it's their right to do so, many doctors say. After an embryo screening, "I tell them it's normal and I tell them it's male or female," says PGD expert Yury Verlinsky of the Reproductive Genetics Institute in Chicago. "It's their embryo. I can't tell them which one to transfer."

It's one thing to allow infertile couples to choose gender after PGD. Creating embryos solely to sort boys from girls sets off ethical and moral alarm bells. In the last year or so, several clinics have begun to offer the procedure for gender balance without restrictions. Steinberg, of Fertility Institutes, says his team methodically debated the pros and cons before doing so. The logic, he says, is simple: "We've been offering sperm sorting for 20 years without any stipulations. Now, in 2004, I can offer almost 100 percent success with PGD. Why would I make it less available?" Steinberg.'s clinic, which also has offices in Las Vegas and Mexico, will soon perform its 100th PGD sex-selection procedure. So far, about 40 babies have been born, every one of them the desired sex. It's unclear how many couples will actually want to endure the hefty cost, time commitment and physical burden of fertility drugs and IVF just to ensure gender. But the idea is intriguing for a lot of couples. "I've had friends and neighbors discreetly inquire," says Dr. David Hill, head of ART Reproductive Center in Beverly Hills, Calif., where about 5 to 10 percent of patients are requesting PGD solely for sex selection. Hill has no problem offering it, but he respects colleagues who say no. "This is a really new area," he says. "It's pretty divided right now as to those who think it's acceptable and those who don't."

Dr. Mark Hughes, a leading PGD authority at Wayne State University School of Medicine in Detroit, is one of the latter. "The last time I checked, your gender wasn't a disease," he says. "There is no illness, no suffering and no reason for a physician to be involved. Besides, we're too busy helping desperate couples with serious disease build healthy families." At Columbia University, Dr. Mark Sauer balks at the idea of family balance. "What are you balancing? It discredits the value of an individual life." For those few patients who ask for it, "I look them straight in the face and say, 'We're not going to do that'." And at Northwestern, Dr. Ralph Kazer says bluntly: " 'Gattaca' was a wonderful movie. That's not what I want to do for a living."

One of the most vexing concerns is what some consider gender selection's implicit sexism. When you choose one sex, the argument goes, you reject the other. In Asia girls have been aborted or killed, and populations skewed, because of favoritism toward boys. Could the same thing happen here? GIVF's Blauer says the vast majority of MicroSort couples want girls, not boys, though that could change if Y-sort statistics improve. At Hill's clinic, about 65 percent request boys; at Steinberg's, 55 percent. "It's not going to tip the balance one way or the other," he says. But what if a couple doesn't get the boy or girl they desire? PGD comes as close as it gets to guaranteeing outcome, but there remains the thorny question of what to do with "wrong sex" embryos. Opponents worry that they'll be destroyed simply because they're male or female, but the options are identical for everyone going through IVF: discard the extras, freeze them for later use, donate them or offer them up for scientific research. As for MicroSort, of the more than 500 pregnancies achieved so far, four have been terminated at other facilities (GIVF won't perform abortions) because of "non-desired gender," says Blauer. "It's important to realize that couples have reproductive choice in this country," he says, but "the vast majority of patients want another healthy child and are happy with either gender."

Just beyond these clinical worries lies a vast swamp of ethical quandaries and inherent contradictions. People who support a woman's right to choose find themselves cringing at the idea of terminating a fetus based on sex. Those who believe that embryos deserve the status of personhood decry their destruction, but gender selection could result in fewer abortions. Choosing sex can skew male-female ratios, but it might also reduce overpopulation. Requesting a girl could mean she will be more desired by her parents, but it's also possible she'll grow up and decide she'd rather have been a boy. "Children are going to hold their parents responsible for having made them this way," says bioethicist Kass, "and that may not be as innocent as it sounds."

And then there is the most fundamental conflict of all: science versus religion. One Korean-American couple, with two daughters has been on both sides. Feeling an intense cultural pressure to produce a son, the woman, 31, attended a MicroSort information session, where Blauer reviewed the technique. Intrigued, she went back for a second session and convinced her husband to come along. When it was time to move forward, though, a greater power took over. "I don't think God intended us to do that," she says. "We decided we should just pray about it and leave it up to God."

There are no laws against performing gender selection in the United States. Many people believe that the safety and effectiveness of reproductive technologies like PGD should be regulated, says Kathy Hudson, of the Genetics and Public Policy Center at Johns Hopkins, which recently polled 1,200 Americans on the topic. But, she says, many Americans "are uncomfortable with the government being the arbiter of how to use these technologies." Meanwhile, fertility doctors look to the American Society for Reproductive Medicine for professional standards. John Robertson, head of ASRM's ethics committee, says preconception techniques like MicroSort "would be fine once safety is established." So far, MicroSort reports, 2.4 percent of its babies have been born with major malformations, like Down syndrome, compared with 3 to 4 percent in the general population. But until the trial is completed, there are no definitive data. As for PGD, the ASRM currently discourages its use for sex selection, but Robertson says he wouldn't rule out the possibility that it might become acceptable in the future.

So what, in the end, should we make of gender selection? Will programming of human DNA before birth become inevitable? "I learned a long time ago never to say never," says Rick Myers, chief of Stanford's genetics department. Still, he says, traits we're all worried about, like height, personality and intelligence, aren't the products of single genes. They're cooked in a complex stew of DNA and environment—a stew that boggles scientists, even those with IQs so high you'd swear they were bioengineered. And even if we could create designer Uma Thurmans, would we want to? Sharla Miller and Mary Toedtman say absolutely not. "That's taking it too far," says Miller.

We wouldn't be human if we didn't fantasize about the sci-fi universe around the corner. Steinberg, who has worked in IVF since its conception in the 1970s, remembers finding notes on his windshield in the early days that said, TEST-TUBE BABIES HAVE NO SOUL. The very idea of creating life outside the womb "was unthinkable," he says. And yet, some 1 million test-tube babies later, the practice has become routine. The same will likely be true of gender selection, says Robin Marantz Henig, author of the new book "Pandora's Baby," a history of IVF "The more it's done," she says, "the less you're going to see concerns."

Lizette Frielingsdorf doesn't have any. She and her husband have three boys—Jordan, 8, Justin, 6, and Jake, 5—and one MicroSort girl, Jessica, who just turned 2. "I call her my $15,000 baby. We felt like we won the lottery," says Frielingsdorf "Probably once a week someone will say, 'You got your girl. How did you do that?' and I'll say, 'Here's the number.' I want others to experience the same joy we have." No doubt, many will.

# MAKING TIME FOR A BABY

## For years, women have been told they could wait until 40 or later to have babies. But a new book argues that's way too late

**By NANCY GIBBS**

LISTEN TO A SUCCESSFUL WOMAN DISCUSS HER FAILURE TO bear a child, and the grief comes in layers of bitterness and regret. This was supposed to be the easy part, right? Not like getting into Harvard. Not like making partner. The baby was to be Mother Nature's gift. Anyone can do it; high school dropouts stroll through the mall with their babies in a Snugli. What can be so hard, especially for a Mistress of the Universe, with modern medical science devoted to resetting the biological clock? "I remember sitting in the clinic waiting room," recalls a woman who ran the infertility marathon, "and a woman—she was in her mid-40s and had tried everything to get pregnant—told me that one of the doctors had glanced at her chart and said, 'What are you doing here? You are wasting your time.' It was so cruel. She was holding out for that one last glimpse of hope. How horrible was it to shoot that hope down?"

The manner was cold, but the message was clear—and devastating. "Those women who are at the top of their game could have had it all, children and career, if they wanted it," suggests Pamela Madsen, executive director of the American Infertility Association (A.I.A.). "The problem was, nobody told them the truth about their bodies." And the truth is that even the very best fertility experts have found that the hands of the clock will not be moved. Baby specialists can do a lot to help a 29-year-old whose tubes are blocked or a 32-year-old whose husband has a low sperm count. But for all the headlines about 45-year-old actresses giving birth, the fact is that "there's no promising therapy for age-related infertility," says Dr. Michael Soules, a professor at the University of Washington School of Medicine and past president of the American Society for Reproductive Medicine (ASRM). "There's certainly nothing on the horizon."

This means, argues economist Sylvia Ann Hewlett in her new book, *Creating a Life: Professional Women and the Quest for Children* (Talk Miramax Books), that many ambitious young women who also hope to have kids are heading down a bad piece of road if they think they can spend a decade establishing their careers and wait until 35 or beyond to establish their families. Even as more couples than ever seek infertility treatment—the number of procedures performed jumped 27% between 1996 and 1998—doctors are learning that the most effective treatment may be prevention, which in this case means knowledge. "But the fact that the biological clock is real is unwelcome news to my 24-year-old daughter," Hewlett observes, "and she's pretty typical."

**27 IS THE AGE AT WHICH A WOMAN'S CHANCE OF GETTING PREGNANT BEGINS TO DECLINE**

**At 20, the risk of miscarriage is about 9%; it doubles by 35, then doubles again by the time a woman reaches her early 40s**

**At 42, 90% of a woman's eggs are abnormal; she has only a 7.8% chance of having a baby without using donor eggs**

## The Limits Of Science

ASSISTED REPRODUCTIVE TECHNOLOGY IS ONE OF THE great medical success stories of the late 20th century. Thanks to fertility drugs, in-vitro fertilization (IVF) and a growing list of even more sophisticated techniques, tens of thousands of healthy babies are born each year that otherwise might never have been conceived. But the process is neither foolproof nor risk free. There are limits to what science can do for infertile couples, and the more doctors have to intervene with drugs, needles and surgery to get sperm to meet egg, the greater the chance that something will go wrong. Among the pitfalls:

**OVARIAN HYPERSTIMULATION** The first step in most assisted-fertilization techniques is to trick the ovaries into producing a lot of eggs at once. But the hormones doctors use to do this are powerful drugs and in rare cases can cause serious complications, including blood clots and kidney damage.

**MULTIPLE GESTATION** Not being able to have a baby can be heartbreaking. But having too many at once can be even worse. About 20% to 35% of IVF pregnancies produce multiple fetuses, usually twins. Having more than two or three babies at once is often a medical disaster. Babies that develop in a crowded uterus or are born too early are at risk for a lifetime of developmental problems, including mental retardation, paralysis and blindness. Trying to reduce the number of fetuses through selective abortion has its own problems, not the least of which is an increased chance of miscarriage.

**LOW BIRTH WEIGHT** Twins and triplets (not to mention septuplets) often weigh less than normal at birth. But a recent study from the U.S. Centers for Disease Control suggests that even single babies conceived through IVF are more likely to be born underweight. Whether that also puts them at greater risk of developmental problems is uncertain.

**BIRTH DEFECTS** An Australian study published in March reported that IVF children are twice as likely to suffer birth defects—such as cleft palate, a hole in the heart or kidney problems—as children conceived the usual way. Several earlier studies have shown no difference between the two kinds of babies, so further research is needed. Even if the apparent increase is real, it might not be clear whether the birth defects are caused by the artificial reproductive technology or by whatever underlying problem caused the infertility in the first place.

Even the most powerful techniques can turn back a woman's biological clock only so far. Women in their early 30s who want to use their own eggs have a better than 30% chance of delivering a live baby by artificial means. After age 43, the success rate drops to a forbidding 3%.

—*By Christine Gorman*

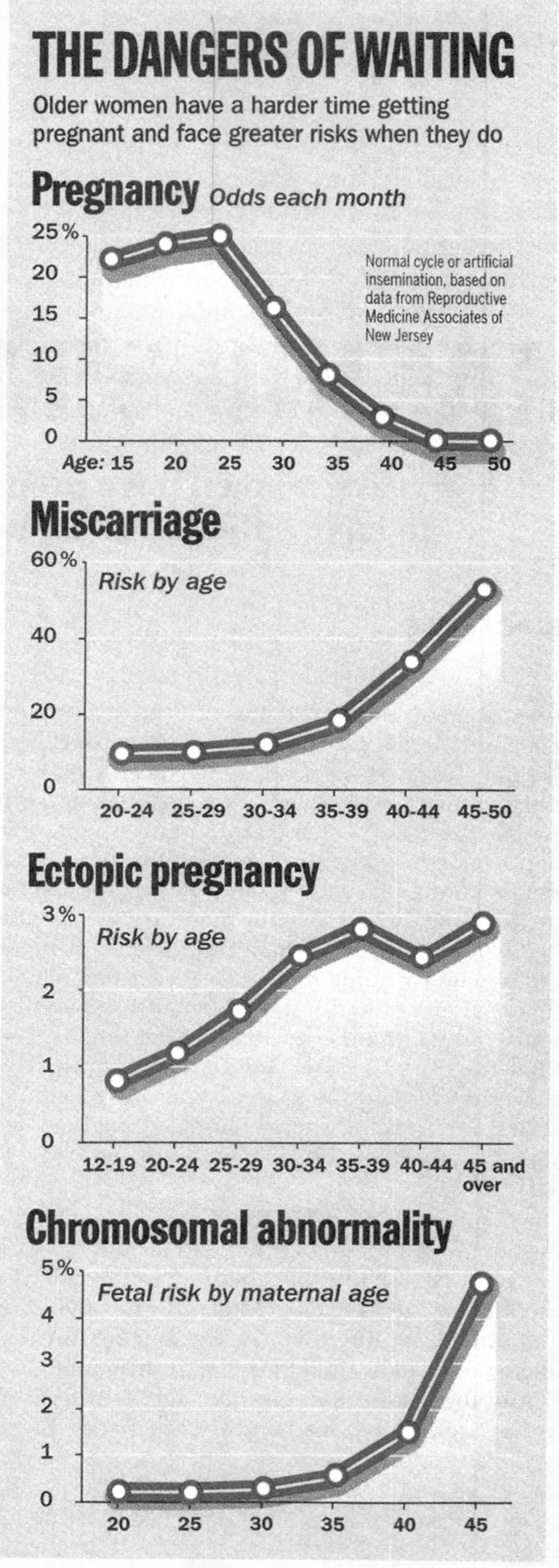


Sources: American Society for Reproductive Medicine; National Center for Health. Statistics; CDC; *British Medical Journal*; Mayo Clinic. TIME Graphic by Lon Tweeten and Ed Gabel; text by Laura Bradford

## THREE WAYS TO GIVE NATURE A HELPING HAND

Sometimes hormone therapy does the trick, but many infertile couples require more sophisticated manipulation of sperm and eggs. Among the techniques that offer the greatest hope for success:

### In vitro fertilization

**HOW THEY DO IT** A woman's eggs are extracted and mixed with her partner's sperm in a Petri dish. The resulting embryo is transferred to her uterus through the cervix

**POPULARITY** At least 60,000 IVF procedures are performed in the U.S. annually, with an average birthrate of 25%

### ICSI (intracytoplasmic sperm injection)

**HOW THEY DO IT** To counteract problems with sperm count, quality or mobility, doctors inject a single sperm directly into a mature egg to increase the chance of fertilization

**POPULARITY** ICSI accounts for approximately 24,000 IVF procedures annually. Average birthrate: 30%

### Egg donation

**HOW THEY DO IT** When the problem is aging eggs, a young woman may donate her eggs to the couple. Fertilized with the man's sperm, the resulting embryo is implanted in the older woman's womb

**POPULARITY** More than 5,000 eggs are donated yearly. After the eggs are fertilized, the birthrate is approximately 40%

Sources: American Society for Reproductive Medicine; National Center for Health Statistics; CDC; *British Medical Journal*; Mayo Clinic; text by Laura Bradford.

Women have been debating for a generation how best to balance work and home life, but somehow each new chapter starts a new fight, and Hewlett's book is no exception. Back in 1989, when Felice Schwartz discussed in the *Harvard Business Review* how to create more flexibility for career women with children (she never used the phrase Mommy Track herself), her proposals were called "dangerous" and "retrofeminist" because they could give corporations an excuse to derail women's careers. Slow down to start a family, the skeptics warned, and you run the risk that you will never catch up.

And so, argues Hewlett, many women embraced a "male model" of single-minded career focus, and the result is "an epidemic of childlessness" among professional women. She conducted a national survey of 1,647 "high-achieving women," including 1,168 who earn in the top 10% of income of their age group or hold degrees in law or medicine, and another 479 who are highly educated but are no longer in the work force. What she learned shocked her: she found that 42% of high-achieving women in corporate America (defined as companies with 5,000 or more employees) were still childless after age 40. That figure rose to 49% for women who earn $100,000 or more. Many other women were able to have only one child because they started their families too late. "They've been making a lot of money," says Dr. David Adamson, a leading fertility specialist at Stanford University, "but it won't buy back the time."

Recent Census data support Hewlett's research: childlessness has doubled in the past 20 years, so that 1 in 5 women between ages 40 and 44 is childless. For women that age and younger with graduate and professional degrees, the figure is 47%. This group certainly includes women for whom having children was never a priority: for them, the opening of the work force offered many new opportunities, including the chance to define success in realms other than motherhood. But Hewlett argues that many other women did not actually choose to be childless. When she asked women to recall their intentions at the time they were finishing college, Hewlett found that only 14% said that they definitely did not want to have children.

For most women Hewlett interviewed, childlessness was more like what one called a "creeping nonchoice." Time passes, work is relentless. The travel, the hours—relationships are hard to sustain. By the time a woman is married and settled enough in her career to think of starting a family, it is all too often too late. "They go to a doctor, take a blood test and are told the game is over before it even begins," says A.I.A.'s Madsen. "They are shocked, devastated and angry." Women generally know their fertility declines with age; they just don't realize how much and how fast. According to the Centers for Disease Control, once a woman celebrates her 42nd birthday, the chances of her having a baby using her own eggs, even with advanced medical help, are less than 10%. At age 40, half of her eggs are chromosomally abnormal; by 42, that figure is 90%. "I go through Kleenex in my office like it's going out of style," says reproductive endocrinologist Michael Slowey in Englewood, N.J.

Hewlett and her allies say they are just trying to correct the record in the face of widespread false optimism. Her survey found that nearly 9 out of 10 young women were confident of their ability to get pregnant into their 40s.

Last fall the A.I.A. conducted a fertility-awareness survey on the women's website iVillage.com. Out of the 12,524 respondents, only one answered all 15 questions correctly. Asked when fertility begins to decline, only 13% got it right (age 27); 39% thought it began to drop at 40. Asked how long couples should try to conceive on their own before seeking help, fully 42% answered 30 months. That is a dangerous combination: a couple that imagines fertility is no problem until age 40 and tries to get pregnant for 30 months before seeing a doctor is facing very long odds of ever becoming parents.

In one sense, the confusion is understandable: it is only in the past 10 years that doctors themselves have discovered the limitations. "I remember being told by a number of doctors, 'Oh, you have plenty of time,' even when I was 38," says Claudia Morehead, 47, a California insurance lawyer who is finally pregnant, using donor eggs. Even among fertility specialists, "it was shocking to us that IVF didn't work so well after age 42," admits Dr. Sarah Berga, a reproductive endocrinologist at the University of Pittsburgh School of Medicine. "The early '90s, to my mind, was all about how shocked we were that we couldn't get past this barrier." But even as doctors began to try to get the word out, they ran into resistance of all kinds.

One is simply how information is shared. Childlessness is a private sorrow; the miracle baby is an inevitable headline. "When you see these media stories hyping women in their late 40s having babies, it's with donor eggs," insists Stanford's Adamson, "but that is conveniently left out of the stories." The more aggressive infertility clinics have a financial incentive to hype the good news and bury the facts: a 45-year-old woman who has gone through seven cycles of IVF can easily spend $100,000 on treatment. But even at the best fertility clinics in the country, her chance of taking a baby home is in the single digits.

In hopes of raising women's awareness, ASRM launched a modest $60,000 ad campaign last fall, with posters and brochures warning that factors like smoking, weight problems and sexually transmitted infections can all harm fertility. But the furor came with the fourth warning, a picture of a baby bottle shaped like an hourglass: "Advancing age decreases your ability to have children." The physicians viewed this as a public service, given the evidence of widespread confusion about the facts, but the group has come under fire for scaring women with an oversimplified message on a complex subject.

"The implication is, 'I have to hurry up and have kids now or give up on ever having them,'" says Kim Gandy, president of the National Organization for Women. "And that is not true for the vast majority of women." Gandy, 48, had her first child at 39. "It was a choice on my part, but in most ways it really wasn't. It's not like you can create out of whole cloth a partner you want to have a family with and the economic and emotional circumstances that allow you to be a good parent. So to put pressure on young women to hurry up and have kids when they don't have those other factors in place really does a disservice to them and to their kids."

To emphasize a woman's age above all other factors can be just one more piece of misleading information, Gandy suggests. "There are two people involved [in babymaking], and yet we're putting all the responsibility on women and implying that women are being selfish if they don't choose to have children early." She shares the concern that women will hear the research and see the ads and end up feeling it is so hard to strike a balance that it's futile to even try. "There is an antifeminist agenda that says we should go back to the 1950s," says Caryl Rivers, a journalism professor at Boston University. "The subliminal message is, 'Don't get too educated; don't get too successful or too ambitious.'"

Allison Rosen, a clinical psychologist in New York City who has made it her mission to make sure her female patients know the fertility odds, disagrees. "This is not a case of male doctors' wanting to keep women barefoot and pregnant," she says. "You lay out the facts, and any particular individual woman can then make her choices." Madsen of A.I.A. argues that the biological imperative is there whether women know it or not. "I cringe when feminists say giving women reproductive knowledge is pressuring them to have a child," she says. "That's simply not true. Reproductive freedom is not just the ability not to have a child through birth control. It's the ability to have one if and when you want one."

YOU CAN TRACE THE STRUGGLE BETWEEN HOPE AND BIOLOGY back to *Genesis*, when Abraham and Sarah gave thanks for the miracle that brought them their son in old age. "She was the first infertile woman," notes Zev Rosenwaks, the director of New York Presbyterian Hospital's infertility program. "It was so improbable that an allegedly menopausal woman could have a baby that her firstborn was named Isaac, which means 'to laugh.'" The miracle stories have fed the hope ever since, but so does wishful thinking. "It's tremendously comforting for a 34- or 36-year-old professional woman to imagine that she has time on her side," says Hewlett, which can make for resistance to hearing the truth.

**"In just 30 years we've gone from fearing our fertility to squandering it—and very unwittingly."**

This is the heart of Hewlett's crusade: that it is essential for women to plan where they want to be at 45 and work backward, armed with the knowledge that the window for having children is narrower than they have been led to believe and that once it begins to swing shut, science can do little to pry it open. And Hewlett argues as well that employers and policymakers need to do more to help families make the balancing act work. "The greatest choice facing modern women is to freely choose to have both, a job and a family, and be supported and admired for it, not be seen as some overweening yuppie."

As it happens, Hewlett knows from personal experience. She says she didn't set out to write about how hard it is for professional women to be moms. She planned to do a book celebrating women turning 50 at the millennium and to look at what forces had shaped their lives. Then she discovered, in interview after interview with college deans and opera divas, a cross section of successful women in various fields, that none of them had children—and few of them had chosen to be childless. Many blamed themselves for working too hard and waiting too long—and waking up to the truth too late. "When I talked to these women," she recalls, "their sense of loss was palpable."

Hewlett had spent most of her professional life writing and lecturing on the need for business and government to develop more family-friendly workplaces; she has a Ph.D. in economics from Harvard. And she has had children and lost them and fought to have more. As a young Barnard professor with a toddler at home, she lost twins six months into her pregnancy: If only, she thought, I had taken time off from work, taken it easier. A year and a half later, she writes, she was turned down for tenure by an appointments committee that believed, in the words of one member, that she had "allowed childbearing to dilute my focus." Hewlett was lucky: she went on to have three more children, including Emma, to whom she gave birth at 51 using her own egg and infertility treatments. Hewlett says she understands "baby hunger."

At least she understands it for women. Men, she argues, have an unfair advantage. "Nowadays," she says, "the rule of thumb seems to be that the more successful the woman, the less likely it is she will find a husband or bear a child. For men, the reverse is true. I found that only one-quarter of high-achieving men end up without kids. Men generally find that if they are successful, everything else follows naturally." But that view of men doesn't quite do justice to the challenges they face as well. Men too are working harder than ever; at the very moment that society sends the message to be more involved as fathers, the economy makes it harder—and Hewlett's prescription that women need to think about having their children younger leaves more men as primary breadwinners. They would be fathers as far as biology goes, but they wouldn't get much chance to be parents. "A lot of my friends who are men and have had families are now divorced," Stanford's Adamson admits. "When you ask them what happened, the vast majority will say, 'Well, I was never home. I was working all the time. I didn't pay enough attention to my family. I wish I had, but it's too late now.'"

Hewlett still insists that men don't face the same "cruel choices" that women confront. "Men who find that they have no relationship with their adult kids at least have a second chance as grandfathers," she argues. "For women, childlessness represents a rolling loss into the future. It means having no children *and* no grandchildren." While her earlier books are full of policy prescriptions, this one is more personal. She salts the book with cautionary tales: women who were too threatening to the men they dated, too successful and preoccupied, too "predatory" to suit men who were looking for "nurturers." The voices are authentic but selective; taken together, it is easy to read certain passages and think she is calling for a retreat to home and hearth, where motherhood comes before every other role.

Hewlett replies that she is simply trying to help women make wise choices based on good information. She is not proposing a return to the '50s, she says, or suggesting that women should head off to college to get their MRS. and then try to have children soon after graduation. "Late 20s is probably more realistic, because men are not ready to commit earlier than that. And the 20s still needs to be a decade of great personal growth." She recommends that women get their degrees, work hard at their first jobs—but then be prepared to plateau for a while and redirect their energy into their personal lives, with the intention of catching up professionally later. "You will make some compromises in your career. But you will catch up, reinvent yourself, when the time is right."

**100% RISE IN PAST 20 YEARS OF CHILDLESS WOMEN AGES 40 TO 44**

**Only 0.1% of babies in the U.S. are born to women age 45 or older**

The problem is that Hewlett's own research argues otherwise: in her book all of the examples of successful women who also have families gave birth in their 20s. These women may escape the fate of would-be mothers who waited too long, but they encounter a whole different set of obstacles when it comes to balancing work and family. Biology may be unforgiving, but so is corporate culture: those who voluntarily leave their career to raise children often find that the way back in is extremely difficult. Many in her survey said they felt forced out by inflexible bosses; two-thirds say they wish they could return to the work force.

Much would have to change in the typical workplace for parents to be able to downshift temporarily and then resume their pace as their children grew older. Hewlett hopes that the war for talent will inspire corporations to adopt more family-friendly policies in order to attract and maintain the most talented parents, whether male or female. Many of her policy recommendations, however, are unlikely to be enacted anytime soon: mandatory paid parental leave; official "career breaks" like the generous policy at IBM that grants workers up to three years' leave with the guarantee of return to the same or a similar job; a new Fair Labor Standards Act that would discourage 80-hour workweeks by making all but the very top executives eligible for overtime pay.

Hewlett calls herself a feminist, but she has often crossed swords with feminists who, she charges, are so concerned with reproductive choice that they neglect the needs of women who choose to be mothers. In the history of the family, she notes, it is a very recent development for women to have control over childbearing, thanks to better health care and birth control. But there's an ironic twist now. "In just 30 years, we've gone from fearing our fertility to squandering it—and very unwittingly." The decision of whether to have a child will always be one of the most important anyone makes; the challenge is not allowing time and biology to make it for them.

*—Reported by Janice M. Horowitz, Julie Rawe and Sora Song/New York*

# Barren

## COMING TO TERMS WITH A LOST DREAM

*by* DEBORAH DERRICKSON KOSSMANN

WHEN I WAS 5, I listed several things I wanted to be when I grew up: teacher, archaeologist (my mother had wanted to be that and had explained what it was), author, and mother. I have always thought of myself as an archaeologist of sorts, dusting off bones from my clients' emotional digs, figuring out how they fit together to make an understandable history. I teach graduate students. I write. But I have not become a mother. What does it mean to be barren, unable to grow anything in the land that is the body?

Infertility is about the body. One's identity becomes defined by what the body does or does not do. During my first miscarriage, I experienced slow, aching cramps and the punch of the uterus as if it were saying, "No, not now, not time." There was no happy announcement of pregnancy, only the feeling of sadness when the bleeding came. By the time we learned I was pregnant, it was already over.

The second pregnancy began with more Clomid, a medication we were using to stimulate ovulation, and a new set of medical procedures, including a test called a hysterosalpingogram. No one understands why some women unexpectedly get pregnant after having this test. Perhaps a slight blockage exists, perhaps the dye they use is like Liquid-Plumr. Envision pipes opening up as the gunky stuff drains away. During the test, I lay on the table with the sheet covering my bottom half, the nurse and the doctor directing me: "Here you relax.... Here you breathe.... We'll see your uterus above on that screen." I had to turn my head from the hard table to see it. But first I focused on an image: blue dye being threaded into me, the shock of its entry almost like sexual intrusion. Not rape; I wanted this, didn't I? The goal was to find the blocked places, to make my body a host that could grow things. The dye entered and my body fought back. Above me, my uterus floated, distinct, not looking like those pictures in biology books. Mine is elongated, a shapely part of me, like a pink heart. Tubes stretched out from it. Momentarily fascinated, I ignored the physical discomfort as I looked inside myself.

The test took place two weeks before my nephew, Michael (my sister's third child), was born. My husband and I visited the hospital, bringing my sister Chinese food—greasy egg rolls, noodles in sauce. She was tired, but happy. She tried not to be too happy, mindful of our struggles with infertility, as she gave Michael to me to hold. Looking back, I wonder if my uterus at that moment opened and if somehow that muscle inside me relaxed, allowing my egg to roll downward and inside. I picture the egg, cartoonlike, smiling.

The night after Michael's birth, we conceived. My husband dreamed that night of a blond boy in a bucket. He told me the next morning we were pregnant, but I didn't believe him. And then, suddenly, we were. It was Christmastime and I was tired, green, and hungry. I told people early: I couldn't contain our news. For a long time after the first miscarriage, we'd waited to try and get pregnant, and we'd waited through more cycles on the medication. Now, I read things about babies. I imagined ourselves dividing over and over inside me. We had a nickname for it. We called it "Pea." I stayed green and tired and full of indigestion. My temperature stayed up. My breasts began to hurt all the time and grow larger. My husband noted this outward sign. He began to buy books about finances, investments. He was worrying about building our nest with enough twigs and sticks to weave securely for the egg—the blond boy in the bucket.

On Super Bowl Sunday, we returned from brunch with friends and some part of me felt different. Several days earlier, I'd finally stopped taking my temperature, believing at last my hormone levels would remain high. Then it appeared: a rusty red spot as I wiped myself. I started to panic. I went to the bathroom every hour. Each time, it was still there, another drop. It was a stop sign, red light, a flashing siren light on the top of a police car telling us to pull over, stop driving. I called the doctor—not *my* doctor, but the doctor on call. He sounded irritated. He was probably watching the game, eating snack foods, and drinking beer. I told him what was happening. "Call tomorrow for an ultrasound appointment," he said. "There's nothing to do today."

Should I rest, lie down?

"You can do that if you want," he said. "It probably won't matter."

In the hours that followed, I thought about my wedding day when my sister was several months pregnant with my second niece, Maddie. Right after the reception, she began bleeding. Her doctor put her on bed-rest for more than a month. We still shiver to think of Maddie's not being; we were so close to losing her. After the phone call to the doctor, I lay in bed and cried because I knew what was happening. My uterus was clenching, not to hold on, but to let go. It was like a star falling. You don't exactly see the trajectory, only the brief light and the memory that once it was reality, if only for the briefest breath. I lay flat and very still. Sometimes, when I was a child with a fever, I'd look at the corners of my bedroom ceiling and imagine walking on it like it was the floor. What a strange possibility if the whole world could be upside-down! In the suspended shadows, I'd hang in the wrong direction and try to experience that fevered moment before the world swung back.

The next morning, when I called for the ultrasound appointment, they told me to drink fluids. I drank, ten, twenty, thirty ounces. I was still drinking on the way to the hospital. I was still bleeding. "Many women spot early in their pregnancies. I've read this and it could be true," I told my husband. "My sister bled and it was bright red and Maddie is here now. It could be true, couldn't it?" My husband nodded a little distractedly and held my hand. It was as if he'd already begun dissembling the nest, knocking twigs everywhere.

*I stripped off all my clothes and put on my* **blue** *gown and bracelet. My husband sat with me. It was a funeral of* **waiting.**

At the hospital, the technician ran the probe over my abdomen. "You didn't drink enough. Go drink more," she said accusingly. I was sitting in a room with pamphlets about sexually transmitted diseases and bladder infections, and I was drowning myself with water. I felt myself float like a balloon, and still the technician said it was not enough water. She said with annoyance now, "We can't read it this way. We'll do a transvaginal. Now go urinate." I peed and peed and peed. Then she brought out the condom-covered probe, which I helped her put inside me. It reminded me of a stick shift on one of those driving video games. She stared at the incomprehensible screen that was turned slightly away from me. My husband seemed not to notice the weirdly pornographic quality to the whole interaction. "I can't see," the technician said, "I'll be right back." But I knew already what I knew—that something had happened. The radiologist came in and said, "I'm sorry. It stopped growing a week or so ago." She compared the size of the yolk with the technicians' developmental chart and moved the probe around again inside me. I began to cry then, just wanted to get up and go somewhere like those animals that howl and howl, deep in the forest.

But first we had to walk back to the obstetrician's office. My doctor was almost tearful at the news. The nurse-practitioner was actually crying. She asked me, "Do you want to wait? Or we can do a dilation and evacuation (D&E) and see if we can get a tissue sample. Then we can maybe figure out what happened. You don't have to wait and then bleed. You can know it's finished." I could barely think because I was that animal howling, but I made the D&E appointment for the next day. I knew that was better: I couldn't stand to wait.

The next day, we checked into the hospital. I told the admissions person the reason for our visit and cried. I told the doctor doing the surgery what had happened when she asked, and I cried again. I stripped off all my clothes and put on the blue gown and bracelet. My husband sat with me. He held my rings because I was not allowed to wear them into surgery. It was a funeral of waiting.

After they came to take me into surgery, he waited in the other room like those old movies where they show the father pacing the waiting area during the baby's delivery. I was still sobbing when they wheeled me into the operating room. The surgical team put my feet up into high stirrups. The anesthesiologist said something that I didn't hear because it was suddenly dark. My obstetrician had cautioned, "Don't worry about whatever you say or do during the procedure." Afterward, when I woke up after the surgery, a nurse was hovering over me, my face was wet, and my hands held a ball of damp tissues. I knew I'd said and done things I couldn't remember as they carefully cleaned out that beautiful elongated space inside me that must have clenched its muscled will against the intrusion, the loss, and the flowing out.

After the second miscarriage, we both took the nest apart. A friend once told me about some misguided birds that had built a nest by her front door inside a large flowerpot. One of the eggs—a finch egg, she thinks—was accidentally knocked out and broken. Thinking about that story, I wondered if the bird missed the shattered egg. After the D&E, I stayed home for a few days in the dark house in stunned silence. I read two murder mysteries in 24 hours. I slept. But mostly, I just sat quietly and took painkillers for the cramps. It was raining outside, a winter rain, the hard, cold kind. I sat in my living room for almost three hours before I noticed that it was raining *inside* the house, a steady drip in the entranceway. I put a pot under it and sat some more. My husband didn't know what to do. He held me, but as is the way with wild animals, I'd found a cave and remained in it.

We visited a high-risk specialist who told us nothing we hadn't figured out already. She offered us a different medication, the possibility of a study. We both underwent full panels of genetic testing and filled vials of blood in the lab. The results of the D&E testing came back. The obstetrician showed us the numbers and pronounced them "normal." He told me they couldn't be sure if they'd obtained the right tissue. It was so early in the pregnancy that the tissue they used may have been from the embryo or my own body. He was gentle and encouraging about trying again. He said, "If you want to, and whenever you feel ready." There seemed to be no answers for what was termed "secondary infertility." After all, I'd finally been able to get pregnant when on medication, hadn't I?

When I visited my sister during this time, I didn't hold my nephew. He was exactly nine months ahead of the child I was missing. My husband and I decided to try again and spent more months on drugs and off drugs with no conception. The anniversary of the first miscarriage passed. Then the anniversary of the due date of the second miscarriage approached. I tried to speak to my husband from the cave. "It's a harder time than I expected," I said, "The 28th will be difficult." He said he understood. The 28th passed, and he said nothing. On the 29th, I climbed out of my cave and tried to beat some conversation out of him. Where had he gone? He no longer guarded the cave, no longer grieved as I did. "I want our old life back," he said. He said he didn't really want children, maybe never did. Men and women grieve differently, the literature claims. I wanted to rip at his seeming indifference with unforgiving claws.

We talked to resolve our differences. But in order to have children, we needed to agree to proceed with the medical process we'd been going through. And then we needed to decide at what level we'd stop treatment. Imagine two posturing like a bull and a matador. After several conversations like this, our battle became scripted. One wave of the cape and we were off. We began to avoid the ring. We began to avoid sex. Once when we were scheduled to have sex—neither of us called these times making love at this point—my husband turned to me and said in a businesslike voice, "Okay, let's pretend we're in a lab and they're forcing us." We took turns elaborating this scenario so much that our laughter rang over the bed and bounced back to us until we could make love.

How can I explain what the infertility journey does to a sex life? First, there's fun, the joy of trying to make something. Then, there's the fear of making something you will lose. Then, there's the stress of having to make something on a schedule and the fact that hoping at all becomes so painful. The pain is like a small, deep cut that won't heal.

When the third miscarriage happened, we barely talked. I knew the pregnancy was over three days before the bleeding started. I was now so attuned to my body that I almost swore I could feel when the egg released. I tried to control what I could. I kept my butt elevated for 20 minutes after sex, even though it was futile. But I told myself maybe it would matter and at least I could do something. When the bleeding for the miscarriage began, I cried in the bathroom at the community mental health center where I worked, big heaving sobs that I tried to stifle, since I told myself the patients used the same bathroom, and I didn't want to upset or have to comfort them. I was glad I'd had the D&E last time, since each change of pads and tampons now made me wonder, Was this life? Was *this?*

In the infertility specialist's office, the new doctor, a reproductive endocrinologist, sat across from me. He said, "You seem stressed by your situation," and asked if I wanted to see their psychologist. This would have been funny at any other time, since I'm a psychologist married to a psychologist, and had already been seeing a psychologist on and off during the whole ordeal. This new doctor seemed to believe that, because I was starting anew with him, the past three years and three miscarriages didn't count. "Here are new vitamins and new blood work and more medication," he said. I wasn't very hopeful, but I took the medication and felt myself ovulate days before I was supposed to. I took the ovulation test at work between patients and brought it home to my husband, because I didn't even trust myself to read its results right any more. He thought I'd ovulated, too. He said this carefully, since I was wild with hormones. When I called the doctor panicked and afraid we'd missed another opportunity to get pregnant, the doctor said I couldn't have ovulated. We scheduled time to have sex as soon as the doctor's office called back because we knew it was the "right" time. We lay on the yellow, sun-warmed afternoon bed and tried to make a baby. We didn't.

## Time to Stop

At the next doctor's visit, when he told us we could try stronger drugs or in vitro fertilization (though there were still no known reasons for the miscarriages) and when he said the words "let's take another blood test," I knew. I knew, just as I knew when it was time to break up with somebody or change jobs, that it was time to stop. I told my husband on the way home. I didn't say it directly, however. I told him (half in the cave) that I was getting rid of all the oversized clothes and borrowed maternity outfits I'd been keeping. Once home, I angrily cleaned out closets and drawers. I was getting rid of the clothes that no longer fit me or were no longer about who I was or wanted to be.

That night and for the whole week following, as my husband and I climbed into bed, we listened to a confused mockingbird singing in the dark, just outside our window. He was looking for a mate, looking to make a bird family. He was singing at the wrong time, but what a song of trills and warbles and fakery! He sang as if his life depended upon finding his mate. The week after his glorious midnight performances brought only silence. In all that darkness, could he have found something?

I began working out every day at the gym and lost all the weight I'd gained, reclaiming my body. I began writing poetry again, stories and words about grief. I quit my 30-hour-a-week administrative job at the community mental heath center. I remembered that I once liked my husband as a friend and that, while neither of us was perfect dealing with our infertility or each other, as a couple, we'd survived.

*I suddenly felt tears push at the back of my eyelids as the* **thought** *welled up that I would never make a cake like this for my daughter.*

Bodily scars linger. I have bigger breasts from the pregnancies and, possibly, some other physical effects from the medications I took. I struggle with my feelings about what it means to be female and not give birth. I recently walked into a hair salon where four pregnant women and one woman with an infant sat. It reminded me in an instant that I'm different from other women: I won't hold a child that looks like my husband and me.

But there are also moments of solace. My husband jokingly holds our favorite cat up next to his cheek and grins. "See the resemblance?" he asks. A few months ago, I attended the opening of an art exhibit held by a young woman who'd been one of my first long-term psychotherapy clients. She made textured and original ceramic pieces symbolizing parts of her personality, and she'd wanted me to see them. (They were too big to bring to my office.) She stood next to me with shining eyes and excitement at the fulfillment of making something, and I recognized that I'd helped in this. The years we'd worked together had created something in her that, in turn, created something else, healthy and full of her life energy.

I'm an aunt. In some cultures this is an important and respected position—someone who doesn't have her own children, but loves others' children as if they were her own. My first niece, Sarah, is 8 years old, as old as my relationship with my husband. We attended her birthday party and watched as she blew out the candles on the orange, pumpkin-shaped cake that my sister had crafted. My family sang "Happy Birthday" in all different keys to her happy face. I suddenly felt tears push at the back of my eyelids as the thought welled up that I'd never make a cake like this for my daughter.

My 5-year-old niece, Maddie, was pleased that I hung her artwork on my kitchen door. "Aunt Debbie," she asked holding a small fistful of tiny yellow flowers she'd bunched up with tape borrowed from my drawer, "Can you hang these up? These are for you." I looked at the small wilted weeds, the same yellow as her hair and her ruffled dress. She was smiling at me and I was acutely aware of the ache her gifts sometimes caused. She was not my own child, yet my love for her touched the emptiness inside me.

My nephew Michael was talking. He said, "Aunt Bebbie." When I visited my sister, he played a new game with me, jumping off the coffee table into my arms over and over, sure that I'd catch him. And I did, every time, though each time he flew into the air and I held him, I remembered what had slipped from my grasp.

How long does it take to give birth to oneself as a childless woman? A year after we'd stopped all the procedures and the medications, given up the idea of trying, and continued along our changed life path, I suddenly became pregnant. On a television show, a surprise situation like ours should have turned out fine. It didn't. I had another early miscarriage. For a while after this, I halfheartedly entertained thoughts about adoption. This was fantasy, a way to imagine a life that ran parallel to this one, in some other universe. That alternative life included a little boy or girl running through our backyard, playing pretend under the peach tree. I began to realize that I'd always be barren if I continued to hold onto the idea that a child should be in me and produced by me. If I believed this idea, planted in me when I was a child myself, I'd always have only a weed-filled field, scrub trees, and emptiness. Here, in this infertile place, I kept the grief about "Pea" and the other lost embryos, along with the fantasies about what might have been.

A second-floor room in our house had been painted bright yellow before we'd moved in, six years ago. I said it would make a great baby's room. Each morning, it filled with sunshine, and several contented cats stretched out in its warm spots. A few weeks ago, my husband suggested moving my home office from the corner of the basement into the yellow room. To take my creativity upstairs meant reorganizing the whole house—moving heavy furniture to different rooms, carrying what seemed like endless numbers of books from bookshelf to bookshelf, opening boxes, tossing files I hadn't looked at in a wile, cleaning out old pictures, and deciding what I should take with me. In the middle of the chaos, my husband leaned over my shoulder as I ordered office furniture online. He joked in a low inviting voice, "Come upstairs, out of the cave, write happy things in the yellow room."

Once I moved into the yellow room, I could see from my windows the neighbors' houses and their children running between the fenced backyards. In our own yard, the peach tree, planted from a dried pit, is now mature enough to begin bearing juicy fruit itself. Inside my new room, I see lots of photographs of my husband and me with our nieces and nephew, snapshots of our friends and family, and pictures of the places the two of us have visited together. High on a bookshelf, almost out of reach, sits a small, closed box, a gift from my husband's aunt, from the days before the second miscarriage. Inside, protected in white tissue paper, nestles a pair of green, hand-knit baby booties.

---

*Deborah Derrickson Kossmann, Psy.D., is a clinical psychologist in private practice and also works in a multidisciplinary medical oncology practice. She is a journalist, essayist, and poet. Address: 1709 Langhorne-Newton Rd., Suite 2, Langhorne, PA 19047. E-mails to the author may be sent to drskoss@aol.com.*

A form of this article originally appeared in "Families, Systems & Health", 18, No. 4, Winter 2000, pp. 479-484. From *Psychotherapy Networker*, July/August 2002, pp. 40-45, 58. 

# Inside The Womb

## What scientists have learned about those amazing first nine months—and what it means for mothers

By J. Madeleine Nash

As the crystal probe slides across her belly, Hilda Manzo, 33, stares wide-eyed at the video monitor mounted on the wall. She can make out a head with a mouth and two eyes. She can see pairs of arms and legs that end in tiny hands and feet. She can see the curve of a backbone, the bridge of a nose. And best of all, she can see movement. The mouth of her child-to-be yawns. Its feet kick. Its hands wave.

Dr. Jacques Abramowicz, director of the University of Chicago's ultrasound unit, turns up the audio so Manzo can hear the gush of blood through the umbilical cord and the fast thump, thump, thump of a miniature heart. "Oh, my!" she exclaims as he adjusts the sonic scanner to peer under her fetus' skin. "The heart is on the left side, as it should be," he says, "and it has four chambers. Look—one, two, three, four!"

Such images of life stirring in the womb—in this case, of a 17-week-old fetus no bigger than a newborn kitten—are at the forefront of a biomedical revolution that is rapidly transforming the way we think about the prenatal world. For although it takes nine months to make a baby, we now know that the most important developmental steps—including laying the foundation for such major organs as the heart, lungs and brain—occur before the end of the first three. We also know that long before a child is born its genes engage the environment of the womb in an elaborate conversation, a two-way dialogue that involves not only the air its mother breathes and the water she drinks but also what drugs she takes, what diseases she contracts and what hardships she suffers.

One reason we know this is a series of remarkable advances in MRIs, sonograms and other imaging technologies that allow us to peer into the developmental process at virtually every stage—from the fusion of sperm and egg to the emergence, some 40 weeks later, of a miniature human being. The extraordinary pictures on these pages come from a new book that captures some of the color and excitement of this research: *From Conception to Birth: A Life Unfolds* (Doubleday), by photographer Alexander Tsiaras and writer Barry Werth. Their computer-enhanced images are reminiscent of the remarkable fetal portraits taken by medical photographer Lennart Nilsson, which appeared in Life magazine in 1965. Like Nilsson's work, these images will probably spark controversy. Antiabortion activists may interpret them as evidence that a fetus is a viable human being earlier than generally believed, while pro-choice advocates may argue that the new technology allows doctors to detect serious fetal defects at a stage when abortion is a reasonable option.

The other reason we know so much about what goes on inside the womb is the remarkable progress researchers have made in teasing apart the sequence of chemical signals and switches that drive fetal development. Scientists can now describe at the level of individual genes and molecules many of the steps involved in building a human, from the establishment of a head-to-tail growth axis and the budding of limbs to the sculpting of a four-chambered heart and the weaving together of trillions of neural connections. Scientists are beginning to unroll the genetic blueprint of life and identify the precise molecular tools required for assembly. Human development no longer seems impossibly complex, says Stanford University biologist Matthew Scott. "It just seems marvelous."

How is it, we are invited to wonder, that a fertilized egg—a mere speck of protoplasm and DNA encased in a spherical shell—can generate such complexity? The answers, while elusive and incomplete, are beginning to come into focus.

Only 20 years ago, most developmental biologists thought that different organisms grew according to different sets of rules, so that understanding how a fly or a worm develops—or even a vertebrate like a chicken or a fish—would do little to illuminate the process in humans. Then, in the 1980s, researchers found remarkable similarities in the molecular tool kit used by organisms that span the breadth of the animal kingdom, and those similarities have proved serendipitous beyond imagining. No matter what the species, nature uses virtually the same nails

## How They Did It

With just a few keystrokes, Alexander Tsiaras does the impossible. He takes the image of a 56-day-old human embryo and peers through its skin, revealing liver, lungs, a bulblike brain and the tiny, exquisite vertebrae of a developing spine.

These are no ordinary baby pictures. What Tsiaras and his colleagues are manipulating are layers of data gathered by CT scans, micro magnetic resonance imaging (MRI) and other visualization techniques. When Lennart Nilsson took his groundbreaking photographs in the 1960s, he was limited to what he could innovatively capture with a flash camera. Since then, says Tsiaras, "there's been a revolution in imaging."

What's changed is that development can now be viewed through a wide variety of prisms, using different forms of energy to illuminate different aspects of the fetus. CT scans, for example, are especially good at showing bone, and MRI is excellent for soft tissue. These two-dimensional layers of information are assembled, using sophisticated computer software, into a three-dimensional whole.

The results are painstakingly accurate and aesthetically stunning. Tsiaras, who trained as a painter and sculptor, used medical specimens from the Carnegie Human Embryology Collection at the National Museum of Health and Medicine in Washington as models for all but a few images. The specimens came from a variety of sources, according to museum director Adrianne Noe, including miscarriages and medically necessary procedures. None were acquired from elective abortions.

*—By David Bjerklie*

and screws, the same hammers and power tools to put an embryo together.

Among the by-products of the torrent of information pouring out of the laboratory are new prospects for treating a broad range of late-in-life diseases. Just last month, for example, three biologists won the Nobel Prize for Medicine for their work on the nematode *Caenorhabditis elegans*, which has a few more than 1,000 cells, compared with a human's 50 trillion. The three winners helped establish that a fundamental mechanism that *C. elegans* embryos employ to get rid of redundant or abnormal cells also exists in humans and may play a role in AIDS, heart disease and cancer. Even more exciting, if considerably more controversial, is the understanding that embryonic cells harbor untapped therapeutic potential. These cells, of course, are stem cells, and they are the progenitors of more specialized cells that make up organs and tissues. By harnessing their generative powers, medical researchers believe, it may one day be possible to repair the damage wrought by injury and disease. (That prospect suffered a political setback last week when a federal advisory committee recommended that embryos be considered the same as human subjects in clinical trials.)

To be sure, the marvel of an embryo transcends the collection of genes and cells that compose it. For unlike strands of DNA floating in a test tube or stem cells dividing in a Petri dish, an embryo is capable of building not just a protein or a patch of tissue but a living entity in which every cell functions as an integrated part of the whole. "Imagine yourself as the world's tallest skyscraper, built in nine months and germinating from a single brick," suggest Tsiaras and Werth in the opening of their book. "As that brick divides, it gives rise to every other type of material needed to construct and operate the finished tower—a million tons of steel, concrete, mortar, insulation, tile, wood, granite, solvents, carpet, cable, pipe and glass as well as all furniture, phone systems, heating and cooling units, plumbing, electrical wiring, artwork and computer networks, including software."

Given the number of steps in the process, it will perhaps forever seem miraculous that life ever comes into being without a major hitch. "Whenever you look from one embryo to another," observes Columbia University developmental neurobiologist Thomas Jessell, "what strikes you is the fidelity of the process."

Sometimes, though, that fidelity is compromised, and the reasons why this happens are coming under intense scrutiny. In laboratory organisms, birth defects occur for purely genetic reasons when scientists purposely mutate or knock out specific sequences of DNA to establish their function. But when development goes off track in real life, the cause can often be traced to a lengthening list of external factors that disrupt some aspect of the genetic program. For an embryo does not develop in a vacuum but depends on the environment that surrounds it. When a human embryo is deprived of essential nutrients or exposed to a toxin, such as alcohol, tobacco or crack cocaine, the consequences can range from readily apparent abnormalities—spina bifida, fetal alcohol syndrome—to subtler metabolic defects that may not become apparent until much later.

IRONICALLY, EVEN AS SOCIETY AT LARGE CONTINUES TO WORRY almost obsessively about the genetic origins of disease, the biologists and medical researchers who study development are mounting an impressive case for the role played by the prenatal environment. A growing body of evidence suggests that a number of serious maladies—among them, atherosclerosis, hypertension and diabetes—trace their origins to detrimental prenatal conditions. As New York University Medical School's Dr. Peter Nathanielsz puts it, "What goes on in the womb before you are born is just as important to who you are as your genes."

Most adults, not to mention most teenagers, are by now thoroughly familiar with the mechanics of how the sperm in a man's semen and the egg in a woman's oviduct connect, and it is at this point that the story of development begins. For the sperm and the egg each contain only 23 chromosomes, half the amount of DNA needed to make a human. Only when the sperm and the egg fuse their chromosomes does the tiny zygote, as a fertilized egg is called, receive its instructions to grow. And grow it does, replicating its DNA each time it divides—into two cells, then four, then eight and so on.

If cell division continued in this fashion, then nine months later the hapless mother would give birth to a tumorous ball of literally astronomical proportions. But instead of endlessly dividing, the zygote's cells progressively take form. The first striking change is apparent four days after conception, when a 32-cell clump called the morula (which means "mulberry" in Latin) gives rise to two distinct layers wrapped around a fluid-filled core. Now known as a blastocyst, this spherical mass will proceed to burrow into the wall of the uterus. A short time later, the outer layer of cells will begin turning into the placenta and amniotic sac, while the inner layer will become the embryo.

The formation of the blastocyst signals the start of a sequence of changes that are as precisely choreographed as a ballet. At the end of Week One, the inner cell layer of the blastocyst balloons into two more layers. From the first layer, known as the endoderm, will come the cells that line the gastrointestinal tract. From the second, the ectoderm, will arise the neurons that make up the brain and spinal cord along with the epithelial cells that make up the skin. At the end of Week Two, the ectoderm spins off a thin line of cells known as the primitive streak, which forms a new cell layer called the mesoderm. From it will come the cells destined to make the heart, the lungs and all the other internal organs.

At this point, the embryo resembles a stack of Lilliputian pancakes—circular, flat and horizontal. But as the mesoderm forms, it interacts with cells in the ectoderm to trigger yet another transformation. Very soon these cells will roll up to become the neural tube, a rudimentary precursor of the spinal cord and brain. Already the embryo has a distinct cluster of cells at each end, one destined to become the mouth and the other the anus. The embryo, no larger at this point than a grain of rice, has determined the head-to-tail axis along which all its body parts will be arrayed.

How on earth does this little, barely animate cluster of cells "know" what to do? The answer is as simple as it is startling. A human embryo knows how to lay out its body axis in the same way that fruit-fly embryos know and *C. elegans* embryos and the embryos of myriad other creatures large and small know. In all cases, scientists have found, in charge of establishing this axis is a special set of genes, especially the so-called homeotic homeobox, or HOX, genes.

HOX genes were first discovered in fruit flies in the early 1980s when scientists noticed that their absence caused striking mutations. Heads, for example, grew feet instead of antennae, and thoraxes grew an extra pair of wings. HOX genes have been found in virtually every type of animal, and while their number varies—fruit flies have nine, humans have 39—they are invariably arrayed along chromosomes in the order along the body in which they are supposed to turn on.

Many other genes interact with the HOX system, including the aptly named Hedgehog and Tinman genes, without which fruit flies grow a dense covering of bristles or fail to make a heart. And scientists are learning in exquisite detail what each does at various stages of the developmental process. Thus one of the three Hedgehog genes—Sonic Hedgehog, named in honor of the cartoon and video-game character—has been shown to play a role in making at least half a dozen types of spinal-cord neurons. As it happens, cells in different places in the neural tube are exposed to different levels of the protein encoded by this gene; cells drenched in significant quantities of protein mature into one type of neuron, and those that receive the barest sprinkling mature into another. Indeed, it was by using a particular concentration of Sonic Hedgehog that neurobiologist Jessell and his research team at Columbia recently coaxed stem cells from a mouse embryo to mature into seemingly functional motor neurons.

At the University of California, San Francisco, a team led by biologist Didier Stainier is working on genes important in cardiovascular formation. Removing one of them, called Miles Apart, from zebra-fish embryos results in a mutant with two nonviable hearts. Why? In all vertebrate embryos, including humans, the heart forms as twin buds. In order to function, these buds must join. The way the Miles Apart gene appears to work, says Stainier, is by detecting a chemical attractant that, like the smell of dinner cooking in the kitchen, entices the pieces to move toward each other.

The crafting of a human from a single fertilized egg is a vastly complicated affair, and at any step, something can go wrong. When the heart fails to develop properly, a baby can be born with a hole in the heart or even missing valves and chambers. When the neural tube fails to develop properly, a baby can be born with a brain not fully developed (anencephaly) or with an incompletely formed spine (spina bifida). Neural-tube defects, it has been firmly established, are often due to insufficient levels of the water-soluble B vitamin folic acid. Reason: folic acid is essential to a dividing cell's ability to replicate its DNA.

Vitamin A, which a developing embryo turns into retinoids, is another nutrient that is critical to the nervous system. But watch out, because too much vitamin A can be toxic. In another newly released book, *Before Your Pregnancy* (Ballantine Books), nutritionist Amy Ogle and obstetrician Dr. Lisa Mazzullo caution would-be mothers to limit foods that are overly rich in vitamin A, especially liver and food products that contain lots of it, like foie gras and cod-liver oil. An excess of vitamin A, they note, can cause damage to the skull, eyes, brain and spinal cord of a developing fetus, probably because retinoids directly interact with DNA, affecting the activity of critical genes.

Folic acid, vitamin A and other nutrients reach developing embryos and fetuses by crossing the placenta, the remarkable temporary organ produced by the blastocyst that develops from the fertilized egg. The outer ring of cells that compose the placenta are extremely aggressive, behaving very much like tumor cells as they invade the uterine wall and tap into the pregnant woman's blood vessels. In fact, these cells actually go in and replace the maternal cells that form the lining of the uterine arteries, says Susan Fisher, a developmental biologist at the University of California, San Francisco. They trick the pregnant woman's immune system into tolerating the embryo's presence rather than rejecting it like the lump of foreign tissue it is.

In essence, says Fisher, "the placenta is a traffic cop," and its main job is to let good things in and keep bad things out. To this

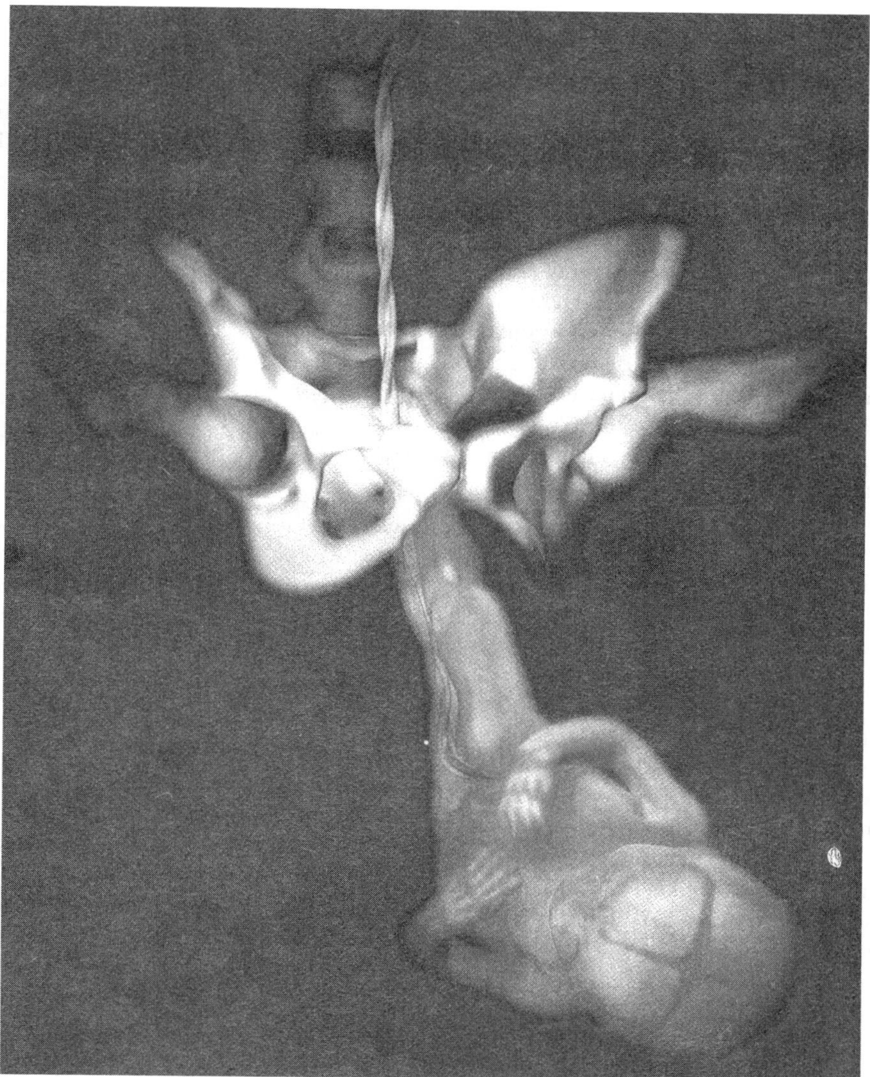

⑨ months—shows how a baby emerges from the birth canal began with an unusual delivery that required doctors to place the mother in a spiral CT scanner. The image was merged with CT and ultrasound data from other babies to create this re-enacted birth.



end, the placenta marshals platoons of natural killer cells to patrol its perimeters and engages millions of tiny molecular pumps that expel poisons before they can damage the vulnerable embryo.

ALAS, THE PLACENTA'S DEFENSES ARE SOMETIMES BREACHED—by microbes like rubella and cytomegalovirus, by drugs like thalidomide and alcohol, by heavy metals like lead and mercury, and by organic pollutants like dioxin and PCBs. Pathogens and poisons contained in certain foods are also able to cross the placenta, which may explain why placental tissues secrete a nausea-inducing hormone that has been tentatively linked to morning sickness. One provocative if unproved hypothesis says morning sickness may simply be nature's crude way of making sure that potentially harmful substances do not reach the womb, particularly during the critical first trimester of development.

Timing is decisive where toxins are concerned. Air pollutants like carbon monoxide and ozone, for example, have been linked to heart defects when exposure coincided with the second month of pregnancy, the window of time during which the heart forms. Similarly, the nervous system is particularly vulnerable to damage while neurons are migrating from the part of the brain where they are made to the area where they will ultimately reside. "A tiny, tiny exposure at a key moment when a certain process is beginning to unfold can have an effect that is not only quantitatively larger but qualitatively different than it would be on an adult whose body has finished forming," observes Sandra Steingraber, an ecologist at Cornell University.

Among the substances Steingraber is most worried about are environmentally persistent neurotoxins like mercury and lead (which directly interfere with the migration of neurons formed during the first trimester) and PCBs (which, some evidence suggests, block the activity of thyroid hormone). "Thyroid hormone plays a noble role in the fetus," says Steingraber. "It actually goes into the fetal brain and serves as kind of a conductor of the orchestra."

PCBs are no longer manufactured in the U.S., but other chemicals potentially harmful to developing embryos and fetuses are. Theo Colborn, director of the World Wildlife Fund's contaminants program, says at least 150 chemicals pose possible risks for fetal development, and some of them can interfere with the naturally occurring sex hormones critical to the development of a fetus. Antiandrogens, for example, are widely found in fungicides and plastics. One in particular—DDE, a breakdown product of DDT—has been shown to cause hypospadias in laboratory mice, a birth defect in which the urethra fails to extend to the end of the penis. In humans, however, notes Dr. Allen Wilcox, editor of the journal *Epidemiology*, the link between hormone-like chemicals and birth defects remains elusive.

THE LIST OF POTENTIAL THREATS TO EMBRYONIC LIFE IS LONG. It includes not only what the mother eats, drinks or inhales, explains N.Y.U.'s Nathanielsz, but also the hormones that surge through her body. Pregnant rats with high blood-glucose levels (chemically induced by wiping out their insulin) give birth to female offspring that are unusually susceptible to developing gestational diabetes. These daughter rats are able to produce enough insulin to keep their blood glucose in check, says Nathanielsz, but only until they become pregnant. At that point, their glucose level soars, because their pancreases were damaged by prenatal exposure to their mother's sugar-spiked blood. The next generation of daughters is, in turn, more susceptible to gestational diabetes, and the transgenerational chain goes on.

In similar fashion, atherosclerosis may sometimes develop because of prenatal exposure to chronically high cholesterol levels. According to Dr. Wulf Palinski, an endocrinologist at the University of California at San Diego, there appears to be a kind of metabolic memory of prenatal life that is permanently retained. In genetically similar groups of rabbits and kittens, at least, those born to mothers on fatty diets were far more likely to develop arterial plaques than those whose mothers ate lean.

But of all the long-term health threats, maternal undernourishment—which stunts growth even when babies are born full term—may top the list. "People who are small at birth have, for life, fewer kidney cells, and so they are more likely to go into renal failure when they get sick," observes Dr. David Barker, director of the environmental epidemiology unit at England's University of Southampton. The same is true of insulin-producing cells in the pancreas, so that low-birth-weight babies stand a higher chance of developing diabetes later in life because their pancreases—where insulin is produced—have to work that much harder. Barker, whose research has linked low birth weight to heart disease, points out that undernourishment can trigger lifelong metabolic changes. In adulthood, for example, obesity may become a problem because food scarcity in prenatal life causes the body to shift the rate at which calories are turned into glucose for immediate use or stored as reservoirs of fat.

But just how does undernourishment reprogram metabolism? Does it perhaps prevent certain genes from turning on, or does it turn on those that should stay silent? Scientists are racing to answer those questions, along with a host of others. If they succeed, many more infants will find safe passage through the critical first months of prenatal development. Indeed, our expanding knowledge about the interplay between genes and the prenatal environment is cause for both concern and hope. Concern because maternal and prenatal health care often ranks last on the political agenda. Hope because by changing our priorities, we might be able to reduce the incidence of both birth defects and serious adult diseases.

***—With reporting by David Bjerklie and Alice Park/New York and Dan Cray/Los Angeles***

# WHO'S RAISING BABY?

## Challenges To Modern-Day Parenting

*Anne R. Pierce*

Drive through the empty streets of our neighborhoods and ask yourself not merely where the children have gone but where childhood has gone. It is most unlikely you will see such once-familiar scenes as these: a child sitting under a tree with a book, toddlers engaged in collecting leaves and sticks, friends riding bikes or playing tag, parents and their offspring working together in the yard, families (in no hurry to get anywhere) strolling casually along. Today's children are too busy with other things to enjoy the simple pleasures children used to take for granted. Preoccupied with endless "activities" and diversions, they have little time for simply going outside.

Where are the children and what are they doing? They are in day-care centers, now dubbed "learning centers." They are in "early childhood programs" and all-day kindergarten. They are acquiring new skills, attending extracurricular classes, and participating in organized sports. They are sitting in front of the computer, the TV, and the Play Station. They are not experiencing the comfortable ease of unconditional love, nor the pleasant feeling of familiarity. They are not enjoying a casual conversation, nor are they playing. They are working—at improving their talents, at competing with their peers, at "beating the enemy" in a video game, at just getting by, at adapting to the new baby-sitter or coach, at not missing Mom or Dad. They, like their computers, are "on." Being, for them, is doing, adjusting, coping. Parenting, for us, is providing them with things to do.

Young children expend their energy on long days in group situations, in preschool and after-school programs, in music and athletic lessons. For much-needed relaxation, they collapse in front of the TV or computer, the now-defining features of "homelife." Relaxation no longer signifies quiet or repose. The hyperactive pace of children's television shows and video games, always accompanied by driving music, exacerbates and surpasses the fast pace of modern life. Children stare at the screen, though the inanity, violence, and doomsday sociopolitical messages of the programming are anything but reassuring.

From doing to staring, from staring to doing. There is little room in this scenario for idle contentment, playful creativity, and the passionate pursuit of interests. Alternatives to this framework for living are provided neither in thought nor in deed by busy parents who, themselves, end their rushed days with television and escapism.

Before nursery school starts, most children who can afford it have attended "classes," from gymnastics to ballet, piano, or swimming. Infant "swim lessons," in which an instructor in diving gear repeatedly forces screaming babies underwater so that they are forced to swim, are now commonplace. Day-care centers claim to give toddlers a head start in academic advancement and socialization. Increasing numbers of bright young children spend time with tutors or at the learning center to attain that ever-elusive "edge."

Children in elementary school now "train" and lift weights in preparation for their sports. Football and track are new options for first-graders. A recent trend in elementary athletic programs is to recruit professional coaches, due to the supposed competitive disadvantage of amateur coaching done by parents. It is more common for young children to "double up," participating in two team sports at a time. A constantly increasing selection of stimulating activities lures modern families, making downtime more elusive.

What used to be "time for dinner" (together) is, more often than not, time for family members to rush and scatter in different directions. A typical first-grade soccer team practices two evenings a week, from 6:00 to 7:30. The stress involved in getting six-year-olds fed and in gear by practice time and, after practice, bathed and in bed at an appropriate hour is obvious. And yet, if you attend a first-grade soccer game, you'll likely find parents eager to discover the activities of other people's children and anxious to sign their children up for—whatever it might be. Some parents appear to be jealous of the activities others have discovered.

### THE NEW CONFORMISM—AFRAID OF MISSING OUT

In asking scores of parents about the purpose of all this activity, I have never received a clear or, to my mind, satisfactory answer. The end, apparently, is unclear apart from the idea, often expressed, that if one's child starts activities later than other children, he (or she) will be "left behind." Some of the more cohesive explanations I have received are these: A mother described herself as being "swept along by the inevitable"; she didn't want her young daughter to be "the only one missing out." A couple explained their determination to expose their toddler to a wide variety of opportunities so that he would know which sports he excelled in "by the time things get competitive." A father said, simply, that he saw his role in terms of making sure his children were "the best at something," and with all the other kids starting activities at such an early age, this meant that his kids "had to start even earlier."

In effect, this is the "do what everyone else does, only sooner and more intensely" theory of child rearing. This theory creates a constant downward pressure upon children of a younger and younger age. This was evident to me when my youngest son entered kindergarten and I discovered he was within a small minority of boys who had not *already* participated in team sports. Only five years earlier, my oldest son was within the sizable majority of kindergartners whose parents had decided kindergarten was a little too early for such endeavors. (First grade was then the preferred starting point.)

The more families subscribe to this "lifestyle," the more there is another reason for pushing kids off to the races: If no children are around to play with, then, especially for only children, organized activities become their only opportunity to "play" with other kids. Playing is thus thoroughly redefined.

The philosophy of child rearing as a race and of homelife as oppressive for women compels families toward incessant action. Love, nurture, and, concomitantly, innocence have been demoted as compared to experience and exposure. The family is viewed as a closedness to experience, the nurturing role within the family as the most confining of all. Indeed, busyness supplants togetherness in many modern families.

One legacy of Freud, Piaget, Pavlov, and the behaviorists, neodevelopmentalists, and social scientists who followed them has been the decreasing respect for the child's being and the increasing emphasis upon his "becoming." The child is seen as "socializable" and is studied as a clinical object whose observable response to this or that "environmental stimulus" becomes more important than his deeper, more complicated features. With the clinical interpretation of childhood, social engineering projects and "activities" that make the child's world more stimulating gain momentum.

In addition to the advantage that all this activity supposedly gives children, there is also the element of convenience. If parents are too busy to supervise their children, it behooves them to keep the kids so busy and under the auspices of so many (other) adults that they are likely to "stay out of trouble." Such is the basis of many modern choices. Children spend much of their time exhausted by activities, the purposes of which are ill construed.

*Conformism, convenience, and new interpretations of childhood are, then, contributing factors in the hectic existence and the premature introduction to academics that parents prescribe for their children.*

Conformism, convenience, and new interpretations of childhood are, then, contributing factors in the hectic existence and the premature introduction to academics that parents prescribe for their children. For example, before the 1960s, it was generally believed that placing young children in out-of-home learning programs was harmful. The concern for the harmfulness of such experiences was abandoned when these learning programs became convenient and popular.

## EDUCATION AS 'SOCIALIZATION'

In *Miseducation: Preschoolers at Risk*, David Elkind expressed dismay at the fact that age-inappropriate approaches to early education have gained such momentum despite the undeniable evidence that pushing children into formal academics and organized activities before they are ready does more harm than good. He lamented, "In a society that prides itself on its preference for facts over hearsay, on its openness to research, and on its respect for 'expert' opinion, parents, educators, administrators, and legislators are ignoring the facts, the research and the expert opinion about how young children learn and how best to teach them.... When we instruct children in academic subjects, or in swimming, gymnastics, or ballet, at too early an age, we miseducate them; we put them at risk for short-term stress and long-term personality damage for no useful purpose."

Elkind pointed to the consistent result of reputable studies (such as that conducted by Benjamin Bloom) that a love of learning, not the inculcation of skills, is the key to the kind of early childhood development that can lead to great things. These findings, warned Elkind, point to the fallacy of early instruction as a way of producing children who will attain eminence. He noted that with gifted and talented individuals, as with children in general, the most important thing is an excitement about learning: "Miseducation, by focusing on skills to the detriment of motivation, pays an enormous price for teaching infants and young children what amounts to a few tricks."

He further observed that those advocating early instruction in skills and early out-of-home education rely upon youngsters who are very disadvantaged to tout early education's advantages. "Accordingly, the image of the competent child introduced to remedy the understimulation of low-income children now serves as the rationale for the overstimulation of middle-class children."

Dr. Jack Westman of the Rockford Institute, renowned child psychiatrist Dr. Stanley Greenspan, and brain researcher Jane Healy are among the many unheeded others who warn of the implications of forcing the "childhood as a race" approach upon young children. Laments Westman, "The result is what is now referred to as the 'hothousing movement' for infants and toddlers devoted to expediting their development. This is occurring in spite of the evidence that the long-term outcomes of early didactic, authoritarian approaches with younger children relate negatively to intellectual development."

*In an interview for* Parent and Child *magazine, Dr. Greenspan insisted that young children suffer greatly if there is inadequate "emotional learning" in their daily lives.*

In an interview for *Parent and Child* magazine, Dr. Greenspan insisted that young children suffer greatly if there is inadequate "emotional learning" in their daily lives. Such learning, he explained, is both a requisite for their ability to relate well with others and the foundation of cognitive learning. "Emotional development and interactions form the foundation for all children's learning—especially in the first five years of life. During these years, children abstract from their emotional experiences constantly to learn even the most basic concepts. Take, for example, something like saying hello or learning when you can be aggressive and when you have to be nice—and all of these are cues by emotions."

In *Endangered Minds: Why Children Don't Think and What We Can Do About It*, Healy states the case for allowing young children to play with those who love them before requiring them to learn academic skills. She intones, "Driving the cold spikes of inappropriate pressure into the malleable heart of a child's learning may seriously distort the unfolding of both intellect and motivation. This self-serving intellectual assault, increasingly condemned by teachers who see its warped products, reflects a more general ignorance of the growing brain.... Explaining things to children won't do the job; they must have the chance to experience, wonder, experiment, and act it out for themselves. It is this process, throughout life, that enables the growth of intelligence."

Healy goes so far as to describe the damaging effect on the "functional organization of the plastic brain" in pushing too hard too soon: "Before brain regions are myelinated, they do not operate efficiently. For this reason, trying to 'make' children master academic skills for which they do not have the requisite maturation may result in mixed-up patterns of learning.... It is possible to force skills by intensive instruction, but this may cause a child to use immature, inappropriate neural networks and distort the natural growth process."

*Play is a way for children to relish childhood, prepare for adulthood, and discover their inner passions.*

Play is important for intellectual growth, the exploration of individuality, and the growth of a conscience. Play is a way for children to relish childhood, prepare for adulthood, and discover their inner passions. Legendary psychoanalyst D.W. Winnicott warned us not to underestimate the importance of play. In *The Work and Play of Winnicott*, Simon A. Grolnick elucidates Winnicott's concept of play.

> Play in childhood and throughout the life cycle helps to relieve the tension of living, helps to prepare for the serious, and sometimes for the deadly (e.g., war games), helps define and redefine the boundaries between ourselves and others, helps give us a fuller sense of our own personal and bodily being. Playing provides a trying-out ground for proceeding onward, and it enhances drive satisfaction.... Winnicott repeatedly stressed that when playing becomes too drive-infested and excited, it loses its creative growth-building capability and begins to move toward loss of control or a fetishistic rigidity.... Civilization's demands for controlled, socialized behavior gradually, and sometimes insidiously, supersedes the psychosomatic and aesthetic pleasures of open system play.

When we discard playtime, we jeopardize the child's fresh, creative approach to the world. The minuscule amount of peace that children are permitted means that thinking and introspection are demoted as well. Thought requires being, not always doing. Children who are not allowed to retreat once in a while into themselves are not allowed to find out what is there. Our busy lives become ways of hiding from the recesses of the mind. Teaching children to be tough and prepared for the world, making them into achieving doers instead of capable thinkers, has its consequences. Children's innate curiosity is intense. When that natural curiosity has no room to fulfill itself, it burns out like a smothered flame.

In an age when "socialization" into society's ideals and mores is accepted even for babies and toddlers, we should remember that institutionalized schooling even for older children is a relatively new phenomenon. Mass education was a post-Industrial Revolution invention, one that served the dual purposes of preparing children for work and freeing parents to contribute fully to the industrial structure. No longer was work something that families did together, as a unit.

The separation of children from the family's work paved the way for schools and social reformers to assume the task of preparing children for life. This is a lofty role. As parents, we need to inform ourselves as to what our children are being prepared *for* and *how* they are being prepared.

Although our children's days are filled with instruction, allowing them little time of their own, we seem frequently inattentive as to just what they are learning. As William Bennett, Allan Bloom, and others have pointed out, recent years have been characterized by the reformulation of our schools, universities, and information sources according to a relativist, left-leaning ideology saturated with cynicism. This ideology leaves students with little moral-intellectual ground to stand on, as they are taught disrespect not only for past ideas and literary works but for the American political system and Judeo-Christian ethics. Such works as *The Five Little Peppers and How They Grew* and *Little Women* are windows into the soul of a much less cynical (and much less hectic) time.

Teaching children about the great thinkers, writers, and statesmen of the past is neglected as the very idea of greatness and heroism is disputed. Thus, the respect for greatness that might have caused children to glance upward from their TV show or activity and the stories about their country's early history that might have given them respect for a time when computer games didn't exist are not a factor in their lives. The word *preoccupied* acquires new significance, for children's minds are stuffed with the here and now.

## THE DEVALUATION OF HOMELIFE

The busyness of modern child rearing and the myopia of the modern outlook reinforce each other. The very ideas that education is a race and that preschool-age children's participation in beneficial experience is more important than playing or being with the family are modern ones that continually reinforce themselves for lack of alternatives. Our busy lives leave insufficient time to question whether all this busyness is necessary and whether the content of our childrens' education is good.

The possibility that children might regard their activities less than fondly when they are older because these activities were forced upon them is not addressed. The possibility that they may never find their own passionate interests is not considered. (I came across an interesting television show that discussed the problem middle-school coaches are having with burned-out and unenthusiastic participants in a wide range of sports. The coaches attributed this to the fact that children had already been doing these sports for years and were tired of the pressure.)

One needs time to be a thinker, freedom to be creative, and some level of choice to be enthusiastic. Families can bestow upon children opportunities for autonomy while at the same time giving them a stable base to fall back upon and moral and behavioral guidelines. Having a competitive edge is neither as important nor as lasting as the ability to lead a genuine, intelligently thought-out, and considerate life.

*Some of the best learning experiences happen not in an institution, not with a teacher, but in a child's independent "research" of the world at hand.*

Some of the best learning experiences happen not in an institution, not with a teacher, but in a child's independent "research" of the world at hand. As the child interprets the world around her, creates new things with the materials available to her, and extracts new ideas from the recesses of her mind, she is learning to be an active, contributing participant in the world. She occupies her physical, temporal, and intellectual space in a positive, resourceful way. Conversely, if she is constantly stuffed with edifying "opportunities," resentment and lack of autonomy are the likely results.

In *The Erosion of Childhood*, Valerie Polakow insists upon the child's ability to "make history" as opposed to simply receiving it. Lamenting the overinstitutionalization of children in day care and school, she warns, "Children as young as a year old now enter childhood institutions to be formally schooled in the ways of the social system and emerge eighteen years later to enter the world of adulthood having been deprived of their own history-making power, their ability to act upon the world in significant and meaningful ways." She adds, "The world in which children live—the institutional world that babies, toddlers and the very young have increasingly come to inhabit and confront—is a world in which they become the objects, not the subjects of history, a world in which history is being made of them."

Day care provides both too much stimulation of the chaotic, disorganized kind, which comes inevitably from the cohabitation of large numbers of babies and toddlers, and too much of the organized kind that comes, of necessity, from group-centered living. It provides too little calm, quiet, space, or comfort and too little opportunity to converse and relate to a loving other.

Imagine, for example, a parent sitting down with her child for a "tea party." As she pours real tea into her own cup and milk into her child's, the "how to do things" is taken seriously. The child is encouraged to say "thank you" and to offer cookies to his mother, and their chat begins. Although they are pretending to be two adults, the ritual is real; it occurs in a real home setting; it provides the child with real food and a real opportunity for "mature" conversation. The mother says, "I'm so glad to be here for tea. How have you been?" The child, enjoying the chance to play the part of his mother's host, answers, "Fine! Would you like another cookie?" "Oh yes, thank you," answers his mother. "These cookies are delicious!" The child is learning about civilized behavior.

*Children living in the new millennium need a refuge from the impersonal, the mechanical, and the programmed. We must provide them with more than opportunities for skill learning, socialization, and competition.*

Then, picture the toy tea set at the learning center. Two children decide "to have tea." They fight over who has asked whom over. When one child asks, "How have you been?" the other loses interest and walks away. Too much of this peer-centered learning and not enough of adult-based learning clearly has negative implications for social development. The child simply cannot learn right from wrong, proper from improper, from other children who themselves have trouble making these distinctions.

Homelife that provides a break from group action has innumerable advantages for older children as well. Think of the different learning experiences a child receives from sitting down at the dinner table with his family and from gulping down a hamburger on the way to a nighttime game. In one case, the child has the opportunity to learn about manners and conversation. In the other, he is given another opportunity to compete with peers. (This is not to deny the benefits of being part of a team but simply to state that homelife itself is beneficial.) I hear many parents of high-school students complain about the competitive, selfish manner of today's students. And, yet, most of these students have not a moment in their day that is not competitive.

How can we expect children to value kindness and cooperation when their free time has been totally usurped by activities wherein winning is everything? At home, winning is not everything (unless the child expends all his time trying to "beat the enemy" in a video game). At home, a child is much more likely to be reprimanded for not compromising with his siblings than for not "defeating" them. If homelife provides children with time to define their individuality and interact with family members (and all the give-and-take implied), then it is certainly an invaluable aspect of a child's advancement.

Children living in the new millennium need a refuge from the impersonal, the mechanical, and the programmed. We must provide them with more than opportunities for skill learning, socialization, and competition. Otherwise, something will be missing in their humanness. For to be human is to have the capacity for intimate attachments based upon love (which can grow more intimate because of the closeness that family life provides); it is to reason and to have a moral sense of things; it is to be capable of a spontaneity that stems from original thought or from some passion within.

We must set our children free from our frenetic, goal-oriented pace. We must create for them a private realm wherein no child-rearing "professional" can tread. Within this secure space, the possibilities are endless. With this stable base to fall back upon, children will dare to dream, think, and explore. They will compete, learn, and socialize as the blossoming individuals that they are, not as automatons engineered for results.

---

*Anne R. Pierce is an author and political philosopher who lives in Cincinnati with her husband and three children. As a writer, she finds that bringing up children in the modern world gives her much food for thought.*

# UNIT 3

# Finding a Balance: Maintaining Relationships

## Unit Selections



## Key Points to Consider

- Is marriage necessary for a happy, fulfilling life? Why is or is not that so? When you think of a marriage, what do you picture? What are your expectations of your (future) spouse? What are your expectations of yourself? What and how much are you willing to give to your marriage?
- What are your views on spanking? Why is it seen as an ineffective parenting tool? What are other alternatives? What do you think of them? Why?
- How important are your siblings in your life? What are the particular challenges faced by aging siblings who would like to repair a damaged sibling relationship after years of conflict?
- What is the role of grandparents in family life? How do they influence the well-being of their grandchildren?

**Links: www.dushkin.com/online/**
These sites are annotated in the World Wide Web pages.

**Child Welfare League of America**
*http://www.cwla.org*

**Coalition for Marriage, Family, and Couples Education**
*http://www.smartmarriages.com*

**The National Academy for Child Development**
*http://www.nacd.org*

**National Council on Family Relations**
*http://www.ncfr.com*

**Positive Parenting**
*http://www.positiveparenting.com*

**SocioSite**
*http://www.pscw.uva.nl/sociosite/TOPICS/Women.html*

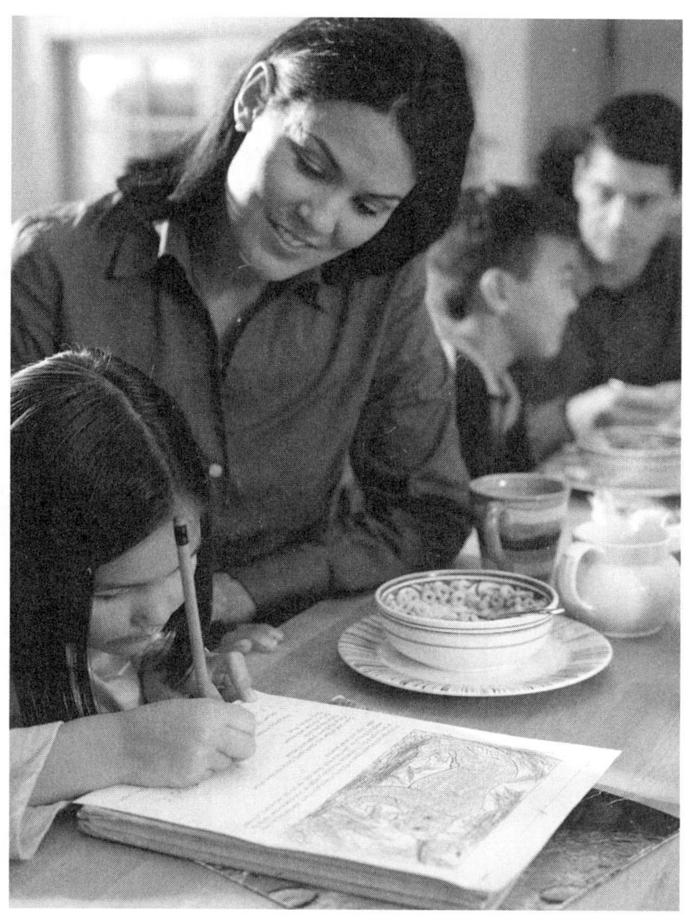

And they lived happily ever after . . . The romantic image conjured up by this well-known final line from fairy tales is not reflective of the reality of family life and relationship maintenance. The belief that somehow love alone should carry us through is pervasive. In reality, maintaining a relationship takes dedication, hard work, and commitment.

We come into relationships, regardless of their nature, with fantasies about how things ought to be. Partners, spouses, parents, children, siblings, and others—all family members have at least some unrealistic expectations about each other. It is through the negotiation of their lives together that they come to work through these expectations and replace them with other, it is hoped, more realistic ones. By recognizing and acting on their own contribution to the family, members can set and attain realistic family goals. Tolerance and acceptance of differences can facilitate this process as can competent communication skills. Along the way, family members need to learn new skills and develop new habits of relating to each other. This will not be easy, and, try as they may, not everything will be controllable. Factors both inside and outside the family may impede their progress.

Even before one enters a marriage or other committed relationships, our attitudes, standards, and beliefs influence our choices. Increasingly, choices include whether or not we should commit to such a relationship. From the start of a committed relationship, the expectations both partners have of their relationship have an impact, and the need to negotiate differences is a constant factor. Adding a child to the family affects the lives of parents in ways that they could previously only imagine. Feeling under siege, many parents struggle to know the right way to rear their children. These factors can all combine to make child rearing more difficult than it might otherwise have been. Other family relationships also evolve, and in our nuclear family-focused culture, it is possible to forget that family relationships extend beyond those between spouses, parents, and children.

The initial subsection presents a number of aspects regarding marital and other committed relationships, decisions about even entering such a relationship, and ways of balancing multiple and often competing roles played by today's couples who hope to fulfill individual as well as couple needs. It is a difficult balancing act to cope with the expectations and pressures of work, home, children, and relational intimacy. "No Wedding? No Ring? No Problem" depicts current trends in the United States toward more and more couples choosing cohabitation as an alternative to marriage. As various cultural groups come to the United States, unwilling to give up the cultural activities and beliefs of their home country, changes have begun to take place in what is expected when we marry. "Marriage at First Sight," the story of arranged marriages in the U.S. Indian community, may be a sample of what to expect. "The War Over Gay Marriage" touches at the heart of what it means to be a socially recognized and valued committed couple.

The next subsection examines the parent/child relationship. In the first article, "New Evidence for the Benefits of Never Spanking," Murray Straus, presents a detailed argument against parents using corporal punishment as a means of child discipline. The next reading, "Father Nature: The Making of a Modern Dad" details ways in which men are changed, at a fundamental, hormonal level by an active involvement in their children's lives. "What About Black Fathers?" proposes that the involvement of low income African American fathers in their children's lives is best facilitated through support for existing family forms. "Adoption by Lesbian Couples" is a detailed analysis of existing literature on children raised in lesbian households and shows that children raised in lesbian households are not significantly different from those raised in heterosexual households. "Are Married Parents Really Better for Children?" is an overview of the research on the parent/child relationship and confronts the assumption that there is a single "best" way to raise children. The final article in this section, "The Perma Parent Trap," depicts a growing trend in the U.S.—that of adult children moving back in with their parents, with the full approval of the parents.

The third and final subsection looks at other family relationships. "Oldest, Youngest, or in Between" documents that the commonly held belief that birth order affects personality, and presents ways in which these effects can be countered. Siblings relationships and the baggage associated with them, are often assumed to improve with age. "Why We Break Up With Our Siblings" questions this assumption. Then, in "The Grandparent as Parent," the role of grandparents as parents to their grandchildren is explored. Many of these grandparents anticipated they would perform a different role in their grandchild's life, and are now becoming principal caregivers and disciplinarians to their grandchildren.

# No wedding? No ring? No problem

## *More and more Americans opt for cohabitation*

BY JAY TOLSON

Before 1970, it was called "living in sin" or "shacking up," and it was illegal in every state of the union. Why then, many social scientists are beginning to ask, has America's 30-year rise in unmarried cohabitation remained a shadow issue in the family-values debate? "Unlike divorce or unwed childbearing, the trend toward cohabitation has inspired virtually no public comment or criticism," note David Popenoe and Barbara Dafoe Whitehead, co-directors of Rutgers University's National Marriage Project. University of Michigan sociologist Pamela J. Smock, whose survey of recent research will appear in the *Annual Review of Sociology* to be published this summer, finds that most Americans are still unaware of the extent or significance of cohabitation, even though more than half of today's newlyweds live together before tying the knot, compared with about 10 percent in 1965.

Scholars are quick to point out that the United States is still a long way from Sweden, where unmarried couples—who have all the rights, benefits, and obligations of married partners—make up about 30 percent of couples sharing households. In America, by contrast, cohabiting couples make up only about 7 percent of the total. And for most of those 4 million couples, living together is a transitory business: 55 percent marry and 40 percent end the relationship within five years. "In this country," says University of Chicago sociologist Linda J. Waite, coauthor of the forthcoming *Case for Marriage*, "it's still mostly up or out."

What Smock has found is that the proportion for whom it's "out" of the union is on the rise. In addition, more and more unmarried women who become pregnant choose to cohabit rather than marry, which means that living together is increasingly a substitute for marriage, particularly, notes Smock, among African-Americans.

One of the biggest revelations of the new research is how many cohabiting arrangements involve children. "About one half of previously married cohabitors and 35 percent of never-married cohabitors have children in the household," Smock reports. She adds that almost 40 percent of all supposedly single-parent families are really two-parent cohabiting families. Unfortunately, that doesn't mean that kids in these households fare as well as kids with two married parents. "The nonparent partner... has no explicit legal, financial, supervisory, or custodial rights or responsiblities regarding the child of his partner," notes Linda Waite in the winter issue of *The Responsive Community*. Studies cited by Popenoe and Whitehead suggest there is also a greater risk of physical or sexual abuse in those situations.

Few romantic notions about cohabitational bliss withstand close scrutiny. While there is a little more sex between unmarried cohabitors than between married couples (one more act per month), there's also more cheating by both partners. Then, too, there's more domestic violence and a higher incidence of depression.

But since living together is still mainly a stage in courtship for the majority of marriagebound Americans, the critical question is how the experience affects the subsequent union. Here the evidence is slightly mixed. According to most research, couples who live together—with the possible exception of those who move in already planning to wed—tend to have rockier marriages and a greater risk of divorce. Why this is so is hard to say. It could be that people who cohabit are less traditional in their ideas and less reluctant to divorce. But it's also possible that the experience itself has an effect. "We need to do more qualitative research," says Smock, "and talk to people in their 20s... to find out why they are doing what they are doing."

**Old rules.** Some of the scholars who are studying the phenomenon—including Popenoe and Whitehead—are also taking sides, urging young adults to reject the argument that cohabitation is good preparation for marriage. Other researchers are taking aim at the economic disincentives to marriage, including the marriage penalty in the tax code and restrictions on Medicaid, both of which often discourage less affluent cohabitors from tying the knot. There is even a movement to bring back an older form of courtship. Leon and Amy Kass co-teach a course at the University of Chicago described by the former as "a higher kind of sex education." Using their own recently published anthology, *Wing to Wing, Oar to Oar: Readings on Courting and Marrying*, they attempt " to train the hearts and minds by means of noble examples for romance leading to loving marriage."

Can such a quaint notion win over minds hardened by the "divorce revolution" of their parents' generation? Steven L. Nock, a University of Virginia researcher, is guardedly optimistic that durable marriages will make a comeback (and in fact, since 1990, have been doing so), whether or not old courtship styles are restored. "My generation," says the 49-year-old sociologist, "was the first to confront equality of the sexes. As a result, many reacted to the changed rules by fleeing from marriage. I suspect that our children, who've grown up with gender equality as a given, will be less likely to flee marriage." That might not be the "horse and carriage" argument, but it makes some sense.

# Marriage
## AT FIRST SIGHT

They date, go to U2 concerts, hit bars with pals. But for the sake of tradition and family, even some highly Americanized Indian immigrants agree to wed strangers

*By* PAULA SPAN

ON THE EVENING BEFORE HER ENGAGEMENT, Vibha Jasani found herself on the rooftop terrace of her uncle's house in India, feeling a breeze begin as the sun lowered, gazing out at the city of Rajkot and the mountains beyond, trying to be calm, and failing. She was about to cry, and not with joy.

When her father asked what was wrong, she just shrugged; she could hardly manage a reply. But he knew anyway.

Marrying a pleasant young man she'd just met was not the romance Vibha envisioned when she was a teenager playing volleyball at Annandale High; it was not the kind of courtship she yakked about with her friends at Virginia Tech or her coworkers in Arlington. This felt like—and was—a custom held over from a previous century. But because she was 25 and not-getting-any-younger, her parents had prevailed on her to do something she'd repeatedly vowed she wouldn't: fly to India to find a husband.

She'd spent the past three weeks meeting men—at least one each day—carefully prescreened by her uncle for their suitability. She'd poured them tea and passed platters of sweets and nuts, enduring awkward half-hour conversations that seemed more like interviews. She chose the one she could talk most comfortably with; they went out together three or four times; she met his family. All parties approved, and suddenly 300 people were about to stream into a rented hall the next day to celebrate their engagement, which everyone seemed delighted about, except the prospective bride.

"Everything's so out of control," Vibha worried. "Things just sort of happened." She'd gone along with the flurry of events, sometimes resentfully and sometimes obligingly, but she wasn't sure she could bring herself to take the next step. Her almost-fiancé, Haresh, appeared to be a nice guy—mature, considerate. But was he the man she wanted to spend the next 50 years with? How could she possibly know after such a brief time? What if, once she returned home to Northern Virginia, she was miserable with someone who'd grown up in such a different culture? Or he was? Divorce was not an acceptable option among Indians, in their home country or their new one.

"It's a shot in the dark," she thought, fearful of making a mistake. Maybe she should put a stop to it. Her eyes started to brim.

Her father, not a demonstrative man by nature, gave her a hug. "We only want you to do this if you're 100 percent sure," he told her in their native Gujarati. "If you're not, you don't have to… We just want you to be happy."

She looked at him—his eyes were reddening, too—and felt her opposition ebb away. "Screw it," she decided. "Okay. I can do it."

So the engagement proceeded last March, Vibha wearing a beautiful turquoise ensemble called a lengha and a blank expression. Guests were laughing and celebrating afterward, and she was thinking, with mingled panic and resignation, "Omigod, I'm engaged. I'm *done*." She packed up that night, flew home the following day and began planning a late-November wedding to a man she barely knew.

Now, with the big event just weeks away, Vibha (pronounced VEE-bah) flits around the Beltway, booking a deejay, making last-minute menu decisions, choosing the elaborate henna designs that will be applied to her hands and feet for the ceremony.

Yet even as she checks off the chores in a notebook she's labeled "wedding journal," uncertainty continues to eat at her. Should she really go through with this? Is she doing the right thing?

### ARRANGED HAPPINESS

Vinay Sandhir used to voice a lot of the same doubts about getting married the traditional way. He'd find his own spouse, he insisted. He didn't want a lot of familial meddling. He wanted to fall in love; in fact, "I wanted to be blown off my feet." But he was still single at 33, so one evening, his parents sat him down at their dining room table and had that same you're-not-getting-any-younger talk. So here he is in his home office in Annandale—he's an MBA and a management consultant in health care—printing out the latest batch of e-mailed responses to a matrimonial ad his parents placed in the weekly newspaper India Abroad. It read:

> *Punjabi parents desire beautiful, professional, never married, US raised girl for handsome son, 34, 5'10"/150, fair, slim, athletic, engineer/MBA, consultant in DC area. Enjoys travel, sports, music. Please reply...*

Some of these criteria come from his parents. Vinay (pronounced Vin-NEIGH) thinks it's pointless to talk about appearances—though he himself actually *is* good-looking, rangy and dark-eyed, with an easy grin—since "everyone thinks their kids are beautiful." Nor does he particularly care which Indian state someone's forebears come from. But on this issue, he's yielded to the elder Sandhirs, who will be visiting this evening and will review the new candidates. They think someone from their home region would prove more "compatible."

Education is something they all agree on. The Sandhir family tree is heavy with doctors, including Vinay's father and two elder brothers and their wives. Vinay's intended need not be a physician, but he wants her to be ambitious and successful, "talented at what she does."

The "US raised" stipulation, on the other hand, comes from Vinay, who was 4 when his family settled in Western Maryland. He plays basketball a couple of times a week, lives to scale mountains (that's Mount Rainier—he's climbed it three times—on his screen saver) and ski and raft, caught five U2 concerts during last year's tour. He can't see himself with a woman raised in India, regardless of her graduate degrees. He wants a partner as Americanized as he is, "someone who's shared my experiences, someone I can laugh about things with, someone I don't have to explain everything to."

If such a prospect should surface in this batch, his parents will e-mail her parents, attaching his photo and "biodata," a document providing particulars and describing him as "intelligent, independent, dynamic... also deeply family-oriented and compassionate." If he passes muster, her parents will provide a phone number or e-mail address. Meanwhile, each family will conduct discreet background checks, making inquiries through friends and acquaintances to ensure the other is cultured, respectable, acceptable.

This week's possibilities, Vinay notices, include a health analyst in Toronto; an MBA from NYU; a Maryland social worker. "She'll probably get nixed just because she's older than me," he predicts. Oops, here's a woman he went out with a few times last year, until she stopped answering his e-mails. Chuck that one.

Which leaves 18 new responses to add to the 30 or so they've already received. "I didn't see anything totally, totally great," Vinay says. But he's loosened his requirements, having learned over the past months that this whole arranged marriage thing is more complicated than he'd foreseen.

## The Lure of a Love Marriage

Love and marriage, in that order. The ethos so dominates mainstream Western culture, from Billboard charts to Hallmark racks, that other matrimonial approaches barely register. But in much of the Muslim world, in many Asian societies, among Hasidic Jews, and certainly in India—which has sent roughly three-quarters of a million immigrants to the United States since 1980—it's still common for people to pair up the other way around: marriage first, set up by one's elders and wisers, and then, with time, love. It's the historic norm, anthropologists say, not only the way kings and queens cemented strategic alliances, but the way ordinary folks—colonial Americans included—got hitched until comparatively recently.

It's how Vinay's parents married in 1959. Though his mother had never seen his father (he'd glimpsed her), she agreed to the engagement because she trusted her eldest sister, who'd set up the match. Vibha's parents had actually met—she silently served him tea—but hadn't exchanged a word. The album they keep to remember their 1975 wedding looks wonderfully romantic, with black-and-white photos of the groom arriving on horseback and the bride garlanded with marigolds, but they were strangers.

The process is so different now that young Indian Americans, who tend to shudder at the term "arranged marriage," cast about for more palatable phrases. "Semi-arranged marriage," for instance, or "arranged introduction." The updated version is no longer coercive (both the bride and groom have veto power), and traditional dowry transactions have largely been replaced, at least among the urban elite, by mutual exchanges of jewelry and clothing.

Some see these matches as a last resort, but since a single person who's reached the mid-twenties (for a woman) or late twenties (for a man) is probably causing an Indian family some anxiety, the need for a last resort can crop up fairly early in life. So if people haven't met spouses through school or work, or at networking events intended to bring marriageable Indians together, or via Web sites like *Indianmatchmaker.com*, or through newer permutations like the speed-dating sessions staged by a District firm called Mera Pyar ("My Love"), their parents may take up the traditional role.

They run ads, canvass Web sites, put the word out on the community grapevine: Dad's aunt knows a nice Bengali family in Atlanta whose nephew is an electrical engineer. Mom's medical school classmate in Detroit has a cousin with a single daughter working with computers in Bangalore.

After their parents perform due diligence—Hindu marriages are considered a union of two families, not merely two individuals, so bloodlines and reputations matter—the children meet and spend time together and decide whether their relationship has a future. A voluntary process, no different from having your friends fix you up, the fixed-up like to say.

But it *is* different. Families—many of whom disapprove of or forbid dating—don't want to introduce their kids to someone to hang out with or move in with; they want a wedding, and soon. Vinay's relatives think that after he's spent three or four evenings with a woman, he ought to know: She's his future bride or she's history. ("Not how it's going to work," he tells them.) And while both generations talk about having choices, most parents hope kids will choose to marry people of the same religious and ethnic background, the proper socioeconomic and educational level, acceptable lineage. Those are the factors that determine compatibility, not whether both parties treasure walking in the rain.

"It's a little like a debutante ball—'You can select freely, from among this preselected group of people,'" says anthropologist Johanna Lessinger, author of *From the Ganges to the Hudson*.

The so-called Second Generation of Indian immigrants (born here) and the 1.5 Generation (born there, raised here) are growing increasingly restive at these restrictions. They go off to college, where many date and have sex while their parents maintain a don't ask/don't tell policy. After that, though there are no reliable statistics, a growing number appear to opt for the do-it-yourself model known as a "love marriage." It's what Vibha and Vinay expected for themselves.

A preliminary analysis of Indian intermarriage rates in the United States by sociologist Maitrayee Bhattacharyya, a Princeton doctoral candidate, documents this trend. The 1990 Census showed that more than 13 percent of Indian men in this country, and 6 percent of women, were married to non-Indians—clearly love marriages, since Indian families might accept but wouldn't actively arrange such matches. But the rates for those born in the United States were dramatically higher, and among U.S.-born Indians under 35, about half had "married out." Those numbers may decline in the 2000 Census (that data is not yet available) because continuing immigration has broadened the pool, making it easier to meet an Indian spouse. Even so, for many immigrant families the love marriage remains a worrisome phenomenon.

So for all the change, the consensus is that most Indian American parents continue to exert significant influence over their children's courtships, and arranged marriages are common in Fairfax County as well as in Gujarat, the northwest Indian state Vibha's family started emigrating from more than 30 years ago.

Elders are better at this, the theory goes. "At least you know a bit about the boy, who he is and what he does, rather than just being emotional, being attracted to physical appearances, 'Oh, he's so cute,'" explains Vibha's aunt Induben Jasani. "Does he come from a good family? Does he have good morals and values? Character is something we can see a little better than youngsters do."

Besides, arranged marriages help keep traditions alive, stem the tendency toward out-marriage. "There's a sense of ethnic identity tied up in it," Lessinger says. "This is a way of holding on to their Indian-ness."

But a bubbly culture-straddler like Vibha—who's lived here since she was 5 and grew up watching "Xena: Warrior Princess," who speaks Gujarati at home but elsewhere uses 80-mph unaccented English punctuated with *like* and *y'know* and *kinda deal*, who loves Bollywood movies but relaxes from pre-wedding stress by seeing the Eminem flick "8 Mile"—isn't always sure how much Indian-ness to keep and how much American-ness to embrace. She calls herself "pretty much a mix," and in trying to negotiate the milestone of marriage, she sometimes finds herself pretty much mixed up.

## Giving It a Shot

"Very hard work, a wedding," says Vibha's father, Ramesh Patel, on a Saturday afternoon with the event bearing down on them. On the living room rug, relatives are helping with the task of the day: dozens of small silver cows, favors for wedding guests, must be enfolded in red or gold foil, then inserted into matching silk bags. Vibha, padding around in bare feet and rumpled clothes, hair in a ponytail, is steeling herself for an afternoon of errands. "Work-run-work-run"—that's her life these days.

This Colonial-style home is what families have in mind when they call themselves, in matrimonial ads, "well settled in U.S.," with a deck overlooking the yard and a Mercedes in the driveway. It looks like any of the other houses along the winding street, except for the rack near the front door where people place their shoes when they enter, and the carved wooden shrine in the dining room where her mother, Shanta, prays daily to Hindu deities. The Patels (Vibha's parents have taken the name of their caste as a surname; Vibha uses the family name Jasani) bought this place in North Springfield 15 years ago, when Ramesh was working 90 hours a week in two different restaurants, saving obsessively to buy a Dunkin' Donuts franchise. He now owns three, in Maryland, while Shanta works at the Postal Service facility at Dulles.

Vibha, who moved home after graduating from Virginia Tech in psychology and management, is in human resources at NCS Pearson, a half-hour drive away in Arlington. She's the eldest of the Patels' three daughters, and by the time she'd been out of school for two years, well, "you have no idea how much the pressure is on for an Indian woman."

"We were worrying," her mother concurs, keeping one eye on the cow-wrapping. "Time was passing." They would have accepted a son-in-law Vibha found on her own, she says. "She had freedom. We didn't tell her no." But "she didn't like anybody. She couldn't find anybody."

To Vibha, this constitutes considerable revisionism. Her own account—mostly related in a series of cell-phone conversations as she drives home from work in her slightly scuffed Honda—reflects the tensions between Indian customs and American expectations.

She had a couple of fairly serious relationships with men in high school and college, for instance, but never dared to tell her parents about them. "It's a no-no; you don't date," she explains one night, steering past the multicultural neon strip malls of Columbia Pike and then along Braddock Road—practically the only time in the day she's alone and free to talk. Anyway, those guys were a "didn't-work-out kinda deal." After graduation, she and her friends went to bars and clubs in the District, drinking and dancing, playing pool with friends, flirting. A smiley extrovert with vast dark eyes, she had no trouble meeting men. It was fun, but "the person you want to marry, you're probably not going to meet in a club," she decided.

Which was starting to matter. Apart from the pointed questions about marriage from family and friends (the Jasani/Patel clan in Northern Virginia, expanding as more relatives immigrate, now numbers about 80), Vibha herself felt increasingly ready to settle down, as virtually all her South Asian friends already had. "I was tired of all these casual relationships," she says. "I wanted something serious."

Her family's first matchmaking effort, an ad in India Abroad, led to a few desultory dates with men who met their ethnic, religious, linguistic, dietetic (the family is vegetarian) and socioeconomic standards. "Didn't click," Vibha found. So her parents returned to a favorite theme. "They'd bring it up, then drop it, then bring it up a month later: 'What do you think of going to India to look for a guy?'"

She resisted for months; she'd spent time in India and feared a "culture gap" with Indian men. "I'm being stereotypical when I say this, but I thought they'd want a wife at home, cooking and cleaning and taking care of them." Vibha had seen her mother play this role daily. "I'm traditional, but I'm not *that* traditional. I wanted someone who'd be fifty-fifty with everything, someone to share the responsibilities." She didn't think she'd find him in Gujarat.

But the Patels didn't drop the idea, and Indian daughters hesitate to defy their parents. Many times her mother had prepared vegetarian meals for Vibha while she was away at college, and her father had driven nearly five hours to Blacksburg to deliver them, then turned around and headed home—how could she now dismiss their wishes? Her father's eldest brother, dying in a nearby hospice with the whole family gathered around, yearned to see her engaged—shouldn't she give him this final pleasure?

"I was just like, okay, I'll give it a shot." She'd get her parents off her case, she told girlfriends from work, assuring them that she expected to return unattached. She and her mother left on their mission a year ago Valentine's Day, with a return flight booked in three weeks.

## Thirty Men in Three Weeks

At her uncle's stucco house in Rajkot, Vibha donned a salwar kameez, a tunic over pants with a long scarf. Her uncle had culled 30 suitors from the hundred who'd responded to local newspaper ads, and day after day, as each came to call, the encounters unfolded the same way. First, her mother and uncle chatted briefly with the potential bridegroom as Vibha served refreshments ("I hate that!"). Then the young people could retreat to another room for a brief stab at getting to know each other.

The first man to call was a physician, "fairly intelligent, attractive kinda guy," accompanied by his parents. Their dialogue consisted of a series of standard questions: Hi, how are you? When did you arrive? How was your trip? Tell me about your family: Do you have brothers and sisters? What are your interests? She ran through the responses—fine, thanks; yesterday; uneventful; two sisters; movies and music and computers—that would soon come to feel routine. Meanwhile, she was muttering to herself, "I don't want to do this. Why do I have to do this?" This guy, she concluded, "wasn't that interested, and I wasn't that interested." Next.

There were engineers and pharmacists and dentists. Some, she could tell in the first two minutes, were ruling her out because her complexion was coppery (there's a cultural preference for light skin) or because she was "normal-sized," not super-slim. That was fine, because anyone who couldn't see beyond looks, who didn't notice that she had a brain and a personality, "I'm like, forget you."

Some seemed a bit intimidated; she wasn't deferential, she was fluent in both Gujarati and English. A few seemed more attracted to her U.S. citizenship, marriage being a legal and comparatively quick route to a green card, than to her. After each session, her family wanted to know how she liked the latest candidate, whether she wanted to get engaged, "like I was going to decide on the spot."

Take the "doctor guy," for whom her family had high hopes. He prattled on about how prestigious his university was and how well he was doing there; he had the self-awareness of a coconut. Her family was disappointed by Vibha's blase response. A doctor! From one of the best schools! "But I didn't believe anything my parents said. They just wanted me to get married." Next.

Though the encounters got easier as the days passed, and she tried to keep an open mind as her uncle had advised, she couldn't really embrace the process. "I'm like, 'No.' 'No.' 'No.'"

The exception was Haresh Umaretiya, slotted in at the last minute when someone canceled. He came by before Vibha had time to dress up or tense up—a tallish engineer her own age, friendly eyes, high cheekbones, "the first one I had a decent conversation with." He was interested in what she had to say. When she asked what he enjoyed doing, "He said, 'I like observing people.' I'm in psychology; we had things in common… He was honest, which was nice… I thought, 'Okay, this could work.'"

He also enjoyed their meeting, it turned out. He thought Vibha was beautiful, but more important, "if you meet local Indian girls, they are shy, they can't reply," he'd found. "She is educated. And she is forward, she can talk." Though frankly, when he called a few days later to see if she'd like to go out, it was her fever to flee the house and the marriage marathon, as much as a desire to see him again, that prompted her to agree.

They went to a local park, bought ice cream cones, sat on the grass and talked. "Totally general, nothing serious. I loved that," Vibha says. "It was like meeting a friend. I felt at ease with him. I had a nice time." A few days later they went to a movie and had dinner together. Three meetings—two more than most local women would've had, an allowance made for Vibha's Western ways—and then it was time to meet his family. "Omigod, a good 20 people came, his father, his brother, his brother's wife, his mom, his aunt, his other aunt… They're all staring at me. Normally, you're supposed to bow your head, not look people in the eye; I'm just sitting there smiling. They're shocked, but they think, 'Well, she's American, she doesn't know.'" They approved anyway.

In Western conceptions of romance, lovers supposedly get carried away by passion. In Indian culture, the wedding process itself sweeps people along, a dizzying round of planning and shopping and crowds and gifts and excitement. Yet even as she agreed to proceed and preparations were underway, Vibha agonized.

From her earlier relationships, she'd learned to be a bit wary of American casualness, people's willingness to dump a girlfriend or boyfriend and then start dating someone new two weeks later. But she had also discovered what it was to fall in love. "This wasn't the same feeling, and I knew the difference so well. I was like, 'Do I really want to be with someone I don't know, and don't know if I'll ever love? Whoa.'"

She swallowed her doubts after her father flew over for the engagement, and they had that teary last-minute talk on the rooftop. After the engagement party, though, when she and Haresh were finally alone in a room, he wanted to kiss her. "And I'm just like, no."

## The Sandhir Scale

Vinay Sandhir managed to stave off such dilemmas for years. He had a grand time in a coed dorm at West Virginia University and still skis, hikes and tailgates with his friends from the honors program there. Afterward, he had an "American" girlfriend for six years, a fact he never shared with his parents and they seemed not to notice, even though she was virtually living with him, retreating to her own apartment when they came to visit.

His family is "really conservative" and wouldn't have accepted it, Vinay believes, "unless I was sure I wanted to marry her and fight for her." But he wasn't sure.

When that relationship ended, he dated a business school classmate and a military administrator. Then came the dining room table confrontation. Like most traditional Indians, his parents don't consider their parental duty done until all their children have married. Vinay protested. "I'd say, 'It *is* done! I'm educated! I'm successful!'" He usually turned their inquiries aside with a vague, "We'll see."

But this time he said, "Okay, try it your way." Since childhood, he had felt more American than Indian, but "some soul-searching" after his breakup had led to a realization: "I don't want to be the person who ends the relationship with India and the culture of Indian-ness."

That meant marrying an Indian American, though on his own terms and timetable. So he's been good-naturedly working with his parents to write his 35-word ad and pass along the responses; he's had long phone conversations with prospects he hasn't met; he's launched the series of dinners and brunches that will reveal if any of them "knock my socks off."

If only he could use that decision software a grad school professor gave him. "It would be absolutely perfect! It takes qualitative criteria and gives them a quantitative score." As it happens, though, Vinay has a nondigital means to the same end—his father has developed numeric rankings for the women whose parents respond to their ad. Call it the Sandhir Scale.

"We're not prejudiced against anybody," says Sikander Lal Sandhir, after he and his wife, Prabhat, an elegant couple, have arrived at their son's townhouse and greeted him with affectionate banter. "We're trying to find common factors, language, ancestral background, ethnicity, education... We might be able to guide Vinay."

Everyone settles in Vinay's living room, the stack of new printouts on the coffee table; his father takes out a pen. Some applicants don't even merit a score. The social worker, as Vinay predicted, gets an inked N for Not Rated. "This girl, unfortunately, is almost two years older than Vinay," his father murmurs in his formal English. "We'd prefer a girl who is younger; that's the norm in our culture. And it makes more sense. To start a family at 36—as a physician, I know there could be problems." On to the MBA from NYU.

His scale awards points for education and professional accomplishment: three for an MD or MBA, two for a CPA, one for a bachelor's degree. A woman gets a point if she's a Punjabi Hindu (half a point if she's northern Indian from another state), a point if she's born or raised in this country (deduct half a point if she's been here less than 10 years), a point for a desirable family background. Various physical attributes—slimness, height, fair skin, general attractiveness—can add up to four points. No one's ever received a perfect 10, but anyone with a 6.5 or higher is worth pursuing.

The MBA from NYU, for instance, "has been here for a while, and her family background is similar to ours; the father is a physician," Vinay's father muses, jotting notes. With an Ivy League undergraduate degree, "she gets good marks for her education." He's unimpressed with her photo ("I think she is so-so"), but overall she gets a 6.5. He passes the pages to his wife, who approves, and to Vinay, who shrugs but will forward his standard biodata package.

Sadly, the Sandhir Scale has proved more useful in theory than in reality. Take the dentist from Upstate New York whom his father had rated a 9. After several promising phone chats, Vinay flew up to visit and discovered "a very proper girl" who hadn't left India until she was 18. They seemed culturally out of synch. "No sparks or anything," he decided. Not wanting to make snap judgments, he invited her to Virginia and planned a lively weekend: an Orioles game, hiking in the Shenandoah Valley, brunch on Capitol Hill. Still no sparks. Trying to be gentlemanly, he called afterward to say he'd enjoyed meeting her but didn't think the relationship would "progress."

Sometimes an intriguing woman never replies to *his* e-mail. He's learned, too, that his initial disinclination to juggle several prospects simultaneously, which struck him as callous, was unwise: By the time he'd decided against Candidate A and was ready to move down his list, Candidate B might already be off the market.

At the moment, he's talking with a gynecologist from Alabama and a Houston computer trainer. The Alabaman was in Washington visiting her brother recently, so he took her to Jaleo for tapas and to a Georgetown piano bar.

"A very smart, talented girl," he reports. "Was a connection made, one way or the other?... I didn't feel like I got any closer to making a decision." The Houston woman will be in town in a few weeks; they've made dinner plans. Tonight's review adds two more possibilities to his roster.

He's getting frustrated with the ups and downs and delays. "It's a lot more give and take than people make it out to be," he's discovered. Maybe all those parental warnings were on target, maybe he's waited too long. Certainly, the long-distance process of phoning and meeting all these people is growing unwieldy.

In fact, he's mislaid the number of that pediatrician in New Jersey who got a ringing 8.0 on the Sandhir Scale. But he'll dig it out and call her, he promises his dad. She grew up on Long Island; she likes music and travel, Vinay's own passions. She sounds interesting.

## A Tradition in Transition

It has worked this way for thousands of years, immigrant parents tell their acculturated and uneasy offspring. It works better than Americans' impulsive love marriages, which so often split apart. "We have less divorce," Vibha's mother points out. "That's what results tell us."

In fact, the advantages and drawbacks of arranged marriages can't be so easily appraised. The incidence of divorce among Indian-born Americans *is* dramatically lower than among Americans generally, but that partly reflects the continuing stigma of divorce. Even as the divorce rate among Indian Americans appears to be increasing, the topic is rarely discussed. Vibha knows people, including several in her own family, who have divorced, but she doesn't want to talk about them. Divorce reflects poorly on an Indian family, and some proportion of arranged marriages endure not because they are successful or rewarding, but because leaving them would bring such shame.

And many endure because the definition of success differs from Western ideas. Traditional Indians don't expect a partner to be that improbable combination of soul mate/confidante/red-hot lover/best friend. "The husband-wife bond is one of reliability and dependability and complementary family roles—raising children, caring for elders," explains Karen Leonard, author of *The South Asian Americans* and a University of California-Irvine anthropologist. "They may communicate very little in intimate ways, and it's still a good marriage."

When marriages do go seriously awry, people like Anuradha Sharma see the fallout. Dozens of support groups have formed across the country for South Asian women victimized by domestic violence. Sharma until recently was executive director of Washington's ASHA (which means "hope" and stands for Asian Women's Self-Help Association). Operating from a secret downtown address, its volunteers accompany clients (primarily Indian, Pakistani and Bangladeshi) to area hospitals and courts and immigration offices, help them find shelter and, sometimes, obtain restraining orders. "I've seen the system of arranged marriage work really well," says Sharma, whose own parents' marriage was arranged. "But the system has a lot of trust built into it, and, in my work, I've also seen men very purposely take advantage of that."

Her vantage point—she's spent a decade with organizations concerned with violence against women—acquaints her particularly well with the most painful stories. Men who live in the United States sometimes visit remote villages in their ancestral countries, accept large dowries and consummate arranged marriages, then leave and don't return. They bring brides here from abroad, exploit and isolate and batter them, then threaten them with deportation or loss of their children if they report the abuse.

"I've had teenagers call, or social workers on behalf of teenagers, to see what we could do for women under 18 who were being whisked off to India or Pakistan and forced into marriage," Sharma says. "I met a couple who tried to have a love marriage, and family members from abroad were stalking and threatening them."

Even without such coercion, some members of the Second Generation find their elders' matchmaking efforts oppressive. "People on the outside think arranged marriage is exotic, it's romantic, it's cute—like that show 'Meet My Folks,'" says Devika Koppikar, a congressional aide weary of fending off attempts to get her married. "It's not."

For years, she laments, her parents have told her she's not accomplished or beautiful enough to land a husband herself, circulated her photo and e-mail address without her permission, enlisted friends and relatives to badger her into accepting men she has no interest in. There is no model, in Indian tradition, of a satisfying life as a single person. Feeling angry and estranged from her family at 31, she's "kind of tempted to just meet someone and head for Vegas."

Koppikar has formed "a two-woman support group" with a friend, a 30-year-old optometrist who broke off one arranged engagement, then nearly cracked under her parents' relentless pressure—"shouts, arguments, tears"—to enter another. She found a South Asian therapist who urged her to move out of her volatile family home, and after one particularly ugly altercation, she did. "I didn't even pack a bag," she says. "I felt I wasn't safe, emotionally."

Even Vibha—whose parents treated her much more respectfully, whose decision to marry Haresh, however difficult, was her own—hopes her youngest sister, just 13, takes a different route. She'd be pleased if Shetal, born here and less tradition-bound than Vibha, could skip "the big ordeal": parental pressures and cross-cultural tensions, a compressed courtship, language difficulties and hassles at the INS office. "I want her to find someone here, on her own, fall in love, get married, be happy," Vibha says.

If young Indian Americans raise their children differently—and people like Vibha and Vinay vow that their kids will be free to date, to be open about their romances, to marry whom they please—then the arranged marriage may not survive more than another generation or two in this country. In India, too, love marriages have grown more common among urban sophisticates.

In matters of courtship and marriage, in fact, young, well-educated Indians often have more social freedom than their American cousins, whose parents' values were fixed when they emigrated decades ago. "They still think of the norms they grew up with as the only acceptable ones. They haven't been able to change, seeing that as a betrayal of Indian-ness," says Padma Rangaswamy, author of *Namaste America* and a Chicago historian. "But Indians in India are happy to change and don't have those hangups. My friends' children in India are all finding their own spouses."

That Vibha didn't shocked her "American" girlfriends. A couple of them met for lunch a few weeks after her Indian sojourn, and she stunned them with her news and her engagement photos. "I looked at her like, 'You're kidding me,'" says Tiffany Obenhein. "Serve somebody tea, have a conversation—and bang, you're getting married? It seemed awfully fast for Vibha, who's so American." It took her friends a moment to recover and offer hugs and congratulations.

But then, the whole venture felt pretty fast to Vibha, too. Back home and back at work, arranging for a priest and a florist and a hall at Martin's Crosswinds in Greenbelt, "everything was so rushed," she says. "I didn't have time to think, and nothing was stopping it."

## Can This Be Love?

Haresh arrived in September, after six months of exchanging e-mail and instant messages with his intended, and moved in with her and her family. They got to kiss, finally, slipping off to the basement rec room for privacy, and Vibha was reassured: "He was a great kisser."

And yet... In mid-October, they'd planned to get their license at the county courthouse and be legally married, in order to speed up the immigration paperwork. Vibha canceled the appointment. "I'm like, no, I'm not going to do it. I wasn't sure. Plus, I was sick."

A week later, however, they went ahead and were married in a quick civil ceremony in a lawyer's office, and afterward Haresh made her a promise: He'd never lie to her. She thought that was sweet, she was "definitely moved," yet she didn't feel married. Or even, she acknowledged, in love. Haresh, the more amorous of this pair, sent her doting e-mail messages and a mushy birthday card, and she kept them all and waited for reciprocal feelings to smite her after the big Hindu wedding still to come. "I can't say I love him, but I'm pretty close," was her assessment. "And I know it's going to happen."

Because the thing was, he'd been growing on her week by week, with his quiet thoughtfulness, his steady support. "He puts up with my dad, who's hard to put up with," she reported from her car one night. "I run around doing all this wedding stuff, and he runs around with me. There's always family around—we haven't really spent much time together—but he hasn't complained once."

To Vibha's amazement, he pitched in with dish-washing and vacuuming and garbage-toting; it turned out he'd lived for a time with his grandparents, and helped with household chores when his grandmother was ill. This was major.

"Indian men don't tend to value the role women play, but he understands what they go through and respects it. He's like, why shouldn't women do what they want to do?" He didn't even care if she changed her last name or not, and since he didn't care, she decided she would.

On the Hindu New Year, Haresh was out doing errands with her dad instead of celebrating with the rest of the family at her aunt's house, and Vibha was ticked. "And then I went home and I was in my room and I'm waiting for him to come tell me 'Happy New Year,' and I'm *fuming*!" she recounts. "And I'm still mad about it the next day—and it hits me. Whoa. I missed him."

So the wedding, a four-day extravaganza for nearly 400 guests, is on.

## 'Body, Mind and Soul'

On Thursday night, a mehndiwalli from Gaithersburg came to the house and painstakingly applied paisley henna patterns to Vibha's hands and feet while her female relatives warbled traditional songs. The darker the mehndi, the more your husband will love you, goes the old saying, by which standard Vibha will have a deeply devoted mate.

Friday night, a few hundred people gathered at the Durga Temple in Lorton for garbas and dandia raas, the traditional Gujarati dances Vibha has loved since childhood, and she and her sisters and Haresh went flying across the floor until they were sweaty and exhausted, and her hair was coming unpinned.

Saturday, the family gathered for prenuptial ceremonies at the house ("Omigod, that was looong").

On Sunday, her wedding day, Vibha surprises even herself with her serenity. The photographer is urging her to smile; the decorator is setting up a glorious gold-embroidered white canopy (called a mandap); there's nothing left to prepare or decide. She might as well relax.

Wearing a ravishing embroidered lengha and extravagant amounts of gold jewelry, her face flecked with traditional bindya dots and her neck encircled by orchids, she's ready to be escorted to the ceremony on her uncle's arm. "Have you seen the mandap?" says Chetan Desai, one of her closest Virginia Tech buddies. "It kicks ass."

Under the canopy, with the bride and groom seated on silvery thrones, the songs and prayers continue for several hours in a mix of Sanskrit and Gujarati with a touch of English. The priest lights the sacred fire in a ziggurat-shaped brazier and Vibha and Haresh slowly circle it four times, symbolizing the stages of life and religious duty. They ask for prosperity and redemption from sin and future calamities. "Let us be like the earth and the sky," which are never separated, the priest intones on behalf of the groom. "Let us join our forces, let us have offspring, let us live a life of 200 years."

"I accept you as my husband and I offer my body, mind and soul to you," is the bride's response.

Vibha's Tech friends, most of whom have love marriages, are keeping a watchful eye on her. They've been a little worried, knowing Vibha's "adventurous spirit," about an arranged marriage to a guy from India. "How's this going to work?" Desai had wondered. "What if he's expecting some old-fashioned, stand-behind-your-man Indian woman?"

But seeing her calm gaze during the ceremony, noticing how glowy she looks at the reception afterward, they feel reassured. "We know her fake smile, her 'everything's all right' mode, but this was real," Desai says afterward, when Vibha and Haresh have left for a week's honeymoon—by a wide margin, the longest time they will ever have spent alone—in Hawaii. "He was happy, she was happy, she was at peace with herself. She was a *bride*."

## The Date From Hell

That pediatrician from New Jersey? "We had a really good conversation" on the phone, Vinay says. "We had the same perspective on this whole India Abroad/meeting people stuff... She's very smart, she has passion for her work." She would shortly head overseas, and he wanted to meet her before she left, so they agreed to rendezvous in Philadelphia on a Friday night. Vinay bought tickets to a Sixers game, feeling upbeat.

Alas. "It was raining. It was miserable," he reports. "She was in a bad mood from the get-go." Arriving 45 minutes late, she stepped into a puddle en route to his car, complained about the long walk across the parking lot to the arena, barely initiated a conversation the entire evening. "I don't know if it was me, I don't know if it was the weather, I don't know if it was her day," Vinay says, nursing his disappointment and a glass of pink guava juice while relating the sorry saga to his visiting parents. Her pager went off, he adds, but she didn't have to leave, although he began to wish she did: "How bad is it that you're hoping some kid is sick enough that she has to go in to the hospital?"

En route to a restaurant in a neighborhood neither knew well, "she proceeds to bitch for 15 minutes in the car about how she couldn't read the map." An awkward dinner, a quick drop-off at the train station, "and I don't anticipate ever having to talk to or hear from her again. Because it was the worst, most miserable date of my life. Number one."

He's starting to wonder about this whole arrangement business. "Deep down, I don't think assessing someone from pictures and biodata tells you anything," he says. "There's probably lots of decent people we overlooked. There really isn't a foolproof way of doing it."

But he's still in touch with the Alabama doctor. He sees the Houston woman when she's in town visiting her brother. And there was an interesting ad in India Abroad his parents recently responded to:

> *Invitation for handsome, caring, outgoing, broad-minded, well-settled professionals, 31-plus; for beautiful, v. fair, slim, educated U.S. raised daughter...*

## 'My Man'

Back from her honeymoon, Vibha Umaretiya seems liberated from frenzy and pressure—and from doubt. When she's with Haresh, she's giggly and charmed; she finds reasons to touch his shoulder, and he squeezes her hand. When she's not with him, when she's finally able to put away her cell phone and actually talk over lunch at the pizza place across from her office, she's expansive, buoyant.

"Now that we're married, I'm okay," she announces. "No more ifs or ands or buts."

Perhaps it's wise that Indian wedding rituals have expanded to incorporate such Western ideas as honeymoons. On Maui there was time to just lie on a beach and listen to the waves, time to get to know the man she'd wed.

"He's really very romantic, more than I am," she confides. On the plane, he kept his arm around her practically the whole flight. At their hotel, he catered to her, fed her morsels from his plate. "So much care, it was just incredible. I'm like, 'Stop the madness.'"

Not that she really wanted him to stop. "He made coffee for me in the morning! I'm like, omigod... He was so sweet; he makes it really easy for me to like him." But what about—that annoying Western question—love? A pause.

"How do you know if you love someone? Does a light come on over your head?" Haresh wants to get his master's degree in engineering; he thinks he could finish in a year and a half. Vibha may decide to start a business one day. They want to buy a condo or a townhouse as soon as they can, have some time as a twosome before the children arrive—at least five years away—and possibly his family arrives, too, if they choose. And because Haresh is soft-spoken and understanding and fair-minded about women's roles, and because she also wants him to do what fulfills him, they will have a good life together.

"He's my man, and he will be my man up until the day I die, or whatever," she muses, launching into a monologue. "The way you feel about a person is constantly changing, y'know?... Maybe there are days when you don't want to deal with him, maybe there'll be days when you don't want to miss a second with him. Do I look forward to spending time with him? Yes. Do I look forward to getting to know him? Yes. Do I like him for what he is? Do I have a deeper understanding of him? Yes."

So how their meeting and their future were arranged, with all the attendant anxieties, is starting to seem beside the point. "For me, it was the right thing," Vibha says. And she laughs. "I never thought I'd do it this way. It's really weird how life works, y'know? But I'm happy with the way it ended up. Seriously happy."

---

**Paula Span (pspan@bellatlantic.net) is a Post staff writer.**

# The War Over Gay Marriage

## In a landmark decision, the Supreme Court affirms gay privacy and opens the way to a revolution in family life

IT WAS A HOMEY SCENE. STANDING in their warm kitchen on a winter's day in 2001, Julie and Hillary Goodridge, a couple for 16 years, played the old Beatles song "All You Need Is Love" for their young daughter, Annie. Hillary asked Annie if she knew any people who loved each other. The little girl rattled off the names of her mothers' married friends, heterosexuals all. "What about Mommy and Ma?" asked Hillary. "Well," the child replied, "if you loved each other you'd get married."

That did it. "My heart just dropped," said Hillary. The gay couple headed for the Massachusetts Department of Public Health to get a marriage license. Julie was optimistic, Hillary less so. "I thought we'd be led away in handcuffs," Hillary recalled. Blood tests and $30 in hand, they anxiously asked for an application. "No, you're not allowed to," responded the woman behind the counter. "I'll need two grooms first." Hillary and Julie asked to speak to the department's director. The woman politely told them, "No, you can't get married, and there's nothing you can do about it."

Actually, there was. With the help of the Gay & Lesbian Advocates & Defenders (GLAD), Hillary and Julie sued for the right to be legally wed. Any day now, the Massachusetts Supreme Judicial Court is expected to decide their case. No court in America has ever recognized gay marital vows. But last week Hillary and Julie—and every gay person who wants to be married or adopt a child or hold a job or receive a government benefit or simply enjoy the right to be respected—received a tremendous boost from the highest court in the land.

The outcome of *Lawrence et al. v. Texas*, handed down on the final day of the Supreme Court's 2002–2003 term, was not unexpected. In a Houston apartment five years ago, Tyron Garner and John Geddes Lawrence had been arrested by police for performing a homosexual act and fined $200. By a 6–3 vote, the high court struck down the Texas anti-sodomy law. In some ways, the Supreme Court was just catching up to public opinion. In 1986, in *Bowers v. Hardwick*, a decision that lived in infamy among gays in America, the court had upheld a Georgia anti-sodomy law. At the time, 25 states had such laws. Some 17 years later, only four states banned sodomy between homosexuals (an additional nine states had laws, on the books but rarely enforced, barring sodomy between any sexual partners).

> Advocates have had to deal with what one called 'the ick factor'—the revulsion some heterosexuals feel about homosexuals.

What stunned court watchers—and what promises to change forever the status of homosexuals in America—was the far reach of the court's reasoning. Gays "are entitled to respect for their private lives," said Justice Anthony Kennedy, reading from his majority opinion from the high court's mahogany bench. His voice was quiet and he seemed a little nervous, but his words rang with lasting meaning. Under the due-process clause of the 14th Amendment of the Constitution, Kennedy ruled, gays were entitled to a right of privacy. "The state cannot demean their existence or control their destiny by making their private sexual conduct a crime," said Kennedy. In the crowded courtroom, some of the gay activists and lawyers silently but visibly wept as they listened.

Justice Kennedy's ruling in the *Lawrence* case "may be one of the two most important opinions of the last 100 years," says David Garrow, legal scholar at Emory University and Pulitzer Prize-winning biographer of Martin Luther King Jr. "It's the most libertarian majority opinion ever issued by the Supreme Court. It's arguably bigger than *Roe v. Wade*," said Garrow, referring to the 1973 Supreme Court decision giving women a right to abortion. At least in symbolic terms, Garrow put the decision on a par with *Brown v. Board of Education*, the landmark 1954

## A Winding Road

### A look back at the highs and lows of gay rights:

**1895** The writer Oscar Wilde is convicted for "gross indecency between males."

**1924** The first formal U.S. gay-activist group is founded in Chicago.

**1969** Patrons of Stonewall Inn resist a police raid in what's considered birth of the gay-rights movement.

**1975** Former NFL player Dave Kopay announces he's gay—the first pro athlete to do so.

**1977** Anita Bryant mounts national crusade to block gay rights.

**1986** Supreme Court rules in *Bowers* that sodomy is a crime.

**1987** ACT UP is born, taking up the fight against AIDS.

**1993** Military adopts "don't ask, don't tell" policy for gays.

**1993** Thousands of gay-rights supporters march on Washington.

**1996** High court: gays enjoy equal rights under the Constitution.

**1997** Ellen DeGeneres's TV-show character comes out.

**2000** Vermont allows gay couples to form civil unions.

**2001** Federal judge upholds law banning gay adoption.

**2003** An openly gay Episcopal bishop is elected in N.H.

ruling declaring that separate was not equal in the nation's public schools.

But it may be years before the ripple effects of *Lawrence* are felt. Just as schools were still segregated in parts of the South a decade after the *Brown* decision, it is likely that attempts to give gays true legal equality with heterosexuals will encounter fierce resistance from people and institutions that still regard homosexuality as morally deviant. The battle—over gay marriage, gay adoption, gays in the military and gays in the workplace—will be fought out court to court, state to state for years to come. Nonetheless, there is no question that the *Lawrence* case represents a sea change, not just in the Supreme Court, a normally cautious institution, but also in society as a whole.

In 1986, when the court had ruled in the *Bowers* case, Justice Byron White curtly dismissed the argument that the Constitution protected the right of homosexuals to have sex in their own homes. Writing for the majority of justices, White had called such an assertion "facetious." But social norms have been transformed over the past two decades. How mainstream is the idea of "gay rights"? Of the six justices who voted to strike down laws against homosexual sodomy, four were appointed by Republican presidents. (Kennedy, David Souter and John Paul Stevens all subscribed to a right of privacy for gays; Justice Sandra Day O'Connor stuck to the narrower ground that it was unfair to punish gays but not heterosexuals for sodomy.) Polls showed that the justices have public opinion behind them: some six out of 10 Americans believe that homosexual sex between consenting adults should be legal.

One veteran gay activist could sense the change in the attitudes of the justices. Kevin Cathcart, executive director of the Lambda Legal Defense and Education Fund, has been part of a small but determined circle of lawyers plotting gay-rights strategy since 1984. In the past, he had to deal with what he called the "ick factor"—the revulsion some heterosexuals feel about homosexual acts. "The Kennedy opinion not only does not have an ick factor," says Cathcart, "but is almost an apology for the ick factor 17 years ago."

One justice was still full of disgust. In a biting, sarcastic voice, Justice Antonin Scalia read his dissent from the bench. He denounced his colleagues for "taking sides in the culture war." He accused the court's majority of having "largely signed on to the so-called homosexual agenda." Most Americans, Scalia warned, "do not want persons who openly engage in homosexual conduct as partners in their business, as scout-masters for their children, as teachers in their children's schools, or as boarders in their homes." Scalia predicted that the court's decision would cause "a massive disruption of the current social order" by calling into question the government's right to legislate morality. While noting the majority's statement that the case did not involve gay marriage, Scalia scoffed, "Do not believe it."

Scalia's fulmination was impressive, but (as even he might privately concede) it was also an overstatement of the legal and political reality, at least for the immediate future. While gays can now claim some constitutional protection—their new right to privacy under the *Lawrence* decision—the federal government and the states can override those rights if they have a good enough reason, a "legitimate state interest." Thus, national security could trump privacy in the military and preserve the Pentagon's "don't ask, don't tell" policy on gays. Or the state's interest in preserving "traditional institutions"—like marriage between different-sex couples—might overcome a homosexual's right to not be "demeaned," as Justice Kennedy put it. After *Lawrence*, gays can no longer be branded as criminals. But that does not mean they will enjoy all the rights of "straight" citizens. The current Supreme Court has shown, albeit erratically, a federalist streak: it will not lightly trample "states' rights"—that is, second-guess the power of states to make up their own rules, especially if popular opinion is running strong.

Inevitably, politics will play a role. Some conservative groups were apoplectic. "People of faith are not going to lie down and allow their faith to be trampled because a politically correct court has run amok," promised the Rev. Lou Sheldon, president of the Traditional Values Coalition. He offered a hint of the battles that lie ahead when a vacancy opens up on the high court. "In this court, you do not have friends of the Judeo-Christian standard. We know who our friends are. And we know who needs to be replaced," said Sheldon. Sandy Rios, president of the Concerned Women for America, predicted moral Armageddon. "We're opening up a complete Pandora's box," she said. Some conservatives, including Justice Scalia, warned that the court's decision would undermine laws barring bigamy, incest and prostitution.

**Blood tests and $30 in hand, the Goodridges asked for a license. 'No,' the clerk told the women. 'I'll need two grooms first.'**

Maybe. But states will still be able to ban sexual practices that are obviously hurtful or exploitative of women or minors. Nonetheless, the fear of legalized wantonness will quickly become a campaign issue. Last week the White House—which decided not to file a brief in the case—was taking cover; White House spokesman Ari Fleischer defensively mumbled that gay rights were a matter for the states to decide. Bush's political handlers were fearful of alienating either gay voters or the legion of Christian conservatives who provided Bush with his electoral base in 2000. "Bush officials apparently think homosexual activists make better leaders than the conservative activists who delivered millions of votes," taunted Bob Knight, director of the conservative Culture and Family Institute.

The fight over gay rights could easily become a "wedge issue" in the 2004 presidential campaign, though Democrats, too, will be wary of getting ahead of public opinion. For the most part, gay rights will be fought out at the local and state level. The struggle will be protracted and there may be a real backlash. An overview of the main battlegrounds:

**Gay Marriage.** Although gay couples routinely have commitment ceremonies and The New York Times wedding pages now run photos of gay and lesbian pairings, no state in the country recognizes or grants gay marriages. (Churches are badly split, with some denominations honoring same-sex unions and others vehemently opposing them.) Vermont comes the closest of any state with "civil unions" that bestow many of the same rights and responsibilities as marriage, but give it a different name—for purely political reasons. A few other states, most notably Massachusetts and California, seem to be edging toward the recognition of gay marriage, either by legislation or judicial fiat. But the stronger movement, at least for now, appears to be in the other direction. Some 37 states—and the federal government—have adopted "Defense of Marriage Acts," which define marriage as applying only to a man and a woman, and—significantly—bar recognition of same-sex marriage from other states.

These laws will inevitably be challenged in the courts under the *Lawrence* decision. On June 11, a court in Ontario, Canada, ruled that same-sex marriages are legal (they are also legal in the Netherlands and Belgium). Last weekend in Toronto, during the city's Gay Pride celebration, the city's marriage office stayed open for extended hours. A dozen of the first 200 customers were Americans who had driven across the border. Legal experts are divided over whether a gay couple with a Canadian marriage license will be recognized back in the States, but they are sure that sooner or later the issue of gay marriage will wind up in the Supreme Court, though probably not for several years.

By then the court may be, as the saying goes, following the election returns. Gary Bauer, the president of American Values and a former presidential candidate, warned that if the Republicans do not take a stand against gay marriage in the 2004 election, then GOP "family values" activists might just sit home rather than work for the party. On the other hand, Bush may pick up votes from libertarians and Republican moderates (the "soccer moms") if he is seen as being compassionate or tolerant of different sexual orientations.

**Adoption and Custody.** Most states now permit single gays to adopt children. Resistance to gay adoption has waned as studies show that children raised by gays look a lot like those raised by straights—and are no more or less likely to be gay. Still, only 11 states permit same-sex couples to adopt children. The rest of the states are a patchwork of conflicting rules. Florida, swayed by Anita Bryant's 1977 "Save the Children" campaign, is the most restrictive, banning adoption by any gay or lesbian individuals. That law, based largely on moral disapproval, seems vulnerable after *Lawrence*.

The most immediate impact of *Lawrence* will be on custody battles. One Virginia judge, for instance, asked a lesbian to detail her homosexual acts in court testimony and

THE NEXT FRONT

Marriage is one thing. But what happens when partners part? For gay couples splitting up, it's still a legal 'no man's land.'

## Breaking Up Is Hard to Do

BY DEBRA ROSENBERG

When Texans Russell Smith and John Anthony traveled to Vermont to join in a civil union in February 2002, they had all the romantic intentions of any couple exchanging "I do's." But like the 50 percent of Americans whose marriages end in divorce, Smith and Anthony later decided to call it quits. Because the two had shared business deals, Smith worried he might one day face financial obligations from his ex. So he filed for divorce in a Texas court. Though a district judge initially agreed to grant one, Texas Attorney General Greg Abbott intervened. He feared granting a divorce would signal that the state recognized the union in the first place—a step Texas and other states aren't yet willing to take. "A judge cannot grant a divorce where no marriage existed," Abbott argued. The judge reversed the divorce and the couple was forced to hash things out on their own. "They were just wanting to legally terminate this relationship," says Anthony's lawyer, Tommy Gunn. "Obviously the divorce route did not work."

If gay couples think it's tough to get married, they may find it's even harder to split up. Few want to think about it on the way to the altar, but "we're not immune to relationship problems," says David Buckel, an attorney who directs the marriage project at Lambda Legal. Though all it takes is a romantic weekend to tie the knot under Canada's just-passed same-sex marriage law or get linked by civil union in Vermont, both places require at least one member of the couple to establish residency for a year before granting a divorce or official dissolution. Of the roughly 5,000 civil unions performed so far in Vermont, the only state that legally recognizes the same-sex commitments, 85 percent went to out-of-staters.

That has left other states grappling with what to do when civil unions sour—and whether standard divorce laws can apply. A West Virginia family-court judge agreed to use divorce laws to dissolve a civil union there last year. But Connecticut courts dismissed the divorce case filed by Glen Rosengarten, who decided to end his 15-year relationship shortly after he and his partner got a civil union in Vermont. Dying of AIDS, Rosengarten wanted to preserve his estate for children from an earlier marriage, says his lawyer Gary I. Cohen. "He had incredible anxiety about it—he really wanted closure in his life," Cohen says. Rosengarten appealed to the state Supreme Court, but died before the case was heard. Medical bills ate up his estate, so inheritance became a moot point too.

Without access to divorce, all the benefits gay couples get with a civil union—shared property, adoption rights, insurance—must be undone one by one. If they can't dissolve the union, they may not be free to enter into a new union or marriage, either. "It shoves gay people into a no man's land where they have to fight it out for themselves," says Evan Wolfson, director of Freedom to Marry. "Because it's not marriage, people don't have one of the automatic protections that comes with marriage." Gay couples can't hope to erase the pain that comes with parting. But after last week, there's at least a chance they may one day get a little more help when things fall apart.

With PAT WINGERT

then told her she would lose her child because her behavior was immoral. That sort of reasoning will likely no longer pass constitutional muster.

**Gays in the Workplace, Schools and the Military.** Big employers have already gotten the message. In 1992 only one of the Fortune 500 companies offered benefits to gay partners. Today the number is 197, including 27 of the top 50. Unfounded worries about getting tagged with massive AIDS bills have been replaced by top companies' desire to compete for gay workers.

Schools and the military will be slower going. Teachers fear harassment or retribution if they support student efforts to form "gay-straight alliances" (even so, there are some 1,700 pro-tolerance clubs in 50 states). The Pentagon will argue that "unit cohesion" will suffer if gays are openly tolerated in the military. Part of the underlying legal basis for the armed services' restrictive "don't ask, don't tell" policy, a federal anti-sodomy law, is likely to be struck down. Still, the courts are very reluctant to interfere with the military.

### PRAYERFUL PROTEST AT THE HIGH COURT
### Critics share Scalia's view that the decision hurts the state's right to legislate morality

Despite the challenges ahead, the alliance of gay lawyers who have been working for two decades to overturn discriminatory laws can feel the ground shifting beneath their feet. Last week Susan Sommer, the supervising attorney at the Lambda Legal Defense and Education Fund, went to an early court hearing in a case aimed at overturning New Jersey's ban on gay marriages. The U.S. Supreme Court's ruling in *Lawrence* "didn't come up," she noted. "But now I feel like when I walk in the courtroom I've got a powerful symbol on our side, the ringing words of Justice Kennedy that *Bowers v. Hardwick* had demeaned gay people."

Lambda is trying to soften up public opinion with town-hall meetings designed to show that gay families are good for the community. "The town halls we're doing tell people, 'Hey, we're just like anyone else—a middle-class, hometown suburban couple that's been called boring'," says Cindy Meneghin, 45, who with her partner, Maureen Kilian, also 45, and their two children, Joshua, 10, and Sarah, 8, are suing to be recognized as a legal family in New Jersey. "You can't look at our beautiful, charming kids and not notice that we're a family, and the myths start tumbling down. What we've found is that people get to know us as people with families and kids, that I coach soccer and take pictures, and Maureen is the best dessert maker in town, and, oh yes, Maureen and Cindy are a gay couple."

At their home in the liberal Boston enclave of Jamaica Plain, Julie and Hillary Goodridge (who adopted the common last name from Hillary's grandmother because it sounded "positive") have found acceptance—except for the time a bunch of high-school kids urinated on their car and yelled "Dyke!" Last week Julie sat down with their daughter, Annie, to explain the *Lawrence* decision. "I had to do it without talking about sodomy," said Julie. "I mean, she's only 7 and three quarters!" "The Supreme Court made an important decision yesterday," Julie told Annie. "They said it was OK for lesbians and gays to love each other." "That's good," said Annie. But she still wants her parents to be married.

---

This story was reported by T. TRENT GEGAX, DEBRA ROSENBERG, PAT WINGERT, MARK MILLER, MARTHA BRANT, STUART TAYLOR JR., TAMARA LIPPER, JOHN BARRY, REBECCA SINDERBRAND, SARAH CHILDRESS and JULIE SCELFO. It was written by EVAN THOMAS.

Social Science and Public Policy

# NEW EVIDENCE FOR THE BENEFITS OF NEVER SPANKING

*Murray A. Straus*

Virtually a revolution has occurred in the last four years in the state of scientific knowledge about the long-term effects of corporal punishment. This article summarizes the results of that research and explains why the new research shows, more clearly than ever before, the benefits of avoiding corporal punishment.

Somewhat ironically, at the same time as these new studies were appearing, voices arose in state legislatures, the mass media, and in social science journals to defend corporal punishment. Consequently, a second purpose is to put these recent defenses of corporal punishment in perspective.

This is followed by a section explaining a paradox concerning trends in corporal punishment. Public belief in the necessity of corporal punishment and the percentage of parents who hit teenagers is about half of what it was only 30 years ago. Despite these dramatic changes, 94 percent of parents of toddlers in a recent national survey reported spanking, which is about the same as it was in 1975 (Straus and Stewart, 1999).

The article concludes with an estimate of the benefits to children, to parents, and to society as a whole that could occur if corporal punishment were to cease.

Defenders of corporal punishment say or imply that no-corporal punishment is the same as no-discipline or "permissiveness." Consequently, before discussing the new research, it is important to emphasize that no-corporal punishment does not mean no-discipline. Writers and organizations leading the movement away from corporal punishment believe that rules and discipline are necessary, but that they will be *more* effective without corporal punishment. Their goal is to inform parents about these more effective disciplinary strategies, as exemplified in the very name of one such organization—the Center for Effective Discipline (see their web site: *http://www.stophitting.com;* see also the web site of Positive Parenting program *http://parenting.umn.edu*).

## Previous Research on Corporal Punishment

In order to grasp the importance of the new research, the limitations of the previous 45 years of research need to be understood. These 45 years saw the publication of more than 80 studies linking corporal punishment to child behavior problems such as physical violence. A meta-analysis of these studies by Gershoff (in press) found that almost all showed that the more corporal punishment a child had experienced, the worse the behavior of the child. Gershoff's review reveals a consistency of findings that is rare in social science research. Thompson concluded that "Although... corporal punishment does secure children's immediate compliance, it also increases the likelihood of eleven [types of] negative outcomes [such as increased physical aggression by the child and depression later in life]. Moreover, even studies conducted by defenders of corporal punishment show that, even when the criterion is immediate compliance, noncorporal discipline strategies work just as well as corporal punishment.

The studies in my book *Beating the Devil Out of Them* are examples of the type of negative outcome reviewed by Thompson. For example, the more corporal punishment experienced, the greater the probability of hitting a wife or husband later in life. Another study of kindergarten children used data on corporal punishment obtained by interviews with the mothers of the children. Six months later the children were observed in school. Instances of physical aggression were tallied for each child. The children of mothers who used corporal punishment attacked other children twice as often as the children whose mothers did not. The children of mothers who went beyond ordinary corporal punishment had four times the rate of attacking other children. This illustrates another principle: that the psychologically harmful effects of corporal punishment are parallel to the harmful effects of physical abuse, except that the magnitude of the effect is less.

Despite the unusually high constancy in the findings of research on corporal punishment, there is a serious problem with all the previous research, these studies do not indicate which is cause and which is effect. That is, they do not take into account the fact that aggression and other behavior problems of the child lead parents to spank. Consequently, although there is clear evidence that the more corporal punishment, the greater the probability of hitting a spouse later in life, that finding could simply indicate that the parents were responding to a high level of aggression by the child at Time 1. For example, they might have spanked because the child repeatedly grabbed toys from or hit a brother or sister. Since aggression is a relatively stable trait, it is not surprising that the most aggressive children at Time 1 are still the most aggressive at Time 2 and are now hitting their wives or husbands. To deal with that problem, the research needs to take into account the child's aggression or other antisocial behavior at Time 1 (the time of the spanking). Studies using that design can examine whether, in the months or years following, the behavior of children who were spanked improves (as most people in the USA think will be the case) or gets worse. There are finally new studies that use this design and provide information on long term change in the child's behavior.

## Five New Landmark Studies

In the three-year period 1997–1999 five studies became available that can be considered "landmark" studies because they overcame this serious defect in 45 years of previous research on the long-term effects of corporal punishment. All five of the new studies took into account the child's behavior at Time 1, and all five were based on large and nationally representative samples of American children. None of them depended on adults recalling what happened when they were children.

## Study 1: Corporal Punishment and Subsequent Antisocial Behavior

This research studied over 3,000 children in the National Longitudinal Survey of Youth (Straus, et al., 1997). The children were in three age groups: 3–5, 6–9, and 10–14. The mothers of all three groups of children were interviewed at the start of the study in 1988, and then again in 1990 and 1992. The findings were very similar for all three age groups and for change after two years and four years. To avoid excess detail only the results for the 6–9 year old children and for the change in antisocial behavior two years after the first interview will be described here.

*Measure of corporal punishment.* To measure corporal punishment, the mothers were told "Sometimes kids mind pretty well and sometimes they don't," and asked "About how many times, if any, have you had to spank your child in the past week?"

*Measure of Antisocial Behavior.* To measure Antisocial Behavior the mothers were asked whether, in the past three months, the child frequently "cheats or tells lies," "bullies or is cruel/mean to others," "does not feel sorry after misbehaving," "breaks things deliberately," "is disobedient at school," "has trouble getting along with teachers." This was used to create a measure of the number of antisocial behaviors frequently engaged in by the child.

*Other Variables.* We also took into account several other variables that could affect antisocial behavior by the child. These include the sex of child, cognitive stimulation provided by the parents, emotional support by the mother, ethnic group of the mother, and socioeconomic status of the family.

*Findings.* The more corporal punishment used during the first year of the study, the greater the tendency for Antisocial Behavior to *increase* subsequent to the corporal punishment. It also shows that this effect applied to both Euro American children and children of other ethnic groups. Of course, other things also influence Antisocial Behavior. For example, girls have lower rates of Antisocial Behavior than boys, and children whose mothers are warm and supportive are less likely to behave in antisocial ways. Although these other variables do lessen the effect of corporal punishment, we found that the tendency for corporal punishment to make things worse over the long run applies regardless of race, socioeconomic status, gender of the child, and regardless of the extent to which the mother provides cognitive stimulation and emotional support.

## Study 2: A Second Study of Corporal Punishment and Antisocial Behavior

*Sample and Measures.* Gunnoe and Mariner (1997) analyzed data from another large and representative sample of American children—the National Survey of Families and Households. They studied 1,112 children in two age groups: 4–7and 8–11. In half of the cases the mother was interviewed and in the other half the father provided the information. The parents were first interviewed in 1987–88, and then five years later. Gunnoe and Mariner's measure of corporal punishment was the same as in the Straus et al. study just described; that is, how often the parent spanked in the previous week.

Gunnoe and Mariner examined the effect of corporal punishment on two aspects of the child's behavior: fighting at school and antisocial behavior. Their Antisocial Behavior measure was also the same as in the Straus et al. study.

*Findings on Fighting.* Gunnoe and Mariner found that the more corporal punishment in 1987–88, the greater the amount of fighting at school five years later. This is consistent with the theory that in the long run corporal punishment is counter-productive. However, for toddlers and for African-American children, they found the opposite, i.e. that corporal punishment is associated with *less* fighting 5 years later. Gunnoe and Mariner suggest that this occurs because younger children and African-American children tend to regard corporal punishment as a legitimate parental behavior rather than as an aggressive act. However, corporal punishment by parents of young children and by African-American parents is so nearly universal (for example, 94 percent of parents of toddlers) that it suggests an alternative explanation: that no-corporal punishment means no-discipline. If that is the case, it is no wonder that children whose parents exercise no-discipline are less well behaved. Corporal punishment may not be good for children, but failure to properly supervise and control is even worse.

*Findings on Antisocial Behavior.* The findings on the relation of corporal punishment to Antisocial Behavior show that the more corporal punishment experienced by the children in Year 1, the *higher* the level of Antisocial Behavior five years later. Moreover, they found that the harmful effect of corporal punishment applies to all the categories of children they studied—that is, to children in each age group, to all races, and to both boys and girls. Thus, both of these major long-term prospective studies resulted in evidence that, although corporal punishment may work in the short run, in the long run it tends to boomerang and make things worse.

An important sidelight of the Gunnoe and Mariner study is that it illustrates the way inconvenient findings can be ignored to give a desired "spin." The findings section includes one brief sentence acknowledging that their study "replicates the Straus et al. findings." This crucial finding is never again mentioned. The extensive discussion and conclusion sections omit mentioning the results showing that corporal punishment at Time 1 was associated with more antisocial behavior subsequently for children of all ages and all ethnic groups. Marjorie Gunnoe told me that she is opposed to spanking and has never spanked her own children. So the spin she put on the findings is not a reflection of personal values or behavior. Perhaps it reflects teaching at a college affiliated with a church which teaches that God expects parents to spank.

## Study 3: Corporal Punishment and Child-to-Parent Violence

Timothy Brezina (1999) analyzed data on a nationally representative sample of 1,519 adolescent boys who participated in the Youth in Transition study. This is a three-wave panel study that was begun in 1966. Although the data refer to a previous generation of high school students, there is no reason to think that the relationship between corporal punishment and children hitting parents is different now that it was then, except that the rate may have decreased because fewer parents now slap teen-agers.

*Measure of Corporal Punishment.* Corporal punishment was measured by asking the boys "How often do your parents actually slap you?" The response categories ranged from 1 (never) to 5 (always). Twenty eight percent of the boys reported being slapped by their parents during the year of the first wave of the study when their average age was 15, and 19 percent were slapped during the wave 2 year (a year and half later).

*Measure of Child Aggression.* The boys were asked similar questions about how often they hit their father and their mother. Eleven percent reported hitting a parent the first year, and 7 percent reported hitting a parent at Time 2 of the study.

*Findings.* Brezina found that corporal punishment at Time 1 was associated with an *increased* probability of a child assaulting the parent a year and a half later. Thus, while it is true that corporal punishment teaches the child a lesson, it is certainly not the lesson intended by the parents.

As with the other four studies, the data analysis took into account some of the many other factors that affect the probability of child-to-parent violence. These include the socioeconomic status and race of the family, the age of the parents, the child's attachment to the parent, child's attitude toward aggression, and child's physical size.

## Study 4: Corporal Punishment and Dating Violence

Simons, Lin, and Gordon (1998) tested the theory that corporal punishment by the parents increases the probability of later hitting a partner in a dating relationship. They studied 113 boys in a rural area of the state of Iowa, beginning when they were in the 7th grade or about age 13.

*Measure of Corporal Punishment.* The mothers and the fathers of these boys were asked how often they spanked or slapped the child when he did something wrong, and how often they used a belt or paddle for corporal punishment. These questions were repeated in waves 2 and 3 of this 5-year study. The scores for the mother and the father for each of the three years were combined to create an overall measure of corporal punishment. More than half of the boys experienced corporal punishment during those years. Consequently, the findings about corporal punishment apply to the majority of boys in that community, not just to the children of a small group of violent parents.

*Measure of Dating Violence.* The information on dating violence came from the boys, so it is not influenced by whether the parents viewed the boy as aggressive. The boys were asked whether, in the last year, "When you had a disagreement with your girlfriend, how often did you hit, push, shove her?"

*Measure of Delinquency at Time 1.* As explained earlier, it is critical to take into account the misbehavior that leads parents to use corporal punishment. In this study, that was done by asking the boys at Time 1 how often they had engaged in each of 24 delinquent acts such as skipping school, stealing, and physically attacking someone with a weapon; and also how often they had used drugs and alcohol.

*Parental involvement and support.* Finally the study also took into account the extent to which the parents showed warmth and affection, were consistent in their discipline, monitored and supervised the child, and explained rules and expectations. In addition, it also controlled for witnessing parental violence.

*Findings.* Simons and his colleagues found that the more corporal punishment experienced by these boys, the greater the probability of their physically assaulting a girlfriend. Moreover, like the other prospective studies, the analysis took into account the misbehavior that led parents to use corporal punishment, and also the quality of parenting. This means that the relation of corporal punishment to violence against a girlfriend is very unlikely to be due to poor parenting. Rather, it is another study showing that the long run effect of corporal punishment is to engender more rather than less misbehavior. In short, spanking boomerangs.

## Study 5: Corporal Punishment and Child's Cognitive Development

The last of these five studies (Straus and Paschall, 1999) was prompted by studies showing that talking to children (including pre-speech infants) is associated with an increase in neural connections in the brain and in cognitive performance. Those findings led us to theorize that if parents avoid corporal punishment, they are more likely to engage in verbal methods of behavior control such as explaining to the child, and that the increased verbal interaction with the child will in turn enhance the child's cognitive ability.

This theory was tested on 806 children of mothers in the National Longitudinal Study of Youth who were age 2 to 4 in the first year of our analysis, and the tests were repeated for an additional 704 children who were age 5 to 9 in the first year. Corporal punishment was measured by whether the mother was observed hitting the child during the interview and by a question on frequency of spanking in the past week. A corporal punishment scale was created by adding the number of times the parent spanked in two sample weeks. Cognitive ability was measured in Year 1 and two years later by tests appropriate for the age of the child at the time of testing such as the Peabody Picture Vocabulary Test.

The study took into account the mother's age and education, whether the father was present in the household, number of children in the family, mother's supportiveness and cognitive stimulation, ethnic group, and the child's age, gender, and child's birth weight.

The less corporal punishment parents use on toddlers, the greater the probability that the child will have an above average cognitive growth. The greater benefit of avoiding corporal punishment for the younger children is consistent with the research showing the most rapid growth of neural connections in the brain of early ages. It is also consistent with the theory that what the child learns as an infant and toddler is crucial because it provides the necessary basis for subsequent cognitive development. The greater adverse effect on cognitive development for toddlers has an extremely important practical implication because the defenders of corporal punishment have now retreated to limiting their advocacy to toddlers. Their recommendation is not based on empirical evidence. The evidence from this study suggests that, at least in so far as cognitive development is concerned, supporters of corporal punishment have unwittingly advised parents to use corporal punishment at the ages when it will have the most adverse effect.

## The Message Of The Five Studies: "Don't Spank"

Each of the five studies I briefly summarized is far from perfect. They can be picked apart one by one, as can just about every epidemiological study. This is what the tobacco industry did for many years. The Surgeon General's committee on smoking did the opposite. Their review of the research acknowledged the limitations of the studies when taken one-by-one. But they concluded that despite the defects of the individual studies, the cumulative evidence indicated that smoking does cause lung cancer and other diseases, and they called for an end to smoking. With respect to spanking, I believe that the cumulative weight of the evidence, and especially the five prospective studies provides sufficient evidence for a new Surgeon General's warning. A start in that direction was made by the American Academy of Pediatrics, which in 1998 published "Guidelines for Effective Discipline" (*Pediatrics* 101: 723–728) that advises parents to avoid spanking.

## Is There a Backlash?

It is ironic that during the same period as the new and more definitive research was appearing, there were hostile or ridiculing articles in newspapers and magazines on the idea of never spanking a child. In 1999, Arizona and Arkansas passed laws to remind parents and teachers that they have the right to use corporal punishment and to urge them to do so. There has also been a contentious debate in scientific journals on the appropriateness of corporal punishment. These developments made some advocates for children concerned that there is a backlash against the idea of no-spanking. However, there are several reasons for doubting the existence of a backlash in the sense of a reversal in the trend of decreasing public support for corporal punishment, or in the sense of non-spanking parents reverting to using corporal punishment.

One reason for doubting the existence of a backlash is that, each year, a larger and larger proportion of the American population opposes corporal punishment. In 1968, which was only a generation ago, almost everyone (94 percent) believed that corporal punishment is sometimes necessary. But in the last 30 years public support for corporal punishment has been decreasing. By 1999, almost half of US adults rejected the idea that spanking is necessary.

### The Advocates Are Long-Time Supporters

In 1968, those who favored corporal punishment did not need to speak out to defend their view because, as just indicated, almost everyone believed it was necessary. The dramatic decrease in support for corporal punishment means that long time advocates of corporal punishment now have reason to be worried, and they are speaking out. Consequently, their recent publications do not indicate a backlash in the sense of a change from being opposed to corporal punishment to favoring it. I suggest that it is more like dying gasps of support for an ancient mode of bringing up children that is heading towards extinction.

The efforts of those who favor corporal punishment have also been spurred on by the increase in crime in many countries. The rise in youth crime in the United States, although recently reversed, is a very disturbing trend, and it has prompted a search for causes and corrective steps. It should be no surprise that people who have always believed in the use of corporal punishment believe that a return to their favored mode of bringing up children will help cure the crime problem. They argue that children need "discipline," which is correct. However, they equate discipline with corporal punishment, which is not correct. No-corporal punishment does not mean no-discipline. Delinquency prevention does require, among other things, discipline in the sense of clear rules and standards for behavior and parental supervision and monitoring and enforcement. To the extent that part of the explanation for crime, especially crime by youth, is the lack of discipline, the appropriate step is not a return to corporal punishment but parental standards, monitoring, and enforcement by non-violent methods. In fact, as the studies reviewed here indicate, if discipline takes the form of more corporal punishment, the problem will be exacerbated because, while corporal punishment does work with some children, more typically it boomerangs and increases the level of juvenile delinquency and other behavior problems.

The criticism in scientific journals of research on corporal punishment is also not a backlash. It has to be viewed in the light of the norms of science. A standard aspect of science is to examine research critically, to raise questions, and to suggest alternative interpretations of findings. This results in a somewhat paradoxical tendency for criticism to increase as the amount of research goes up. There has recently been an increase in research showing long-term harmful effects of corporal punishment. Given the critical ethos of science, it is only to be expected that the increased research has elicited more commentary and criticism, especially on the part of those who believed in corporal punishment in the first place.

### Three Paradoxes About Corporal Punishment

Three paradoxical aspects of the movement away from corporal punishment are worth noting. The first is that, although approval of corporal punishment had declined precipitously in the last generation, almost all parents continue to spank toddlers. The second paradox is that professionals advising parents, including those who are opposed to spanking, generally fail to tell parents not to spank. They call this avoiding a "negative approach." Finally, and most paradoxically of all, focusing almost exclusively on a so-called "positive approach," unwittingly contributes to perpetuating corporal punishment and helps explain the first paradox.

*Paradox 1: Contradictory Trends.* Some aspects of corporal punishment have changed in major ways. A smaller and smaller percent of the public favors spanking (Straus and Mathur, 1996). Fewer parents now use belts, hairbrushes and paddles. The percent of parents who hit adolescents has dropped by half since 1975. Nevertheless, other aspects of corporal punishment continue to be prevalent, chronic, and severe. The 1995 Gallup national survey of parents (Straus and Stewart, 1999) found that:

- Almost all parents of toddlers (94 percent) used corporal punishment that year
- Parents who spanked a toddler, did it an average of about three times a week
- 28 percent of parents of children age 5–12 used an object such as a belt or hairbrush
- Over a third of parents of 13-year-old children hit them that year

The myths about corporal punishment in *Beating The Devil Out Of Them* provide important clues to understanding why parents who "don't believe in spanking" continue to do so. These myths also undermine the ability of professionals who advise parents to do what is needed to end corporal punishment.

*Paradox 2: Opposing Spanking but Failing to Say Don't Spank.* Many pediatricians, developmental psychologists, and parent educators are now opposed to corporal punishment, at least in principle. But most also continue to believe that there may be a situation where spanking by parents is necessary or acceptable (Schenck, 2000). This is based on cultural myths. One myth is that spanking works when other things do not. Another is that "mild" corporal punishment is harmless. All but a small minority of parents and professionals continue to believe these myths despite the experimental and other evidence showing that other disciplinary strategies work just as well as spanking, even in the short run and are more effective in the long run as shown by the first four of the studies described earlier in this article.

Consequently, when I suggest to pediatricians, parent educators, or social scientists that it is essential to tell parents that they should never spank or use any other type of corporal punishment, with rare exception, that idea has been rejected. Some, like one of America's leading developmental psychologists, object because of the unproven belief that it would turn off parents. Some object on the false belief that it could be harmful because parents do not know what else to do. They argue for a "positive approach" by which they mean teaching parents alternative disciplinary strategies, as compared to what they call the "negative approach" of advising to never spank. As a result, the typical pattern is to say nothing about spanking. Fortunately, that is slowly changing. Although they are still the exception, an increasing number of books for parents, parent education programs, and guidelines for professionals advise never-spanking.

Both the movement away from spanking, and an important limitation of that movement are illustrated by publication of the "Guidelines For Effective Discipline" of the American Academy of Pediatrics. This was an important step forward, but it also reflects the same problem. It recommends that parents avoid corporal punishment. However, it also carefully avoids saying that parents should *never* spank. This may seem like splitting hairs, but because of the typical sequence of parent-child interaction that eventuates in corporal punishment described in the next paragraph, it is a major obstacle to ending corporal punishment. Omitting a never-spank message is a serious obstacle because, in the absence of a commitment to never-spank, even parents who are against spanking continue to spank. It is important to understand what underlies the paradox of parents who are opposed to spanking, nonetheless spanking.

*Paradox 3: Failing To Be Explicit Against Spanking Results in More Spanking.* The paradox that fewer and fewer parents are in favor of spanking, but almost all spank toddlers reflects a combination of needing to cope with the typical behavior of toddlers and perceiving those behaviors through the lens of the myth that spanking works when other things do not.

When toddlers are corrected for misbehavior (such as hitting another child or disobeying), the "recidivism" rate is about 80 percent within the same day and about 50 percent within two hours. For some children it is within two minutes. One researcher (who is a defender of corporal punishment) found that these "time to failure" rates apply equally to corporal punishment and to other disciplinary strategies (Larzelere, et al., 1996). Consequently, on any given day, a parent is almost certain to find that so-called alternative disciplinary strategies such as explaining, deprivation of privileges and time out, "do not work." When that happens, they turn to spanking. So, as pointed out previously, just about everyone (at least 94 percent) spanks toddlers.

The difference between spanking and other disciplinary strategies is that, when spanking does not work, parents do not question its effectiveness. The idea that spanking works when other methods do not is so ingrained in American culture that, when the child repeats the misbehavior an hour or two later (or sometimes a few minutes later) parents fail to perceive that spanking has the same high failure rate as other modes of discipline. So they spank again, and for as many times as it takes to ultimately secure compliance. That is the correct strategy because, with consistency and perseverance, the child will eventually learn. What so many parents miss is that it is also the correct strategy for non-spanking methods. Thus, unless there is an absolute prohibition on spanking, parents will "see with their own eyes" that alternatives do not work and continue to find it is necessary to spank.

## "Never-Spank" Must Be The Message

Because of the typical behavior of toddlers and the almost inevitable information processing errors just described, teaching alternative disciplinary techniques by itself is not sufficient. There must also be an unambiguous "never-spank" message, which is needed to increase the chances that parents who disapprove of spanking will act on their beliefs. Consequently, it is essential for pediatricians and others who advise parents to abandon their reluctance to say "never-spank." To achieve this, parent-educators must themselves be educated. They need to understand why, what they now consider a "negative approach," is such an important part of ending the use of corporal punishment. Moreover, because they believe that a "negative approach" does not work, they also need to know about the experience of Sweden. The Swedish experience shows that, contrary to the currently prevailing opinion, a never-spank approach has worked (Durrant, 1999).

In short, the first priority step to end or reduce spanking may be to educate professionals who advise parents. Once professionals are ready to move, the key steps are relatively easy to implement and inexpensive.

> Parent-education programs, such as STEP, which are now silent on spanking, can be revised to include the evidence that spanking does *not* work better than other disciplinary tactics, even in the short run; and to specifically say "*never* spank."

> The Public Health Service can follow the Swedish model and sponsor no-spanking public service announcements on TV and on milk cartons.
>
> There can be a "No-Spanking" poster and pamphlets in every pediatrician's office and every maternity ward.

There could be a notice on birth certificates such as:

> WARNING: SPANKING HAS BEEN DETERMINED TO BE DANGEROUS TO THE HEALTH AND WELL BEING OF YOUR CHILD—**DO NOT EVER, UNDER ANY CIRCUMSTANCES, SPANK OR HIT YOUR CHILD**

Until professionals who advise parents start advising parents to *never* spank, the paradox of parents becoming less and less favorable to spanking while at the same continuing to spank toddlers will continue. Fortunately, that is starting to happen.

The benefits of avoiding corporal punishment are many, but they are virtually impossible for parents to perceive by observing their children. The situation with spanking is parallel to that of smoking. Smokers could perceive the short run satisfaction from a cigarette, but had no way to see the adverse health consequences down the road. Similarly, parents can perceive the beneficial effects of a slap (and, for the reasons explained in the previous section, fail to see the equal effectiveness of alternatives), they have no way of looking a year or more into the future to see if there is a harmful side effect of having hit their child to correct misbehavior. The only way parents can know this would be if there were a public policy to publicize the results of research such as the studies summarized in this article.

Another reason the benefits of avoiding spanking are difficult to see is that they are not dramatic in any one case. This is illustrated by the average increase of 3 or 4 points in mental ability associated with no-corporal punishment. An increase of that size would hardly be noticed in an individual case. However, it is a well established principle in public health and epidemiology that a widely prevalent risk factor with small effect size, for example spanking, can have a much greater impact on public health than a risk factor with a large effect size, but low prevalence, for example, physical abuse. For example, assume that: (1) 50 million US children experienced CP and 1 million experienced physical abuse. (2) The probability of being depressed as an adult is increased by 2 percent for children who experienced CP and by 25 percent for children who experienced physical abuse. Given these assumptions, the additional cases of depression caused by CP is 1.02 times 50 million, or 1 million. The additional cases of depression caused by physical abuse is 1.25 time 1 million or 250,000. Thus CP is associated with a four times greater increase in depression than is physical abuse.

Another example of a major benefit resulting from reducing a risk factor that has a small effect, but for a large proportion of the population, might be the increase in scores on intelligence tests that has been occurring worldwide. Corporal punishment has also been decreasing worldwide. The decrease in use of corporal punishment and the increase in scores in IQ tests could be just a coincidence. However, the results of the study described earlier in this article which showed that less spanking is associated with faster cognitive development suggest that the trend away from corporal punishment may be one of a number of social changes (especially, better educated parents) that explain the increase in IQ scores in so many nations.

The other four prospective studies reviewed in this article and the studies in *Beating the Devil Out of Them* show that ending corporal punishment is likely to also reduce juvenile violence, wife-beating, and masochistic sex, and increase the probability of completing higher education, holding a high income job, and lower rates of depression and alcohol abuse. Those are not only humanitarian benefits, they can also result in huge monetary savings in public and private costs for dealing with mental health problems, and crime.

I concluded the first edition of *Beating the Devil Out of Them* in 1994 by suggesting that ending corporal punishment by parents "portends profound and far reaching benefits for humanity." The new research summarized in this article makes those words even more appropriate. We can look forward to the day when children in almost all countries have the benefit of being brought up without being hit by their parents; and just as important, to the day when many nations have the benefit of the healthier, wealthier, and wiser citizens who were brought up free from the violence that is now a part of their earliest and most influential life experiences.

### *Suggested Further Readings*

Brezina, Timothy. 1999. "Teenage violence toward parents as an adaptation to family strain: Evidence from a national survey of male adolescents." *Youth & Society* 30: 416–444.

Durrant, Joan E. 1999. "Evaluating the success of Sweden's corporal punishment ban." *Child Abuse & Neglect* 23: 435–448.

Gershoff, Elizabeth Thompson. In press. "Corporal punishment by parents and associated child behaviors and experiences: A meta-analytic and theoretical review." *Psychological Bulletin.*

Gunnoe, Marjorie L., and Carrie L. Mariner. 1997. "Toward a developmental-contextual model of the effects of parental spanking on children's aggression." *Archives of Pediatric and Adolescent Medicine* 151: 768–775.

Larzelere, Robert E., William N. Schneider, David B. Larson, and Patricia L. Pike. 1996. "The effects of discipline responses in delaying toddler misbehavior recurrences." *Child and Family Therapy* 18: 35–37.

Neisser, Ulric. 1997. "Rising scores on intelligence tests: Test scores are certainly going up all over the world, but whether intelligence itself has risen remains controversial." *American Scientist* 85: 440–447.

Schenck, Eliza R., Robert D. Lyman, and S. Douglas Bodin. 2000. "Ethical beliefs, attitudes, and professional practices of psychologists regarding parental use of corporal punishment: A survey." *Children's Services: Social Policy, Research, and Practice* 3: 23–38.

Simons, Ronald L., Kuei-Hsiu Lin, and Leslie C. Gordon. 1998. "Socialization in the Family of origin and male dating violence: A prospective study." *Journal of Marriage and the Family* 60: 467–478.

Straus, Murray A., and Anitia K. Mathur. 1996. "Social change and change in approval of corporal punishment by parents from 1968 to 1994." Pp. 91–105 in *Family violence against children: A challenge for society.*, edited by D. Frehsee, W. Horn, and K-D Bussmann, New York: Walter deGruyter.

Straus, Murray A., and Mallie J. Paschall. 1999. "Corporal punishment by mothers and children's cognitive development: A longitudinal study of two age cohorts." in *6th International Family Violence Research Conference.* Durham, NH: Family Research Laboratory, University of New Hampshire.

Straus, Murray A., and Julie H. Stewart. 1999. "Corporal punishment by American parents: National data on prevalence, chronicity, severity, and duration, in relation to child, and family characteristics." *Clinical Child and Family Psychology Review* 2: 55–70.

Straus, Murray A., David B. Sugarman, and Jean Giles-Sims. 1997. "Spanking by parents and subsequent antisocial behavior of children." *Archives of pediatric and adolescent medicine* 151: 761–767.

---

*Murray A. Straus is professor of sociology and co-director of the Family Research Laboratory at the University of New Hampshire. He is the author or coauthor or editor of 18 books including* Stress, Culture, and Aggression. *This article is adapted from Chapter 12 of* Beating the Devil Out of Them: Corporal Punishment in American Families and Its Effects on Children, *2nd edition, published by Transaction.*

# Father Nature: The Making of a Modern Dad

It takes a lot more than testosterone to make a father out of a man. New research shows that hormonal changes in both sexes help shape men into devoted dads. If testosterone is the defining hormone of masculinity, it's time to redefine manhood.

**By Douglas Carlton Abrams**

"One of my first memories growing up was wishing that my father would be home more," recalls Andrew Hudnut, M.D., a family doctor in Sacramento, California. "I was 8, and we had just returned from a canoe trip. I remember thinking, 'I don't want a bigger house or more money. I just want my dad around.'"

When his wife gave birth, Hudnut arranged his practice so he could be home to take care of his son, Seamus, two days a week; he sees patients on the other three workdays. "It was a very natural transition," he reports. "I'm grateful to have the opportunity my father never had."

Part of a new generation of men who are redefining fatherhood and masculinity, Hudnut, who is 33, is unwilling to accept the role of absentee provider that his father's generation assumed. With mothers often being the breadwinners of the family, many young fathers are deciding that a man's place can also be in the home—part-time or even full-time.

According to census figures, one in four dads takes care of his preschooler during the time the mother is working. The number of children who are raised by a primary-care father is now more than 2 million and counting. By all measures, fathers, even those who work full-time, are more involved in their children's lives than ever before. According to the Families and Work Institute in New York City, fathers now provide three-fourths of the child care mothers do, up from one-half 30 years ago.

### Is Father Nurture Natural?

Many men and women wonder if all of this father care is really natural. According to popular perceptions, men are supposedly driven by their hormones (primarily testosterone) to compete for status, to seek out sex and even to be violent—conditions hardly conducive to raising kids. A recent article in *Reader's Digest,* "Why Men Act As They Do," is subtitled "It's the Testosterone, Stupid." Calling the hormone "a metaphor for masculinity," the article concludes, "...testosterone correlates with risk—physical, criminal, personal." Don't men's testosterone-induced chest-beating and risk-taking limit their ability to cradle and comfort their children?

Two new Canadian studies suggest that there is much more to masculinity than testosterone. While testosterone is certainly important in driving men to conceive a child, it takes an array of other hormones to turn men into fathers. And among the best fathers, it turns out, testosterone levels actually drop significantly after the birth of a child. If manhood includes fatherhood, which it does for a majority of men, then testosterone is hardly the ultimate measure of masculinity.

In fact, the second of the two studies, which was recently published in the *Mayo Clinic Proceedings,* suggests that fathers have higher levels of estrogen—the well-known female sex hormone—than other men. The research shows that men go through significant hormonal changes alongside their pregnant partners, changes most likely initiated

## The Daddy Dividend

Beyond birth and infancy, researchers are finding, a father's presence makes a big difference in a child's long-term development. Ross Parke, Ph.D., a psychologist at the University of California at Riverside, explains that children of involved fathers regulate their own emotions better.

They also have better social skills than children whose fathers are not involved in their lives and have better success in school. "It is clear that fathers affect their children's social, cognitive and emotional development," he says.

A father's influence seems to come, at least in part, through the unique ways that fathers play and interact with their children, says Kyle Pruett, M.D., a child psychiatrist at Yale. "Fathers are more likely to encourage their kids to tolerate frustration and master tasks on their own before they offer help," he explains, "whereas mothers tend to assist a fussing child earlier."

More than any particular social or cognitive skill, however, a father's love and affection may be the most significant gift he can give his children, says Ronald Rohner, Ph.D., a psychologist-anthropologist at the University of Connecticut, who for the past 40 years has been studying the effects of father love on children's development. "A father's love is often a significant buffer against depression, conduct problems and substance abuse," he finds.

"Children who experience their father's love are often more emotionally stable, less angry, have better self-esteem and have a more positive worldview," Rohner says. To his surprise, he discovered that "father love is often as influential as mother love on a child's happiness and sense of well-being." Rohner and his colleagues reviewed 100 U.S. and European studies; their results can be found in the *Review of General Psychology*.

Although researchers are just beginning to study the children of involved fathers, there is a mountain of research on the children of absent fathers. Those children are at a higher risk for school failure and dropout, drug use, teen pregnancy, delinquency and teen suicide. Fathers clearly play an important role in the psychological and social survival of their kids. —D. A.

by their partner's pregnancy and ones that even cause some men to experience pregnancylike symptoms such as nausea and weight gain. It seems increasingly clear that just as nature prepares women to be committed moms, it prepares men to be devoted dads.

"I have always suspected that fatherhood has biological effects in some, perhaps all, men," says biologist Sue Carter, Ph.D., distinguished professor at the University of Maryland. "Now here is the first hard evidence that men are biologically prepared for fatherhood."

The new studies have the potential to profoundly change our understanding of families, of fatherhood and of masculinity itself. Being a devoted parent is not only important but also natural for men. Indeed, there is evidence that men are biologically involved in their children's lives from the beginning.

### Is Biology Destiny for Dads?

It's well known that hormonal changes caused by pregnancy encourage a mother to love and nurture her child. But it has long been assumed that a father's attachment to his child is the result of a more uncertain process, a purely optional emotional bonding that develops over time, often years.

Male animals in some species undergo hormonal changes that prime them for parenting. But do human dads? The two studies, conducted at Memorial University and Queens University in Canada, suggest that human dads do.

In the original study published last year in *Evolution and Human Behavior,* psychologist Anne Storey, Ph.D., and her colleagues took blood samples from 34 couples at different times during pregnancy and shortly after birth. The researchers chose to monitor three specific hormones because of their links to nurturing behavior in human mothers and in animal fathers.

The first hormone, prolactin, gets its name from the role it plays in promoting lactation in women, but it also instigates parental behavior in a number of birds and mammals. Male doves who are given prolactin start brooding and feeding their young. Storey found that in human fathers, prolactin levels rise by approximately 20 percent during the three weeks before their partners give birth.

"THIS IS THE FIRST EVIDENCE THAT MEN ARE BIOLOGICALLY PREPARED FOR FATHERHOOD."

The second hormone, cortisol, is well known as a stress hormone, but it is also a good indicator of a mother's attachment to her baby. New mothers who have high cortisol levels can detect their own infant by odor more easily than mothers with lower cortisol levels. The mothers also respond more sympathetically to their baby's cries and describe their relationship with their baby in more positive terms. Storey and her colleagues found that for expectant fathers, cortisol was twice as high in the three weeks before birth than earlier in the pregnancy.

Biologist Katherine Wynne-Edwards, Ph.D., who conducted the research with Storey explains that while cortisol is seen as the "fight or flight" hormone, it might more accurately be described as the "heads-up-eyes-forward-something-really-important-is-happening" hormone. It may help prepare parents for approaching birth. Cortisol levels normally increase in women as pregnancy advances; indeed, a cumulative rise in stress-hormone levels sets off labor and delivery.

The third hormone, testosterone, is abundant in male animals during mating but decreases during nurturing. If bird fathers are given testosterone, they spend more time defending their territory and mating than taking care of exist-

## Hormones vs. Culture By Michael Lamb, Ph.D.

The view that fathers are reluctant caregivers may be a thing of the past. New findings show that hormonal changes of parenting are not limited to mothers. The reason we haven't discovered the hormonal changes in human fathers before now lies in a combination of scientific progress and cultural change.

Early studies on rats found that males could learn to become involved fathers after prolonged exposure to their pups but did not experience any hormonal changes. The fact that these reluctant dads could learn to nurture led to the so-called bonding hypothesis. It claimed that fathers, including human fathers, could *learn* to become competent caregivers.

But changes in mothers' work roles have forced a redefinition of fathers' nurturing roles. When I began studying families in the mid-1970s, half the fathers had never changed a diaper. Now, most dads do diaper duty. A father's role is increasingly multifaceted. He is, ideally, a breadwinner, a coach, a moral guide, a source of love and inspiration.

Here's the shocking news: In 90 percent of birds and the majority of fish, fathers care for the young. Mammals are the only major group of vertebrates in which mothers are more involved. Among mammals, 90 percent of fathers take off after conception or birth. But the offspring usually are either self-sufficient from the start or can survive with the sole care of the mother.

So why should human dads stick around and burp a baby? It turns out there's a big evolutionary advantage for the kids who get coddled.

Father care seems to boost the chances of survival significantly for human babies. Born helpless and dependent, babies demand an enormous amount of care. Having two parents to provide food and protection increases the odds an infant will function well and make it to adulthood.

Most children today survive physically, whether or not they have an involved father. But this may not have always been the case. In hunter-gatherer cultures the presence of a father counted heavily.

Even in advanced industrial societies, where food and physical survival are rarely the issue, social survival still is. Children who grow up without their fathers are at greater risk for everything from school failure to teen suicide (see "The Daddy Dividend").

So why, if fathers have a hormonal connection to their children, aren't all fathers more involved dads? "There are cultural scripts that have precluded fathers from being involved," observes Jay Belsky, Ph.D., a psychologist at the University of London. "A generation ago fathers weren't allowed into birthing rooms and didn't change diapers. When social norms work against father involvement, hormones may have less of an effect on their actual behavior." Men have moderate to high contact with infants in only 40 percent of cultures, according to an international survey.

In other words, humans aren't held in hormonal thrall—research suggests that hormones simply facilitate a transition into fatherhood. The definition of that fatherhood will no doubt depend on culture.

*Michael Lamb, Ph.D., is at the National Institute of Child Health and Human Development.*

ing offspring. Research has shown that human males experience a surge in testosterone when they win sporting events and other competitions.

> "MY BEST GUESS IS THAT WOMEN'S HORMONE LEVELS ARE TIMED TO THE BIRTH—AND MEN'S HORMONE LEVELS ARE TIED TO THEIR PARTNERS"

In Storey's study, testosterone levels plunged 33 percent in fathers during the first three weeks after birth. Levels then returned to normal by the time the babies were four to seven weeks old. However brief the dip in testosterone, it may have effects that endure for the life of the child. According to University of California at Riverside psychologist Ross Parke, Ph.D., it may "let the nurturing side of men come to center stage." The dip may set in motion the more-cooperative, less-competitive enterprise of parenting. By encouraging fathers to interact with their kids, the brief hormonal change might actually induce the bonding process.

### Estrogen and the Daddy Brain

Wynne-Edwards and graduate student Sandra Berg designed another, just-published study to test Storey and Wynne-Edwards' earlier findings. They measured the hormone levels of the fathers over a longer period of time and incorporated into the study a control group of men who had never had children. The control group was matched by age, season and time of day tested—all of which can affect hormone levels. Finally, by using saliva samples instead of blood draws, they were able to test the fathers and the men in the control group much more frequently.

In addition to confirming the earlier findings for testosterone reduction and cortisol change the researchers also found that the fathers had elevated levels of estrogen. The increase started 30 days before birth and continued during all 12 weeks of testing after birth. Although estrogen is best known as a female sex hormone, it exists in small quantities in men, too. Animal studies show that estrogen can induce nurturing behavior in males.

Acting in the brain as well as in other parts of the body, estrogen in men, and testosterone in women, makes humans extremely versatile behaviorally. "We spend an awful lot of time looking for differences between the sexes and trumpeting them when we find them," observes Wynne-Edwards, "but our brains are remarkably similar, but from the same DNA."

In fact, going into the study, Wynne-Edwards predicted that the "daddy brain" would use the same nerve circuits, triggered by many of the same hormones, as the "mommy brain." "If Mother Nature wanted to turn on parental behavior in a male," she reasoned, "the easiest thing would be to turn on pathways already there for maternal behavior."

The studies also found that a father's hormonal changes closely paralleled those of his pregnant partner.

### The Intimacy Effect

The researchers believe that intimate contact and communication between partners may induce the hormonal changes that encourage a father to nurture his children, Storey explains. "My best guess is that women's hormone levels are timed to the birth—and men's hormone levels are tied to their partners."

Exactly how this occurs is unknown. There may be actual physiological signals exchanged between partners in close contact, such as the transmission of pheromones. Similar to odors, pheromones are volatile chemical substances that animals constantly give off through their skin or sweat but that are undetectable. Pheromones can stimulate specific reactions—especially mating—in other animals. Think of a female dog in heat attracting all those barking male dogs in the neighborhood.

Classic studies show that menstruation is communicated, and synchronized, through pheromones among dorm mates in college. If women in dorms respond to one another's pheromones, then a man and a woman who share intimate space could certainly communicate chemical messages. These pheromones could biologically cue a man that his partner is pregnant and kick off the hormonal changes that prompt him to be a dad in deed as well as in seed. Pregnancy certainly could, in fact, be signaled.

The level of intimacy within a couple seems to be a factor in how a mother's body chemically signals approaching birth to a father. All of the men tested were living with their pregnant partners. Emotional closeness may also generate hormonal changes, although the possibility was not examined in detail. Still, couples reported feeling closer to their partner if they were talking about the baby and sharing details about the pregnancy.

Whether this is the cause or the result of hormonal changes remains unknown for now. But the intimacy effect and the subsequent hormonal shifts may also be the reason many men experience pregnancylike symptoms.

### Honey, We're Pregnant

When he is not taking care of Seamus, Hudnut treats both men and women in his practice. He recalls several patients who came to him complaining of such typical pregnancy symptoms as weight gain and nausea—all of whom were men. He remembers one second-time father who knew that his wife was pregnant even before she told him: He started having morning sickness, just as he had during her first pregnancy.

Pregnancy symptoms in men are actually more common than most people believe. Two studies found that approximately 90 percent of men experience at least one pregnancy related symptom, sometimes severe enough to prompt an expectant father to seek medical help.

According to a study reported in *Annals of Internal Medicine,* more than 20 percent of men with pregnant wives sought care for symptoms related to pregnancy "that could not otherwise be objectively explained." Unfortunately, like pregnancy symptoms in women, there is little that can be done to make the symptoms go away—except wait.

"PREGNANCY SYMPTOMS IN MEN ARE GENERALLY DISMISSED AS BEING ALL IN THE FATHER-TO-BE'S HEAD, NOW IT SEEMS THEY MAY ALSO BE IN HIS HORMONES"

Pregnancy symptoms in men, however well documented, are generally dismissed as being all in the father-to-be's head. Now it seems they may also be in his hormones. Storey and her colleagues found that the men who experienced more pregnancy symptoms actually had higher levels of prolactin. They also had a greater reduction in testosterone after exposure to sounds of crying and other "infant cues" that simulated the experience of being with an actual baby.

For men who feel nauseated or gain weight, no one yet knows for sure whether the changes in hormones are to blame. Surging hormones, however, have long been blamed for women's morning sickness and other pregnancy side effects. The fact that men also experience hormone changes suggests it is more than empathy that causes many of them to feel their partner's pain.

### Changed by a Child

While it now seems a father may accompany his wife on her hormonal roller coaster during pregnancy, interacting with the baby may keep his hormones spinning even after the birth.

It's no secret that hormone levels can change in response to behavior. Sex, sports and work success can all send testosterone production spiraling upward. Might not nurturing a child—or conversely, the sight, sound and smell of a newborn—also change fathers' levels of testosterone?

In the original study, the researchers asked couples to hold dolls that had been wrapped in receiving blankets worn by a newborn within the preceding 24 hours. (After their wives gave birth, fathers held their actual baby.) They listened to a six-minute tape of a real newborn crying and then watched a video of a baby struggling to breast feed. The investigators took blood from the men and women before the test and 30 minutes later.

What they found is startling. Men who expressed the greatest desire to comfort the crying baby had the highest prolactin levels and the greatest reduction in testosterone. And testosterone levels plummeted in those men who held the doll for the full half-hour.

Even though scientists have long observed changes in animal and human behavior as a result of shifting hormone levels, they do not yet understand exactly how hormones accomplish such changes. The hormone-behavior link remains one of the great mysteries of the brain. Perhaps hormones stimulate more neuron connections in the part of the brain responsible for nurturing. Or perhaps hormones encourage neurons in nurturing pathways to fire more quickly.

Wynne-Edwards thinks hormones might turn a two-lane pathway in the father's brain into a four-lane superhighway. A neural road expansion might make fathers better able to recognize the smell or sound of their baby. It might even act on smell receptors in the nose to mitigate the smell of a baby's dirty diaper. Countless are the ways in which hormones could influence a father's brain to be more responsive to his baby.

## Home on the Range

Although testosterone may be the "primary" male sex hormone, the new research makes it clear that other hormones are also significant, especially during the transition into fatherhood. Wynne-Edwards believes the new research is "a validation of the experiences that many men know they have had. It also goes a long way to bumping testosterone off its pedestal as the only hormone that is important to men."

Parke believes that the research suggests something even more radical: "Men are much more androgynous than we think. We have the capability to be aggressive and nurturing. The traditional view of men as predominantly aggressive really sells men short and denies their capability to experience the range of human emotions."

The new research suggests that a man's hormones may play an important role in helping him experience this full range of emotions, especially in becoming a loving and devoted dad. In fact, it offers the first evidence that to nurture is part of a man's nature.

---

*Douglas Carlton Abrams writes frequently on men, sexuality and parenting. He has recently completed* Touching the Moon: A Boy, His Father, and the Discovery of Wonder, *a manuscript about his experiences as a primary care parent.*

# What about Black Fathers?

## By placing so much emphasis on marriage, public policy could set back efforts to bring unmarried fathers into more constructive contact with their children.

BY RONALD B. MINCY

EMBOLDENED BY THE REDUCTION IN THE WELFARE ROLLS, conservatives have renewed their demands that our welfare system reflect traditional family values, specifically marriage. But if marriage becomes the heavily favored family strategy of welfare policy, family-service providers and other supporters of responsible fatherhood will find it harder to help families as they actually exist—families that are not always headed by married couples.

President Bush, an outspoken supporter of strong marriages, has responded to this conservative social agenda with several policy initiatives. First, the administration's new welfare-reform proposal adds a few key words to the fourth goal of the 1996 welfare-reform act: "to encourage the formation and maintenance of healthy two-parent *married* families and responsible fatherhood [emphasis added]." Next, it dedicates $300 million in federal funds to support marriage-promotion efforts. Then, the plan encourages states to provide (pared-down) child support and commits the federal government to share in the costs.

This proposal may soften the opposition from some women's groups to the marriage emphasis. However, the plan only pays lip service to responsible fatherhood and provides no dedicated federal funds to support such efforts. Thus, responsible-fatherhood groups will have to rely exclusively upon Temporary Assistance for Needy Families or other state funds, for which there are many competing priorities.

Anticipating this new political and policy climate, several fatherhood groups that work in predominantly black communities are preparing to expand services to include marriage. The most important and innovative groups include the Center for Fathers, Families and Workforce Development (CFWD), the National Center for Strategic Nonprofit Planning and Community Leadership (NPCL), and the Institute for Responsible Fatherhood and Family Revitalization (IRFFR).

CFWD is a community-based responsible-fatherhood program that also provides job placement and wage- and career-growth services to disadvantaged fathers in Baltimore. The goal is to encourage fathers, whether married or not, to become more involved in their children's lives, both emotionally and financially, and to develop a better relationship with the child's mother. NPCL is a national intermediary organization that has trained more than 2,500 community-based practitioners and agencies that sponsor them. It works, through federally funded demonstration projects, to combine child-support enforcement and workforce-development efforts in support of fragile families, so that fathers have both the means and the commitment to contribute to the support of their children. The organization's recent international conference brought together more than 1,200 responsible fatherhood practitioners from the United States and around the globe. Both organizations are now developing marriage curricula. IRFFR, founded in the 1980s, is perhaps the oldest community-based responsible-fatherhood program in the country. These groups, and others with roots in the black community, did not need to be persuaded by the current political climate that marriage was vital to rebuilding strong black families.

Some observers may accuse them of opportunism or of selling out to the conservative agenda. However, few of these groups opposed marriage in principle, though they did object when the early rhetoric made marriage seem like a panacea—and when proposals began to surface to make marriage a condition of services or bonus payments. The rhetoric has now become more reasonable. The Bush administration intends to promote "healthy, stable, and happy marriages" and will target its marriage-promotion efforts at couples who choose to receive such services. Like most Americans, black fatherhood groups support this and wish that all the unwed parents who come to them for help were in a position to benefit from such services. As Andrew Billingsley points out in his book *Climbing Jacob's Ladder*, blacks generally have strong family values; however, they often struggle under difficult conditions that make it tough to act on those values. For this reason, Billingsley argues, black communities have had more diverse and complex family systems than whites for as long as blacks have been in this country.

## UNMARRIED BUT NOT UNINVOLVED

Fatherhood groups who work in low-income black communities see this diversity and complexity every day. They also know that many young unwed parents, especially fathers, simply are unprepared to assume the responsibilities that would produce the kind of marriages that increase child well-being. For this reason, these groups have expanded their services to help fathers make positive contributions to their children, even while unmarried, and to position themselves to assume the responsibilities that would make it possible for them to one day sustain happy marriages. The new services focus on job retention, wage and career growth, and job placement. Besides employment services, groups are providing legal, educational, team-parenting, substance-abuse, child-support, health, mental-health, spouse-abuse, and other services to meet the needs of clients and their families. They are also improving their capacity to measure program outcomes and diversifying their staff or strengthening existing staff, in hopes that welfare reauthorization would provide additional resources to improve their work with fathers and families. These efforts are consistent with the 1996 goal of encouraging the formation and maintenance of two-parent families.

BUT NOW THE BUSH ADMINISTRATION HAS RAISED THE standard to emphasize marriage per se. And responsible-fatherhood groups that seek to promote marriage in predominantly black communities will find it hard to achieve this higher standard for several reasons. First, there are demographic realities. The percentage of black women of childbearing age (say, 15 to 44 years old) who have never married (41 percent) is just about double the percentage of comparable white women. Second, although cohabitation and unwed births have been rising while marriage has been declining among all race and ethnic groups, these trends are far from convergent for whites, blacks, and other groups.

For example, unwed births are more common among cohabiting Puerto Rican women than among black or non-Hispanic white women. However, an unwed first birth hastens the transition to marriage among non-Hispanic white cohabiting women, has no effect on the transition to marriage among black cohabiting women, and reduces the prospects of marriage among Puerto Rican cohabiting women.

Given these apparent differences in family formation by race and ethnicity, our research team at Columbia University and Princeton University has been using data from a new birth cohort survey to study the likely effects of the administration's approach on black and nonblack children and families. We assume that marriage is the best option even for the children of unwed parents, if only because marriages tend to last longer than cohabiting relationships. However, we also acknowledge the diversity of family systems. In particular, we acknowledge that in black communities (both here and abroad), father-child contact often occurs through nonresidential, visiting relationships between unwed parents, which are less stable than cohabiting relationships. This means that, unlike traditional models of family formation, unwed parents have four options to choose from: no father-child contact, some father-child contact, cohabitation, and marriage. Moreover, it turns out that Billingsley's metaphor powerfully predicts what could happen if the Bush administration's marriage initiatives could be used flexibly to strengthen families, because these options resemble a ladder leading to more intense and enduring forms of father-child contact.

That is, policies often have unintended effects. Thus, the responses of some unwed parents to policies that promote marriage may fall short of the administration's ideal but still result in more intense and enduring forms of father-child contact than would have occurred otherwise. For example, throughout the past two decades, the fraction of low-skilled men who are either working or looking for work has shrunk, despite strong economic growth interrupted by brief recessions. If welfare programs were able to help these men find jobs, some fathers who are not now in regular contact with their children might begin to be. Other fathers who now visit their children might live with them. And still other fathers who are living with their children (and their children's mother) would be married. Moreover, such a policy might have large effects on family formation and father-child contact for black unwed parents and, to a lesser extent, for nonblack unwed parents. Other policies might have the same effects on family formation and father-child contact for black and nonblack unwed parents.

## STRENGTHENING FAMILIES AS THEY EXIST

Our study shows that fathers' employment benefits black and nonblack children, no matter where their parents begin on the ladder to more intense and enduring forms of father-child contact. Compared with children whose fathers did not work, children with working fathers were more likely to have some contact with their fathers, more likely to live with their fathers (and mothers in cohabiting relationships), and more likely to live with their fathers in a traditional married family. Having children with one partner rather than multiple partners also increases the odds of maintaining relationships with children, all the way up the ladder, in black and nonblack families alike. However, a mother's work history prior to giving birth increases the odds of cohabitation and marriage among black unwed parents but has no statistically significant effect on the odds of moving up the ladder for nonblacks. Thus, by providing employment services (for men as well as women) and an emphasis on preventing out-of-wedlock births, welfare policy could increase marriage and other forms of father-child contact for blacks and increase (or leave unchanged) the same outcomes for nonblacks.

Other policies would affect these groups or outcomes differently. Higher cash benefits increase the odds that black and nonblack fragile families have some father-child contact and the odds that they cohabit, but have no effect on the odds that they marry. By contrast, more effective child-support enforcement increases the odds of marriage among nonblacks but reduces the odds of father-child contact, without affecting the odds of marriage among blacks.

UNFORTUNATELY, THESE PROMISING POLICY INSTRUMENTS have been sidelined in the current debate. Instead, the administration is placing its entire emphasis on promoting marriage. Our research suggests such efforts would produce mixed results. They might encourage some unwed mothers to marry. We find, for example, that nonblack unwed mothers with some religious affiliation are more likely to marry the fathers of their children than those without a religious affiliation. Black unwed mothers affiliated with faith communities that hold conservative views on family issues are more likely to marry the fathers of their children than are black unwed mothers with no religious affiliation.

However, great caution is required before black communities would embrace such approaches—because the approaches are likely to celebrate the virtues of marriage while stigmatizing unwed births, something blacks traditionally have not done because of historical experience. Although rates have risen in recent decades, single motherhood has been much more common among black families for more than 100 years. The reasons for this are complex. Some black women became single mothers because they (and the fathers of their children) violated social and religious prohibitions against nonmarital sex. Others became single mothers because they were raped or their husbands were lynched. Still others became single mothers because their husbands migrated north in search of employment but never returned after job discrimination dashed their hopes.

Often in the painful history of race relations in this country, desertion and victimization were as likely the causes of single motherhood as was moral failure. In any individual case, who could know? Who would ask? In response, the black community developed a tradition of embracing all of its children, even the fair-skinned ones. Under these circumstances, stigmatizing unwed births was impossible. Fortunately, in many respects the circumstances have changed.

THERE IS MOUNTING EVIDENCE THAT CHILDREN ARE BETTER off if they grow up in healthy, married-couple families. This poses a unique challenge for the black community, because the substantial retreat from marriage in the black community has created extraordinarily high rates of childbearing and child rearing among unwed blacks. Marriage proponents would be wise to let this evidence prick the conscience of the nation with this question: How did we allow childbirth and child rearing to divorce themselves from marriage? The diverse race and ethnic groups that now constitute America will have different answers—and different strategies for creating or re-creating the most supportive family arrangements for children.

As they wrestle with this question, each group will be forced to reflect on its past and its future and to develop responses. If the issue is forced by heavily subsidizing marriage, the response that is easiest for whites but hardest for blacks will only provide a common threat against which blacks will rally. This will only distract them from the kind of private, searching dialogue the black community needs to reach into its own soul and find what is best for all its children, those whose parents marry and those whose parents do not.

---

RONALD B. MINCY *is the Maurice V. Russell Professor of Social Policy and Social Work Practice at Columbia University.*

# Adoption by lesbian couples

## *Is it in the best interests of the child?*

The report of the American Academy of Pediatrics in February[1] supporting the introduction of legislation to allow the adoption by co-parents of children born to lesbian couples sparked enormous controversy not only within the medical profession but among the public as well. Almost without exception, only the mother who gives birth to or adopts the child may currently be the legal parent, even in cases where a couple plan a family together and raise their child in a stable family unit. The academy has taken the view that children in this situation deserve the security of two legally recognised parents in order to promote psychological wellbeing and to enable the child's relationship with the co-mother to continue should the other mother die, become incapacitated, or the couple separate. This position is based on evidence derived from the research literature on this issue.[2] The *Washington Times* described the stance of the academy as "an unfortunate surrender to political expediency" and accused the academy's Committee on Psychosociological Aspects of Child and Family Health of sacrificing scientific integrity in order to advance an activist agenda.[3] Is it the case that children born to lesbian couples "can have the same advantages and the same expectations for health, adjustment, and development as can parents who are heterosexual," as stated by the academy? Alternatively, is the academy simply pandering to a politically correct agenda?

Two main concerns have been expressed in relation to lesbian mother families: firstly, that the children would be bullied and ostracised by peers and would consequently develop psychological problems, and, secondly, that they would show atypical gender development such that boys would be less masculine in their identity and behaviour, and girls less feminine, than boys and girls from heterosexual families. Lack of knowledge about these children and their parents in the light of a growing number of child custody cases involving a lesbian mother prompted the first wave of studies in the 1970s. This early body of research focused on families where the child had been born into a heterosexual family and then moved with the mother into a lesbian family after the parents' separation or divorce. Regardless of the geographical or demographic characteristics of the families studied, the findings of these early investigations were strikingly consistent. Children from lesbian mother families did not show a higher rate of psychological disorder or difficulties in peer relationships than their counterparts from heterosexual homes. With respect to gender development, there was no evidence of confusion about gender identity among these children, and no difference in sex role behaviour between children in lesbian and heterosexual families for either boys or girls.[4 5]

A limitation of the early investigations was that only school age children were studied. It was argued that sleeper effects may exist such that children raised in lesbian mother families may experience difficulties in emotional wellbeing and in intimate relationships when they grow up. Further, they may be more likely than other children to themselves adopt a lesbian or gay sexual orientation in adulthood, an outcome that has been considered undesirable by courts of law. To address this question, a group of children raised in lesbian mother families in the United Kingdom was followed up to adulthood.[6 7] These young adults did not differ from their counterparts from heterosexual families in terms of quality of family relationships, psychological adjustment, or quality of peer relationships. With respect to their sexual orientation, the large majority of children from lesbian families identified as heterosexual in adulthood.

In recent years, attention has moved from the issue of child custody to whether lesbian women should have access to assisted reproduction procedures, particularly donor insemination, to enable them to have children without the involvement of a male partner. The findings from studies of these families, where the children grow up without a father right from the start, indicate that the children do not differ from their peers in two parent, heterosexual families in terms of either emotional wellbeing or gender development.[8-11] The only clear difference to emerge is that co-mothers in two parent lesbian families are more involved in parenting than are fathers from two parent homes.

A limitation of the existing body of research is that only small volunteer or convenience samples have been studied, and thus mothers whose children are experiencing difficulties may be under-represented. Nevertheless, a substantial body of evidence indicates that children raised by lesbian mothers do not differ from other children in key aspects of psychological development. On the basis of this evidence it seems that the American Academy of Pediatrics acted not out of political correctness but with the intention of protecting children who are likely to benefit from the legal recognition of their second parent. At present in the United Kingdom, lesbian women are individually eligible to adopt children, whether living with a partner or not. However, members of parliament have recently voted to allow unmarried couples, whatever their sexual orientation, to adopt children jointly.

## References

1. Committee on Psychosocial Aspects of Child and Family Health. Co-parent or second-parent adoption by same-sex parents. *Pediatrics* 2002;109:339–40.
2. Perrin EC. Technical report: coparent or second-parent adoption by same-sex parents. *Pediatrics* 2002; 109:341–4.
3. Dobson JC. Pediatricians vs children. *Washington Times* 2002 Feb 12.
4. Patterson CJ. Children of lesbian and gay parents. *Child Dev* 1992;63:1025–42.
5. Golombok S. Lesbian mother families. In: Bainham A, Day Sclater S, Richards M, eds. *What is a parent? A socio-legal analysis*. Oxford: Hart Publishing, 1999.
6. Golombok S, Tasker F. Do parents influence the sexual orientation of their children? Findings from a longitudinal study of lesbian families. *Dev Psychol* 1996;32:3–11.
7. Tasker F, Golombok S. *Growing up in a lesbian family*. New York: Guilford Press, 1997.
8. Flaks DK, Ficher I, Masterpasqua F, Joseph G. Lesbian choosing motherhood: a comparative study of lesbian and heterosexual parents and their children. *Developmental Psychology* 1995;31:105–14.
9. Golombok S, Tasker F, Murray C. Children raised in fatherless families from infancy: family relationships and the socioemotional development of children of lesbian and single heterosexual mothers. *J Child Psychol Psychiatry* 1997;38:783–91.
10. Brewaeys A, Ponjaert I, Van Hall E, Golombok S. Donor insemination: child development and family functioning in lesbian mother families. *Hum Reprod* 1997;12:1349–59.
11. Chan RW, Raboy B, Patterson CJ. Psychosocial adjustment among children conceived via donor insemination by lesbian and heterosexual mothers. *Child Dev* 1998;69:443–57.

---

Susan Golombok *professor*
Family and Child Psychology Research Centre, City University, London EC1V 0HB (S.E.Golombok@city.ac.uk)

---

# Are Married Parents Really Better for Children?

*by Mary Parke, Policy Analyst, Center for Law and Social Policy*

Over the past four decades, the patterns of family structure have changed dramatically in the United States. An increase in the numbers and proportion of children born outside of marriage and a rise in divorce rates have contributed to a three-fold increase in the proportion of children growing up in single-parent families since 1960. These changes have generated considerable public concern and controversy, particularly about the effects of these changes on the well-being of children. Over the past 20 years, a body of research has developed on how changes in patterns of family structure affect children. Most researchers now agree that together these studies support the notion that, on average, children do best when raised by their two married, biological parents who have low-conflict relationships.

> On average, children do best when raised by their two married, biological parents who have low-conflict relationships.

This research has been cited as justification for recent public policy initiatives to promote and strengthen marriages. However, findings from the research are often oversimplified, leading to exaggeration by proponents of marriage initiatives and to skepticism from critics. While the increased risks faced by children raised without both parents are certainly reason for concern, the majority of children in single-parent families grow up without serious problems. In addition, there continues to be debate about how much of the disadvantages to children are attributable to poverty versus family structure, as well as about whether it is marriage itself that makes a difference or the type of people who get married.

## How has family structure changed?

Single-parent families are much more common today than they were 40 years ago. Rates have increased across race and income groups, but single parenthood is more prevalent among African Americans and Hispanics.

In 1996, 71.5 million children under the age of 18 lived in the U.S. The large majority of these children were living with two parents, one-quarter lived with a single parent, and less than 4 percent lived with another relative or in foster care. Two-thirds of children were living with two married, biological parents, and less than 2 percent with two cohabiting, biological parents. Less than 7 percent lived within a step-family. Twenty percent of children lived with a single mother, 2 percent with a single father, and almost 3 percent lived in an informal step-family—that is, with a single parent and his or her partner.

> The majority of children in single-parent families grow up without serious problems.

Many children live in more than one type of family during the course of their childhoods. For instance, the majority of children in step-families have also lived in a single-parent family at some point.

## Are children better off if they grow up with their married, biological parents?

In 1994, Sara McLanahan and Gary Sandefur, using evidence from four nationally representative data sets, compared the outcomes of children growing up with both biological parents, with single parents, and with step-parents. McLanahan and Sandefur found that children who did not live with both biological parents were roughly twice as likely to be poor, to have a birth outside of marriage, to have behavioral and psychological problems, and to not graduate from high school. Other studies have reported associations between family structure and child health outcomes. For example, one study found children living in single-parent homes were more likely to experience health problems, such as accidents, injuries, and poisonings.

Of course, most children in single-parent families will not experience these negative outcomes. But what is the level and degree of risk for the average child? The answer depends on the outcome being assessed as well as other factors. For example, McLanahan and Sandefur reported that single-parent families had a much higher poverty rate (26 percent) than either two-parent biological families (5 percent) or step-families (9 percent). They also found that the risk of dropping out of high school for the average white child was substantially lower in a two-parent biological family (11 percent) than in a single-parent family or step-family (28 percent). For the average African American child, the risk of dropping out of high school

## Utah has highest proportion of married-couple households

Sixty-three percent of all households in Utah in 2000 were maintained by married couples, the highest in the country. Idaho (59 percent) and Iowa (55 percent) were the second and third highest. The states with less than one-half of their households maintained by married couples were geographically dispersed. Massachusetts, Rhode Island, New York, Louisiana, Mississippi, and Nevada. Only 23 percent of households in the District of Columbia were maintained by married couples.

—*U.S. Census Bureau*

was 17 percent in a two-parent family versus 30 percent in a single- or step-parent family. And for the average Hispanic child, the risk of dropping out of school was 25 percent in a two-parent family and 49 percent in a single- or step-parent family.

Up to half of the higher risk for negative educational outcomes for children in single-parent families is due to living with a significantly reduced household income. Other major factors are related to disruptions in family structure, including turmoil a child experiences when parents separate and/or re-couple with a step-parent (including residential instability), weaker connections between the child and his or her non-custodial parent (usually the father), and weakened connections to resources outside of the immediate family—that is, other adults and institutions in the community that the non-custodial parent may have provided access to.

## How do child outcomes vary among types of families?

Comparing two-parent families with all single-parent families often masks important subtleties. Subsequent research has added to our understanding of the range of family structures by examining separately the data for divorced, widowed, never-married, and cohabiting parents, married stepparents, and same-sex couples. While this research has revealed important nuances about the effects of these different family types on children, many questions remain unanswered.

**Divorced families.** Before they reach adulthood, nearly four out of 10 children will experience the divorce of their parents, and roughly one million children experience their parents' divorce every year. Research shows that, on average, children of divorced parents are disadvantaged compared to children of married parents in the area of educational achievement. Children of divorce are more than twice as likely to have serious social, emotional, or psychological problems as children of intact families—25 percent versus 10 percent.

Most divorced families with children experience enormous drops in income, which lessen somewhat over time but remain significant for years—unless there is a subsequent parental cohabitation or remarriage. Declines in income following divorce account for up to half the risk for children dropping out of high school, regardless of income prior to the divorce. The effects of divorce on children often last through adulthood. For instance, adult children of divorce are more likely to experience depression and their own divorces—as well as earn less income and achieve lower levels of education—compared with adults whose parents remained married.

**Never-married mothers.** Among children living with single mothers, the proportion living with never-married mothers increased from 7 percent to 36 percent between 1970 and 1996. In 1996, 7.1 million children lived with a never-married parent. Children of never-married mothers are at risk of experiencing negative outcomes and are among those most likely to live in poverty. Roughly 69 percent of children of never-married mothers are poor, compared to 45 percent of children brought up by divorced single mothers. Never-married mothers are significantly younger, have lower incomes, have fewer years of education, and are twice as likely to be unemployed as divorced mothers. A child born to an unmarried mother is less likely to complete high school than a child whose mother is married. While we know the number of children born to never-married mothers, we don't really know how many spend their entire childhoods living with a mother who never marries or cohabits. Part of the increase in children living with never-married mothers is attributable to the increase in children born to cohabiting couples, which are often reported as single-mother families.

**Cohabiting-parent families.** In 1970, there were 523,000 unmarried-couple households, while in 2000 4.9 million opposite-sex couples cohabited. About 40 percent of cohabiting households in 2000 included children. While this equates to a small proportion of the total children in the U.S., the proportion of children who will live in a cohabiting household at some point during their childhoods is estimated to be four in 10.

Six out of 10 children in cohabiting-parent families live with an informal step-parent, while four out of 10 live with both biological parents. (In comparison, nine out of 10 children in married-couple households live with both biological parents.)

Research suggests that children in cohabiting families are at higher risk of poor outcomes compared to children of married parents partly because cohabiting families have fewer socioeconomic resources and partly because of unstable living situations.

Research also suggests the importance of distinguishing between cohabiting families with two biological parents and those with a biological parent and another partner. Some evidence indicates that school achievement and behavioral problems are similar among children living with both biological parents—regardless of marital status—and that children in both formal and informal step-families also fare similarly in these areas.

**Step-families.** In 1996, about 7 percent of children, or five million children, lived with a step-parent, and estimates indicate that about one-third of all children today may live with step-parents before reaching adult-hood. More than 90 percent of step-children live with their mother and a step-father. Step-families are at greater risk of dissolution than other marriages; about 60 percent of step-families are disrupted by divorce.

In spite of their better economic circumstances on average, children in step-families face many of the same risks as children of never-married or divorced parents. They are more likely to have negative behavioral, health, and educational outcomes, and they tend to leave home earlier than children who live with both married biological parents. However, the effect sizes are small for many of these differences, and risk levels may vary according to race and level of socioeconomic disadvantage.

**Same-sex couple families.** The 2000 Census revealed that out of 5.5 million cohabiting couples, about 11 percent were same-sex couples—with slightly more male couples than female. About 163,000 same-sex households in total, lived with children under 18 years old. (This compares with about 25 million married-couple households with children under 18.)

Although the research on these families has limitations, the findings are consistent: children raised by same-sex parents are no more likely to exhibit poor outcomes than children raised by divorced heterosexual parents.

## Does family structure or reduced income make the difference?

If the negative effects of single parenthood on child well-being were primarily due to a lack or loss of income, one would expect children living with two adults to do as well as those living with their married, biological parents. But this is not the case. The research shows that children living with cohabiting parents or in a step-family do not do as well as children living with married, biological parents on a number of variables.

## Is it marriage itself or the kind of people who marry that makes the difference?

It is often suggested that the positive effects of marriage on child well-being are likely derived not from marriage itself but from the distinctive characteristics of the individuals who marry and stay married.

Marriage may have certain benefits, such as access to health insurance and tax advantages, that contribute to the increased likelihood of child well-being. It is also possible that those who marry also have attributes unmeasured in existing surveys—such as commitment, loyalty, and future orientation—that distinguish them from those who don't marry and stay married. It is also possible that marriage itself—the actual act of getting married—changes the attitudes and behaviors of couples in positive ways, as well as those of others towards them.

## Doesn't the quality of the relationship matter more than the piece of paper?

The quality of the relationship between parents matters to child well-being. Children who grow up in married families with high conflict experience lower emotional well-being than children who live in low-conflict families, and they may experience as many problems as children of divorced or never-married parents. Research indicates that marital conflict interferes with the quality of parenting. Furthermore, experiencing chronic conflict between married parents is inherently stressful for children, and children learn poor relationship skills from parents who aren't able to solve problems amicably.

## What is the relationship between marriage and poverty?

Children living with single mothers are five times as likely to be poor as those in two-parent families. Some economists have attributed virtually all of the 25 percent increase in child poverty between 1970 and 1997 to the growth of single-parent families. But are single parents poor because they are not married, or would they have remained poor even if they married available partners? While it is difficult to disentangle the effects of income and family structure, clearly the relationship operates in both directions: poverty is both cause and effect of single parenthood. For example, research evidence indicates that in low-income, African American communities, the high rate of male unemployment is one of the factors that explains why low-income mothers do not marry.

But recent economic simulation studies have found that if two poor unmarried parents marry they are less likely to be poor. Economist Robert Lerman found that married parents suffered less economic hardship than cohabiting parents with the same low income and education. Among the apparent explanations were that married parents are more likely to pool their earnings, husbands work longer hours and earn more, and married families receive more assistance from family, friends, and the community. While marriage itself will not lift a family out of poverty, it may reduce material hardship.

## What more do we need to know?

Much remains to be learned about how living in different family structures affects child well-being, including:

- How does moving into and out of different family situations affect children? At what ages are children most vulnerable to these changes? How much of the risk to children is caused by living arrangement instability itself?
- What are the long-term effects of some of these family structure patterns—for example, for children who live in long-term cohabiting families or in long-term, single-parent, never-married families?
- How are children in families from different minority and cultural backgrounds affected by family structure?
- From a child well-being perspective, what are the relevant measures of a "healthy" or "good enough" marriage?

---

*This article was excerpted and reprinted with permission from a policy brief published by the Center for Law and Social Policy (CLASP). The entire brief, including notes and charts, can be downloaded in PDF form from www.clasp.org/Pubs/Pubs_Couples. For more information, contact mparke@clasp.org or call (202) 906-8014.*

# The Perma Parent Trap

By Pamela Paul

There's always an explanation: A 22-year-old college grad wants to hold out for the right job rather than jump into an underpaid makeshift position. Rents are so inflated, a 25-year-old moving out of her boyfriend's apartment couldn't possibly afford a place of her own. With two bedrooms to spare, parents can rehouse the kids and everyone will benefit.

Whatever the reason, young adults are returning home in increasing numbers—following graduation, the dissolution of a relationship or the loss of a job. They often live rent-free and subsidized, with no scheduled date for departure. But while much attention has been paid to live-at-home "adultescents," little has been said about their parents, many of whom are Baby Boomers who greet their boomerang kids with open arms. For a variety of emotional and demographic reasons—their desire to be close with their kids, a yearning for youth—many of today's parents (the original Peter Pan generation) just don't want their adult children to grow up.

"Parents used to let go when their children reached age 18," says David Anderegg, professor of psychology at Bennington College in Vermont and author of *Worried All the Time: Overparenting in the Age of Anxiety*."The idea was, if you can go to jail, I'm no longer responsible for you." But that changed during the 1990s, when Baby Boomers' children turned 18 and devoted parents realized that they had poured their emotional and financial resources into their children from the get-go. "Hyper-investment," says Anderegg, "is hard to turn off."

Some argue that permaparenting stems from the indulgence of an immature and spoiled generation. Others blame the phenomenon on the heavy hand of social and economic forces, especially the current recession. And our very definition of adulthood is in flux—with a homestead no longer a key component of adult identity.

But a rising chorus of psychologists and sociologists says parents simply aren't letting go when they ought to—not only impeding their children's adult independence but also hampering their own post-parenting lives. In the absence of an acute crisis or devastating financial setback, the consensus is that parents should look twice at the reasons they continue to shelter their grown offspring. "If parents can get over the idea that they're not being 'parent enough' or that their kids still 'need' them, then they can get on with their new lives," says Roberta Maisel, author of *All Grown Up: Living Happily Ever After with Your Adult Children*.

The combination of high rents and an unstable job market, increased college attendance and delayed marriage and parenting conspire to inch the age of perceived adulthood upward. Bianca Mlotok, an unemployed college graduate who lives with her parents in New Jersey, admits that even at age 27, she doesn't feel like a grown-up. "I'm a mature person, but I think I'm probably not capable of being on my own," she says. "I feel like an adult sometimes, but in other ways I still feel like a child. I guess I see being an adult as more about a certain level of maturity than about some kind of outward sign. Though probably when I start my own family, I'll finally have my own adult identity."

***Living on one's own is considered a lesser signpost of adulthood than completing an education or supporting a family.***

Bianca isn't the only twentysomething grappling with delayed adulthood. According to a 2003 study by the National Opinion Research Center, most Americans today don't consider a person an adult until age 26, or until she or he has finished school, landed a full-time job, and begun to raise a family. Living independently from one's parents is expected by an average age of 21, yet living on one's own is considered less of a determining factor in reaching adulthood (only 29 percent say it's an "extremely important" step) than completing an education (73 percent) and supporting a family (60 percent).

Shifting parental attitudes toward boomerang kids have much to do with generational differences, the result of each generation correcting and overcorrecting the excesses of the previous one. The wave that preceded the Boomers, the Swing, or Silent, generation (born during the Depression and World War II, 1930-1945) and their children. Generation X (born 1965-1978), were brought up during eras of economic recession, reduced birthrates and familial instability, when raising kids was not a societal focal point. Parents of Boomers "were eager for their kids to grow up and leave the household so that they could be free to pursue their own lives," says generational historian William Strauss. "Boomeranging home was a mark of failure for both children and parents."

In contrast, the Baby Boomers themselves (born between 1946 and 1964) and their Echo Boomer offspring (1979 and 1994) have had the happy fortune to be born during periods of prosperity and family growth that place an emphasis on parenthood. From the 1980s hit *The Cosby Show* to kidcentric TV like Nickelodeon, Boomers were awash in media celebrating the rewards of child-rearing and the joys of childhood. Five times more parenting books are published today than in 1970. Ann Hulbert, author of *Raising America: Experts, Parents and a Century of Advice About Children,* says the resultant professionalization of parenting marked a shift from "what was once considered an intuitive, instinctive endeavor into a systematic, intellectualized enterprise."

## KEEPING THE LINES OF COMMUNICATION OPEN

All this attention, it turns out, has been directed toward raising well-adjusted and well-rounded kids, and guiding those self-same kids into fulfilled adulthood, creating patterns along the way. According to Jane Adams, a social psychologist and author of *When Our Grown Kids Disappoint Us,* previous generations emphasized education and financial independence over all else for their children. In contrast, "Boomers are the first generation for whom their children's emotional fulfillment is a primary goal. Their parental mantra has been, 'Be happy or I'll kill you.'" In an effort to gratify their kids, Boomers have become unusually invested in their lives—determined to have an authentic, intimate relationship with their children.

***The Boomer parental mantra: "Be happy or I'll kill you."***

To achieve this level of chumminess, parents have often acted less like stern grown ups and more like their kids' peers, joining the youth culture wholeheartedly at the mall, even purchasing the same teen-oriented clothes for themselves. This closeness continues and strengthens as Echo Boomers reach early adulthood. "The generation gap used to be a significant barrier between parents and adult kids," says Roberta Maisel. "But today's fiftysomething parent and twentysomething child have a lot of the same values and desires."

Therese Christophe, a 54-year-old long-separated woman who lives with her 25-year-old son, Alexandre, says the arrangement works well precisely because her son and his friends don't view her as very different from themselves. "They see me as an adult, but they know I'm cool enough to be their friend," she explains. "I don't try to play this mother role. There's always been an equal relationship, and we're very tight. I'm not judgmental of him and he isn't judgmental of me." The result: "Living with my kid is like having a roommate, only a lot better."

Today's twentysomethings and their parents communicate better and are closer, finds family therapist Betty Frain. Indeed, in a recent survey of 1,003 high school students, a whopping 78 percent said that "having close family relationships" ranked highest (above money and fame, among other things) in defining success. But closeness also creates problems. "It becomes hard for these parents to say, 'I'm the leader in this family and it's time for you to go,'" says Frain. "We've gotten too friendly with our kids."

Studies suggest that grown kids' well-being is a major determinant of well-being for midlife parents. But overidentification with adult children means parents can lose perspective on what's best for one or both parties. "You see your kids' successes and failures as your own and thus try to immunize your child against failure:" says Frank Furedi, professor of sociology at the University of Kent in the United Kingdom. With such a high level of emotional and financial investment, many parents see the status of their adult children as a final parental exam. And parents don't want a bad grade either for themselves or for their kids.

Not surprisingly, parental involvement in kids' lives has pushed its way onto campuses, where "helicopter parents" hover, trying to help their kids through college financially, emotionally and even academically. Parents have been known to intervene in roommate disputes following an emotional e-mail plea from a child, or call a professor to question a grade. In response, universities are scheduling special parent orientation events, hiring parental "liaisons" to handle questions and demands, and firing off terse-but-diplomatic guidelines.

The days when parents simply dropped their kids off and waved goodbye are as antiquated as the college mixer. Today, *The Harvard College Handbook for Parents* is rife with messages to back off: "Parents are often tempted to call advisers or administrators or even rush back to Cambridge to 'make sure' that problems are quickly resolved," the 2000-2001 booklet warns. "In fact, these well-intentioned efforts invariably slow the process by which freshmen learn to take responsibility for their dealings with individuals and institutions."

## NO HELP LIKE HOME

The most blatant manifestation of permaparenting is the phenomenon of boomerang kids. According to the 2000 census, 4 million people between the ages of 25 and 34 live with their folks. In a 2003 Monster/JobTrak.com poll of college seniors, 61 percent say they expect to move back home after graduation. Buzzword maven Faith Popcorn has coined a new term, "B2B" or Back-to-Bedroom, which she describes as "the phenomenon of jobless Gen Xers and

Gen Ys returning to their parents' homes." NBC's fall lineup includes *Happy Family,* a sitcom about a middle-aged couple who can't get rid of their adult children.

Yet many Boomers don't seem to be trying all that hard to empty the nest. "Boomerang kids are staying at home so they can save money to rent or buy a place of their own instead of living with roommates," says Jane Adams. "Often, they're spending lots of money on clothes and cars and vacations in the process. Unless we put our foot down, why should they move out?"

***Parents of college kids intervene in roomate disputes and question grades with professors.***

Whereas pre-Boomer parents—the GI and Depression/War Generations—reminded their children constantly of their sacrifices and taught them to be grateful for opportunities (what some might call "guilt-tripping"), Baby Boomers didn't want to do that to their kids. According to Adams, having grown up in an era of relative stability, Boomers inadvertently raised the next generation to feel entitled.

But it's not just privileged white kids hanging out at home. Working-class twentysomethings have long boomeranged following high school or vocational training because entry-level wages make independent living a financial challenge. Still, lower income Americans today are even less able to be independent than just a decade ago, according to Frank Furstenberg Jr., professor of sociology at the University of Pennsylvania and head of the Network on the Transition to Adulthood study. Furthermore, America's growing diversity means more adult children at home come from immigrant and ethnic communities in which living at home during one's twenties is normative and even favorable. A 2002 national survey of Latinos found that 78 percent agreed "it is better for children to live in their parents' home until they get married."

Leaving home is getting tougher across social classes and ethnic backgrounds. In the absence of a stable labor market, and with a lack of federal support (such as the GI Bill for education), "we're throwing a lot of things back on the family that the government was doing before, in terms of job training and housing subsidies," says Stephanie Coontz, professor of history and family studies at Evergreen State College in Washington state. Kids today aren't necessarily slackers, she argues; they're just coming of age when economic and federal forces thwart independence. Parents are stepping in, Coontz says, because they don't really have a choice.

Perhaps expectations are higher as well. Many experts say today's twentysomethings don't want to downscale by sharing a walk-up with three roommates when their middle class parents have a house where they can crash. Boomers don't want their kids to rough it either. "Emotional and financial dependence is a two-way street," says Adams, a Baby Boomer herself. "Our generation has taken it upon ourselves to make our grown kids happy. We've abrogated our responsibility to insist they make a life for themselves. Instead we're providing it for them." Often, if parents don't house their grown kids, those with extra cash will help an adult child purchase a home.

Keith and Virginia Edwards, both 59, have allowed all three of their twenty- and thirtysomething kids to live at home, with spouses and grandchildren in tow, for periods of up to three years. The Edwards's latest boomeranger, Jon, 32, moved back—along with his wife and daughter—two years ago. That way, he could train for a job change and his wife could be a full-time mother while they saved up to buy a home.

Keith says he doesn't mind that his adult kids have returned home, and has even encouraged it. "In each case, they wouldn't have been able to save for a down payment if they'd had to rent an overpriced apartment:" he explains. "We wanted them to buy a home rather than rent, so the best solution all around was for them to come back and live with us."

## THE PARENTAL TOLL

Permaparents suffer potential financial and emotional repercussions. The empty-nest years are a crucial time for adults to bone up for retirement, rather than payoff their child's credit cards or feed another mouth. Keeping the kids also prevents couples from reconfiguring their lives in a post-parenting marriage, when, historically, many marriages break up. When marriages do end in divorce, or when one spouse dies, parents may be especially inclined to reconnect with their adult kids.

***Avoiding the empty nest and yearning for youth, many of today's parents (the original Peter Pan generation) just don't want their adult children to grow up.***

"The empty nest is doubly empty when you don't share it with a partner," says Betty Frain, who sees close relationships between single mothers and their adult children so often that she labels it a phenomenon. Nevertheless, as Roberta Maisel explains, "For women who find themselves widowed or divorced in their 50s or 60s, being too involved in adult children's lives can be a big mistake. They have decades ahead and need to find a way to approach their lives as individuals."

Married or not, adults who re-feather the nest past its prime postpone their own personal development. During the late 1990s, a spate of books with titles like *Give Them Wings* or *As You Leave Home: Parting Thoughts From a Loving Parent* appeared to address the challenge of accepting children's adulthood. But despite the temptations—pleas for help from adult children, the desire to pitch in financially, the urge not to let go—experts agree that having kids at home is generally a bad idea. Unless the child is suffering from a crisis, adult children belong on their own; empty nest parents have their own lives to attend to. Jeffrey Arnett, author of the upcoming book *Emerging Adulthood: The Winding Road from the Late Teens Through the Twenties,* believes boomeranging home may not be best for parents. "Parents like being in a position to help their kids, and they like the fact that they get along well enough to live together," he says. "But parents are usually ready by then to move on with their own lives."

Indeed, many psychologists believe the post-parenting period is one in which people have the opportunity to reconfigure their identities—to relocate, downshift or change a career, become more involved in the community, take continuing education courses or learn new creative skills. Carl Jung in particular emphasized the importance of this last stage of development. Having an adult child lurking around the house and feeding off the parental nest egg robs parents of some of this latitude. "These parents end up impeding their own transition into a new period of adulthood," say Furedi. "It's a flight from life." Permaparents, perhaps it's time to grow up.

---

*Pamela Paul is the author of* The Starter Marriage and the Future of Matrimony.

---

# Oldest, Youngest, or in Between

## How your child's birth order can affect her personality—and what you can do to influence its impact

By Margaret Renkl

MY TWO OLDER SONS are very different kinds of boys. Ten-year-old Sam, for example, hates birthday parties, preferring to ask just one other child to go to the movies rather than have 12 kids over to play games. Henry, 5, has adored every big birthday bash he's ever attended. Sam's a dynamo on the baseball field; Henry's opinion of sports can be summed up in a single word: boring.

Certainly, many individual traits and tendencies among brothers and sisters are the products of a unique arrangement of genes. But birth order also plays a key role in shaping a child's personality: Sam and Henry, as well as their 3-year-old brother, Joe, are all different from one another in part because of the order in which they were born.

We've all heard the stereotypes: Firstborns tend to be perfectionists; middle kids, peacemakers; babies, spoiled rotten. But the reality is much more nuanced. Though kids in the same birth position often do share certain character traits, the variables within each family determine the degree to which they fulfill or defy the propensities of birth rank. The youngest of any family may be more freewheeling than the firstborn but won't necessarily turn out to be a brat.

"A firstborn may not be a neat freak or reliable or conscientious," says Kevin Leman, Ph.D., author of *The New Birth Order Book: Why You Are the Way You Are*. But if you're aware of the potential advantages and disadvantages of a child's rank, you can help your kids resist any negative stereotypes. So here's what to expect:

### Firstborns

*Natural Leaders*

**ADVANTAGES:** Before any siblings come along, oldest children get the lion's share of parents' attention, says Meri Wallace, author of *Birth Order Blues: How Parents Can Help Their Children Meet the Challenges of Birth Order*. Mom and Dad have the time to sing songs with them during baths or read them extra books before bed. As only children for a while, they're the first to be the focus of their parents' love and affection and the first to wow the grown-ups by reaching major childhood milestones.

All that undivided attention can translate into a highly successful individual. "If a parent is there providing encouragement, a child can gain tremendous amounts of self-confidence," says Wallace. So the oldest kid in a family often does very well both in school and at work because she tends to be focused and detail-oriented and works hard to please authority. Nanette Kirsch, a mother of three in Wexford, PA, says that her firstborn child, Nathan, now 5, has always been very businesslike about what he needs to do. On his fourth birthday, for example, Nathan handed over to his mom the stuffed bear he'd slept with every night since infancy. "I think I'm ready to give up my bear now," he announced. And he's never looked back.

And once firstborns become older siblings, they have the opportunity to lead. "The younger child often adores the older one because she can do so many things," says Wallace. This chance to teach and nurture a younger sister or brother further boosts the firstborn's self-esteem.

Barb Waugh, a mom of two in Houston, says that she can already see her 4-year-old daughter leading her baby brother. "Now that Sean is two, Eleanor mothers him a lot. I hear her repeat everything that comes out of my mouth to him."

**CHALLENGES:** The greatest strengths of the firstborn can also become her biggest obstacles. For instance, a child who's a natural leader can have trouble making and keeping friends if she's always bossing them around.

Firstborns also risk becoming perfectionists because of the scrutiny they're subjected to by doting parents, who, though well-meaning, may focus on tiny flaws, making their child feel inadequate. Even when parents are supportive, firstborns can still put enormous pressure on themselves to succeed. Christine Ives, a mother of three in Morrison, Colorado, says of her oldest son, Jacob, 5: "We really have to help him stay positive when things don't go his way because he gets so frustrated."

**HOW YOU CAN HELP:** Don't be too domineering. Refrain from correcting minor imperfections. If your child's bedspread is crooked, don't straighten it; if her attempt to style her hair goes awry, leave it be. Brush off mistakes with a "Good try," then move on. And show how you can roll with the punches yourself—accept compliments gracefully, apologize when you've made a mistake, and let your child know when something didn't go as you'd planned.

Acknowledge her, not the products of her efforts, says Leman. Well-intentioned praise like "That's the most beautiful picture you've ever painted" may make a child think she has to create even more impressive art next time. More effective: open-ended encouragement—"I bet you're really happy with those bright colors"—that shows you're proud of how hard she's working.

## Second-borns

*Innovators*

**ADVANTAGES:** Kids in the number-two spot have the luxury of more relaxed parents. In part, that's because Mom and Dad are too busy juggling the demands of a growing family to focus as much anxious energy on him as they did the firstborn, or perhaps because they feel more confident about their decisions. Either way, their calmer demeanor tends to transfer to a second child, who'll typically recover from setbacks more easily than his older sibling and be more creative and playful.

Waugh says of her children: "When she was a baby, Eleanor was nicknamed 'The Fussa'—she's very dramatic and demanding. But Sean has been laid-back since birth; he's content just to watch the scenery go by." She attributes much of their differences in personality to her attitude as a mother. "I can't give Sean as much attention as I gave Eleanor at the same age. I had time to sit with her while she fell asleep after her bedtime story. But Sean has learned to be perfectly happy taking his book to bed until he nods off."

Second-born kids also try to be different just to get noticed by their parents, which can make them real innovators. "The firstborn establishes the theme, and the younger child, to be an individual, develops a variation on the theme," says Wallace. Even if the kids share the same talent, they rarely express that gift in the same way. One child may play the piano, while the other sings in the chorus.

At the same time, second-borns tend to be more competent than firstborns of the same age because they've worked hard to emulate their older brother or sister and they're more independent—they've had an older sibling to show them the way.

**CHALLENGES:** A second child may feel inadequate when he compares himself to his older sister. If Mom and Dad are constantly applauding her accomplishments, he may worry that they love her more. To get attention, he may become a show-off or be extra competitive with other kids. And by the age of 3, he may also resent the fact that his older sister had Mom and Dad all to herself before he came along.

**HOW YOU CAN HELP:** Encourage him to talk about his feelings, giving him words to express himself. Show him pictures of his sister at the same age and remind him that he'll grow up and be able to do what she can do. Also explain that jealousy is normal. Say, "We know it's hard for you to share us, but we have enough love to go around." Let him know that you love him for who he is and that he doesn't need to outdo anyone to gain your attention.

Then be sure to praise him for his own strengths and abilities: It's fine for him to excel in baseball and for his sister to be a great figure skater. If you rejoice in each child's uniqueness, says Leman, you'll end up with kids who are very different, but each will feel that he's a cherished member of the family.

If you have a third baby, your second-born, of course, becomes a middle child, a birth position that comes with its own set of potential traits:

## Middle Kids

*Sharp Negotiators*

**ADVANTAGES:** A child who has both an older and a younger sibling has someone to learn from and someone she can nurture—and she has two playmates instead of just one. Like her older sibling, she has the opportunity to be a leader—an experience that will help build her self-confidence. As one of three (or more) kids, she's able to learn how to relate to a group, how to share, listen to others, and join in activities—so she'll probably get along well with others. My own middle child, Henry, has learned to negotiate both the demands of an older brother who tends to be very bossy and a little brother who insists on doing everything he's doing. Middle kids are usually less pressured than firstborns but are taken more seriously and aren't as overprotected as the youngest.

**CHALLENGES:** When a third child is born, the second's status takes on a new variation: Middle kids may feel left out and overlooked and may be anxious and insecure as a result. If this pattern continues throughout childhood, it can make a child less likely to speak up for herself.

To get her parent's attention, a middle child may act out. She also has to struggle to maintain her identity; to define herself, she may become obsessed with a hobby or be overly competitive. Some middle children may become people pleasers to win affection, and others will withdraw, especially if their parents are always engaged in battles with the other two kids.

**HOW YOU CAN HELP:** Work hard to make a middle child feel special. Try to spend at least some time alone with her every day—and with each of your kids. A ten-minute cuddle at bedtime in a child's room goes a long way.

Ask her opinion, to help build her confidence. When you're dressing for work, for instance, hold up two outfits and let her choose, or remind her that Dad's birthday is coming up and have her help think of a great gift for him.

Whether it's your second, third, or later child, someone will be the baby, with the quirks that go along with that position:

## Babies

*Free Spirits*

**ADVANTAGES:** Like the middle child, the youngest benefits from having more relaxed parents and having older siblings to follow. He's also exposed to more than other kids his age because he's watched his brothers and sisters develop and reach milestones, says Wallace. Since he wants to be like them, he'll insist on doing things by himself.

Jess Hill, a mother of three in Nashville, says her youngest child, 8-year-old Noni, has always been eager to catch up to her older brother and sister. "She set her own alarm clock and made her bed at a very early age to be like Becca and Morey."

Sometimes the baby is the most creative, since he has so much time to himself. And he often has fewer responsibilities than his siblings because others always lend him a hand. Babies often become fun-loving, affectionate, and outgoing people.

**CHALLENGES:** Because the family may be more lax with the youngest, he may have difficulty respecting authority later on. And since people often take over for him, he may become too dependent on others and struggle with handling his own problems. He may also feel less competent than his older siblings—though he learns from them, they can still do much more than he can. Older kids can become jealous of the little one, especially if they feel that he gets extra privileges, says Wallace. They'll say things like "You're just in baby school, but I have real homework."

**HOW YOU CAN HELP:** There will be sibling rivalry, but step in if your baby's being bullied—kids need help developing the skills to work it out. If your kindergartner's dominating the dinner conversation, ask your preschooler to share his day. Give him responsibilities—even a small task like helping to clear the dishes will be beneficial. Let him hear you remind older siblings that they also used to take longer to put their coats on and had a tough time learning to play Candy Land.

Birth-order traits often emphasize the differences between siblings, but it's important to remember that they have a lot in common too. My son Sam once heard me call his little brother "sugar pie," to which he replied, "Joe's not a 'sugar pie.' I'm the big boy, I'm the 'sugar pie'; Henry's the medium boy, he's the 'sugar cookie'; Joe's the littlest, he's the 'sugar lump.'"

## What About Onlies?

Studies show that only children can turn out to be higher achievers and more motivated than kids with siblings. They tend to mature faster than other kids their age; since they're the center of their parents' universe, expectations can be high. And without a brother or sister to play with, they spend more time in the company of adults.

As much as an only child may enjoy being alone or with adults, it's a good idea to try to expand her network of other kids. Preschool, daycare, or any group setting is an important way to allow an only to develop friendships that can stand in for sibling bonds. And it's equally vital that you not inflate expectations. Give her a sense of privacy and her own identity, something she would automatically get if you were caring for more than one.

## Defying the Stereotypes

Two factors that can affect how birth order shapes a child's personality and behavior:

**SIBLING SPACING** Houston mom Pia Byrd, whose three kids were all born about five years apart, says that each of them behaves like a firstborn. Even 4-year-old Dane, the baby, has had his mom entirely to himself during these early years while his older siblings, Brit, 9, and Isabella, 15, are in school. Likewise, a second-born child who's already, say, 4 when the third child is born will probably show both middle- and youngest-child tendencies because during infancy and early childhood she was the baby.

**GENDER** Many parents have specific assumptions about their sons that are different from those about their daughters, influencing the way they treat their kids. A girl who's born after an older brother will often show qualities of both a second- and a firstborn because she's the only daughter. If a youngest child is the only boy following several daughters, he can seem more like a firstborn than the baby for the same reason—he's the first child in the family to grow up influenced by his parents' notions of maleness.

---

Contributing editor MARGARET RENKL wrote about family rituals in the May issue.

# WHY WE BREAK UP WITH OUR SIBLINGS

## As baby boomers age, more are becoming estranged from their brothers and sisters. And they feel the loss especially during the year-end holidays

BY LISE FUNDERBURG

JONDA CYNECKI HASN'T SEEN HER TWIN sister Wanda in 13 years and doesn't hold out much hope that she ever will. Their last contact came at a family gathering in Ohio for Christmas, after which Wanda returned to her home in Key West, Fla. Then she disappeared. She didn't call, didn't write and couldn't be reached. When her parents died several years later, her siblings had to use intermediaries to get through to her. She called to borrow money about a year ago. Since then, the only sign she's still alive is that no one has heard anything to the contrary. And yet Jonda, 54, a school librarian, says wistfully of Wanda, "There isn't a day that goes by that something doesn't remind me of her."

Usually that something is doing the laundry. Whenever Jonda goes down to her basement to wash clothes, she sees, tucked under the stairs, an old tandem stroller. Her father crafted it from spare parts, painted it white and wrapped rubber around its wooden wheels. Jonda won't get rid of the stroller, even though it provokes sorrow and anger toward the sister who walked out on her family. What Jonda doesn't know—and might never know—is why.

Estrangement from siblings is a powerful ache not only for Jonda but for millions of other Americans as well—especially during the year-end holidays, when the absence of relatives is most poignant. Many of the 77 million baby boomers, now well into middle age, live farther from their brothers and sisters than did previous generations. And with each passing year, they face more of the life passages that often trigger splits with siblings, particularly arguments over the care of elderly parents or over their estates. At the same time, boomers have more divorces and fewer children and are less tethered to neighbors than were their parents and grandparents, so they are more in need of strong relationships with sisters and brothers—the most-enduring ties many of us have in our lives. Eighty-five percent of adult Americans have at least one sibling, yet an estimated 3% to 10% have completely severed contact with a brother or sister.

Such absolute estrangements may not be the norm, but experts who study family relationships believe they are on the rise. Psychologist Carol Netzer, author of *Cutoffs: How Family Members Who Sever Relationships Can Reconnect*, thinks that today's broader cultural freedoms have made it easier for people to say goodbye to traditions and to relatives. "The nuclear family is not as tight as it once was," she says. Some rifts reflect larger trends. The Woodstock generation, Netzer explains, was full of young people leaving their families to lose themselves in drugs or join religious groups, political movements and communes. "Often, when that ripple in the culture passes," says Netzer, "people go back to their families." Terry Hargrave, family therapist and author of *Families and Forgiveness*, believes that while the psychological self-help movement has been largely positive, "it teaches the individual that 'you're the most important thing; family is not.'"

The origins of a sibling breach often can be traced to childhood. Psychologist Stephen P. Bank, co-author of *The Sibling Bond*, observes that eldest children who are expected to care for younger siblings may feel overburdened and resentful. Children born too many years apart, says Bank, may never share common interests or developmental stages. For them, slender ties are sometimes easy to cut.

Nancy B. (who asked that her full name not be used) is a management consultant with a sister older by six years and a brother older by 12. She doesn't speak to either of them but for differing reasons. "The age gap was so significant," she says. As a child, she worshiped her brother, whose trips home from college were cause for celebration. A few years ago, he stopped returning her calls. She doesn't know why.

On the other hand, she was never comfortable with her sister. "There was always tension between us," Nancy, now 52, says. "I couldn't figure it out." Nancy ended contact after the sister attached herself to yet another violent man, and Nancy felt relegated to the role of caretaker—for someone who didn't want to be helped. The three siblings were last together 25 years ago at their mother's funeral. Nancy still feels the loss, she says, "but my heart isn't breaking anymore. I've figured out a way to be in the world without trying to make love happen where it isn't."

Yet in other families, psychologist Bank says, large age differences can help alleviate competition for toys, friends and parental attention. Some older siblings enjoy being caregivers, often in exchange for adoration. Studies show bonds among sisters tend to be strongest, epitomized by Bessie and Sadie Delany, co-authors of *Having Our Say: The Delany Sisters' First 100 Years*. And when parents are absent, neglectful or abusive, siblings often fill the void by forming tight bonds, as did the brothers in the movie *Radio Flyer*.

Major life changes such as marriage, divorce, birth, illness or death can trigger a separation, Netzer says, but usually only if tensions have been building for years. Consider, for example, the case of Michael Carr, 42, a money manager, and his older brother Steven, who ended contact with each other two years ago. When they were growing up, Michael saw Steven, two years older, as his best friend and guardian angel. "We were really close," Michael says. "He was the ringleader in the neighborhood. He was my hero." (Steven did not respond to requests for an interview.)

In the early '70s, Michael says, Steven became temperamental and less reliable, no longer resembling the person Michael had admired. Steven wasn't crazy, Michael says, just increasingly moody and self-centered. About six years ago, their father was hospitalized, and the brothers went to Florida to see him. They stayed with their stepmother, with whom Steven had a quarrel. Steven told Michael he was going to the hospital to tell their father about it. "It was ridiculous," Michael says. "My father was at death's door, and my brother wanted to complain to him about my stepmother! I had to physically restrain him from going."

Their father died that night, and Michael hasn't seen his brother since the funeral. "I wouldn't be surprised if I never see him again," Michael says. "If I saw him on the street I would talk to him, but I wouldn't let him back in my life. I don't know who he is."

Money issues are a common source of strife between brothers and sisters: Why wasn't that loan repaid? Who can afford the bigger house? How should the family business be run? Behavior outside the family's value system can also trip the switch: coming out of the closet, marrying interracially or converting to a new religion. Then there are cutoffs linked to extreme emotional states, the reasons for which—such as untreated mental illness, substance abuse, incest and violence—may never be brought out into the open.

Wanda's older brother Charles Bucklew has only a few clues as to what might have caused his sister's self-banishment, including her drinking in the midst of their nearly teetotaling Lutheran family. Wanda, who no doubt has her own analysis of the split, never explained; her siblings never asked. And she could not be located by TIME reporters in Key West and New York. "There may be some reason out there that if you knew, it'd bring you to your knees, and you'd say, 'Oh, my God!'" says Bucklew. "But I don't know."

The drive to create sibling bonds or something like them is to some experts primordial—even for an only child. Parents always have a disproportionate power over offspring, but siblings teach peer-level tolerance, loyalty and constancy—qualities that later apply to colleagues, friends and lovers. In moderation, sibling discord is useful, says psychologist Bank. "If the frustration is too great, it cripples you. But we all need a level of frustration in our lives in order to move ahead."

IN A 1996 STUDY OF PEOPLE AGES 18 TO 86, 33% of those surveyed described their sibling relationships as "supportive," and only 11% were "hostile," with the rest falling somewhere in between. "I understand that there is sibling rivalry because I have two brothers and a sister," says Robert Stewart, chairman of the psychology department at Michigan's Oakland University. "But if something came up, and I needed to be on the other side of the country because one of them called, I'd go. There's not a whole lot of people in the world I'd do that for." Most people think of "rivalry" and "siblings" as synonymous and negative, he says, "but I think of it as a close affectional relationship where affection is not necessarily shown in a Hallmark card kind of way."

The sibling relationship of D.B. (who asked that her name not be used) won't ever be confused with a greeting card. As a child, she looked up to her brother, 3½ years older. After his marriage broke up, though, D.B. didn't like the way he treated his ex-wife. Well after the two divorced, he abandoned their original settlement agreement, demanding half the house and full custody of their daughter. D.B. saw his demands as unfair—and didn't think much of his parenting skills. "I just felt he was such a pig," she says. So she stopped talking to him—for seven years. "I come from a long line of grudge holders," she says. "They like their grudges. They air them and walk them and make jokes about them—embellish them."

The silence ended, though, when an aunt died, and D.B. and her brother were the only relatives left to arrange her burial. "I remember thinking, Damn, now I have to see my brother." But the two reconciled somewhat and now talk occasionally on the phone. D.B., now 54, says if she ever needed money, she wouldn't hesitate to ask him for it. She has no money to offer him if the situation were reversed but says, "I would give him lots of time."

Often, estranged siblings are struck by a sudden yearning to reconnect. Says Bank: "Your children leave home, your friends are sick, the leaves fall off the trees, and you say, 'Well, what do I have from my past?' And for better or worse, you've got this sibling who might have been a pain in the neck but who probably knows more about what it was like to live in your childhood home than anybody else."

Yet even for siblings who wish to reconcile, breaking the ice is hard. "The difficulty most of us have is how do you pick up the telephone after so many years?" says Stewart. "People get into a pattern, and even though they're not comfortable in it, they can't imagine an alternative. Or the amount of courage and energy it would take to try to change may be beyond what they're capable of doing right now."

The ability to overlook imperfections for the sake of a relationship is one hallmark of maturity. Siblings may decide to forgive one another once they have their own children. For Mark Horton, 44, a recent falling-out he had with his eldest sister still baffles him. He's not sure what happened or why. Now that they are back in tentative contact, they still haven't talked about it. "It was kind of a *Twilight Zone* episode," he says. But he does hope things heal. Horton (whose sister declined to be interviewed) says she has done remarkable things for him—sending him money when he was a poor college student and then being the only one to show up at his Harvard graduation. And he wants his four children to know their aunt. "It places them in the world," he says. "They're not comets flying through space randomly; they're part of a solar system."

Reconciliation, experts say, is almost always worth an attempt. But about 40% of the families in Hargrave's clinical practice fail at reconciliation, mostly because when difficult issues get stirred up, no one is willing to take responsibility for what happened. Says Hargrave: "The person who has left just seals off again."

For Douglas Matthews, 49, a human-resources consultant, finally breaking off from his parents and three brothers three years ago brought immense relief—and not just to him. "I see it as the best thing he could have ever done for himself," says his wife Teri-Ann, "and for me and the kids."

MATTHEWS HAS ALWAYS BEEN reluctant TO discuss his family situation because he felt that well-meaning people just wouldn't get it that his parents and siblings were harmful to his happiness. "I learned early on that very few people understand the positive aspects of estrangement," he says. For decades, Matthews waffled between trying to be part of the family and retreating. He would try to initiate changes but says no one was willing to join in. Over time, and with therapy, he discovered that the yearning he felt was based on an unrealizable ideal of what his three brothers might have been to him. "A real brother would be there no matter what," Matthews says, "and not have an agenda for you—just accept where you are and listen. But it would be unconditional—nothing could break it. And also do the stupid things, you know. Go to a ball game together." But what Matthews has with his wife and two sons is no fantasy. "I have a home," he says, "and that's what I didn't have before. And I cherish it."

Cutting off can be beneficial in some cases, says psychology professor Stewart, if what you're getting is nothing but negativity or grief. But it's "escape learning," he says, and if the other people involved are ever willing to work on the problem, "you won't know it because they're gone."

For 15 years Keith Bearden, 33, had given up on his family, including his elder brother Dean, 38. Their parents' divorce cleaved the family into separate camps, and Keith wanted no part of either one. "I was really angry," he says. He also felt that he, a self-described "meek intellectual," had nothing in common with his tattooed, motorcycle-riding, machinist brother. Then Dean started telephoning a couple of years ago, just to see how Keith was doing. Keith, to his surprise, was happy to get the calls. Dean says he had no particular plan, that he had never even thought about the years when they were out of contact. "If you were never close," he says, "you never miss it."

But becoming a parent got Dean thinking about family, and as Keith says, Dean was never judgmental or bitter about what had happened in childhood. Now the brothers talk regularly. They visit each other every few months and have realized they have the same sense of humor, the same taste for adventure, and they notice the same things—someone's weird shoes on the subway or a cute woman in a bar.

Keith says he's much happier accepting rather than resenting the differences in his family, that it's helped him with all his relationships and that Dean deserves the credit for helping him reconnect. "Dean kept the door open, and I eventually walked back in," he says.

Jonda Cynecki hasn't closed the door on her sister but is at a loss as to how anyone can pass through it. Since the death of their parents, Jonda has felt an increasingly acute sense of the irreplaceable nature of family. "There's that line that connects you," she says of her missing twin, "and I don't know if it'll ever be broken. Certainly when one of us passes away—and she could be gone now—I don't know if I'll ever know that." Cynecki pauses, wipes away tears, and collects herself. "Someday, I really need to find her. But just not today. Not today."

***—With reporting by Rachele Kanigel/ Oakland***

# The Grandparent as Parent

In the void created by irresponsible parents, the job of rearing six million North American children is being left to an aging population that may well regret not having been better parents themselves

**by Pat Hansard and Candis McLean**

Living with my grandparents is kind of weird because they are so old, explains 14-year-old Joel Dombroski (not his real name) of Medicine Hat, Alta. "When I was living with my [adoptive] mom I never used to tell anyone I was adopted, but it's okay to say I'm living with my grandparents, because so many kids do." Nevertheless Joel has one key concern: "I worry a lot about them dying. Then what would happen to me?"

- 6% (6 million) of North American children under 18 are being raised by grandparents.
- At some time, one in 10 grandparents has been primary support for one or more grandchildren.
- 43% of seniors raising children have health problems that interfere with holding a job, making it difficult to take even part-time work to help out with expenses.
- Grandparents raising grandchildren are 60% more likely to live in poverty than those who are not.
- The four main reasons cited by grandparents for taking on the challenge of child-rearing in later life: 1. need of the children; 2. preservation of family ties; 3. community and ethnic/cultural consistency; 4. reduced trauma of separation.

Joel's grandparents are among the staggering eight million North American boomers and seniors for whom retirement is turning out very differently than planned, as they struggle to provide homes for grandchildren whose parents are less than adequate. Grandparents sometimes take on raising their children's children because of debilitating illness or injury, but most often dysfunctional parents are the root of the problem. All-too-common threads of drug abuse, alcoholism and crime run through the lives of their adult children. Taxpayers often pick up the tab for welfare, counseling, legal aid and health care as relatives battle for visitation rights and custody of six million children caught in the confusion over whose job it is to raise them. There is very little golf, traveling or leisure for older folks who tap into their savings and retirement savings plans or mortgage their homes to provide food, clothing, healthcare and education for a second and sometimes even a third generation. The moral seems to be: raise your children well, or you will be raising your grandchildren and possibly even your great-grandchildren until you get it right.

As a young woman, Gloria Dombroski, now 56, stayed home with her son and three daughters to give them the foundation they needed to become productive adults. All that changed when her husband of 17 years left their strained marriage for another woman. Mrs. Dombroski took on two jobs, doing her best to keep all systems around the children running smoothly. "For years I had to be a really strong woman, but upon reflection," Mrs. Dombroski says, "it may not have been good for my son, having as his main role model a mom who could do everything, while not having his father in the home. He came to expect women to be in charge and take care of things." According to Mrs. Dombroski, this handicapped her son's ability to parent. While her daughters became exceptional parents, Donald has struggled; at the age of 25 he became involved with a 19-year-old prostitute with whom he had three sons.

As ugly battles ended Donald's marriage, Social Services placed the children in protective custody to keep them safe from their mother who allegedly sexually abused them. Her vengeful counter-accusations resulted in Donald losing custody, as well. For eight years Mrs. Dombroski and her second husband fought for access to her grandsons, during which time one of the boys was placed with a permanent foster family, and two were adopted. The Dombroskis spent $50,000 fighting their daughter-in-law, but other costs were far greater. "The time, energy and emotional toll brought us to a point where we just had to stop," she explains, "But I tried for so long because I wanted those boys to know they were loved and wanted by family."

The battle for her grandchildren has placed Gloria Dombroski on the cutting edge as an advocate fighting for gender equality in divorce law. She sees feminists driving the agenda that discriminates against fathers in child custody cases. "I certainly did not equip my son to deal with vicious women and a vicious court system," she says. So serious was she about her goal to change the system which prevents children from having access to fathers and grandparents when divorce tears families apart, that at 52, she enrolled in college, obtaining, with distinction, a BA in Psychology. Plans for her late-in-life career were put on hold a year ago, however, when Joel was given back to them after his single, adoptive mother took a job in another country.

There is great irony in the fact that the very thing this grandmother fought for, she got, but when the opportunity came to take her grandson, in a moment of fear she said to her second husband of 21 years, "I don't think we need this right now." Mr. Dombroski replied, "We may not need this, but Joel does." The Dombroskis are raising that grandson. "Be careful what you wish and fight for," warns Mrs. Dombroski. "You just might get it."

On a bad day, the Dombroskis ask, "What did we do wrong?" On a good day, they are proud to have the chance to teach their grandson how to love and care for people. They are glad that Joel is healing and these days seldom punishes or sabotages himself for mistakes made by both his natural and adoptive parents. Mrs. Dombroski candidly acknowledges nagging questions which haunt her. She wonders if daycare is creating another generation that will not know how to nurture its children. She asks, "Where are the parents of all these kids who are being raised by my generation? Where are the fathers? Kids need their dads. I raised my kids alone. I could teach them a lot, but I could not teach my son how to be a man."

"We are at the beginning of an entire intergenerational revolution in North America," says Sarah Wenig, spokesperson for Boston Aging Concerns... Young and Old United. Families from all socio-economic levels are affected with a stunning 76% increase since 1970 in the number of grandparents-as-parents. This trend is not the same as the time-honoured lifestyle of the elderly living in an extended family arrangement with their younger families, but rather grandparents being responsible for rearing young children in a home they provide without a parent present.

"It's one of the most remarkable demographic changes in American society over the last few decades," states Meredith Minkler, University of California professor of Community Health Education. She insists the foster care system would collapse under the load were it not for the work of the older generation that continues to rise to the challenge. It is estimated that 150,000 children have been orphaned in the U.S. by the ravages of AIDS alone. In addition, children are being grand-parented in overwhelming numbers because of divorce, neglect, teen pregnancy, family violence, poverty, unemployment, their parents' mental health problems, substance abuse, incarceration and death.

Statistics Canada research analyst Ron Cunningham reports there is no specific question on the Canadian census form which would allow government to derive clear numbers regarding grandparent-led households in this country. "This is a cutting edge subject you are tackling," Mr. Cunningham comments, "because I can tell you each year there are increasing numbers of people making written comments on their census forms regarding 'skip-generation' child rearing. This suggests Census Canada should add a question to determine exactly how many such households there are." The U.S. Census already poses the question and Internet searches reveal over 16,700 organizations and individuals addressing grand-families and grandparents' rights and access issues.

As a result of fighting for custody and access rights to her granddaughter whom she had raised from infancy, Annette Bruce of Legal, Alta. founded Orphaned Grandparents Association. She cautions, "The legal system puts you in a position of having to destroy your child in order to protect your grandchild...or you have to just forget it. Forgetting it isn't really an option." Her husband, Gordon Thielan, recalls the 10 years they parented their granddaughter until she was returned by court order to her mother and is saddened by his daughter's addictions. "We did our best and were good parents, but alcohol made her very hard to handle." He chokes back emotion in recounting the struggle: "In order to go to court with this, you have to make your daughter your enemy."

Ms. Bruce's organization strives to educate the public, judicial and legal systems as well as offer support and information to those caught in battles of their own. "People need help because you enter into a grieving over the death of relationships, but there is no closure, no body to mourn, no gravesite to visit." Her words are tinged with the bitterness of loss and frustration. "Even when there is valid reason to be given custody, the legal system makes a simple solution impossible. As far as the courts are concerned, you get to babysit, pay and give, but don't you dare ask for any rights." A decade of loving and parenting did not weigh as heavily as biology in the court's decision to grant custody to their daughter despite years of mental illness and addictive behavior. "In the court's eyes, we are now legal strangers to our granddaughter."

ParentLink, a Missouri-based research organization reports that challenges in performing everyday tasks can be overwhelming for many seniors who must look after youngsters at a time in their lives when their need to look after themselves is increasing. Some have trouble doing housework, climbing stairs or walking short distances. Shirley Sogah, founder of Grandparents Resource Centre in Denver, Colorado, adds that the cost is high in terms of personal sacrifice for senior members of grand-families. "There is less financial security than in traditional families and most retired people do not have health benefit plans to cover the children, which is a serious problem in the U.S. We're in real trouble down here," she stresses. "The children often come to us with emotional problems and are angry that their family of origin is not intact. They may take that anger out on their grandparents. Most kids are very appreciative, at some level, for their home and care, but long to be with their parents."

Grandparents' marriages often fall apart under the strain of parenting again, while family conflict and resentment may result when the group of grandchildren being parented by grandparents leaves little time or energy for the rest of

## Wisdom

### *Wisdom from grandparents who had it to do over again*

- Cultivate an attitude of sacrifice for your children. But don't be too easy on them.
- Avoid daycare. Impersonal, paid caregivers cannot nurture family relationship bonds.
- Children were never meant to be raised by only one set of parents; it is too hard. They need extended family and societal supports to do the job right.
- Make sacrifices to make family happen. Do everything to keep your marriage together, and I mean everything.
- Stop destroying children in divorce. Get help with your marriage; refuse to divorce, except in cases of violence.
- Do everything you can to get help for your family before social services or the courts step in. Once they do, it is a forever thing.
- If you get a divorce, don't divorce your kids. Stop using children as hand grenades to hurt each other.
- Make children responsible for the consequences of their actions; don't let them blame others for their own mistakes.
- Teach children to earn what they want and to wait for reward; the pursuit of instant gratification in adult life destroys families.
- Take parenting classes, especially when issues begin to surface.
- Have few rules. Give them clearly. Make some non-negotiable and be sure your kids know that violating the ones about drugs, sex and alcohol can destroy them.
- Mentor your children to be good parents.
- For those raising grandchildren:
- Expect that your heart will break daily.
- Tell kids the truth when they ask why their parents aren't raising them. It's one of the things that will break your heart, but it helps them understand how to be good parents when they grow up.
- Boomers need a reason, a cause to live for. Grandchildren are a good cause.

the grandchildren. In addition, a difficult grieving process takes place when the grandparents' circle of friends suddenly drops them because they don't want to be bothered with the children. "We just don't fit our friends' lifestyle of freedom and spontaneity anymore," she says.

Ms. Sogah's efforts to influence the U.S. government to support grandparents raising grandchildren will be aided by initiatives in Canada. The province of Alberta is actively working to establish a Kinship Care program to enhance and improve the foster care system. Bill Mead, CEO for Edmonton and Calgary Children's Authorities, is "absolutely committed" to the this idea of kinship care because it is what is best for the children. He believes the basic cost of foster care should be given to anyone providing such care, including extended family. He wants to see families receive respite care, counseling and financial support so they can do this important work. "We cannot be blowing families apart by putting this burden on them and then not support them properly. Yes, there are costs, but two years of experience with this program in Calgary has shown the costs to be one-half of the least expensive foster care placements."

Elaine Shelton in West Palm Beach, Florida, founded "Off Our Rockers" six years ago when she could find only two sites on the Web dealing with the issue she had never dreamed, as a young mother, she would be part of. "People had always complemented me on my daughter's behavior. Without being disciplined, she was a good kid, involved at church; she didn't seem to need restrictions. But at 14 she went from being a sweet, loving young lady to a hateful, spiteful, violent individual. I tried to set limits and use disciplinary skills, but it was too late," she explains.

"Being able to work part time or at home would have made a big difference, but I had to work. It is important to be there for our children. The big catch phrase at that time was 'quality' time, not 'quantity' time. Baloney! You should spend as much time with your children as they need. I trusted my daughter to do the right thing. I should have been there to make sure she did. Even when kids are out of the house, it is important for them to know that someone is at home waiting for them, instead of them being at home waiting for someone to show up." A legal secretary, Ms. Shelton now takes work home so her 10-year-old grandson will not be a latch-key kid. "I don't want to lose another child by being too busy to deal with how and whom he is spending his time," she says.

Another grand-family, Bea and Jim Daily, had spent nearly 28 years traveling the world with the U.S. Air Force, finally retiring in Ft. Walton Beach, Florida. A cabin on Black Creek was a planned retreat where they would spend much of their leisure time together. The sudden arrival of four grandchildren aged six, five and two (twins), altered their lives forever.

As a newly-married couple, the Dailys had wanted children right away. They

## NEIGHBOUR

Family mobility is a drastic factor in parents' failure raise their own children, according to Alan Mirabelli, Executive Director of the Vanier Institute of the Family who points to the need for roots. "Community cannot happen under the strain of constant moves, and we cannot survive without community," he argues. With many families moving every three to five years, people don't get to know or care about each other. "This reduces the likelihood that neighbors would even know that a family in their midst needs help. People today are reluctant to ask for help and have little expectation they will receive help, even if they do get up the courage to ask for it," Mr. Mirabelli continues. "Instead, we should cultivate an attitude that it is not a bother to be asked for help.

"We overvalue family privacy, autonomy and isolation and thereby have created a culture which has given a very clear message that we should all take care of our own," he says. "The isolation in which we raise our children makes it less possible for others to step in and help in times of crisis. Yet we should not think of helping only in times of crisis. It is more about attending to the business of helping our neighbor rather than coming to the rescue," Mr. Mirabelli maintains.

"We need a cultural shift: companies need to re-evaluate transfers for the sake of transfer and move families only when absolutely necessary. If a family can put down roots, outsiders have the opportunity to speak into the lives of children to keep them out of trouble, and into the lives of parents to help them stay together. People need to invest themselves in their own neighborhoods, get to know the kids, and welcome them into our homes. We have a corporate responsibility to the children around us."

had two sons and a daughter, and over the years did everything together as a family...trips to the beach, picnics, fishing, even hunting for gold in the mountains. "We raised our own kids, hardly ever leaving them with others. Jim wanted me at home with the kids and I wanted to be there. It was a good life," Mrs. Daily recalls, pointing out that they joined the Lutheran Church when the oldest child was five. "Our Larry was always in opposition, leaning to the darker side of things, in spite of a good family life. I don't know how to explain it, but it was a fact," she explains. When the children became teenagers, Mrs. Daily took part-time work so she could be home when the kids were. As a teen, Larry introduced his younger sister to drugs and alcohol, then started shoplifting. Later he joined the Navy, but went AWOL when someone murdered his bunkmate. He met his wife at a drunken party; they had four children and were soon writing bad cheques for rent and groceries, which the Dailys covered, trying to fix the things they could. A violent fight between Larry and his wife resulted in a neighbor calling Children's Services. Frightened, the two older children, Shaina and Matthew, ran across a six-lane highway to their grandmother's house, leaving the twins at home because they were too heavy to carry in the flight to safety. By the time the Dailys got to the twins, the authorities were there. They spent six months in a foster home before being returned to the Dailys.

The young dad's addictions had a firm control over him; three prison sentences for "driving under the influence" and 12 years later, the Dailys, now 69 and 64, are still raising the twins. Shaina, became pregnant at 15 and gave birth to a baby boy, Jamison. Mrs. Daily insisted that she would not start over raising a third generation at this stage of her life. Plans were made to surrender the child for adoption, but the mother of the baby's father intervened. Shaina went to live with that family, but six months later returned to her grandparent's home to complete school. Much of the baby's care fell to Mrs. Daily. Shaina has since graduated, works in retail and lives with her son in a mobile home purchased by the Dailys. Matthew, now 17, spent his entire childhood dreaming that if he could go live with his mom, he could "fix" her. Years of disappointment and his own maturity have brought the realization this family reunion will never happen; he recently moved in with his sister and her baby.

The Dailys pray that Larry will stay on the right side of the law when he is released from prison in a few months. Long divorced, he has a home with his daughter, son and grandson waiting for him. They see the twins going off to college in four years and light at the end of the tunnel. How much life they will have left on the other side of that light remains to be seen.

Mrs. Daily expresses sorrow that all of her grandchildren don't go to church, but says, "It is too much at my age to fight them anymore." She regrets that she and her husband have no social life together. Most of their former friends dropped them when they took on the children. Few gestures of support or offers of respite care have been made by family, friends or church. Quick to forgive, the hurt still registers in her voice. Mr. Daily expresses regret at having had so little time with his wife, but adds, "You have to try when something like this happens to your family. They are your flesh and blood."

## Grandparents as Beneficiaries

"Sure raising grandkids is hard work, people get tired, they feel put-upon and resent their children for leaving their responsibility on their doorsteps. But when we get to the core of what life, family and children are about, the love for their grandchildren transcends all that," states psychiatrist Arthur Kornhaber who has been researching grandparenting issues since 1970. As founder of California's Foundation for Grandparenting, he mentors grandparents through initiatives like Grandparent University as well as websites, radio broadcasts, books and articles.

"Grandparents are not victims here," he argues, "rather, they are beneficiaries. The impact on seniors is not only good, it is fantastic, even sacred. They rediscover the meaning of life, a sense of purpose that diminishes any suffering they are experiencing."

Studies have shown that the older person's immunity is bolstered. They feel vital, useful, necessary. "There is nothing worse than being irrelevant. To suddenly know you are indispensible, that a child needs you to live...well, it is beyond labelling," states Dr. Kornhaber. "How long can you have fun playing Bridge?" he asks. "Besides, the idea that retirement should be a big vacation is a myth, a lie."

Dr. Kornhaber believes grandparents need to become saint-like to be good at this new role, but grandchildren illuminate their lives. He maintains that children know what is going on and view their grandparents with great love and esteem. "The older the grandchild in this situation, the more they understand the power of what the grandparent did. They know what the alternative would have been, too." As one grandchild wrote him, "My grandparents reassured me that my whole world wasn't falling apart and I would survive."

He has found grown children reciprocate with undying devotion, nursing grandparents on their sickbeds and into death. "This arrangement is good for the kids and good for the grandparents," he continues, "and it is the right thing to do. When children need you, the question answers itself."

The key? "You have to love your child more than you, and grandparents can do that. Kids come out really well and eventually most parents grow out of their misery."

"I knew my grandchildren were in trouble the moment I heard my daughter was pregnant," says Shirley Sogah. Her first grandson was born following his mother's motorcycle accident, resulting in multiple disabilities for the child. Her life spiraled out of control until the Colorado Department of Human Services finally placed her two sons in foster care, where they went from one home to another. Ms. Sogah spent seven years battling social services for their custody, then founded the Grandparents Resource Center in Denver, Colorado. Her research became the foundation upon which the Colorado State Legislature passed a House Bill for grandparents' rights in 1991.

Searching for a way to raise public awareness about the plight of grand-families, the idea for a quilt came to her in a dream. "Quilts have been a way of preserving family history and making important statements through the ages. It seemed to be inspired and came together so beautifully," she says. E-mail letters were sent to 100,000 people who gave themselves Internet titles like grandma, nana or grandfather. Ms. Sogah picked a respondent from each of the 50 states and asked them to outline their handprints and give names of grandchildren they were raising.

The 12 feet square quilt, titled "Grand Hands and Hearts Across America," was to be presented to President Bill Clinton, but the Monica Lewinsky scandal erupted. "Somehow it didn't seem right to give a family-oriented quilt to a man who was behaving so shamefully while in office," Ms. Sogah explains. "We waited for the affair to die down, but it hounded him to the end of his presidency." Awaiting the opportunity to present the quilt to President Bush, she smiles, "while the White House drags its feet, Canada is breaking the story." A similar quilt is now being made in Canada for presentation to Prime Minister Chretien.

# UNIT 4

# Crises—Challenges and Opportunities

## Unit Selections

31. **Hitting Home**, Cara Feinberg
32. **The Myths and Truths of Family Abduction**, Nancy B. Hammer
33. **Is Your Dog (Cat, Bird, Fish) More Faithful Than Your Spouse?**, Emily M. Brown
34. **What Kids (Really) Need**, Nancy Gibbs
35. **For Better or Worse: Couples Confront Unemployment**, Marilyn Gardner
36. **The Binds That Tie—and Heal: How Families Cope With Mental Illness**, Herbert Gravitz
37. **Tough Medical Tasks Fall to Families**, John Keilman
38. **Home Alone**, Adam Piore
39. **Terrorism, Trauma, and Children: What Can We Do?**, Linda Goldman
40. **Marriage and Divorce American Style**, E. Mavis Hetherington
41. **Dating After Divorce**, David Anderson and Rosemary Clandos
42. **Divorced? Don't Even Think of Remarrying Until You Read This**, Hara Estroff Marano
43. **Managing a Blended Family**, Sheryl Nance-Nash

## Key Points to Consider

- How does an abusive relationship develop? What, if anything, can be done to prevent it?
- If you felt your sexual relationship was troubled, how would you act? Would you discuss it with your partner? Would you hope that it would correct itself without your doing anything?
- How does the family impact the mental illness of one of its members? What can it do to help the ill family member? What should the role of families be when a family member is seriously and chronically ill?

**Links: www.dushkin.com/online/**
These sites are annotated in the World Wide Web pages.

**Alzheimer's Association**
*http://www.alz.org*

**Caregiver's Handbook**
*http://www.acsu.buffalo.edu/~drstall/hndbk0.html*

**Children & Divorce**
*http://www.hec.ohio-state.edu/famlife/divorce/*

**National Crime Prevention Council**
*http://www.ncpc.org*

**Widow Net**
*http://www.fortnet.org/WidowNet/*

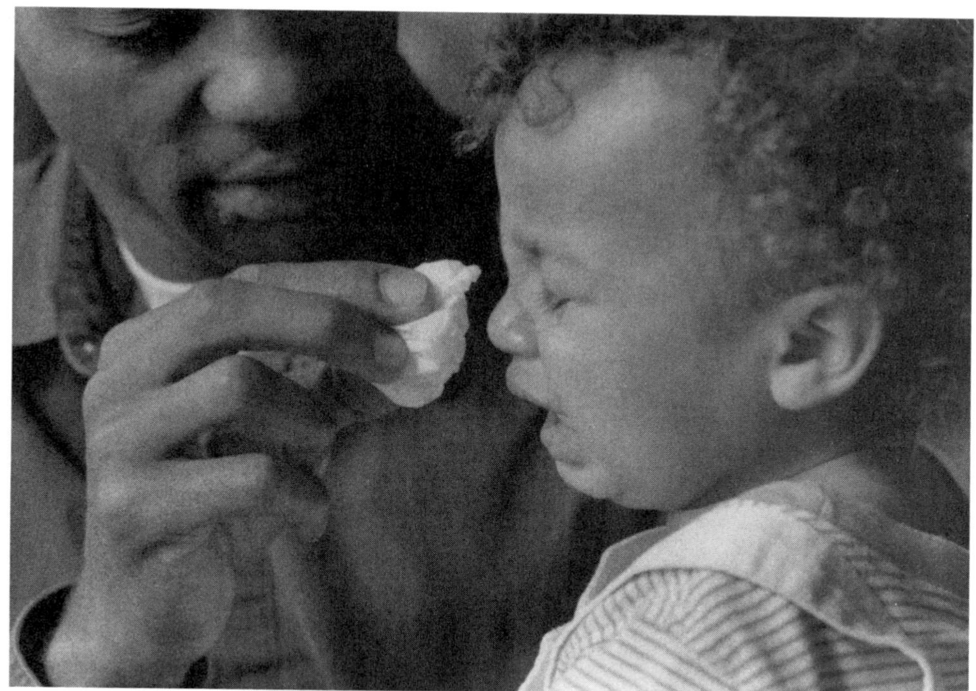

Stress is life and life is stress. Sometimes stress in families gives new meaning to this statement. When a crisis occurs in families, many processes occur simultaneously as families and their members cope with the stressor and its effects. The experience of a crisis often leads to conflict and reduces the family members' ability to act as resources for each other. Indeed, a stressor can overwhelm the family system, and family members may be among the least effective people in coping with each other's responses to a crisis.

Family crisis comes in many forms; it can be drawn out or the crisis event can be clearly defined. The source of stress can be outside or inside the family, or it can be a combination of both. It can directly involve all family members or as few as one, but the effects will ripple through the family, affecting all of its members to one degree or another.

In this unit, we consider a wide variety of crises. Family violence is the initial focus. "Hitting Home" argues that greater awareness of the cycle of violence and the complexity of an abusive relationship can only benefit us as a nation.

"The Myth and Truths of Family Abduction" confronts commonly held, but incorrect beliefs about child abduction. Stranger abduction is much more rare than abduction by family members. With this in mind, the article suggests several tips for anticipating and preparing children for the risk of family abduction.

The next subsection deals with problems in sexuality and sexual relationships. "Is Your Dog (Cat, Bird, Fish) More Faithful Than Your Spouse?" presents six examples of affairs that indicate specific underlying problems between spouses.

The subsection that follows looks at the work/family connection, with interesting results. Employment is explored in "For Better or Worse: Couples Confront Unemployment." Involving the whole family and maintaining communication are found to be essential to helping the family to survive the crisis of unemployment.

Health concerns are the focus of the next section. Mental illness is addressed in "The Binds That Tie–and Heal: How Families Cope With Mental Illness." As this article clearly shows, families can add to the stress of mental illness, but they can also be a major factor in the management of the illness. "Tough Medical Tasks Fall to Families" address the stress families, especially parents, face when required to provide medical care to their chronically ill child. In some cases, these parents are being asked to perform medical procedures that, only a few years ago, were done by skilled medical personnel.

In the next section, the crisis of war is portrayed in "Home Alone." Military personnel, many of them single parents, must find child care when they are called up and sent to war. The strain of the service person facing death as the children also must deal with disruption of their lives is depicted. A related phenomenon, terrorism, is addressed in "Terrorism, Trauma, and Children: What Can We Do?" How do we, as caring adults, respond to questions children have about the dangers of terrorism and war? Because children personalize the threat, the suggestions for how to respond to a child's concerns are highly pragmatic and focused on building a sense of safety and comfort for the child.

Divorce and remarriage are the subjects of the next two subsections. In the first article in the first subsection, Mavis Hetherington presents an overview of "Marriage and Divorce American Style." One of the life-skills that newly divorced individuals may have gotten rusty on is discussed in "Dating After Divorce." Divorce among baby-boomers, sometimes after many years of marriage, is increasingly common.

The other side of divorce–remarriage–is the focus of the next two articles. "Divorced? Don't Even Think of Remarrying Until You Read This" provides insights on what should be dealt with before one remarries. A particular concern of blended families is finances and financial management. How do they blend their financial houses? Should they? "Managing a Blended Family" addresses these concerns and provides tips for merging two different financial systems.

# Hitting Home

## Domestic violence is the issue that embarrasses traditionalists. Today, despite greater awareness and a variety of model programs, partner abuse is still far too prevalent.

**BY CARA FEINBERG**

A LEATHERY WOMAN WITH A DARKENING BLACK eye smokes cigarettes through the spaces of her missing front teeth and tells the police how her boyfriend slapped and bit her because he didn't like her grandchildren. Another woman tells a counselor at a shelter that she's tried to leave her husband 15 times in the two years that she's been married to him. Still another can't speak at all, her moans incoherent as she's wheeled out of her house on a stretcher covered in blood, her cheek slashed into two loose flaps from the corner of her mouth.

These graphic details of domestic abuse come to us courtesy of documentary filmmaker Frederick Wiseman, whose camera has been mercilessly recording the often unpleasant aspects of our social reality for three decades. In the years since 1967, when his first documentary, *Titicut Follies*, garnered artistic awards and journalistic respect—and an injunction from the Massachusetts Superior Court, which banned the film in the state for the next 24 years—Wiseman has captured everything from the crumbling walls of a housing project to the locker-lined hallways of a high school, from a ballet company to a state prison for the criminally insane. Using his signature cinema verité style—there is no narration, music, or overt editorializing in his films—Wiseman has become a barometer of our values and mores, revealing our culture and progress by observing our social organizations, institutions and institutional practices.

It is therefore telling that Wiseman has chosen to take on the issue of domestic violence at precisely this moment. While the scenes from his latest film, *Domestic Violence*, are explicit, we've seen these types of images before. Hardly a news cycle goes by nowadays without a domestic-violence story. The media attention is a salutary development; not long ago, domestic violence didn't exist as a legal or social concept.

Yet while we've come incredibly far in our struggle to recognize domestic violence as a national, public problem, battered women now face a new set of challenges—preeminent among them, the religious right's efforts to portray marriage as the panacea for all social and moral problems. If only we could all just pair up in happily heterosexual matrimony and stay that way, the logic goes, social ills such as violence, crime, and poverty would simply wither away.

While ample data suggest the social and personal benefits of a happy marriage, the get-married-and-stay-married-at-all-costs ethos often ignores the damage that bad marriages can do both to adults and to children. And domestic abuse? Social conservatives often pretend that the problem would disappear if only more people got and stayed married. They make it more difficult for women to leave abusive relationships—not only by steeling social attitudes against divorce but by making it contractually harder (through such vehicles as "covenant marriages") for domestic-violence victims to escape.

> "Everyone asks why she continues to stay; no one thinks to ask, 'Why does he hit her in the first place?'"

Moreover, social conservatives tend to confuse marriage policy with welfare policy; indeed, they would like to replace the latter with the former. This is the "get-married-and-stay-married-and-you-won't-need-welfare" argument. Robert Rector, a senior fellow at the Heritage Foundation, argues that marriage incentives must be built into Temporary Assistance for Needy Families (TANF)—the basic federal welfare program, designed to provide assistance and work opportunities—and that divorced and out-of-wedlock mothers should get diminished levels of welfare assistance for not being married. This is a typical conservative argument that not only gets the relationship between poverty and welfare backward—and this is a great source of liberal-conservative argument generally—but also makes it much harder for wives to leave their abusive husbands, for fear of being financially penalized.

## DOMESTIC VIOLENCE AND THE LAW

It is this sort of rhetoric that threatens to roll back the heroic—and remarkably recent—achievements of the battered-women's movement. As late as the 1960s, if you looked at American newspapers, police reports, medical records, and legal texts, you would find little mention of domestic violence anywhere. "In the last few decades, there has been a great surge in attention to this issue," says Clare Dalton, Northeastern University's Matthews Distinguished University Professor of Law, who is a leading feminist legal scholar and a pioneer in the development of legal education about domestic violence. A founder of Northeastern's domestic-violence clinical program and the Domestic Violence Institute (an interdisciplinary educational, research, and service organization), Dalton served as a consultant on Wiseman's film and led discussions about the issue at several showings of *Domestic Violence* in the Boston area.

"Right up into the 1980s, we still had states in the Union with out-of-date immunity laws based on common law from the 1800s, protecting men who beat their wives," Dalton says. "It was only 10 years ago now that the Supreme Court was even ready to recognize the severity of domestic violence in our country—only eight years ago that Congress addressed it on a federal level with the Violence Against Women Act [VAWA]."

> ... the number of women dying in domestic-violence situations hasn't changed. The problem is as widespread as ever.

That legislation, passed initially in 1994 and renewed by Congress in 2000, was a milestone: It was the first federal law ever to address the issue, and it came at the problem with a variety of solutions, including funding for women's shelters, a national domestic-abuse hot line, rape education-and-prevention programs, training for federal and state judges, new remedies for battered immigrants, and criminal enforcement of interstate orders of protection.

As Dalton points out, VAWA would have been impossible without the work that began with the feminist movement of the 1960s and 1970s. "Our latest campaign against domestic violence grew directly out of the movement," she says. "For the first time, women were getting together and talking about their experiences and discovering the great prevalence of these unspoken terrors. Emerging feminist theory allowed women to connect with each other and to the ideas that feminists had been arguing for all along: that women's legally sanctioned subordination within the family was denying them equality."

Taking their cue from the civil-rights and antiwar movements earlier, feminist activists began to see the law not only as an important tool for protecting victims but as a way to define domestic violence as a legitimate social problem. Local legal groups and grass-roots advocacy organizations began to develop legal remedies based on the link between sexual discrimination and violence. Starting in the sixties, lawyers began to seek civil-protective or restraining orders to keep batterers away from their victims. Courts began to create special rules for domestic-violence cases and custody cases involving children from violent homes. And by the mid-1990s, Congress had passed VAWA. Today, feminist advocates for battered women have begun to draw important interconnections among battering, poverty, welfare reform, homelessness, immigration, employment, gun control, and many other areas of concern. They are working with all sorts of organizations to step up education and reform.

## THE PSYCHOLOGY OF ABUSE

While the stories of domestic violence in Wiseman's film are horrifying, even the most compassionate viewer's sympathy can run thin when victims shun opportunities to abandon their own torture chambers. Of the three women in the opening scene who have called the police, not one is prepared to listen to advice about legal options or free social services. Rather, each one simply continues recounting her abuse, speaking as if she had never even heard the officers' recommendations.

"We have always looked at the victim and said, 'Well, why doesn't she just leave?'" says Lynn Rosenthal, executive director of the Washington, D.C.-based National Network to End Domestic Violence. "We've got cops and judges and lawyers who get upset when victims don't flee, or fail to report their abusers, or don't show up in court to press charges." This past January, a judge in Lexington, Kentucky, sparked outrage among victims' advocates when she fined two women for contempt of court because they returned to their alleged abusers despite having obtained protective orders against them. "But this attitude places the burden on the victim, not the abuser," Rosenthal says. "Everyone asks why she continues to stay; no one thinks to ask, 'Why does he hit her in the first place?'"

Dr. Judith Lewis Herman, an associate clinical professor of psychiatry at Harvard Medical School and the training director of the Victims of Violence Program at Cambridge Hospital, has been fighting to change this perception of victims for more than 30 years. "The tendency to blame the victim has always influenced the direction of psychological study," Herman said in an interview in her office at Harvard. "Research had always looked at what the woman did to provoke her batterer, or it focused on her own 'personality disorders.'" In 1964, for example, researchers conducted an egregious study of battered women called *The Wife-Beater's Wife*, in which the inquiries were directed toward women simply because the men refused to talk. The clinicians identified the women as "frigid" or "indecisive" and went on to *treat* the women so they would stop "provoking" their husbands.

In the mid-1980s, when the diagnostic manual of the American Psychiatric Association came up for revision, this misdiagnosis of victims—and the tendency to blame them for their partners' violence—became the center of a heated controversy. A group of male psychoanalysts proposed that "masochistic personality disorder" be added to the manual to describe any person "who remains in relationships in which others exploit, abuse, or take advantage of him or her, despite opportunities to alter the situation"—a proposal that outraged women's groups around the country. Herman was one of the leaders in the fight to formulate a new diagnosis that accurately described the psychological conditions of battered women. Herman proposed "complex post-traumatic stress disorder," which describes a spectrum of conditions rather than a single disorder, and is now listed as a subcategory of post-traumatic stress disorder in the latest edition of the standard diagnostic manual.

ALTHOUGH WISEMAN RECOUNTS NONE OF THIS POLITICAL or legal history explicitly in *Domestic Violence*, the evidence of these years of struggle pervades every frame he shoots. In the opening sequence, a lean, tattooed, middle-aged man wearing only his undershorts asks, "Why do you always take the woman's word?" as police officers cuff and arrest him.

"When it comes to domestic violence," they respond, "that's the way it is. If she says you hit her, you hit her."

This brief exchange may not seem particularly significant—after all, if a stranger had assaulted a woman in a parking lot, we would expect the police to haul him away. But the very fact that the Tampa, Florida, officers responded immediately to a call for domestic violence and then removed the batterer from his home without hesitation or an arrest warrant is a testament to the progressive laws, police training, and legislative reform developed and implemented in the past 30 years.

According to Elizabeth M. Schneider, a professor at Brooklyn Law School and the author of *Battered Women and Feminist Lawmaking* (2000), one of first and most important legal issues to come to the attention of the feminist movement in the 1960s was the failure of police to protect battered women from assault. By the 1970s, class-action lawsuits were filed in New York City and Oakland, California. All of a sudden, domestic violence was considered a crime against the public and the state, not just the individual.

Yet even these victories and others like them initially made little headway in police attitudes and practices. Nineteen years ago, a woman named Tracey Thurman was nearly beaten to death in Torrington, Connecticut, before the police came to her aid. Though Thurman had reported her estranged husband's threats and harassment to the police repeatedly for over a year, it wasn't until she called in utter desperation, fearing for her life, that the police responded. They sent only one officer, however, who arrived 25 minutes after the call was placed, pulled up across the street from Thurman's house, and sat in his car while Thurman's husband chased her across the yard, slashed her with a knife, stabbed her in the neck, knocked her to the ground, and then stabbed her 12 more times.

Permanently disfigured, Tracey Thurman brought what became a landmark case to the Supreme Court, which found that the city police had violated her 14th Amendment right to "equal protection of the laws" and awarded her $2.3 million in compensatory damages. Almost immediately, the State of Connecticut adopted a new, comprehensive domestic-violence law calling for the arrest of assaultive spouses. In the year after the measure took effect, the number of arrests for domestic assault increased 92 percent, from 12,400 to 23,830.

"We'd all like to look at our progress and be optimistic," says Clare Dalton. "But if you look at the most recent statistics from the Justice Department, the number of women dying in domestic-violence situations hasn't changed. The problem is as widespread as ever.

"But there is one interesting thing here," Dalton notes. "While the number of deaths among women hasn't changed, fatalities among men have dropped significantly. This, in truth, is our first real triumph. If women feel they can get help—if they believe the police will come when they call them, if they understand they will get support and have a place to go where they will be safe with their children—then fewer are pushed to the wall. Fewer will resort to killing or dying at the hand of their abuser."

## THE TAMPA EXAMPLE

Such wisdom has not been lost on the City of Tampa Police Department, whose progressive, community-wide response to the problem Frederick Wiseman chose to film for *Domestic Violence*. Tampa's network of coordinated, cooperative services—from law enforcement, to social services, to the legal system—is a model example of similar programs around the country.

"We now have a zero-tolerance policy toward domestic violence here in Tampa," said Lieutenant Rod Reder, a 24-year veteran of the Hillsborough County Sheriff's Office in Tampa, when reached by phone. A former supervisor for the Sex Crimes Division and onetime member of the Governor's Domestic and Sexual Violence Task Force, Reder is now widely considered to be an expert in the field of domestic and sexual violence. Under the auspices of the U.S. Department of Justice, he runs training sessions for law-enforcement officers at conferences nationwide. "We discovered there were so many simple things we weren't doing... to help victims of domestic violence," Reder said. "And we found there really is only one way to make things work. All the community players have to come to the table; otherwise, it's the victim's safety that gets compromised."

"In the past, many officers looked at domestic-violence calls as a waste of time or a private family matter. Now we consider them some of the most dangerous calls there are."

The catalyst for Tampa's adoption of community cooperation was a woman named Mabel Bexley, who in 1981 pushed Reder to bring police practices in line with new domestic-violence laws, and who two years later became the director of a women's shelter called the Spring. In her 19-year tenure there, Bexley, now 65 and recently retired, expanded the Spring—which is the focus of much of Wiseman's documentary—from a three-bedroom house with more than a dozen women and children huddled inside to a 102-bed facility with 120 employees and a $4-million budget.

Reder and Bexley teamed up again in 1995, when Tampa hit an all-time high in domestic-violence-related homicide, to work alongside members of the state attorney's office and the 13th Judicial Circuit Court to form the zero-tolerance campaign against domestic abuse. Reder and the Hillsborough County police then formed a special domestic-violence unit and developed a three-day training seminar for all seven local law-enforcement agencies.

"We do all sorts of things now to make the system work," said Reder. "When police answer a domestic-violence call, they are required to file a report—even if there is no arrest—just so the incident is documented. We had deputies who would walk away from incidents saying, 'No harm, no foul,' and would leave with no report," he recalled. "But now officers are required to document domestics by state law. You start dinging a few deputies and taking disciplinary action, and word gets out real quick: If you go to a domestic, write a report."

According to Reder, Tampa officers have also become very aggressive about arrests: "We used to think we were doing the right thing by not arresting the man—we didn't want to get him any angrier than he already was. In the past, many officers looked at domestic-violence calls as a waste of time or a private family matter. Now we consider them some of the most dangerous calls there are."

Hillsborough County has also addressed other gaps in the system. "We've sent advocates to go pick up victims at their homes so they'd be sure to get to court," said Reder. "We used to have communal waiting rooms in the courthouse, but now we have separate ones so victims won't have to face their abusers before their trial begins. To file an injunction, you used to have to fill out a complicated 25-page form that was only available in English. This alone used to scare people away, so now we have bilingual advocates and lawyers available to help people fill them out."

This is where the Spring comes in. Though most victims who arrive at the shelter are running for their lives and have no desire even to consider legal action against their abusers at that point, the facility employs an on-site attorney to help them navigate the judicial system and pursue the available options. In addition, each one of the Spring's hot-line operators is a deputy of the court who can file injunctions at any hour of the day or night. This is crucial, because the most dangerous time for abuse victims actually begins the moment they choose to leave their homes. "The Bureau of Justice statistics say that one-third of all women murdered in the U.S. are killed by an intimate," says Jennifer Dunbar, who works at the Spring. "But of those 30 percent, 65 percent are murdered when they leave. It's our job to make sure [victims are] protected at this point."

NEARLY 40 YEARS AFTER THE FIRST FEMINIST ACTIVISTS in the women's movement brought domestic violence to the nation's attention, the policies have largely been set and the laws are finally on the books. Now it's a question of making sure that the systems work and helping the larger community to understand, recognize, and accommodate the needs of battered women. "Right now, we're working on expanding efforts into other systems, like job placement, affordable housing, welfare reform, and child-protective services," says Lynn Rosenthal of the National Network. "A number of states now have special domestic-violence provisions within their welfare systems and housing programs. For instance, under the original job-placement programs in the TANF program, people who showed up tardy three times to the program would lose their benefits. A battered woman might have tremendous problems meeting these criteria—her husband could still be sabotaging her efforts." Rosenthal adds: "It's easy to see how our own well-intended programs could send her right back to her batterer."

... in communities where awareness of partner abuse remains limited... reform movements lag well behind their counterparts in more progressive places.

Throughout the country, states have begun to integrate their systems and have developed new, progressive programs to deal with domestic violence. Though they vary in their specific reforms, many have expanded their legal definition of domestic violence to include nonmarried and nontraditional couples. And some, shifting their focus from punishment to rehabilitation, have begun to examine the root causes of violence in the first place. Programs like EMERGE in Cambridge, Massachusetts, work with batterers to find nonviolent ways to express their anger; many others educate children and teens—ideally, before any battering starts. A number of states have created specialized domestic-violence courts so that the judges hearing these cases are not only familiar with and sympathetic to the special circumstances surrounding battering cases but can follow them from start to finish.

Yet for all the progress that has been made in addressing domestic violence, Wiseman's film makes clear that there is a long way yet to go. One problem is how practically and psychologically difficult it can be for a victim to leave her batterer. But another is the complexity of the political environment itself. As elected officials come and go, their varying agendas affect the winds of legislative change and shift fiscal priorities along with idealistic convictions. According to Robin Thompson, the former executive director of the Florida Governor's Task Force on Domestic Violence, in order for a state to stay vigilant in its fight against domestic abuse there must be "a bedrock of political commitment"—be it a designated task force or a group of grass-roots activists invested in educating and uniting their community. Awareness alone is not enough.

And while states may have implemented great judicial and law-enforcement reforms, if these are not closely monitored and coordinated, they can still fall short of their goals. For instance, if an accused batterer is arrested right away but then must wait six months for a trial, the victim is still largely unprotected. Or if a judge orders a defendant to participate in an intervention program but no one checks to see if he complies, the sentence may be useless.

Obstacles to reform certainly don't fall neatly along partisan lines. A liberal judge might opt for a surprisingly lenient sentence for a defendent, while a conservative judge might make an equally counterintuitive ruling, viewing the court as the woman's traditional protectorate. Yet in communities where awareness of partner abuse remains limited—and partisan issues such as welfare, gun ownership, and "family values" remain entwined with domestic violence—reform movements lag well behind their counterparts in more progressive places.

So far on a national level, what little government funding there is for community-based programs like the community courts or the Spring has not been cut by the Bush administration. But Rosenthal remains worried about the potential for an "unholy merger" between social conservatives and the growing movement for fathers' rights. Though she respects much of the work that fathers' rights groups have done in calling for more paternal responsibility and accountability, she fears that some men will latch on to the claims of right-wingers who resent gains by the battered-women's movement—and by the feminist movement generally—and will seek to cripple these movements' effectiveness by demanding their defunding.

In a tableau that echoes the opening scene of *Domestic Violence*, Wiseman returns at the end of his documentary to police officers responding to a call. This time, it seems, the outcome will be more hopeful: The call was placed not by a battered woman but by a potential batterer seeking intervention—a last-ditch effort to stave off the violence brewing in his household. But when the police arrive, the couple refuses to listen to their suggestions or take any steps to change the situation. When neither the man nor the woman agrees to leave the premises, the police ultimately return to their squad car shaking their heads, leaving behind only words of advice and a volatile couple "afraid of what they might do." It is an ominous ending to a celebration of progress—an eerie mirror of the problem we continue to face.

---

Prospect *assistant editor* CARA FEINBERG *writes the "World Responds" column for Prospect Online.*

# The Myths and Truths of FAMILY ABDUCTION

By Nancy B. Hammer

THE VERY IDEA of child abduction is met by parents in equal measures of fear and disbelief—it can't happen to us. The series of high-profile abductions of children in 2002 raised the country's awareness. The kids spanned the ages of two to 15 and came from all types of families and environments, both urban and rural, across the U.S. In the more horrific cases, the abductor was someone the child did not know. Yet, a recently published study by the U.S. Department of Justice confirms that, compared to the frightening, but relatively rare, kidnappings by strangers, family abductions are commonplace.

In 1988, the Federal government first attempted to count the number of children who become missing each year. In 2002, the Second National Incidence Studies of Missing, Abducted, Runaway, and Thrownaway Children (NISMART-2) was published. The study confirms, once again, that offspring taken by a family member without the knowledge or consent of the custodial parent continues to represent the second-largest category of missing children, with a total of 203,900 youngsters abducted by a family member, as opposed to 115 stereotypical kidnappings by a stranger. Indeed, in your lifetime, you are likely either to experience within your own family or know someone who has gone through some type of family abduction.

Despite the fact that so many kids are abducted by a family member, many people do not fully understand this issue. The public generally views these incidents as infrequent, minor occurrences best handled privately. "After all," people believe, "the child is with a parent; it can't be that bad." Or can it?

On a clear autumn day, John Cramer (name changed) did not return his daughter, age 11, or son, age nine, from his scheduled weekend visitation. John and his wife Sandy (name changed) had separated several months earlier and had begun divorce proceedings. After Sandy contacted police, John's car was found inside a storage locker with a hose running from the tailpipe to the driver's side window. Inside, police found the lifeless bodies of John and the two children. Although it was known that he was unhappy about his failing marriage, no one suspected the level of John's despondency or that he was capable of taking his children's lives as well as his own. While the typical incident of family abduction does not end in death, every time it occurs there is the potential for horrible consequences.

> Though the public believes the incidences of these kidnappings are infrequent, they rank as the second-largest category of missing children in the U.S.

In family abduction cases, kids typically are taken by a parent, although in a few cases, a grandparent or other relative may be the abductor. Parents who abduct often do so when they feel their relationship with the child somehow is threatened. Research indicates that fathers, who are slightly more likely to abduct than mothers, often flee before a custody order is issued, perhaps spurred on by the fear that they are about to lose meaningful contact with their offspring. Mothers, however, typically kidnap after a custody order has been issued, perhaps reacting when the terms of the custody and visitation don't meet their expectations. Regardless of who the abductor is, the overriding motivation is a desire to control the child's relationships and hurt the other parent. The abducting parent often is unable to consider the effects on the youngster and thinks only of his or her immediate situation. One father, after the eight-year abduction of his children, reflected that his actions were motivated by his own inadequacies and need to control, not for the love of his kids.

The public has a tendency to minimize the risk to offspring involved in a family abduction in the mistaken belief that a child is safe in the hands of a parent. A simple scan of the headlines of any major newspaper reveals stories of child abuse, neglect, and even death of kids at the hands of their own parents. In this way, abduction is no different from any other crime committed against a child—kids often are at risk from those they know. Official statistics may not fully reflect the danger inherent in family abduction situations. Some cases resulting in death may be counted as murder or suicide, without reference to the family abduction incident that started it all.

This oversight may leave family abduction out of the crime statistics, yet abduction of a child, even if perpetrated by a parent, is a felony in every state. The state laws often are referred to as "custodial interference" statutes and, if charged as felonies, carry a jail sentence of one year or more and allow the abducting parent, when caught in another state, to be extradited for prosecution in the state from which he or she fled. A conviction of child abduction can have a serious effect on subsequent custody decisions in family court. The FBI can become involved under Federal law if the abducting parent flees with the child across state lines. Further, if the abducting parent takes the child outside the U.S., he or she has violated the Federal international parental kidnapping law, thus involving the FBI and other Federal resources to locate and prosecute the abducting parent.

Research conducted on the consequences of family abduction confirms the seriousness of these cases. In the best-known study of this issue, researchers Geoffrey Greif and Rebecca Hegar interviewed 371 parents whose kids were abducted by a noncustodial parent and found a seven percent incidence of sexual abuse, 23% incidence of physical abuse, and five percent incidence of both physical and sexual abuse.

In addition to statistical information, adults who were parentally abducted as children have begun to raise their collective voices through a new organization called Take Root. This group formed after an initial meeting hosted by the National Center for Missing & Exploited Children (NCMEC) and provides an online venue (`www.takeroot.org`) for the sharing of stories—in addition to hosting a newsletter called "The Link." One of the members of the organization chronicles her own struggle for identity and self-awareness after having lived on the run and under many aliases during the period of her abduction. She writes, "I have had many [names] in my life. The first, my birth name, the name lovingly bestowed upon me as a newborn child, was Cecilie ... until my abduction at age four I was called Sissi or Sisselina, in the sweet custom of nicknaming a young child. After my abduction my father changed my name to Sarah Zissel, the first of many aliases, and for all intents and purposes my birth name was no more."

It can be very difficult to locate the abducting parent and captive child. An abductor can find many hiding places. While some abductors simply adopt new names, others seek to alter their identities illegally. Information on forging birth certificates and creating assumed identities is only a click away on the Internet. Other abductors get assistance from relatives willing to hide a child in violation of the law, or from more formal groups, sometimes known as underground networks, which help abductors violate the law by providing funds and housing. Many abducting parents seek refuge in a foreign country. Not all international abduction cases involve parents of two nationalities. Often, American parents choose to flee to a foreign destination in order to better hide their crime or to be with a new partner.

## Parents as abductors

Regardless of the method or the destination, parents considering abduction must realize that, one day, they could be found. NCMEC's nationwide poster distribution program leads to the recovery of one in six children featured. A growing awareness of missing children and an increasingly vigilant public shed light into the dark corners where abducting parents once hid their children from the other parent, extended family, friends, and law enforcement. In the past year, the U.S. has seen several recoveries of children who had been missing for more than five years.

Abducting parents find, upon their return, that the problems they tried to run away from still exist. In addition, their actions have created new ones. Facing the issues now, however, requires being honest with the child about the left-behind parent, often for the first time since the abduction, and may result in a sense of betrayal in the child who does not know whom to trust. Moreover, the child frequently suffers emotional confusion and depression, as he or she is left to wonder what will subsequently happen. The irony for some parents is that the same child they fought so hard to keep for themselves can become estranged once he or she learns the full truth of the abduction.

If you are concerned about the potential of family abduction, there are steps that can be taken to lessen the risk. Every parent should strive to reduce the tension with the other parent throughout the separation, divorce, or custody process. As difficult as it may be to go through divorce and resolve the custody issues, children need both parents in order to become the individuals they were meant to be. For some families, seeking help from a mediator to define custody and visitation helps both parties to feel as though their concerns have been addressed. A resolution reached together may help prevent one side from feeling like he or she "lost," and therefore, prevent a potential "lashing out" through abduction. In addition, a mediator can talk openly about how parents should strive to remember that their child's need for access to both parents must come first.

Parents should take any threats of abduction seriously and evaluate the risk. Additionally, lawyers should encourage the court handling custody issues to do the same. Recently, California enacted legislation requiring courts to consider whether such a risk exists. The law is modeled on a Department of Justice report, "Early Identification of Risk Factors for Parental Abduction," and can be obtained at `www.ojjdp.ncjrs.org`. If the court finds a risk of flight, it is required to consider certain measures designed to prevent the abduction from occurring. They include:

**Child custody bond.** The court may require parents to post a financial bond or give some other guarantee that they will comply with its order. Such a bond may be obtained from an insurance carrier or bail bonding company. The Professional Bail Agents of the U.S. maintains information on how to find a company able to write this type of bond and may be reached at 1-800-883-7287.

**Supervised visitation.** The terms may allow visits only at certain places, such as the custodial parent's home or a visitation center to be supervised by a professional or other intermediary. This may be appropriate in cases in which an abduction has occurred previously; where there is violence in the relationship; or when threats of abduction have been made.

**Restrict child's removal from state or country.** The court may require either parent to obtain legal permission prior to removing the child from the state. If there is a risk of international abduction, the court will issue a bulletin with the U.S. Department of State's "Children's Passport Issuance Alert Program." It requires a written request to enter the child's name and enables the Department of State to notify a parent before issuing a U.S. passport for the child. Information can be obtained at `www.travel.state.gov`.

Parents also should take certain practical steps to reduce the risk of family abduction and ensure swift action to locate the child:

- Keep a current photograph of your offspring.
- Maintain a complete description of your child, including height, weight, birthmarks, and other unique physical characteristics. Fingerprints also are provided by most law enforcement agencies. All copies of the fingerprints should be turned over to the parent for safe keeping.
- Teach kids to use the telephone. Make sure they know their home phone number, including area code, as well as emergency numbers such as "911" and "0."
- Notify schools, babysitters, and day care centers of the terms of your custody order and who is permitted to pick up the child.
- Maintain identifying data about your former spouse, including description, date of birth, social security number, and contact information for friends and relatives.

Once it is determined that the child is missing, a parent immediately should take the following steps: Contact the local law enforcement agency to make a missing child report; ask that the child be entered into the National Crime Information Center computer as missing (NCIC is the national law enforcement database, operated by the FBI, that allows law enforcement in other states access to information about the child's disappearance); call NCMEC at 1-800-843-5678 and report the child as missing; ask local missing child organizations for assistance; aid law enforcement's search by providing all information available to help locate the child and the abductor; and obtain temporary or sole custody if it was not already court-ordered.

Family abductions are real crimes with real child victims and no winners. If you are considering abducting your child or are concerned that your child might be abducted, help is available. Besides maintaining a 24-hour hotline, NCMEC provides information on family abduction and other child protection issues on its website, www.missingkids.com.

Despite the frequency of these cases and the trauma caused to the families involved, there is hope in every child recovery. The public's understanding of this issue and awareness in looking at the pictures of missing children and reporting suspicious circumstances involving children will yield even more happy endings.

---

*Nancy B. Hammer is the director of the International Division of the National Center for Missing & Exploited Children, Alexandria, Va.*

# Is Your Dog (Cat, Bird, Fish) More Faithful than Your Spouse?

*Affairs are never just about sex.*

by Emily M. Brown

An affair is not about whether or not your spouse loves you. An affair sends a message about a particular problem between spouses. Six examples follow:

**1. Nice couples who never fight.** In reality, they're terrified to be anything but nice for fear that conflict will lead to abandonment. They never resolve their differences, so their marriage erodes.

**2. Couples who are frightened of intimacy.** These couples are afraid of being emotionally vulnerable, so they keep the barriers high between them by fighting. Frequent and intense battles are the emotional connection between them. Sometimes they are verbal, accentuated by slamming doors or other dramatic actions—and in other cases these fights escalate into physical violence. These couples fear closeness more than conflict. They fear that if they let their emotional guard down, they will get hurt, or even be abandoned, or feel trapped.

**3. Spouses who use affairs to fill the emptiness inside—much as alcoholics use alcohol—are sexual addicts.** Sexual addiction is often viewed as a joke, or as an excuse to be promiscuous, but sexual addiction is real. It is not about sex, however, nor is it about romantic love. Charlotte Kasl, a psychologist, says, *"Sexually addicted adults are seeking parents to love them unconditionally"*.

**4. Spouses who are sick of sacrificing their own feelings and needs to take care of others.** The affair begins when someone comes along who stirs the vestiges of life in one of the spouses. The affair is serious, long-term and passionate. Once fully involved, the betraying spouse struggles to decide between the marriage and the other person.

This kind of affair is often regarded as midlife crisis, but it is much more. Your spouse was not looking for an affair, but the years of not attending to his own feelings made him a prime candidate. He was charmed and excited when a friendship with a colleague began to blossom. He had been starving emotionally, so he acted impulsively, although not without the sense of betraying a trust. He and his colleague became seriously involved—even while he was trying to decide which one was the right person for him. He doesn't really want to end his marriage. Yet he certainly doesn't want to end the affair, although he knows he should. So change lies ahead.

**5. Exit Affairs.** An exit affair is the *vehicle* for ending the marriage—not the reason. This is the kind of affair that a spouse launches when the marriage is deteriorating, and endings are hard for him. The affair provides a way of sliding out the door.

What you need to do is understand what each of you contributed to the collapse of your marriage. However, it is unlikely that you will put this kind of marriage back together.

**6. What about affairs that are not acted upon sexually?** Are they really affairs, or are they only friendships? These relationships should be considered as affairs when they consume time and energy that would more appropriately be going into the marriage. These relationships have a sexual current, even if sexual activity is not involved.

You may overlook the seriousness of your spouse's non-sexual affair, however, you would do well to pay attention to two common danger signals: If your spouse is spending more quality time with the other person than with you, and if your spouse's primary confidant is the other person, and not you. If either of these patterns is present, get help now, before the non-sexual affair becomes a sexual affair.

You probably know, consciously or unconsciously, whether your spouse is having an affair. You know deep down that your marriage is off track, but you really don't want to know, so you explain away the evidence you see.

The signs often show up on long-distance phone bills or charge accounts. Or suddenly, your spouse starts criticizing you, your sex life changes, a friend's name suddenly drops into the conversation (or drops out); your spouse's physical appearance suddenly spiffs up, or your spouse becomes moody and unavailable. Sometimes the third party tells you of the affair, hoping to provoke you into ending the marriage.

When you are ready for the truth, it is time to confront your spouse. But if you don't have hard evidence, simply say, *"I think you're having an affair"*, and wait for an answer. It will be more difficult for your spouse to lie if you make a statement than if you asked, *"Are you having an affair?"* This question asks for only a yes or no. Make your statement, then stay silent, and wait for your spouse to respond. Don't give your spouse time to come up with a "good answer", or you'll miss your spouse's initial reactions.

Is there an embarrassed silence? Is there fumbling denial or a beating around the bush? Are there questions that put you on the defensive, such as *"What makes you say that?"*

Any of these responses is probably a "yes". If your spouse does not admit to the affair—and your jealousy is not working overtime—there could be another big secret, but it's not an affair.

Usually, when there's a secret, it's an affair. In the few instances when the secret is not an affair, it is a secret with relevance for your marriage, such as a large financial gift made to a relative without your knowledge.

If your spouse confesses to an affair, you will feel shock—edged with relief, to be followed by pain and fury. Your heart doesn't really want to believe what your head knows is the truth. You're afraid of what will happen next: Will your marriage survive? Will you survive?

Even though you're increasingly furious, ignore the advice of friends and relatives to rush to the nearest divorce attorney. *Legal proceedings don't resolve emotional issues.* See if you can keep your focus on your own pain and anger rather than on attacking your spouse. And whatever you do, leave your children out of it for now. There is time enough later for deciding how to talk with the children about the turmoil in the family.

*Forget the temptation to separate immediately.* Going home to visit your mother for a few weeks so that you don't have to deal with the situation—or telling your spouse to leave—will not help. Fleeing gives the illusion that you can avoid your pain, but the pain goes with you. Separate bedrooms in the same house are OK for a while. Each of you may need some space when you feel so raw and vulnerable. Just don't separate.

*"I can't trust you"* is a common theme. Of course you can't. Right now, neither of you can trust each other. You need to express your pain, and you need for your spouse to hear it.

Your spouse will probably want to appease you in order to avoid having to witness your pain. However, resist any attempts by your spouse to get you to "be nice", and suppress your anger. Don't let your voice be shut off by a quick *"I love you"* or a guilty *"I'm sorry"*. Neither love nor guilt makes it OK. If your spouse offers a lame excuse, such as, *"She came after me, and I didn't know what to do"*, don't believe him. You want it to be over, but blaming the third party won't work. It's your spouse who betrayed you.

But don't assume divorce—though it might seem like the only answer. It's not. It's not even the most common result of an affair. An affair doesn't automatically mean divorce. You have a variety of choices, and you owe it to yourself to take plenty of time to check them out so that you can choose a solution that fits you.

This is not the time for major decisions, because you can't see the whole marriage if you're looking at only one part—and decisions driven by an emotional crisis tend to be poor ones.

You may find that neither of you wants the marriage to end. Or it may be that your spouse's affair really is the announcement that your marriage is ending—that life as you know it is over.

But if your marriage has a chance of making it, your next moves are critical. It is easy to sabotage yourself by asking your spouse question after question about the affair: *"Why didn't you tell me if you thought things weren't right? When did you see her last? Are you still seeing her? How can I believe that?"*

You wake up your spouse at three in the morning, insisting, *"We have to talk now!"* You ask, *"Do you love her? How many times did you have sex? What does she have that I don't have? How could you do this to me?"* No matter what your spouse says, you lose: If he says he loves her, you're devastated, and if he says he doesn't love her, you don't believe him. You think about the affair so much that it becomes your life. You're so obsessed that it's as if you're having an affair with the affair.

Getting over the obsession with the affair requires that you express your anger, pain and powerlessness:

If you tell your spouse that he's lower than low, and ask, *"How could you do this to me?"* this is a statement of your thoughts about your spouse, not an expression of your anger. Anger sounds more like this: *"I am furious at you!"* or *"I am angry at you for lying to me!"* Pain might sound like this: *"I am so hurt that you've done this"*. Powerlessness might be: *"I don't know what to do. Nothing I do makes any difference right now."* See whether your words and your tone of voice are connected to what you are feeling inside. You don't need to scream to convey just how hurt and angry you are—neither do you have to explain nor justify your anger.

Moving beyond obsession is harder when your spouse is leaving the marriage, especially when your spouse is leaving to be with the third party. You are facing a double whammy: It will be hard to resist the temptation to blame it all on your spouse (or the third party). Doing that, however, would be a tragedy. Opportunities are often created out of painful circumstances. This is the time to grow rather than to make yourself a living monument to betrayal. Letting go of obsession is more difficult when you have been married for a long time, and have sacrificed parts of yourself along the way. If you have put aside your needs for the good of your spouse or your marriage, you may feel as if you have little self left, but as you reclaim the lost parts of yourself, you will be able to let go of the obsession.

If the affair was with your best friend, it is not quite incest, but it may feel close to it. When this happens, shock waves wipe out one of your main sources of psychological support. Even so, you must give up the friendship. That is a violation of friendship that goes too deep to be rectified.

Many affairs are with a work colleague. Knowing that the spouse who betrayed you will continue to have daily contact with the third party makes it hard to believe that the affair has really ended. Yet many times it has. It's even harder when you have to have contact with the third party on a regular basis, as for example when that person answers the phone in your spouse's office. If your spouse really seems to have ended the affair, and is working on the marriage, see if you can rise above the temptation to be rude. Make yourself a class act. While it is not always possible or practical for your spouse to change jobs, it is something the two of you might seriously consider for business as well as personal reasons.

In a few cases, the third party won't let go. There are phone calls, letters or other attempts to contact your spouse. Sometimes, this means the affair is continuing, but in other situations, it's because the third party is having difficulty giving up the affair. If your spouse is clear and firm about ending the affair, these contacts should end fairly soon.

How *do* you go about rebuilding your life? Will you ever be able to trust again? Will your marriage survive? If it does, will you feel that bond of belonging that you crave? How *do* you rebuild trust?

Rebuilding involves ruling out separation and divorce for now. By the end of three months, you will know whether you can make the marriage fit you both. However, for the two of you to work together, the affair must be over—physically and emotionally.

You're ready to work on rebuilding trust when the following indicators are in place:

- The affair has been revealed.
- The affair has ended.
- Any ongoing contact between the affair partners, such as at work, is being handled openly and appropriately.
- You still like and care about each other.
- You know how the two of you created an opening for the affair.
- You are both committed to working on yourselves and on the marriage, knowing that it will be painful, and will take longer than you want, and that you have no guarantees of how it will all come out.

If you and your spouse want your marriage, you will both need to make changes in how you interact with each other. One spouse can't rebuild the relationship alone. There is no healing without willingness to risk, but you've got a good chance of rebuilding a better relationship when you both can discuss the changes needed, and share your emotional ups and downs.

Your emotions are critical in connecting with your spouse. Trust is rebuilt by each of you developing the skills of intimacy: Being honest, becoming emotionally vulnerable, and developing reasonable expectations for your marriage.

The affair doesn't mean that your ability to love and care are gone. They were overshadowed by your pain and anger. Your spouse was looking outside your relationship for what he didn't know how to find inside. Thus an important part of rebuilding is looking inward at yourself and at your marriage.

Intimacy doesn't mean constantly being with your spouse. So you must tell each other when you need some physical or emotional space, and when you'll be available again.

Expect your rebuilding process to have its ups and downs. It takes tremendous energy to change habits. Sometimes there is sadness at letting go of your dreams of your perfect future together. Giving up your dreams hurts, but it frees you to move on to new dreams that are based on reality—that are a better fit for who you are today.

---

*Emily M. Brown, LCSW, MSW, is the founder and director of the Key Bridge Therapy and Meditation Center in Arlington, VA. She is a noted international expert on the issue of affairs.*

---



This article appeared in *Bonkers,* July/August 2001, pp. 32-36 and was excerpted from AFFAIRS by Emily M. Brown. Copyright © 1999 by Jossey-Bass. Reprinted by permission of John Wiley & Sons.

# What Kids (Really) Need

**Here's a question to drop in the center of the breakfast table and break in two: What if day care makes our children smarter—and meaner?**

**BY NANCY GIBBS**

It is the season again for working parents to brace themselves and shudder as the latest study on child care lands in the headlines to stoke their quiet fears. But not just theirs. Last week's survey, funded by the National Institutes of Health and the largest ever on the subject, had something awful for just about everyone.

> 17% of kids who spend more than 30 hours a week in day care have aggressive tendencies by kindergarten

The more hours children spend away from their mothers, researchers concluded, the more likely they are to be defiant, aggressive and disobedient by the time they get to kindergarten. Kids who are in child care more than 30 hours a week "scored higher on items like 'gets in lots of fights,' 'cruelty,' 'explosive behavior,' as well as 'talking too much,' 'argues a lot' and 'demands a lot of attention,'" said principal researcher Jay Belsky. It didn't matter if the children were black or white, rich or poor, male or female, and—most confounding—whether the care was provided by a traditional child-care center, a nanny, a grandmother, even Dad. Only Mom will do.

But just in case those stay-at-home moms found comfort in the choices and sacrifices they have made, the study also suggests that kids in strong child-care programs tend to develop better language and memory skills, are in certain respects better prepared for school. Would you take that trade, Mom and Dad?

The news refueled some ancient rivalries, revived the most basic questions about what price our children pay for the hours we work and the choices we make. Parents peered into the data looking for themselves, but clear distinctions were hard to find. So far, the unpublished study has offered us only two kinds of children: those raised at home by their mothers (about 1 in 4 children) and everyone else. Which begs the question that the researchers didn't even pretend to answer: Why would kids who are cared for by anyone other than Mom develop disruptive behaviors, and what should we do about it?

For that matter, should we even be worried at all? The researchers noted that almost all the "aggressive" toddlers were well within the range of normal behavior for four-year-olds. And what about that adjective, anyway? Is a vice not sometimes a form of virtue? Cruelty never is, but arguing back? Is that being defiant—or spunky and independent? "Demanding attention" could be a natural and healthy skill to develop if you are in a room with 16 other kids.

Some experts in the field argue that the problem is not child care but bad child care. Across the nation there is a numbing range in child-care quality, rules and regulations. Some states allow only six babies in one room, others allow 20. States require all different kinds of licensing and accreditation. Child-care workers get paid about $7 an hour on average, roughly the same as parking-lot attendants; no wonder good care is hard to find. "There is a crisis in this country," says Mary Kakareka, a child-care consultant in Rockville, Md. "Middle-class families pay a lot to get into bad centers—and then down the line, pay again to get their kids in special programs to help solve the problems."

But what constitutes good care, whether in the home or outside it? What is the healthiest way for children to spend their time, especially in the years before school soaks up most of the day? Many anxious parents, wanting the best for their children and willing to pay for it, fill their kids' days with oboe lessons and karate classes, their rooms with phonics tapes and smart toys. And yet if you ask the experts to name the most precious thing you can provide your child, they often cite things you cannot buy: time and attention, the appreciation that play is children's work. Maybe, as the study results suggest, mothers have a special gift for giving that kind of gentle company. But it's hard to believe they are the only ones who can, as anyone with a great baby sitter, grandmother, husband or day-care provider can tell you.

This is the challenge to busy parents, working long hours, strung out at home. What would it take to create an easy, quiet space where you can just hang out with your kids, read a story or make one up, build a fort, make something goopy together? If in the process your children grow secure in the knowledge that you will forgive them for whatever they break or spill or forget, if they learn to share because you are sharing, if they don't have to fight for your attention, those skills may serve them better in the adventure that is kindergarten than being able to distinguish the octagon from the hexagon or fuchsia from lilac. The best news about raising a super child is that the secret to doing it is not to try too hard.

---

# For better or worse

## Couples confront unemployment

When the pink slip arrives, it signals changes not only in employment, but also in a marriage.

**By Marilyn Gardner**
Staff writer of The Christian Science Monitor

SOMETIMES IT'S BEST not to count certain things.

Just ask Marilyn and Tom Middleton. They no longer tally the number of times he's been laid off when companies have merged, restructured, or failed. Nor do they keep precise track of the job-related moves they've made—15? 16?

They're not even sure how many years they've spent working in separate cities, commuting to see each other on weekends. She thinks it's about seven. He guesses closer to 10.

What they do know with certainty is that the job losses, moves, and separate addresses have strained their marriage almost to the breaking point at times. Like many couples dealing with unemployment, they have struggled with economic and emotional challenges. They even went through bankruptcy.

"Our marriage has had such incredible highs and lows," says Mrs. Middleton. "But we've hung in there. Now we're enjoying some of the good things."

"Hanging in there" is a skill more couples are honing these days as joblessness rises. More than three-quarters of unemployed Americans say family stress has increased since they lost their job, according to a new study by the National Employment Law Project.

Last month the unemployment rate rose to 6 percent—an eight-year high. In the past three months alone, more than half a million jobs have disappeared. Nearly 2 million people have been searching for at least six months.

In the first rush of pink-slip blues, a couple's concern is typically financial: how to keep the family afloat. As they settle into routines involving résumés, interviews, and rejections, other challenges may test a marriage.

"Work is so important to men in particular that when they lose that, they lose a pretty important part of their life. It affects relationships," says Larry Flaccus of Lexington, Mass., founder of a job-search group for executives called WeWantWork-Boston.com.

### 'How many résumés did you send?'

At work, he explains, people get positive feedback. But during unemployment, feedback may be negative.

"It's critical for the spouse to fill in some of the feedback that might be missing and say, 'I still love you,'" Mr. Flaccus says. "But it's also difficult for them." Almost no support groups exist to let spouses talk about unemployment issues.

Those issues can include loneliness, a lack of communication, changes in the balance of power, housework, too much togetherness, and not enough money.

When the Middletons exchanged wedding vows in 1970, the promise to stay together "for richer, for poorer; for better, for worse" seemed easy enough to make. Love conquers all, right?

That's the fairy-tale version. What they hadn't counted on was unemployment. In 1987, the company where Mr. Middleton worked merged with another company and laid off 95 percent of its staff. The couple had just bought a "dream house," and their two daughters were attending private school.

"It was devastating," he says. "You ask yourself, How am I going to provide for my family, a role I take very seriously?"

His wife remembers it as "a really rough time for us as a couple. You just don't think anything like that can ever happen to you."

For nine months Mr. Middleton looked for work. Eventually, they began an odyssey that took them from Toledo to a job in Colorado Springs. But that job disappeared before the moving van arrived from Toledo. Desperate, Mr. Middleton, a health-insurance executive, drove a taxi in Colorado Springs, while his wife worked two jobs at the mall. "We were barely making it," she says.

## Job loss is a family affair

*By Judy Lowe*

Some years ago, when experts began saying that wage earners would probably be employed by a number of different companies in their lifetimes, I wondered just how that would work.

The predictions were right: Rarely these days do people stay with the same company their whole careers. But my apprehensions were correct, too. No one explained—or planned for—a process by which someone could easily change professions several times.

Now we know that working for multiple companies and reinventing our careers often involves stretches of unemployment. And that can be demoralizing not just for the former job holder but also for the spouse.

When my husband's job was in peril through downsizing, and again when it ended, our marriage went through plenty of ups and downs.

Some of his fellow employees got divorces. I've often wondered what made the difference for us. Several things stand out, although they wouldn't necessarily be the same for others. We had always been used to discussing and sharing every aspect of our lives, including finances. How to allocate funds became a real problem for husbands and wives we knew who were used to keeping their earnings separate.

We have found, as did the couples Marilyn Gardner interviewed, that the lessons we learned during that period continue to strengthen our marriage. But if given a choice, I would rather have learned them some other way.

• *E-mail the Homefront at* **home@csps.com**.

## Family involvement

At one low point, the couple separated. But her father intervened, she recalls. "He told Tom to get his act together. He came to me and said, 'You have no business leaving.' I was mad at him for several years. But we took his advice to heart and were grateful."

Still, challenges—and moves—continued. A business partnership failed. Their daughters faced serious problems, and Mr. Middleton dealt with major illness.

How did the couple manage? Mrs. Middleton began a career as a foster-care therapist, which provided essential income. Their families and close friends gave emotional support. Their church and their faith also sustained them.

In one moment of despair, Mrs. Middleton remembers looking out the window and thinking, "You are going to make a commitment to go through this, and in the process you're going to learn to be joyful and content." She adds, "I've learned that that is not based on my husband."

Later she started a "gratitude journal," each day listing something she was thankful for.

Efforts like these paid off. After their earlier rocky patches, Mr. Middleton now calls his wife his "biggest cheerleader," explaining that she constantly reassured him that everything would be all right.

Now they are optimistic about a new chapter. Last month they moved from San Antonio to Baltimore, where he took up an executive position. They hope this job will take them to retirement.

## When the wife is unemployed

For working women, unemployment brings many of the same challenges, with an added factor: domestic responsibilities. Lucille Wilson of Waltham, Mass., a software developer, was laid off 19 months ago. She has 3-year-old twins and a husband she describes as "wonderful."

Yet household tasks intrude. "Now that I have 'so much free time,' I'm given all these other jobs that need to be done," says Mrs. Wilson, who, like others in this story, was interviewed by phone. "How am I supposed to look for a job, keep my skills up, clean the house, and do all the other things on the 'honey-do' list?"

Housework also becomes an issue when a man is jobless. Monica Leahy of Los Angeles avoids asking her unemployed husband to cook or clean, even though she works full time.

"He's going through such a tough period," she says. "To add this would be much more of a burden on him than it is on me." At the same time, she appreciates the help he gives. "He has done the dishes without me asking. He's helped with the laundry. He's kept the apartment very clean."

Then there is the essential issue of communication. At a time when couples need to air concerns and consider solutions, an out-of-work husband may become defensive or silent, while a wife may pepper him with too many questions. Mrs. Leahy emphasizes the importance of avoiding an interrogating tone.

## Honest communication

Her husband, she says, "was appreciative that I wasn't badgering him each day or asking him, 'Did anyone call? Do you have any interviews?' If he does, he'll let me know. I know how hard he works to find a job. I would never question that."

In the networking groups Flaccus leads, members complain about pressure at home. "Spouses say, 'Why don't you just go get a job?' There seems to be a difficulty in understanding that when there are no jobs available, you can't just go get a job."

Communication is a two-way street, of course. "You have to be able to vent your feelings, telling him once in a while, 'I'm scared, I'm upset,'" says Donna Birkel of Winston-Salem, N.C., whose husband, Damian, has been out of work twice.

Mr. Birkel, now the author of "Career Bounce-Back!" suggests that couples meet weekly to update their situation, rather than face daily grilling. He also urges them to focus on abundance wherever they can, instead of scarcity.

Sometimes dual-career couples find themselves sending résumés and reading want ads at the same time. A couple in Lee,

N.H., who wish to be identified only as Elizabeth and Patrick, lost their jobs in quality assurance at separate companies a year and a half ago. Now both are "totally reinventing" themselves, trying to start new businesses.

With three children, money is tight. "Sometimes we sit there and think, 'If only you would find a job. Why aren't you looking for a job at this very moment?'" she says. "We don't say it, but that's the undercurrent."

To gain fresh perspectives, Elizabeth and others emphasize the value of getting out of the house regularly, enjoying free or low-cost activities. Cabin fever is not conducive to family harmony.

When Birkel was unemployed, he and his family went to the art museum on the day admission was free. They also enjoyed picnics and "one-tank" trips. The Middletons like to take walks and talk along the way. Elizabeth and Patrick often head for their networking group, which offers a change of scenery and a welcome upbeat mood.

"Trying to stay positive is really key," Elizabeth says. "If you can find people to help you stay positive, it's important."

No one pretends that staying positive is easy. But Susan and Larry Flaccus, who have been married 32 years, find that a long-term perspective helps.

"There have been better times, and you know there will be better times again," Mrs. Flaccus says. "You have faith that somehow, together, you'll work something out. Which is not to say that I don't have terrible days. It isn't easy, but it isn't all bad."

While her husband job-hunts in Boston, she runs the couple's bed and breakfast in Shelburne, Mass. She thinks the fact that her income is secondary makes her husband's unemployment easier. "He doesn't have the feeling, 'Oh, I'm not making the money, she's making the money.'"

NOW EMPLOYED: Billy Skinner was laid off from his job just before young Will was born, so Rachel had to return to work right away.

Young couples face different challenges. Two weeks before Rachel and Billy Skinner's baby was born in 2001, Mr. Skinner lost his job in public relations in Austin, Texas. Suddenly Mrs. Skinner's plan to take 12 weeks of maternity leave changed. To bring in needed income, she returned to work when their son, Will, was 6 weeks old.

"It was very difficult," he says. "My wife obviously felt torn, as most mothers do, about going back." Yet he praises her for being supportive and encouraging during his job search, which he describes as "a real roller coaster." At 28, he was competing with experienced 45-year-olds who were willing to take a big pay cut just to get a job.

## Encouraging words

For her part, Mrs. Skinner focused on "getting through each day in the most supportive way." She thought of positive things in their lives—their baby, their health, their abilities. And she reminded her husband that he is smart, confident, capable.

"Sitting home and being mean to each other isn't going to change the situation," she says.

The couple also received encouragement from their parents. "They were reminding us to love each other and continue supporting each other, and were reinforcing our abilities."

After Mr. Skinner was turned down by several employers, the couple theorized that having a job would help him get a job by imposing a routine. He took a minimum-wage post at the Gap.

"Going to my mall job and working with 18- and 20-year-olds put a lot of things in perspective for me."

—Billy Skinner of Austin, Texas, who was laid off from a public-relations job and temporarily took a minimum-wage position just to get back into the workforce.

"Going to my mall job and working with 18- and 20-year-olds put a lot of things in perspective for me," he says. He began interviewing for positions paying considerably less than the $50,000 he had been earning.

Eventually, he received two job offers. He now works as marketing director for an auto-leasing company in Austin.

Looking back, he reflects on how they made it. "There was lots of prayer from lots of people, and a lot of effort on my wife's part. We had to be cheerleaders for each other."

Humor, philosophy, and gratitude help couples live through unemployment. It's good to realize it's not the end of the world.

The experience has also given him a reminder: "All of us forget to be as thankful as we should be when things are good."

Humor helps couples get through jobless periods, too. "We joke about all the character-building experiences we've had," says Teri Nelsen of Fort Collins, Colo., a mother of four, explaining that her husband declared bankruptcy after a franchise failed.

She would tell him, "You're a good person, and we'll get through this." He is graduating this spring with a master's degree in family therapy, which is her field as well.

Other job-seeking families also grow philosophical. "It's a phase," Leahy says. "This isn't permanent. This, too, shall pass."

**HAPPY DAYS: In the 32 years Marilyn and Tom Middleton have been married, they have seen many job-related ups and downs. These have strengthened their bonds.**

Elizabeth looks at the larger picture, saying, "This isn't the end of the world, and it shouldn't be the end of the marriage either. Keep track of what's important. You didn't marry this person just to be rich. Marriage is hard work whether you're out of work or not."

As the Middletons settle into their latest home, she calls these the "gift years," their reward for staying together. In San Antonio they even gave premarital seminars called Building a Solid Foundation at their church to help other couples avoid problems they faced.

"I would not for the world trade where we are as a couple," she says. "Is it perfect? No. Do I wish we could settle down? Yes. Life hasn't gone the way I would have chosen, but I've been blessed. Tom tells me daily that he loves me and that he's glad I'm a part of his life. We feel that if we can make it, there are few people out there who can't."

---

# THE BINDS THAT TIE—AND HEAL: HOW FAMILIES COPE WITH MENTAL ILLNESS

**Psychologist Herbert Gravitz, Ph.D., talks about the importance of families for the mentally ill. While the family may not cause mental illness, it may be one of the most powerful factors affecting the outcome.**

By Herbert Gravitz, Ph.D.

When I lean back in my chair and think about the Parker family, I know they have changed. Instead of fear, isolation and shame, there is love, connection and meaning. And most important, hope has replaced dread and despair. Millions of families throughout the country suffer just as the Parkers did, but many aren't as fortunate. These families are ignored at best and blamed at worst by a society that doesn't understand their needs. But the Parker family (not their real name) is an example of what can happen.

Our first family meeting took place on a cool November afternoon four years ago in my Santa Barbara office. To my left sat Paul Parker, a young man unable to perform his duties as a bookkeeper. He had lost two jobs in one month. In this time, other self-care behaviors had deteriorated as well, making it hard for him to live independently. He had become so increasingly bizarre that he was a concern and embarrassment to his entire family. To my right sat Paul's parents, Tom and Tina. And next to them were their two younger children, 16-year-old Jim and 23-year-old Emma.

Paul has a neurobiological disorder (NBD) and psychiatric illness caused by a brain dysfunction. NBDs currently include major depression, schizophrenia, bipolar disorder and obsessive-compulsive disorder. Although different types of mental illnesses present different challenges, there are similarities in the way these illnesses impact family members and loved ones.

The session unfolded. "You just don't understand, doctor," Paul's father bursted out. "Nobody listens to us, his family. It's not easy dealing with Paul. I hate to say this, but he can be such a burden. My wife and I can't do anything without considering its effect on Paul—and he is 30 years old. Half the time we feel crazy." Tom added, "Paul seems like a stranger to us. It's as though aliens have taken our son and left an impostor."

Almost mindless of the children, Tom and Tina shared the devastation of Paul's illness on their marriage. They were so drained and so angry with each other that they rarely made love, and they seldom went out together. When they did, they argued about Paul. Tom thought that many of Paul's problems were exaggerated and that he was taking advantage of them. Like many mothers, Tina was more protective and accommodating of her son, especially during the early years. These differences led to quarrels in front of the children, which the family dreaded almost as much as Paul's strange and peculiar behavior. Both parents had little compassion left for Paul or each other. Even less time was left for Jim and Emma, because they seemed so normal and caused no problems.

Without warning Jim interrupted, "Not again. Why does Paul get all the attention? I never feel important. You always talk about him." Ignoring her own fears, Emma tried to reassure the family that Paul would be okay. "We've handled Paul's problems before," she pleaded. There were many unspoken feelings, such as the overwhelming responsibility Tom and Tina suffered, the resentment that Emma and Jim felt, as well as the family's guilt, exhaustion and demoralization. And there was a half-wish that Paul would just disappear.

Despite everything, the family loved Paul. They each had powerful—even fierce—loyalties toward him. This was evident when Tom explained: "We brought Paul here, we care what happens, we sit in the waiting room while his life is on the line, and we will take care of Paul when everything is said and done." Paul was important to all of them.

## Stopping the hurt

The family had sought help from other mental health professionals. Paul's parents recounted being blamed for his disorder by several professionals, and they reported feeling confused and helpless. Emma and Jim felt like outcasts, they were ignored by their parents and shunned by their friends. Everyone wanted the hurt to stop. At the very least, the family wanted someone to recognize their pain and say, "This must be very hard for all of you."

The Parkers are not rare or unusual. One in five Americans has a psychiatric disorder at any given time, and half will have one at some point in their lifetime.

More than 100 million Americans have a close family member who suffers from a major mental illness. Of the 10 leading causes of disability, half are psychiatric. By the year 2020, the major cause of disability in the world may be major depression. Further, it has been estimated that only 10 to 20% of those requiring care in the United States receive it in institutions; the rest receive their primary care from the family.

Devoted to their ill member, the family may be the best-kept secret in the arsenal of healing. Yet, family members are considered the support team; they are not known as the stressed and the grieving. These tired mothers and fathers, daughters and sons, husbands and wives deserve attention as well.

Mental illness can weave a web of doubt, confusion and chaos around the family. Unwittingly, the person with mental illness can dominate the entire family through control and fear or helplessness and incapacity. Like a bully, the mental illness bosses the primary sufferer as well as the loved ones. Instability, separation, divorce and abandonment are frequent family outcomes of mental illness.

## Under the influence

I have observed five factors that bind families to the despair of their loved one's illness: stress, trauma, loss, grief and exhaustion. These factors provide a useful framework to understand the underlying structure of the family under the influence.

- Stress is at the foundation of the family experience of mental illness. There is constant tension, dread and worry because the illness can strike at any time. It's common for family members "to walk on eggshells." The Parkers liken the atmosphere to a pressure cooker and the possibility of the ill loved one "going off the deep end" looms. Stress accumulates and leads to psychosomatic illness. Tom has high blood pressure, while Tina suffers ulcers.
- Trauma also lies at the core of the family's experience. It can erode members' beliefs about control, safety, meaning and their own value. While victims of NBDs rarely assault others physically, they do assault with words, and their words can pull apart the family. Another form of trauma is "witness trauma," where the family watches helplessly as loved ones are tortured by their symptoms. This type of family atmosphere can often induce the development of traumatic symptoms like invasive thoughts, distancing and physical disorders. The result can be traumatic stress or posttraumatic stress disorder. Much of the family's despair results from trying to manage and control what it cannot. Knowing when to intervene is one of most difficult lessons a family must learn.
- Loss lies at the very nature of family life. Family members report losses in their personal, social, spiritual and economic lives. They suffer losses in privacy, freedom, security and even dignity. "What we miss most is a normal life," said Mrs. Parker. "We have lost being just an ordinary family." The family may be the only place where we cannot be replaced. So it can be devastating if we cannot have effective family relationships.
- Grief occurs from this steady diet of loss. Family members can go through protracted grieving, which often goes undiagnosed or untreated. Grieving centers around what life will not be. "It's as if we are in a funeral that never ends," said Tom. Grieving can become compounded because our culture does not sufficiently acknowledge and legitimize the grief of those under the influence of mental illness. A lack of appropriate entitlement can follow. "I really have no right to feel bad. Paul is the one who is ill," said Tom. Therefore, mourning fails to occur, preventing acceptance and integration of loss.
- Exhaustion is the natural result of living in such an atmosphere. The family becomes an endless emotional and monetary resource, and must frequently monitor the concerns, issues and problems of the ill loved one. Worry, preoccupation, anxiety and depression can leave the family drained—emotionally, physically, spiritually, economically. Tina summarized it, "There's no rest." Tom added, "We can't even get a good night's sleep; we lie awake wondering what Paul is doing. This is 24 hours a day, 365 days a year."

## Leaving it to fate

Living in an environment of chronic stress, trauma, loss, grief and fatigue can also lead other family members to their own parallel disorder. Parallel disorders of family members are also known as secondary or vicarious traumatization. The family members can develop symptoms including denial, minimization, enabling, high tolerance for inappropriate behavior, confusion and doubt, guilt and depression, and other physical and emotional problems.

Other more recent terms include learned helplessness, which occurs when family members find that their actions are futile; depression fallout, the consequence of living in close proximity to a loved one's despair; and compassion fatigue, burnout that comes from intimate relationships when family members believe they cannot help their loved one and are unable to disengage from the illness long enough to get restored. "I'm just too tired to care," said Tina.

The symptoms of families under the influence of NBDs can be devastating, but they are also very treatable. Research consistently shows that four elements lead to healing: information, coping skills, support and love.

Healing begins with an accurate diagnosis; from there core issues can be confronted. The family moves beyond their loved one's illness—not away from their loved one.

In response to pain, the family can learn to develop a disciplined approach to dealing with their situations. Tina, for example, has embraced spirituality and has learned to ask herself, "What is the lesson that I am supposed to learn in this very moment?" Tom adds, "When I gave up caring about what was supposed to be, I got back my footing and now have something to offer Paul other than my temper."

To create a new life, the Parkers made five key transitions that facilitated healing. Although not every family member made all of these shifts, most family members made enough of them to change their lives. First, to transform the way they thought and felt, they shifted from denial to awareness. When the reality of the illness was confronted and accepted, healing began. The second transition was a shift in focus from the mentally ill person to attention to self. This shift requires the establishment of healthy boundaries. The third transition was moving from isolation to support. Facing the problems of living with mental illness is too difficult to do alone. Family members worked within a framework of love. This makes it easier to relate to the illness with distance and perspective. The fourth change is family members learning to respond to the person instead of the illness itself.

The fifth and final shift toward healing occurs when members find personal meaning in their situation. This elevates the personal, private and limited stories of the family to a much larger and more heroic level. This shift doesn't change what happened or even take the hurt away, it just makes people feel less alone and more empowered. It creates choices and new possibilities.

It has been a little over three years since my first encounter with the Parker family. Yesterday, I met with them for the first time in over a year. As they sat in their familiar seats, I reminisced. I remembered the moment the family's denial was broken: when Tina said to her son Paul, "I have your pain and I have my pain—I have both."

When we first met, they were trying to save a past; now they are building a future. The session was punctuated by laughter as the Parkers learned to reduce their expectations to more realistic levels. They also learned to take better care of themselves. Because family members who get help and support demonstrate healthier functioning, Paul has become more responsible for his own recovery.

Change has occurred for many other reasons. Newer medications, for example, have helped Paul significantly. Almost 95% of what we have learned about the brain has occurred in the last 10 years. Initially, family members couldn't talk to one another. Now, they turn to each other and speak openly about their concerns. Tom and Tina have found a new life through their advocacy and support group work. Emma has married. And Jim is studying to be a psychologist and wants to help families.

Healing a family entails discipline. With love and commitment, family members can break the spell of the illness by broadening their sense of meaning. And meaning can be found in such diverse areas as religion, raising children, contributing to charities, forming organizations, developing a 12-step program, writing, running for office, or helping the boy next door who lost his father.

Families like the Parker's are among a growing number of people who are recognizing that they have been impacted by the mental illness of a loved one. They are choosing to acknowledge their plight, grieve their losses, learn new skills and connect with others.

Living under the influence of mental illness calls us to confront the darker as well as deeper sides of life. It can be a terrifying, heart-breaking, lonely and exhausting experience or it can forge the latent, untapped strengths of individuals and families. There is more hope than ever for families. And it is never too late to have a happy family.

Said Tina Parker, "While I don't believe life is a bowl of cherries, it isn't a can of worms anymore either." And Tom adds, "Hardly a day goes by where I am not grateful for my family and being alive. I savor the good days and let the bad ones pass. I have learned to make the most out of every moment."

### READ MORE ABOUT IT

*The Burden of Sympathy: How Families Cope with Mental Illness* By David A. Karp (Oxford University Press, 2001)

*Obsessive Compulsive Disorder: New Help for the Family* By Herbert Gravitz (Healing Visions Press, 1998)

---

*Herbert L. Gravitz, Ph.D., practices in Santa Barbara, California. He is a founding board of director for the National Association for Children of Alcoholics.*

# Tough medical tasks fall to families

**By John Keilman**
Tribune staff reporter

Carina Borst isn't a nurse, but you'd never know it watching her clinical detachment as she vacuums fluids from the hole in her 1-year-old son's throat, or monitors his blood oxygen level, or medicates him through the tube in his stomach.

If Borst, 32, were paid to do these things, she would need a nursing license. But because she is Zachary's mother, she's allowed to give him this medical care at home, with or without training. In fact, she has little choice.

While her son is supposed to get 16 hours of nursing care a day paid for by the state, a nursing shortage means he's lucky to get eight. Consequently, said Borst, who lives in the northwest suburbs, "most of the time, it's just all me."

Borst is among the growing number of ordinary people who provide sophisticated medical care for their loved ones at home. As hospital stays grow shorter, insurers stingier and visiting nurses scarcer, relatives find themselves giving injections, maintaining intravenous lines and operating dialysis machines.

For some, it's a positive trend, giving them more control over medical care and keeping their loved ones out of hospitals and nursing homes.

Others, though, feel overwhelmed by the responsibility, which they say is thrust upon them without adequate preparation or support.

"It's scary having to do it yourself," said Jennifer Rembrecht, 40, of Naperville, whose son, Jake, 3, breathes through a tube in his throat and eats through a tube in his stomach. She received informal hospital training on how to manage the equipment but said it was "definitely above my level for the first year."

And because mistakes are likely to go undetected and unreported, nobody is certain how this has affected the quality of medical care for patients who are dependent on family members.

Families have always played a crucial role in taking care of relatives. What's changing, experts say, is that these caregivers are performing more and more medical duties once handled by skilled professionals.

"You had the managed care revolution, kicking people out of hospitals quicker and sicker, and at the same time you had people designing nifty gadgets to allow those people to get high-tech medical care at home," said John D. Arras, a University of Virginia biomedical ethics professor who has studied the phenomenon.

"Treatments that would have been available previously only in intensive care units were finding their way into people's living rooms," he said, citing the operation of complicated equipment such as ventilators, infusion pumps, computerized feeding tubes and dialysis machines.

## Fewer professionals

But the number of professionals trained to offer those treatments in the home has been shrinking. As Medicare, Medicaid and private insurers cut back on what they'll cover and how much they'll pay, visiting nurses are in short supply.

"We had 14,000 home health agencies in 1997. We're now down to 7,000 or so," said Carolyn Markey, president of the Visiting Nurse Associations of America.

So medical duties are falling to family. In Illinois, as in other states, laws prohibiting the practice of nursing without a license do not apply to family members. In fact, no law requires that family members be trained at all.

A 1998 national survey of 1,000 family caregivers by the United Hospital Fund of New York found that one-third of those who changed bandages or used medical equipment received no instruction.

When training does take place, it is often inadequate, the fund's Carol Levine said.

"Family members are really put in a terrible situation, with a half-hour training in the hospital, maybe, and a 1-800 number to call, which is practically of no use, and you're on your own," she said.

Home care does not have to be high-tech to induce high stress in loved ones. Diane Lawson of Des Plaines said she spent five months this year dressing sores on the feet of her 80-year-old mother, a chore handled primarily by visiting nurses until Medicare slashed their visits.

Lawson never received formal instruction, and the task proved trickier than she expected. She had to wash her hands before putting on gloves, rub salve on the wounds, prevent the bandages from touching non-sterile surfaces and change gloves as she moved from one foot to the other. It came to be a juggling act done twice a day.

## CAREGIVER:
## 'It's scary having to do it yourself'

"I guess I would have rather had someone talk me through it, because I was very klutzy with the bandages," she said. "[The nurses] had their little tricks, and I didn't catch onto them."

The sores eventually became infected, Lawson said, and she wonders whether she might have been responsible.

Some agencies are more systematic about training family members.

Linnea Windel, chief executive officer of the Visiting Nurse Association of Fox Valley in Aurora, said that as her nurses demonstrate procedures, they use a checklist to ensure the caregiver is following each step. Training can take several visits, she said, and nurses judge the family member's competence.

"There have been situations where we have said this family is not capable of doing a procedure," Windel said.

In that case, the agency will assign a nurse to handle the job even if the insurance company refuses to pay for it, she said.

That gray area has led to tactical maneuvering by some caregivers. Marty Beilin of the Well Spouse Foundation, which runs support groups for caregivers, said the organization warns its members about allowing themselves to be trained for medical procedures they don't feel comfortable performing.

"Once the insurance company feels that you can do this, then they take it off the list of skilled care needs," he said. "If I can give an injection, they will not pay for a nurse to come once a week to give the injection.

## Quality in question

Lenard Kaye, director of the University of Maine's Center on Aging, said it's hard to measure because mistakes are unlikely to be detected.

While many family caregivers say their devoted attention more than makes up for a lack of experience, some evidence suggests problems exist. The United Hospital Fund survey found that 1 in 8 caregivers who administered a loved one's medication was aware of making a mistake.

The federal government in 2000 issued a $141 million grant to help caregivers, and Joseph Lugo, planning specialist for the Illinois Department on Aging, said some of that money is paying for hands-on training programs, including medication management.

But some say far more help is needed for family members increasingly expected to do more on the medical front lines.

"Nobody really thought through what that meant for the family member," Levine said. "People can learn how to do things, but I often wonder if you don't speak English, or you haven't had some sort of education in computers or how machines work, how do you manage? I really, really worry about people."

## Family

# Home Alone

Single parents in the armed forces face some special problems as they ship out for the Gulf

**BY ADAM PIORE**

MASTER SGT. SUE HARPER STANDS IN HER KITCHEN CLUTCHING a drawer so tightly her knuckles turn white. Oblivious to the dinner chatter in her dining room, the rail-thin blonde with the ponytail and glasses presses a telephone to her ear. "Master Sergeant Harper, sir. I was told to check in every couple hours," she says. After a moment, she hears what she was hoping for. "Well, good! Thank you, sir." Harper hangs up, relieved. There will be no deployment to Turkey tonight. Instead, she can sleep at home in the same bed with her 12-year-old daughter, Maria, on the Kaiserslautern military base in Germany. From her smile, you'd think she won the lottery. But this simple reprieve is better than money. Harper is a single mom, and living alone with Maria has forged an unusually strong bond between mother and daughter. Saying goodbye is never easy; saying goodbye as she heads off to war is almost more than Harper can bear. "Every parent feels they are the only person who understands their kid and can do things for them," says Harper, 39, a public-affairs officer with the 21st Theater Support Command, a logistics unit. "I worry that other people just won't get her like I do." Then she asks the question that haunts her most: "What if I don't come back?"

These are lonely times for parents like Harper. Those familiar media images of husbands and wives bidding each other tearful farewells on docks and airfields tell only part of the story. According to the Pentagon, the number of single moms and dads in the military has nearly doubled since the last gulf war from 47,685 in 1992 to almost 90,000 today. Despite the dramatic increase, however, the Pentagon has no special programs in place for them. Military officials aren't even sure why the numbers are up. "That's not something we could speculate on," says Lt. Col. Cynthia Colin, a Pentagon spokeswoman. "We recruit people, and the people in the military reflect society."

While there are no hard data to explain the jump, it's clear that jobs in today's much smaller forces are more demanding than in the past. Between 1992 and 2002, the military shrank from about 1.8 million to 1.4 million active-service members; those who remain have seen their burdens increase. "Certainly, frequent deployments and long separations are challenging for marriages," says Shelley MacDermid, a professor and co-director of the Military Family Research Institute at Purdue University. "One hypothesis is that as the tempo has gone up, it's been harder to stay married."

**The prospect of war brings parents agonizing choices. Perhaps the most difficult of them all: what to do with your children while you're gone?**

Raising a child in the military—moving from base to base, surviving on a paltry government salary—has never been easy. But life as a single military parent these days poses special challenges. The prospect of war brings agonizing choices: How to explain to your child the need to leave? How much to reveal about the danger ahead? Perhaps most difficult of all: What to do with your kids while you're gone?

**FAMILY MATTERS: Sgt. Gatson sent her sons, Cori and Dashon, to stay with her ex-husband, Elton, in Louisiana**

For Sgt. Shala Gatson, 24, also stationed in Germany, the solution lay about 5,000 miles away. In January, Gatson delivered her two young sons, Cori, 7, and Dashon, 5, to her ex-husband

(and Dashon's father), Elton, in Alexandria, La. Because the Army doesn't pay the cost of flying children back to the United States, Gatson, a supply specialist also with the 21st who makes roughly $2,000 a month, had to borrow from friends to come up with the $800 airfare. During the all-too-brief time with his mother in Louisiana, Dashon one day nonchalantly asked, "Mama, are you going to die?" "No," she told him. "I'm going to do my best to come back. Mommy has to go and protect the other people from the bad guys. Mommy is going to go work on computers." After she left, the boys struggled to adjust. They were happy to be spending time with Elton, but their mother was ever in their thoughts. "My mama is fighting a war," Cori told his teacher one day, "and after the war we're all going back to Germany."

Harper chose to bring a friend from Arkansas to Germany to care for Maria. Theresa Snuffer, or "Ms. Theresa," is a silver-haired former stay-at-home mom whose husband served five tours in Vietnam. She understands the needs of children like Maria. "I don't think a kid should be uprooted," says Snuffer, who arrived in Europe last month. "It's OK for summer vacation. But during the school year, they should be around their own things." In addition to a tight-knit group of military neighbors to help Snuffer look after Maria, there is a school staff experienced in handling deployments. In recent weeks counselors at Kaiserslautern Middle School have been gathering the names of students whose parents are deploying. They will be watching for several telltale signs. "Some children start acting out," says counselor Harriet Scofield. "We often see grades falling, uncompleted homework. Other children will start having problems with peers, picking arguments."

Ironically, the increase in the number of single parents in the military may be in part the result of recent Pentagon successes. In 1989, Congress created a new network of mostly five-day-a-week child-care centers for parents in the military, and offered subsidies based on family income. The moves made the military a more viable career option for all parents, singles and couples alike. Still, there are gaps. Child care is usually available only weekdays from 9 to 5 and soldiers are fined if they are late picking up their kids. More broadly, no consideration is given to the special needs of single parents. "We have a lot of different people in different situations," says the Pentagon's Colin. Providing more assistance for single parents being sent to the Gulf is "really not feasible," Colin says. "It would just be way too much work. Each situation is different, depending on where you are stationed and what your situation is. Some people might live near a grandparent. Others may live in another country."

While they were still together in Germany, Sue and Maria made the best of it. Maintaining the ordinariness of life, the little daily rituals, seemed to bring the most comfort. There were dinners at their favorite restaurant, Alt Landstuhl, where waitresses still wear traditional German costumes, and where Maria and her mother like to order "the grossest things" on the menu. "That's how I fell in love with snails," says Maria. In those precious final days, special events took on new meaning. In an auditorium festooned with balloons, men and women in camouflage sat among students for an awards ceremony that was likely to be the last school event many of the parents would attend for a long time. Maria was called to the stage three times: for good citizenship, for making the honor roll and, most important, for winning the school competition in the National Geographic Geography Bee. She received a medal on a ribbon and placed it squarely over her mother's shoulders. Sue won't be able to attend the regional finals, to be held this month. But for a little while, at least, things were as they should be. Mother and daughter shared a moment of celebration together, and Iraq and the looming thunder of war seemed far, far away.

Gatson and Harper finally shipped out to Turkey the last week of February. It was easier for Gatson—by the time she left, she could barely stand the sight of her sons' rooms. "The house is so empty," she said. "Nobody fussing, nobody coming in and saying, 'How you doing?'" Harper found it difficult. Every morning before school, she said a tearful goodbye, never knowing if she would be there when Maria came home. Finally early one morning a little past 4 a.m., Harper kissed her sleepy daughter and slipped away.

With ARIAN CAMPO-FLORES

# Terrorism, trauma, and children: What can we do?

By Linda Goldman

***"I never knew grief could feel so much like fear."***

—*C. S. LEWIS*

On September 11, 2001, our children, either directly or vicariously, witnessed the terrorist assault upon our nation, watching over and over again as fanatics crashed American planes into the World Trade Center, the Pentagon, and the fields of Pennsylvania. Our young people witnessed adults running frantically out of control, jumping blindly out of windows, screaming, crying, and appearing bewildered—through black smoke-filled skies and burning buildings—as an insidious and non-locatable enemy emerged to wreak pandemonium and panic upon their lives. The media acted as a surrogate parent and extended family *before* this horrific event, and shared with our children *during* this event visually, aurally, and viscerally. These were sounds and images so graphic that they will forever be imprinted upon their psyche and ours. This unprecedented horror is now a traumatic overlay, potentially triggering all of the pre-existing grief-related issues that our children were carrying before September 11.

Death-related tragedies involving suicide, homicide, and AIDS, and non-death-related traumas such as bullying and victimization, divorce and separation, foster care and abandonment, violence and abuse, drugs and alcohol, and sexuality and gender identification had left many youth living their lives with overwhelmed feelings and distracted thoughts. After September 11, these issues still prevail, infused with the paradigm of terrorism, war, biological destruction, and nuclear annihilation—ideas that are entirely new for our children, for whom "war" is part of a history lesson. In the adult world our children look to for security and comfort, they now see or sense a world of terror, panic, and anxiety, with too many questions and too few answers about their future.

Children processing their grief and trauma may not necessarily progress in a linear way through typical grief phases. The four phases of grief are shock and disbelief, searching and yearning, disorganization and despair, and rebuilding and healing (*Life and Loss,* 2002). These phases may surface and resurface in varying order, intensity, and duration. Grief and trauma work can be messy, with waves of feelings and thoughts flowing through children when they least expect them to come. Kids can be unsuspectingly hit with "grief and trauma bullets" in the car listening to a song or the news, seeing or hearing an airplane overhead, or watching the video of the New York devastation or the Pentagon crash. A fireman's siren, a jet fighter, a soldier in military uniform, a letter in the mailbox, or a balloon bursting can trigger sudden intense feelings without any warning.

## Children's voices

Children's reactions to terrorism, war, anthrax, and the perceived loss of safety and protection provide a window into their psyches and help suggest ways the adults around them can help. Our ability to listen to questions, thoughts, and feelings is paramount in creating a safe zone for our children to process these life-changing times.

Children normally assume they live in a friendly, safe, and caring world. The terrorist attacks of September 11 amplified the pre-existing signs that their world is unprotected, scary, and contains an uncertain future. This deepened loss of the assumptive world of safety for our children creates a new set of voices that all parents, educators, and health professionals must heed.

Five-year-old Tommy, after sitting and listening to his Mom's careful explanation about the terrorist attack, explained why he was really upset about the terrorism: "This is a real tragedy, because I kept searching and searching all day and couldn't find any of my cartoons on TV."

## Talking to children about terrorism, trauma, and war

One question weighing heavily on the minds of parents, educators, and mental health professionals is "How do we talk to our children about war, terrorism, prejudice, biochemical attack, and nuclear destruction?"

Sometimes it may help to ask children if they have been "thinking about world events" and if they are, open a dialogue. Some children don't want to talk about it. Some live in fear they will be killed, others say there is nothing to worry about. Some may want to know the facts; therefore we need to choose words

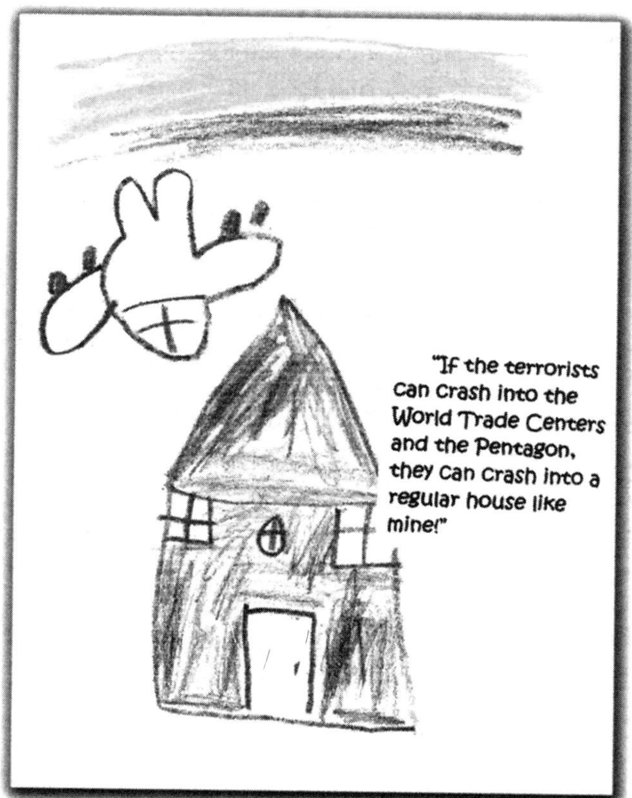

"If the terrorists can crash into the World Trade Centers and the Pentagon, they can crash into a regular house like mine!"


Darian, age 6, illustrates his fear for his own safety after September 11.

that will help them understand what is happening around them. Because so many of us feel "it's just too big," we need to be able to discuss each piece of this huge experience a little at a time. The following are examples of definitions helpful to initiate dialogue with children.

***Terrorism*** *is an act or acts of violence, abuse, murder, or devastation against unsuspecting people and countries by a person or group of people that believe their cause is more important than human life or property. Their feeling of "being right" is sometimes more important to them than their own lives. Terrorists can be big or small, black or white, or any color, American or foreign. Their goal is to create terror, disruption, and vulnerability.*

***Trauma*** *is an experience that can be scary and difficult. It may create feelings of fear, anger, rage, and revenge. A trauma can be a death of someone close to use, caused by a car accident or a terrorist bombing. It can also be from knowing something scary that happened on TV, or to someone we know, or even to a stranger we see on a news video.*

## Creating dialogues

When creating dialogues with children, use accurate, real, and age-appropriate language, avoiding clichés or denial of their experience. Concentrate on giving the facts, and keep responses to questions simple and age-appropriate. This helps adults follow the lead of children as to how much information they choose to take in. Especially with young children, minimize the scope of the tragedy, without contemplating with them what did or may happen.

Keeping explanations developmentally appropriate allows children to process this experience at their own level. Young elementary school children need simple information balanced with reassurance that trustworthy adults are bringing stability to their day-to-day life. Middle school children may seek out more facts and want to know more about what is being done to keep them safe and healthy at home, school, and in the community. High school students may outspokenly voice opinions about what happened and why, and may need to develop ways to combat terrorism, rationalize war, and prevent world annihilation. (Adapted from National Association of School Psychologists, NASP, www.nasponline.org.)

Telling children the truth in an age-appropriate way is very important. They often have a conscious or unconscious knowledge of events happening around them and can sense the impact of the terrorist trauma on the adult world. One mom shared just such an experience in the car with her four-year-old son, Andy. She was "sneaking" a listen to the news on the day of the attack. As the reporter began talking about the destruction of the World Trade Center, she quickly turned it off so Andy couldn't hear. Andy immediately explained his level of awareness: "Mommy, they are talking about the plane crash that blew up buildings today."

He just knew about it. If Andy had then been told his experience wasn't real, he may have begun to doubt himself and/or the adult world and question his mother's truthfulness. If Andy felt his mom was hiding the truth about what happened, he might worry more, thinking his mom was too afraid to tell him what really happened. Either way, Andy may have another loss—the loss of the trust in the adult world. Teachable moments for all children can evolve with teachers and parents on subjects such as bullying, violence, prejudice, sexual discrimination, and conflict resolution.

It's OK to let children know you are upset and worried too. Using mature modeling of this upset and worry can create examples for children to follow. It's often hard for them to reconcile a message of "Don't worry; everything is fine" with the enormity of anxiety they may feel coming from the adult world. Find out what they may know about the traumatic event, remembering that they may process what they see and hear inaccurately. Search for faulty perceptions and replace these with simple truths. Young children usually worry about their immediate environment, their family and friends and pets, and their ongoing day-to-day routine. Kids may worry something will happen to their dog, their home, or their friend.

## Prepare children for dialogue

Reassure children that what they are feeling is very common. Emphasize to them that adults are feeling the same things that they are. Remind them that everyone has different ways of showing their feelings and that is OK. Restore confidence by reassuring them that problems are being handled, people who were hurt are being cared for, buildings are being cleared, and that things are getting a little better each day.

## *Helping our children grieve can only help the grieving child in each one of us.*

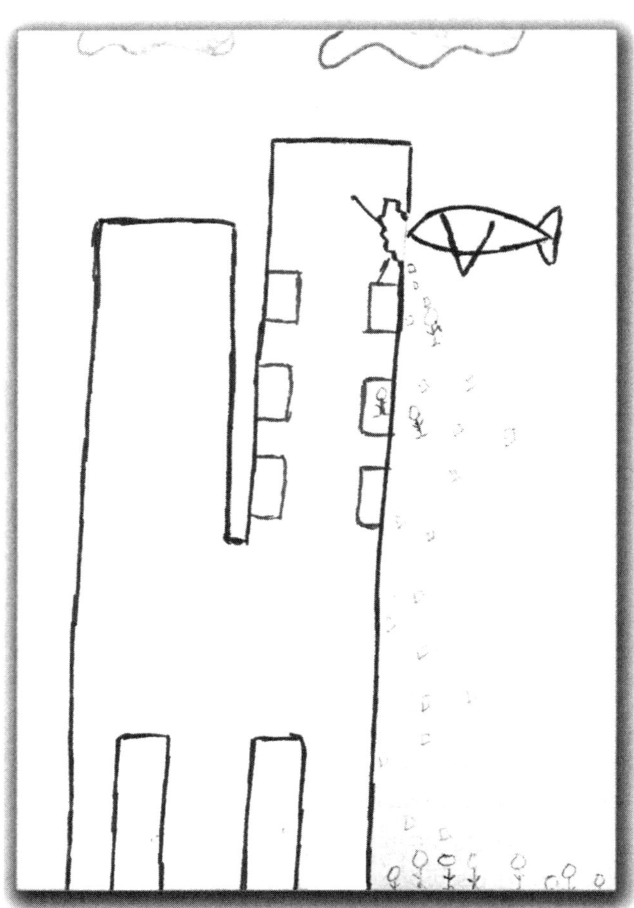

With this recreation of the World Trade Center destruction, 13-year-old Tiara illustrates her grief over the horrific footage she viewed on TV.

Mature modeling guides children to create responsible ways to be helpful during the crisis. Emphasize ways that adults can help. Parents can volunteer to give blood, food, time, and money. Relief agencies such as the Red Cross issued appeals for help. Contributions of needed goods and family money can be taken to needy areas. Children can be included in planning ways families can help and joining in delivering food and clothing. Families and schools may want to join together in saying a prayer for the victims that were attacked, for their families, and for world leaders to bring about peace.

### Accept children's reactions

While there are several commonly seen reactions to trauma in children, these reactions range widely. Some children will listen to your explanation and then go out to play. Others will want to stay near you and talk about it for a length of time, or maybe ask you to drive them to school instead of taking the bus. Still others may be angry that adults can't immediately fix the problem.

Children can use many activities to safely tell their story. Props like firefighter and police hats, doctor kits, toy soldiers, and hand puppets can be used to reenact the tragedy and war. Toys, puppets, art, clay modeling, collage, letter writing, journaling, and other projective play can be used for role-play and expression of emotions. Positive visualizations and breathing exercises can help kids to relax.

### Activities to help children participate in world events

Children can create rituals that allow commemoration and avenues to voice feelings. Lighting candles, planting flowers, writing letters, raising money for victims, or saying prayers for survivors or world peace allow children to be recognized mourners. Thirteen-year-old Helen lived in a New Jersey community where many families, especially those of firefighters and police, had been deeply affected by the World Trade Center disaster. "Let's make brownies," she told her younger brother and sister, "and sell them to raise money for the firefighters. Everybody likes brownies."

Communities can involve children in participating in fundraisers for the survivors of terrorist attacks. Making patriotic pins and selling them to raise money to help victims and survivors, creating Web sites for world peace, or having a poster contest at school on "What We Can Do to Feel Safe" are ways to give children back a sense of control and participation in their own lives.

### What kids can do about terrorism

**1.** Talk about their feelings. Allow children ways to tell their story as much as they need to. Draw pictures, create poems, write letters, or offer suggestions about ways to help.

**2.** Make a fear box. Cut out pictures from newspapers and magazines about what frightens them and paste these around the box. Write down their fears and put them inside.

**3.** Create a worry list. Make a list of worries from 1 to 5; number 1 is the biggest. Suggest that children talk about this list with someone they trust, like their mom or dad, their sister or brother, their guidance counselor, or a good friend.

**4.** Put together a "peaceful box." Ask kids to find toys, stuffed animals, and pictures that make them feel safe and peaceful, and keep these items in the box.

**5.** Help others. Help boys and girls give food or clothing to people who need it. Suggest that the family donate money to a good cause, like the Red Cross, the fund for victims and survivors of terrorist action, or the children in Afghanistan.

**6.** Display an American flag and create an original global flag. Children can place these flags together outside their house to remind everyone of their support for their country and their hope for world peace.

**7.** As a family, say a nightly prayer and light a candle for world peace.

## Helping our children grieve

We are now a nation and a world of grieving, traumatized children, and the terror of bullying lives inside most of us on this planet and threateningly looms over our everyday life. Our children fear terrorism from foreign strangers and bullying from well-known classmates, siblings, and adult figures. If we can help our kids to see the relationship between terrorist attacks, bullying behaviors, and issues of power and control, we can begin rooting out the behaviors that create oppression, prejudice, misguided rage, and destruction of people and property as a justification for a cause or self-serving purpose.

Responsible adults need to help children cope with trauma and loss and grief from the terrorists outside their country and the bullying within their homes, schools, and community. Providing information, understanding, and skills on these essential issues may well aid them in becoming more compassionate, caring human beings and thereby increase their chances of living in a future world of inner and outer peace.

When the crisis interventions have passed, we will need extensive training in schools and universities to prepare to work with kids in the context of a new paradigm of trauma and grief. Educators, parents, health professionals, and all caring adults must become advocates in creating understanding and procedures to work with our children facing a present and future so different from their past. Our task is to help our children stay connected to their feelings during the continuing trauma of terrorism and war.

The terrorist attack has transformed us all into a global community joining together to re-instill protection and a sense of safety for America and for the world. Helping our children grieve can only help the grieving child in each one of us.

---

*Read more about children and complicated grief issues in Linda Goldman's book* Breaking the Silence: A Guide to Help Children With Complicated Grief/Suicide, Homicide, AIDS, Violence, and Abuse *(Taylor and Francis, 2002). To contact Linda Goldman, e-mail her at lgold@erols.com or visit her Web site at www.erols.com/lgold.*

# Marriage and Divorce American Style

A destructive marriage is not a happy family.

By E. Mavis Hetherington

ON AVERAGE, RECENT STUDIES SHOW, PARENTS AND CHILDREN in married families are happier, healthier, wealthier, and better adjusted than those in single-parent households. But these averages conceal wide variations. Before betting the farm on marriage with a host of new government programs aimed at promoting traditional two-parent families and discouraging divorce, policy makers should take another look at the research. It reveals that there are many kinds of marriage and not all are salutary. Nor are all divorces and single-parent experiences associated with lasting distress. It is not the inevitability of positive or negative responses to marriage or divorce that is striking, but the diversity of them.

Men do seem to benefit simply from the state of being married. Married men enjoy better health and longevity and fewer psychological and behavioral problems than single men. But women, studies repeatedly have found, are more sensitive to the emotional quality of the marriage. They benefit from being in a well-functioning marriage, but in troubled marriages they are likely to experience depression, immune-system breakdowns, and other health-related problems.

We saw the same thing in the project I directed at the Hetherington Laboratory at the University of Virginia, which followed 1,400 divorced families, including 2,500 kids—some for as long as 30 years—interviewing them, testing them, and observing them at home, at school, and in the community. This was the most comprehensive study of divorce and remarriage ever undertaken; for policy makers, the complexity of the findings is perhaps its most important revelation.

## GOOD MARRIAGES, BAD MARRIAGES

By statistical analysis, we identified five broad types of marriage—ranging from "pursuer-distancer" marriages, (which we found were the most likely to end in divorce), to disengaged marriages, to operatic marriages, to "cohesive-individuated" marriages, and, finally, traditional marriages (which had the least risk of instability).

To describe them briefly:

- Pursuer-distancer marriages are those mismatches in which one spouse, usually the wife, wants to confront and discuss problems and feelings and the other, usually the husband, wants to avoid confrontations and either denies problems or withdraws.
- Disengaged marriages are ones where couples share few interests, activities, or friends. Conflict is low, but so is affection and sexual satisfaction.
- Operatic marriages involve couples who like to function at a level of extreme emotional arousal. They are intensely attracted, attached, and volatile, given both to frequent fighting and to passionate lovemaking.
- Cohesive-individuated marriages are the yuppie and feminist ideal, characterized by equity, respect, warmth, and mutual support, but also by both partners retaining the autonomy to pursue their own goals and to have their own friends.
- Traditional marriages are those in which the husband is the main income producer and the wife's role is one of nurturance, support, and home and child care. These marriages work well as long as both partners continue to share a traditional view of gender roles.

We found that not just the risk of divorce, but also the extent of women's psychological and health troubles varies according to marriage type—with wives in pursuer-distancer and disengaged marriages experiencing the most problems, those in operatic marriages significantly having fewer, and those in cohesive-individuated and traditional marriages the fewest. Like so many other studies, we found that men's responses are less nuanced; the only differentiation among them was that men in pursuer-distancer marriages have more problems than those in the other four types.

The issue is not simply the amount of disagreement in the marriage; disagreements, after all, are endemic in close personal relations. It is *how* people disagree and solve problems—how they interact—that turns out to be closely associated with both the duration of their marriages and the well-being of wives and, to a lesser extent, husbands. Contempt, hostile criticism, belligerence, denial, and withdrawal erode a marriage. Affection, respect, trust, support, and making the partner feel valued and worthwhile strengthen the relationship.

## GOOD DIVORCES, BAD DIVORCES

Divorce experiences also are varied. Initially, especially in marriages involving children, divorce is miserable for most couples. In the early years, ex-spouses typically must cope with lingering attachments; with resentment and anger, self-doubts, guilt, depression, and loneliness; with the stress of separation from children or of raising them alone; and with the loss of social networks and, for women, of economic security. Nonetheless, we found that a gradual recovery usually begins by the end of the second year. And by six years after divorce, 80 percent of both men and women have moved on to build reasonably or exceptionally fulfilling lives.

Indeed, about 20 percent of the women we observed eventually emerged from divorce enhanced and exhibiting competencies they never would have developed in an unhappy or constraining marriage. They had gone back to school or work to ensure the economic stability of their families, they had built new social networks, and they had become involved and effective parents and socially responsible citizens. Often they had happy second marriages. Divorce had offered them an opportunity to build new and more satisfying relationships and the freedom they needed for personal growth. This was especially true for women moving from a pursuer-distancer or disengaged marriage, or from one in which a contemptuous or belligerent husband undermined their self-esteem and child-rearing practices. Divorced men, we found, are less likely to undergo such remarkable personal growth; still, the vast majority of the men in our study did construct reasonably happy new lives for themselves.

As those pressing for government programs to promote marriage will no doubt note, we found that the single most important predictor of a divorced parent's subsequent adjustment is whether he or she has formed a new and mutually supportive intimate relationship. But what should also be noticed is that successful repartnering takes many forms. We found that about 75 percent of men and 60 percent of women eventually remarry, but an increasing number of adults are opting to cohabit instead—or to remain single and meet their need for intimacy with a dating arrangement, a friendship, or a network of friends or family.

THERE IS GENERAL AGREEMENT AMONG RESEARCHERS THAT parents' repartnering does not do as much for their children. Both young children and adolescents in divorced and remarried families have been found to have, on average, more social, emotional, academic, and behavioral problems than kids in two-parent, non-divorced families. My own research, and that of many other investigators, finds twice as many serious psychological disorders and behavioral problems—such as teenage pregnancy, dropping out of school, substance abuse, unemployment, and marital breakups—among the offspring of divorced parents as among the children of nondivorced families. This is a closer association than between smoking and cancer.

However, the troubled youngsters remain a relatively small proportion of the total. In our study, we found that after a period of initial disruption 75 percent to 80 percent of children and adolescents from divorced families are able to cope with the divorce and their new life situation and develop into reasonably or exceptionally well-adjusted individuals. In fact, as we saw with women, some girls eventually emerge from their parents' divorces remarkably competent and responsible. They also learn from the divorce experience how to handle later stresses in their lives.

Without ignoring the serious pain and distress experienced by many divorced parents and children, it is important to underscore that substantial research findings confirm the ability of the vast majority to move on successfully.

It is also important to recognize that many of the adjustment problems in parents and children and much of the inept parenting and destructive family relations policy makers have attributed to divorce actually are present *before* divorce. Being in a dysfunctional family has taken its toll before the breakup occurs.

Predicting the aftermath of divorce is complex, and the truth is obscured if one looks only at averages. Differences in experience or personality account for more variation than the averages would suggest. A number of studies have found, for instance, that adults and children who perceived their pre-divorce life as happy and satisfying tend to be more upset by a marital breakup than those who viewed the marriage as contentious, threatening, or unfulfilling. Other studies show that adults and children who are mature, stable, self-regulated, and adaptable are more likely able to cope with the challenges of divorce. Those who are neurotic, antisocial, and impulsive—and who lack a sense of their own efficacy—are likely to have these characteristics exacerbated by the breakup. In other words, the psychologically poor get poorer after a divorce while the rich often get richer.

THE DIVERSITY OF AMERICAN MARRIAGES MAKES IT UNLIKELY that any one-size-fits-all policy to promote marriage and prevent divorce will be beneficial. Policy makers are now talking about offering people very brief, untested education and counseling programs, but such approaches rarely have long-lasting effects. And they are generally least successful with the very groups that policy makers are most eager to marry off—single mothers and the poor.

In their recent definitive review of the research on family interventions, Phil Cowan, Douglas Powell, and Carolyn Pape Cowan find that the most effective approaches are the most comprehensive ones—those that deal with both parents and children, with family dynamics, and with a family's needs for jobs, education, day care, and health care. Beyond that, which interventions work best seems to vary, depending on people's stage of life, the kind of family or ethnic group they are in, and the specific challenges before them.

Strengthening and promoting positive family relationships and improving the many settings in which children develop is a laudable goal. However, policies that constrain or encourage people to remain in destructive marriages—or that push uncommitted couples to marry—are likely to do more harm than good. The same is true of marriage incentives and rewards designed to create traditional families with the husband as the economic provider and the wife as homemaker. If our social policies do not recognize the diversity and varied needs of American families, we easily could end up undermining them.

---

E. MAVIS HETHERINGTON *is a professor of psychology at the University of Virginia and the co-author (with John Kelly) of* For Better or for Worse: Divorce Reconsidered.

# DATING AFTER DIVORCE

## 5 TIPS FOR NAVIGATING THE SINGLES SCENE

**THE RATE OF DIVORCE IN AMERICA REMAINS HIGH, LEAVING MANY ADULT MEN AND WOMEN ALONE, AVAILABLE AND WONDERING HOW TO MANEUVER ON THE PLAYING FIELD. AFTER YEARS OF BEING IN A RELATIONSHIP, PUTTING YOURSELF BACK IN THE SINGLES MARKET CAN BE A DAUNTING ENDEAVOR. HERE, DAVID A. ANDERSON, PH.D., OFFERS ADVICE GLEANED FROM HIS OWN RESEARCH AND THAT OF OTHER EXPERTS TO HELP YOU GET BACK INTO DATING MODE.**

AFTER 19 YEARS OF WAKING UP NEXT TO THE SAME person, 44-year-old Yolanda*, a marketing consultant, suddenly found herself greeting mornings alone. Recently divorced, she was overwhelmed by the mere thought of dating again. Yolanda's self-esteem was so damaged by her tumultuous breakup that she worried about her ability to start a new relationship, not to mention her rusty dating skills. And the pool of single men looked more like a droplet compared with the ocean available to her during her younger years.

***Approximately nine in 10 people will marry, but about one half of first marriages end in divorce.***

Yolanda may have felt alone on the playing field, but she was far from it. According to the U.S. Census Bureau, approximately nine in 10 people will marry, but about one half of first marriages end in divorce. Between 1970 and 1996, the number of women living alone doubled to 14.6 million, and the number nearly tripled for men, jumping from 3.5 million to 10.3 million.

With so many single adults out there, one might guess that there's also a lot of dating going on. Instead, it seems that the older we get, the less we date. In one study conducted at the University of Michigan Institute for Social Research, social psychologist Jerald G. Bachman, Ph.D., found that nearly 50 percent of 18-year-olds go out at least once a week, compared with only approximately 25 percent of 32-year-olds.

While it's true that some people simply choose not to date, others want to but don't know how to go about it or can't overcome their negative self-thoughts. So how can those who are struggling with these obstacles successfully and healthfully re-enter the dating arena? First, it's important to set appropriate personal standards. In particular, will you play hard to get or be an easy catch? I call the manifestation of these standards one's "social price." The more you have to offer in a relationship, the more you can expect in return, thus increasing your appropriate social price. Factors that help determine your social price include your ability to bring desirable traits such as inner strength, kindness, intelligence and affection to a relationship.

### *Abby, 31*

"I started dating the day my divorce was final. I found myself desperate for confidence and I thought I might find it by dating. But nobody really wants that kind of burden. However, a little later, nobody measured up to my standards. I've met people on buses and airplanes and in airports, even walking down the street. I don't think I ever had a date that resulted from a bar experience. I dated some real morons. I jumped in too quickly. My first few relationships were definitely physical. They weren't the kind of people who, in my right mind, I would have dated. I'm still dating. And now I've met somebody really great online. We e-mailed back and forth for two weeks before we started talking on the phone. It's a fun and great way to get to know someone. I think it's a whole lot more honest. You get a better view of a person when you start off corresponding."

Working with Shigeyuyki Hamori, an economist at Kobe University in Japan, I researched methods for estimating the qualities and contributions of marriage prospects. We hypothesized that singles seeking relationships assess unseen qualities in others based on social price as it is reflected in actions, body language and verbal communication. We concluded that those exhibiting self-confident assertions of dating standards are perceived as holding relatively more promise as marriage partners. Conversely, those who appear insecure and desperate, call a love interest excessively or engage in sexual activity too soon send signals that they hold inferior unseen traits.

## *Those who believe they have a lot to offer set higher standards for potential partners*

So just as we tend to assume that expensive cars are better than similar, cheaper ones, we may also conclude that those demonstrating high social prices have unobserved qualities superior to those with lower social prices. But be wary: Overselling also occurs. For instance, individuals with a substantial income but little else to offer may exaggerate their social price. And as with any type of price misrepresentation, true quality eventually surfaces. In the dating market, this can translate into a broken relationship.

At the core, inaccurate social pricing is a by-product of low self-esteem and other negative self-emotions. "Fear absolutely devastates some people," says clinical psychologist Michael S. Broder, Ph.D., a former radio-talk-show host and author of *The Art of Living Single*. "It can be the fear of being hurt, rejected or involved, and it can stem from a history of having been hurt or of traumatic relationships. People can be very proficient in other parts of their lives, but the fear of dating can make them stay alone—or pine for the relationship they left."

### *Alex, 28*

"After my divorce, I had to face dating. I didn't know what dating was. I had never dated. I came from France with my girlfriend whom I married. Dating is a process and there are rules. Every time I met with someone, I was thinking of my wife—where she was, what she was doing. Dating was a decision, not a random encounter. I started using the Internet. But even when the criteria were right, the people were wrong. When I did meet someone through the Web, it didn't work. In France, one could sweet-talk with a complete stranger, without a phone number exchanged. Here, even a gentle smile across the train platform is not well received. Maybe I tend to overanalyze things. I should seize the day and stop asking questions."

Others rebound or get involved in another relationship too soon. Their desperation usually stems from sadness, guilt, anger or anxiety about being alone. "You get this feeling that you're in the worst possible situation in your life," Broder explains. "Then you may do what you later consider desperate: a one-night stand, calling the ex or ignoring intuitive warnings and jumping into a bad relationship you would never choose if you weren't feeling reckless."

Fortunately, it is possible to avoid these and other pitfalls when seeking out a new partner. If you're ready to get back in the saddle again, here are five key tips to help you on your way.

## 1 DEVELOP A (NEW) SUPPORT GROUP

It's natural to turn to old friends for support. They know and care about you, and they typically have your best interests in mind. But more often it's new friends who will better help you adjust to your new life. That's because friends shared with your ex often unwittingly take sides, and either alliance can prove a hindrance when introducing someone new into your life. Old friends may lack the proper interest or compassion, and they may even be jealous of your newfound freedom.

"My divorce split our extended families and friends," says Yolanda of her and her ex-husband. "But my new friends had a fresh perspective that helped my self-esteem. Those who were single had confidence that was contagious; that really helped me when I started going out again as a single person. And sometimes they offered good advice."

Do use discretion when listening to others' words of wisdom, advises Broder. "Solutions that worked for a friend may be a disaster for you. If you don't want advice, be assertive and let people know that advice giving is off-limits unless it's requested."

For the most part, however, friendship is a vital ingredient in the recovery process. "Facing things alone can take a toll on you," says Broder. "Friends can help you see that dating doesn't have to be so serious."

## 2 ASSESS YOUR SELF-WORTH

People with low self-esteem tend to create relationships with others who evaluate them negatively, suggests one study on self-concept done by William B. Swann Jr., Ph.D., a University of Texas psychology professor. If you're suffering from a negative self-image, it's vital you take steps to create a positive, healthy self-concept.

> ***Patricia, 38***
>
> "I've been divorced for 10 years. And since then, I have been focusing on raising my teenage daughter as well as on my career in commercial real estate. So it leaves no time for dating. I tried the Internet, but it is so time-consuming. It was work. You have to get online and check your messages and then figure out who these people were. I got tired of looking at the computer too. In the end, I don't think I lasted for more than a week. The best way to meet people, I find, is through friends. I ask them, 'Do you know anyone?' Still, it is very difficult to meet people. I met the man I am spending time with now at my daughter's school. I've also been introduced to other people through friends and work. What's really important, though, is maintaining a positive outlook."

Begin by making a list of your positive qualities, then hang it in your home where you'll see it regularly, suggest Bruce Fisher, Ed.D., Robert Alberti, Ph.D., and Virginia M. Satir, M.A., in their book *Rebuilding When Your Relationship Ends*. Sharing your list with your support group and asking for honest feedback will help you to work on clearing up any discrepancies between your self-image and the real you. Broder also recommends making a list of new beliefs and affirmations that you'd like to incorporate into your thinking system. Read aloud these new self-concepts often, regardless of how you're feeling, to help solidify them in your mind.

***"It can be the fear of being hurt, rejected or involved, and it can stem from a history of having been hurt or of traumatic relationships. People can be very proficient in other parts of their lives, but the fear of dating can make them stay alone—or pine for the relationship they left."***

For Yolanda, a brief relationship five years after her divorce made her realize she had to adjust her mind-set. "I felt ashamed about all of the times I'd say yes when my answer was really no," she says now. "The consequences were painful, but I didn't believe I could completely change the pattern. Then I took the advice you hear about in 12-step programs and turned it over to God—my higher power. Moving forward and forgiving myself became easier."

People who feel victimized after a breakup may do well to develop a bold—or even defiant—attitude. Psychologists at the University of Washington and Canada's University of Waterloo recently found that feelings of resignation and sadness make people with low self-esteem less motivated to improve their mood. "When you feel defiant you become excited, confident and ready to take action," says Broder. "You take care of yourself, making it pretty clear that you are not going to be ruined by divorce. It's a very healthy thing to do."

## 3 PLAN ACTIVITIES

You won't find a new mate—or even a new friend—while sitting on the couch, your television on, curtains drawn. Consider your post-relationship time as an opportunity to do the things you couldn't do while you were with your ex. Create a list of 20 activities you would enjoy doing with a perfect partner, then give the list a second look. "Rarely do people have more than three or four things on their list that they cannot do if they're not in a relationship," says Broder. "Be active; don't feel like your whole life is on hold."

Today's singles are finding luck—and love—in nonconventional ways. After her 17-year relationship ended, Lili*, a 43-year-old writer, re-entered the dating arena by joining a telephone dating service. Instead of meeting men for dinner, she invited them for daytime walks in a well-populated park. "They weren't dates; they were interviews," says Lili, who admits that taking the first step was difficult. "If I liked them, we went for coffee." Laura*, a 49-year-old financial adviser, also missed companionship after her 24-year marriage dissolved. "I don't sit with problems for very long," she says. "I knew what I wanted and went after it." Laura joined an online dating service and eventually met her soon-to-be second husband.

Joseph Walther, Ph.D., an associate professor of communication, language and literature at Troy, New York's Rensselaer Polytechnic Institute, found that people who use Internet dating services such as Match.com may achieve more beginning-stage emotional intimacy than they do in face-to-face situations. Single surfers don't have to worry about common first-impression concerns such as bad-hair days and wrinkled clothes, Walther points out. Plus, they don't see body-language cues such as shrugging and smirking that can create barriers in communication. Currently, cyber researchers believe that as much as 33 percent of friendships formed online eventually advance to face-to-face meetings.

## 4 CURB UNHEALTHY CRAVINGS

When we are in emotional pain, our feelings often don't coincide with our intellect and instead manifest themselves as cravings that can prove unhealthy and self-destructive. Cravings usually plague people who have zero tolerance for a single lifestyle and want to jump into a new relationship as soon as their breakup is final. Also susceptible are individuals with low self-evaluation who are convinced they can't make it alone. Fortunately, while such cravings may feel overwhelming and unavoidable, Broder asserts that they don't have to be.

### *Brian*, 35*

"Soon after my wife and I were separated, I felt it was very difficult to be alone. I forced myself to go out almost every night, just to be out of the house. I did a lot of things, such as listening to music at clubs, going to bars. I was being open to the world—it was almost a Renaissance. It wasn't a matter of getting back into the scene—I was never in the scene. I had never been aggressive about dating. So I really didn't know what I was doing. I wanted to go out and meet people. After a relationship ends, though, loneliness is the hardest thing. It's important to learn how to be with yourself and not force a new relationship to compensate for that loneliness. I've also learned that it's important to know how to accept help. Before my divorce, I never felt the need to rely on friends for emotional support. It had been more difficult for me to accept support rather than give it. For the first time, I reached out."

Take Julie*, a 42-year-old college student in Southern California whose need for immediate passion led her to make decisions despite intuitively knowing they were unwise. "I kept going out with men who did not have the potential for a long-term relationship," she confesses. "One had problems with his ex-wife, another wouldn't marry outside of his religion. After getting hurt many times, I finally decided to be more careful when choosing men. I'm still prone to my old behavior, but I'm more apt to say no to men who are a poor match for me."

***People with low self-esteem tend to create relationships with others who evaluate them negatively in turn***

To short-circuit cravings, Broder suggests doing something that actively breaks the pattern and makes you approach the situation in a healthier way. Call someone in your support group, share your unwanted tendencies and ask that he or she invite you out when you fall into bad habits. And consider keeping a journal of the things that successfully distract you from your urges, such as renting a funny movie or going for a long walk, that you can turn to the next time cravings crop up.

## 5 PREPARE FOR PITFALLS

Certain times of the year—holidays, anniversaries and birthdays, for instance—are harder to navigate than others because they are loaded with expectations and memories. After a separation or divorce, social configurations change, making feelings of loss and loneliness more intense. Perfectionists tend to struggle most during the holidays, according to Broder. High expectations lead them to dwell on favorite memories of their past and compare them with current situations.

Garrett*, an optometrist in his mid-40s, remembers that his first Christmas alone was a tough one. "Weeks prior to the holidays were extremely difficult because the traditions were highly disrupted," he says. "Not being in my own home and not having a closeness with someone was difficult, and I felt very much afraid of not finding someone again."

***Ultimately, the best tip for re-entering the dating game is to explore various action strategies and choose those that are most comfortable for you***

To cope, Garrett stuck close to his family. "You stitch together the connections that you have," he says. "It was piecemeal and patchwork, but it was critical for me. I also looked for other ways to divert my attention. I organized a staff party, participated in a musical and cooked at other people's homes."

### *Elli, 65*

"There have been some periods in my life when I couldn't find a match—I would fall for someone who didn't want me or reject someone whom I didn't want. But I never had a problem with dating after my divorces. I met my first husband on the second day of college when I was 18 years old, and I abandoned my studies to marry him—this was the kind of choice women made in those days. Immediately after we were separated, I moved away to resume my studies. Coincidentally, I met my next guy on the second day of classes. When we broke up, I immediately began dating again."

Garrett got it right, according to Sally Karioth, Ph.D., R.N., an associate nursing professor at Florida State University and an expert on stress, grief and trauma. Karioth points again to planning as the key to reducing stress and meeting new people. Don't be afraid to ask for help organizing new activities, and break tasks into smaller chores to fend off feelings of being overwhelmed. Broder also suggests avoiding holiday comparisons and focusing instead on the enjoyable aspects of current and future ones. "You'll get through, and then you won't fear it anymore," says Broder. "It may not be the best of your life, but it may not be the horror you thought it would be."

Ultimately, the best tip for re-entering the dating game is to explore various action strategies and choose those that are most comfortable for you. For some, getting into the right frame of mind before taking the leap is essential. For others, simply trying something new or even uncomfortable works. You know yourself best, so trust your in-

### LEARN MORE ABOUT IT:

***The Courage to Love Again: Creating Happy, Healthy Relationships After Divorce***
*Sheila Ellison (Harper San Francisco, 2002)*

***Resilient Identities: Self Relationships and the Construction of Social Reality***
*William B. Swann Jr. (Counterpoint Press, 1999)*

***Rebuilding When Your Relationship Ends***
*Bruce Fisher, Robert E. Alberti and Virginia M. Satir (Impact Publishers, 1999)*

www.Match.com
www.Lavalife.com

ner wisdom. If you are ready to find new love, take heart: More than 40 percent of weddings in America are remarriages. But don't feel obligated to rush into another marriage, either—the U.S. Census Bureau reports that 60 percent of second marriages end in divorce. Now that you're single it's perfectly acceptable to remain so if that's what you prefer. As Broder says, "What you do with your life now is up to you."

* Identities have been changed.

---

*David A. Anderson, Ph.D., is an associate professor of economics at Centre College in Danville, Kentucky. Rosemary Clandos is a freelance science writer in Calabasas, California.*

# DIVORCED?

## Don't Even Think of Remarrying Until You Read This

**Divorce rates prove that conventional wisdom is wrong: The dirty little secret is that when it comes to relationships, experience doesn't count. Experts take a close look at why we don't learn from our mistakes and how we can start—right now.**

**By Hara Estroff Marano**

Americans are an optimistic lot. Perhaps nowhere is our optimism more apparent than in our approach to marriage.

One of every two marriages can be expected to end in tears. Still, 90% of Americans marry. Surveys consistently show that marriage holds an honored place on our wish list, something we believe is necessary for attaining life happiness—or its slightly wiser sibling, fulfillment.

If our optimism steers us into marriage, it goes into overdrive with remarriage. Despite the disappointment and the pain and the disruption of divorce, most of us opt to get back on the horse. An astonishing 75% of the broken-hearted get married all over again. And if you count among the remarried those who merge lives and households without legal ratification, the de facto remarriage rate is even higher.

Yet a whopping 60% of remarriages fail. And they do so even more quickly; after an average of 10 years, 37% of remarriages have dissolved versus 30% of first marriages.

If divorce and remarriage rates prove one thing, it is that conventional wisdom is wrong: When it comes to remarriage, experience doesn't count. A prior marriage actually *decreases* the odds of a second marriage working. Ditto if you count as a first marriage its beta version, living together; three decades of a persistently high divorce rate have encouraged couples to test the waters by living together before marrying. But this actually dims the likelihood of marital success.

"It's so counterintuitive," says Diane Sollee, M.S.W., a family therapist and director of the Coalition for Marriage, Family and Couples Education, based in Washington, D.C. "It seems obvious that people would be older and wiser. Or learn from the mistake of a failed first marriage and do better next time around. But that's like saying if you lose a football game you'll win the next one. You will—but only if you learn some new plays before you go back onto the field."

Remarriage may look a lot like any other marriage—two people, plenty of hope, lots of love and sex, and a desire to construct some form of joint life. It even smells like an ordinary marriage—the kitchen is busy once again. But it has its own subversive features, mostly invisible to the naked eye, that make it more tenuous. It's not impossible to make remarriage work, but it takes a concerted effort.

### Why Experience Doesn't Count

No, when it comes to relationships, people don't automatically learn from experience. There seems to be something special about relationships that prevents them from recognizing their failures. A close look at marriage suggests several reasons why.

• **Love deludes us.** The rush of romance dupes us into believing our own partnership uniquely defies the laws of gravity. "We feel that this new, salient, intense relationship fills the firmament for us," observes William J. Doherty, Ph.D., director of the Marriage and Family Therapy Program at the University of Minnesota and author of *The Intentional Family* (Avon, 1999). "You really think 'problems are for regular people and our relationship certainly isn't regular,'" Doherty adds. "Partners bring to remarriage the stupidity of the first engagement and the baggage of the first marriage."

• **Marriage deflects us.** Marriage, in fact, contains a structural psychological loophole: Being a two-party event from the get-go, it affords us the (morally slippery) convenience of thinking that any problems reside in our partner. We simply chose the wrong person last time. Or despite our shining presence and best efforts, the other person developed some critical character flaw or craziness. Either way, we focus—wrongly, it turns out—on the characteristics of our partner rather than on the dynamics of the relationship, by definition involving both people.

"Till our last dying breath we still think, 'Someday I'll meet a mensch and it will be perfect; he will fit with all my wonderfulness in such a way that it will all work,'" says Diane Sollee. "We indulge the illusion that, with the right partner, conflict will be minimal."

Jeffry Larson, Ph.D., psychology professor at Brigham Young University, confirms, "Partners don't reflect on their own role. They say 'I'm not going to make the same mistakes again.' But they do make the same mistakes unless they get insight into what caused the divorce and their role in the marriage failure." Larson is quick to admit that our culture generally provides us with no road map for assessing ourselves or our relationships. And some people are just too narcissistic to admit they had any role in the relationship's failure. They will never understand what went wrong. And that makes them lousy bets as new partners.

What's more, we are deeply social creatures, and even distant rumblings of a threat to our most intimate social bond are intolerable. When problems develop, marriages become so painful that we can't bear to look at our own part in them.

• **Conflict confuses us.** Our ability to learn about relationships shuts down precisely when marriage begins to get tough—and they all get tough. Conflict is an inevitable part of relationships. But many people have no idea how to resolve the conflict; they see it instead as a sign that there's something wrong with the relationship—and their partner. With low expectations about their own ability to resolve conflict, explains psychologist Clifford Notarius, Ph.D., professor of psychology at Catholic University in Washington, D.C., people go into alarm mode. This distorts the couple's communication even further and prevents any learning from taking place. "When a husband hears 'let's talk about money,' he knows what's coming," says Notarius. "He doesn't think anything different can happen. He shuts down."

• **Conflict rigidifies us.** Arguments engage the Twin Terminators of relationship life: blame and defensiveness. These big and bad provocateurs destroy everything in their path, pushing partners further apart and keeping them focused on each other.

Invariably, marriage experts insist, whether in the first marriage or the fourth, couples tend to trip over the same mistakes. No. 1 on the list of errors is unrealistic expectations. A decline in intensity is normal and to be expected, says Notarius. In its own way, it should be welcomed. It's not a signal to bail out. "You will be disappointed—but that opens the potential for a relationship to evolve into something wonderful, a developmental journey of adult growth. Only in supportive relationships can we deal with our personal demons and life disappointments. We get the reassurance of having a partner who will be there no matter what, someone who can sit through our personal struggle for the hundredth time and support us. The promise of long-term relationships is the sharing of the secret self."

Absent this awareness, partners tend to start down the road to divorce as soon as the intensity wanes. Happiness, observes Pat Love, Ph.D., a marital therapist based in Austin, Texas, is the ratio between what you expect and what you get. "You have to suffer the clash of fantasy with reality in some relationships," adds Notarius. "Either you do it in the first relationship or you have 10 first relationships."

## How To Remarry

Why is remarriage so difficult? The short answer is because it follows divorce. People who divorce are in a highly vulnerable state. They know what it's like to have a steady dose of love, that life's burdens are better when shared. But, says Love, "They go out, so they're hungry. And when you're hungry, you'll eat anything." The longing for comfort, for deep intimacy, impels the divorced to rush back into a married state. Says Love: "People tend to want to go back into the woodwork of marriage."

Yet prospective remarriage partners need to build a relationship slowly, experts agree. "They need to know each other individually and jointly," says Robert F. Stahmann, Ph.D., professor of family sciences and head of the Marriage Preparation Research Project at Brigham Young University. "This means time for bonding as a couple because the relationship will be under stress from each partner's various links to the past," none more tangible than children and stepchildren.

Couples also need enough time to allow for the cognitive and emotional reorganization that must take place. Says Love, "You've got to replace the image in your head of what a man or a woman is like based on your ex. It happens piece by piece, as with a jigsaw puzzle, not like a computer with the flick of a switch."

When choosing a mate the second time around, people typically look for traits and tendencies exactly opposite those of their first partner. A woman whose first husband was serious and determined will tend to look for someone more fun. "Unfortunately," observes Howard K. Markman, Ph.D., "to the extent that they are making conscious choices, they are looking at the wrong factors." At the University of Denver, where he is professor of psychology, Markman and his colleagues are videotaping couples in a second marriage who were also studied in a first marriage.

"The motivation to do it differently is there," says the researcher, "and that is good. But they don't know exactly what to do differently. They're not making changes in how they conflict, which is predictive of relationship quality."

Further, he notes, both parties need to use the second marriage to become better partners themselves. "They both need to nourish the relationship on a daily basis... and refrain from things [such as hurling insults at one another] that threaten the marriage in the face of disappointments."

- **Learn to Love Complexity.** There is even more opportunity for conflict and disappointment in remarriages because the challenges are greater. "There are always at least four people in bed," says Love. "Him, her, his ex and her ex. Not to mention the kids." The influence of exes is far from over with remarriage. Exes live on in memories, in daydreams, and often in reality, arriving to pick up and deliver the kids, exerting parental needs and desires that have to be accommodated, especially at holiday and vacation times. The ex's family—the children's grandparents, aunts, uncles and cousins—remains in the picture, too. "When you remarry," says Brigham Young's Larson, "you marry a person—and that person's ex-spouse." It just comes with the territory.

- **Defuse Anger, Vent Grief.** Nothing keeps exes, and the past itself, more firmly entrenched in the minds of one-time spouses than anger. But we can minimize anger by finding ways to minimize the impact of ghosts from the past.

Unless people grieve the loss of the prior relationship and the end of the marriage, they are at risk of staying covertly attached to it. "When they don't grieve, often they remain angry," Larson says. "Exploring the feelings of sadness, and understanding the ways in which the first marriage was good, is a way of unhooking from it."

Many are the sources of loss that require acknowledgment:

*The loss of an attachment figure.* "It has nothing to do with how you were treated," says Love. "You lost someone you once cared about."

*Loss of intact family.* We all harbor the idea of a perfect family, and it's one in which emotions and biology are drawn along the same tight meridians.

*A sense of failure.* "A powerful element contributing to vulnerability in a second marriage," observes Love, "is a sense of shame or embarrassment stemming from the relationship's failure," denial of any role in the marital breakdown notwithstanding.

"There is pain and fear from the fact that former relationships did not go well," adds Hawkins, "which inhibit commitment to the new relationship and distort communication between partners."

*A sense of grief.* Grief is bound to be especially great for those who were dumped by their first spouse. "You can't grieve and try to get used to a new relationship at the same time," says Jeff Larson, who recommends waiting at least one or two years after a divorce before remarrying.

## Digging Up the Past

Stahmann emphasizes that for remarriage to be successful, couples need to look at their previous relationships and understand their history. How did they get into the first marriage? What were their expectations, hopes and dreams? Through the soul-searching, people learn to trust again.

"It is essential that they do this together," Stahmann says. "It helps each of them break from the past relationship and sets a precedent for the foundation of the new one."

Pat Love stresses that this joint exploration must include a look at the partners' own role in the failure of the past relationship. "You have to list what you didn't like in your partner and own your own part in it. If you don't understand your part, then you are bound to do it again."

"When you do something that reminds me of my old partner," Love explains, "I project all the sins of that partner onto you. If you don't want sex one night, then you are 'withholding,' just like the ex." The fact is, Love insists, "the things you didn't like in your old partner actually live on in you."

But such joint exploration doesn't always take place. Couples are often afraid that a partner who brings up the past will get stuck there. Or that a discussion will reignite old flames, when in fact, it helps extinguish them. "Couples often enter remarriage with their eyes closed more than the first marriage," reports Hawkins. "It's as if they are afraid the marriage won't happen if they confront the issues."

Once a couple has opened up and explored their past, they need to bring the kids in on the discussion. "Kids don't have the same understanding of how and why the prior relationship ended," explains Stahmann. "Yet they need it." On the agenda for discussion: how the adults got together, why the past failed, how contact with the biological parents will be maintained, and all the couple's dreams and hopes for the future. Most experts would reserve this conversation for after the wedding.

- **Clearing Customs.** In any marriage, each partner to some degree represents a different culture with different traditions and rituals and symbols. The two distinct sets of highly structured traditions are not simply deeply emotionally resonant; they carry the force of commandment. The subtlest departure from them can make anyone feel like an outsider in his own home. One or both partners is bound to feel bad, even unloved, when their current family does a celebration "the wrong way."

The problem is, culture clash is built in to marriage, says Frank Pittman III, M.D., an Atlanta-based family therapist whose most recent book is *Grow Up! How Taking Responsibility Can Make You a Happy Adult* (Golden Books, 1998).

That, however, is where the fun begins. "The conflict causes electricity and the need to discuss things and compare perspectives, and thus come to know one another and oneself. That is the source of a marriage's energy," he says.

It's wise for couples heading into remarriage to explicitly discuss and agree on which ritual styles will prevail when. Even the everyday ones: Will dessert be served with dinner? Are evening snacks allowed? Then there are the big celebrations sprinkled throughout the calendar, culturally designated as holidays but more likely hurdles of stress in remarriage households.

• **Negotiating External Forces.** As if there aren't enough internal hurdles, remarriage can be undermined by outside forces, too. "People who lived independently before remarriage often have jobs, friend networks and hobbies that are anti-relational," says Stahmann. "These are spheres in which they have come to invest a lot of themselves as a regular source of gratification." He counts among them learned workaholism. "Such individual-gratifying activities can be hard to give up. Couples need time to work out these patterns."

• **Coping with Kids.** Nothing challenges a remarriage more than the presence of children from a prior marriage, and 65% of remarriage households contain kids. Their failure rate is highest in the first two years, before these multiplex families have even sorted themselves out.

"All you need is one active conspirator," says Minnesota's Doherty. "It's not uncommon for an ex to play on the ambivalence or outright hostility that kids have for a remarriage, especially at the beginning. An ex can have you talking about him every day."

Take one of his clients for example: Bob, who is remarried, gets a visit from his two children. After the weekend, the kids mention to their mother that the house felt cold. She calls her ex-husband, furious. When he agrees to turn up the thermostat, the new spouse feels powerless in her own home and angry at her husband because she thinks he is not standing up for himself, or her.

With kids present, partners in a remarriage do not get time to develop as a couple before becoming parents. Their bond is immediately under assault by the children. Family experts agree that this is yet another reason for couples heading into remarriage to prolong the period of courtship despite the incentives to merge households.

Even noncustody can pose problems. "Custody is a legal solution," says Stahmann. "It implies nothing about the emotional reality of family. A parent who shares custody or one who has only visitation rights is already experiencing some degree of loss regarding the children."

And the children themselves are in a state of post-divorce mourning over the loss of an intact family and full-time connection to a parent. No matter which parent a child is with, someone is missing all the time. "This leads to upset, depression and resentment at the new marriage," says Emily Visher, Ph.D., a psychologist in California and co-founder of the Stepfamily Association of America. The resentment is typically compounded by the fact that the children do not have the same perspective as the adults on how and why their parents' marriage broke up.

Financial obligations add more stress. Many a stepfather thinks: "I don't want to be putting my money into your kids' college education when I didn't put it into mine."

"There is an existential, moral dimension to remarriage families that is not talked about," says Minnesota's Doherty. "The partners will always be in different emotional and relational positions to the children. One is till death do us part. The other is till divorce do us part. The stepparent harbors a deep wish that the children did not exist, the very same children the parent could not live without."

People need to develop "a deep empathic understanding of the different emotional worlds parent and stepparent occupy." To be a stepparent, Doherty adds, "is to never be fully at home in your own house in relation to the children, while the original parent feels protective and defensive of the children. Neither 'gets' it until each describes what the emotional world is for him or her." Each partner is always an outsider to the experience of the other.

The role of the nonbiological parent is crucial—but fuzzy. "Twenty plus years into the divorce revolution and remarriage is an incomplete institution," observes Andrew Cherlin, Ph.D., professor of sociology at Johns Hopkins University. "It's not clear what rules a stepparent should follow." In successful families, the stepparent is somewhere between a friend and a parent, what he calls "the kindly uncle role." Using first names can help enhance that relationship.

But most importantly, "the more a couple can agree on expected roles, the more satisfied they will be," says Carlos Costelo, a Ph.D. candidate focusing on the dynamics of remarriage at the University of Kansas.

The key to remarriage, says Stahmann, is for couples to be less selfish that they used to be. "They have to realize there is a history there. They can't indulge jealousy by cutting off contact with kids. They can't cut off history." Selfishness, he insists, is the biggest reason for failure of remarriages.

"We all have a lot to learn from them," notes Doherty. "Remarriage families hold the secrets to all marriage. Remarriage with stepchildren illuminates the divergent needs and loyalties that are always present but often invisible in original families."

## It Takes a Village

With so much vulnerability, and the well-being of so many people at stake, prospective partners in a remarriage need a little help from others. "The impression of family and friends on whether this remarriage will work is important," says Stahmann.

Pat Love, herself in a remarriage, couldn't be more emphatic. "You've got to do it by consensus. It takes a village. You've got to listen to friends. You're in an altered state by way of infatuation. The failure factor is there, making you fragile."

In fact, Stahmann contends, the opinion of family members and friends is predictive of remarriage success. "Friends and family know who you are. They knew you married, and they can see how you are in the context of the new relationship." The trick is to listen to them.

## READ MORE ABOUT IT

*Stepfamilies: Love, Parenting and Marriage in the First Decade,* James H. Bray, Ph.D., and John Kelly (Broadway Books, 1998)

*How To Win as a Stepfamily,* Emily B. Visher, Ph.D., and John S. Visher, M.D. (Brunner/Mazel, 1991)

---

*Hara Estroff Marano is PT's editor-at-large and author of* Why Doesn't Anybody Like Me? *(William Morrow, 1999).*

# Managing a BLENDED Family

CRAFTING A FINANCIAL PLAN FOR TWO *FAMILIES* THAT MERGE THROUGH MARRIAGE IS SERIOUS BUSINESS. HERE'S HOW TO DO IT RIGHT.

**BY** SHERYL NANCE-NASH

**FROM THE OUTSET, KOFI AND YVETTE MOYO FIRMLY** believed that their union would add value to all members of their growing brood. Combining his eight children and her one child could have easily led to emotional upheaval and financial discord—but the Moyos had a plan.

First, they adopted the concept of a village raising a child. Yvette and Kofi needed unity to raise nine children (who now range in age from 18 to 33) over their 15-year marriage. The couple garnered support from both sets of grandparents as well as Kofi's former wives and Yvette's former partner. Some of the children stayed with the Moyos full time for a stretch, but Kofi and Yvette didn't have primary custody. The children would journey from Cincinnati to join them in Chicago for the summer months, weekends, holidays, and birthdays. "We had a commitment to harmony," maintains Yvette.

So, how did the Moyo's keep their financial house in order? Yvette, 50, an advertising sales and marketing executive, and Kofi, 64, a photojournalist, author, and amateur chef, quit their jobs to start Resource Associates International (PAI), a marketing firm best known for its Real Men Cook for Charity fund-raising events, and the Marketing Opportunities in Business and Entertainment (MOBE) conference series. The company grossed annual revenues of approximately $600,000, generating enough income to support the growing clan and pay for everything from summer camp and family trips, to child support and the first year of college tuition for everyone. (By the second year, the children have to pay for their tuition by working or gaining scholarships or other forms of financial aid.)

Next, the family went on an austerity program. "I shopped at Burlington Coat Factory instead of downtown at Lord & Taylor," Yvette explains. Furthermore, Kofi is a frugal and savvy shopper. For example, he drives a mint condition 1988 Land Cruiser that he purchased online. (Yvette owns a 1971 Mercedes, which is also in excellent condition.) Over the years, they have been able to realize more savings since Kofi makes repairs around the house. "We gave up luxuries like new suits and expensive stuff and settled for what mattered," says Yvette. "[The children] knew we cared for them. If one of them had a prom, they'd go and I'd do without if necessary. The priority was to expose them to a variety of things and make them feel good about themselves."

As the Moyos demonstrate, bringing two households together—each with its own culture, traditions, financial habits, and values—is no small matter. Entering a new relationship with children, former spouses, and expanded financial responsibilities can be downright daunting. But many couples are willing to take on the challenge. According to the Lincoln, Nebraska-based Stepfamily Association of America (SAA), about 75% of divorced people eventually remarry and about 65% of those remarriages involve children from prior unions.

While the divorce rate is nearly 62%, blended families can and do succeed. Making it work, however, requires a strong commitment from the couple—to each other and to the newly formed family.

Poor planning and disagreement on goals can quickly unravel recently constituted stepfamilies. For one thing, the second or third time around, finances can be an even

## How to Blend Your Family's Finances

**Re-evaluate all of your insurance needs.** Review your policies—health, property, auto, and, especially, life. Your expanded family will likely mean you need to increase coverage. Consult with your financial adviser.

- **Update all financial documents.** Any paperwork that named your previous spouse as a beneficiary should be changed.
- **Create a budget and stick to it.** With a bigger family, there is less wiggle room for money mistakes if you want to achieve your financial goals. Be sure that budget includes a fund for emergencies and savings for the short and long term.
- **Rethink your asset allocation.** Before it was just you and now it's you and your spouse. Look at both portfolios closely. You don't have to merge accounts, but it's important to note, for example, if you both have shares of the same stock or if your respective portfolios are heavily weighted in a particular asset class or sector. In all cases, think diversification.
- **Develop a will or living trust.** If you already have one, it will need to be changed to reflect your current situation. If you don't have one, by all means complete one. In the document, name guardians for your children. This is a tough issue for any parent, but particularly when there are different sets of children and possibly multiple guardians.

greater issue since both spouses usually have more assets, more debts, and contradictory money-management styles. Also, asserts Marilyn Bergen, a certified financial planner with CMC Advisers in Portland, Oregon, "the children may have very different spending habits and values. How will you get everyone on the same page?

### ACHIEVING FINANCIAL HARMONY

Few things are as unromantic as finances. Before you get too deep into the prospects of marital bliss, you must engage in straight talk about money. There are a myriad of issues to deal with, including child support, prenuptial agreements, property ownership, retirement finances, and estate planning. First, you need to gain a full accounting of your loved one's assets, debts, legal issues, and tax liabilities. "You want to know what sort of verbal agreements they may have, say to help pay their parent's prescription drug costs, or to buy a child a car," says SAA President Margorie Engel.

Take a good look at each other's spending habits. "Poor spending habits are often what caused the first marriage to break up. You should work to come up with a common financial plan and a debt-elimination plan," advises Pierre Dunagan, president of The Dunagan Group, a Chicago-based financial services firm. "Commit your plan to paper. Having a document that you both agreed on and signed makes a huge difference. It's a little hard to dispute."

Dunagan says once couples are married, they should schedule weekly or monthly meetings to review the family's finances. The two need to determine whether financial goals are on track or, if not, factors that have stalled progress. Other issues include deciding how money will be managed. You should answer the following questions before you take the plunge: Will you have separate accounts, joint accounts, or a combination of the two? How much will each contribute to household expenses?

COMMIT YOUR PLAN TO PAPER. HAVING A DOCUMENT THAT YOU BOTH AGREED ON AND SIGNED MAKES A HUGE DIFFERENCE.

Dunagan says there's another important matter to address: What will the combined financial needs of the children be? Maybe you already made plans for college financing for two children, but how do you now make adjustments for your spouse's other two? Or, what if you and your new spouse are contemplating having a child together? Have you considered the expenses of daycare, larger living quarters, and the like?

### MAKING ADJUSTMENTS

These are matters that the Moyos had to take into account when their family expanded. In fact, the entrepreneurs made some rather smart financial moves along the way. They bought a house with a four-car garage, which was spacious enough to provide living quarters for Yvette's mother, an office for a staff of four, and the family's living quarters. "It's a major resource," says Yvette. "We've used the equity to assist the business, make home repairs, and otherwise keep the family going."

Another decision they made early on was to get substantial life insurance for each other ($1 million for Yvette, and $1.5 million for Kofi) and for their children ($10,000 per child). However, some would argue that life insurance is about income replacement, so it's not necessary to obtain it for a child. But when tragedy struck—one of Kofi's daughters was killed in a car accident—they realized that it was a wise decision.

All stepfamilies have to make major adjustments to their lifestyles and to their spending habits. Take the Hales of Long Branch, New Jersey.

When Kim, 37, and William, 39, were married seven years ago, they had six children between them. Since then, they've added one foster child from Guatemala, Kim gave birth to another, and one more is on the way. Initially, the family moved into a three-bedroom apartment in Kim's building because she didn't want to live in the home that William had rented with his former wife. The newly formed family was a bit cramped, and within a couple of years, the Hales purchased a four-bedroom home.

## Resources for Stepfamilies

### Websites:

Family and Stepparenting Tips:
**www.blended-families.com**

Stepfamily Matters:
**www.step-family-matters.com**

The Stepfamily Association of America:
**www.saafamilies.org/index.htm**

### Books:

*Blending Families: A Guide for Parents, Stepparents, and Everyone Building a Successful New Family*
(Berkley Books, $14.00)

*Money Advice for Your Successful Remarriage: Handling Delicate Financial Issues Intelligently and Lovingly*
(iUniverse.com, $14.95)

*The Complete Idiot's Guide to Step-parenting*
(Alpha Books, $16.95)

Largely due to Kim's influence, the Hales have learned to be frugal in their spending. Concedes William: "I made some bad financial decisions in my first marriage. We were over-spenders. I thought I could work overtime and make it work, but that wasn't the case."

In fact, when William and Kim married, he didn't have a checking or savings account. Kim proved to be a good teacher and he was a willing student. They opened joint accounts and William has learned from her thriftiness. "Saving is hard with a big family," says Kim, who spends as much as $250 each week on groceries. "I learned from my mom to save on small stuff. When you have a family this size and everybody saves a dollar here and there, it adds up. I shop with coupons."

They have also spent considerable time teaching their children to have respect for the value of a dollar. When the children were younger, they received allowances of $5–$10 a week, but now the teens must earn their money—especially since they have developed a taste for FUBU, Sean John, and other designer goodies. The older children have jobs and the Hales require them to fork over 10% of their paycheck as a tithe, another 10% for long-term savings, and the remainder for personal items such as school clothes, cell phones, and leisure activities.

These days, the Hales have been forced to batten down the hatches. Before William lost his job 18 months ago due to a legal complication with his employer and Kim was unable to handle the physical demands of nursing as a result of her pregnancy, their household income was $120,000. Today, their household income has been downsized to $35,000. To make ends meet, William sells health plans for AmeriPlan USA and Kim sells real estate. The two also generate limited income from Pure Word Ministries (William is a licensed and ordained evangelist). Over the past two years, they have tapped William's entire 401(k) account—roughly $40,000—to maintain living expenses.

The good news, however, is that William will return to the electric company as well as gain 18 months in back pay. He plans to use the money to pay off debt that the family has accumulated, build up retirement savings, and develop a fund to help their children finance their college education. Kim and William hold life insurance policies but admit that they have yet to complete their wills. "With a blended family, it's more than a notion about what to do about the kids," says Kim. "Somebody's not going to like the decisions you make, like the children's mother. It's a sticky situation because we haven't legally adopted each other's children though we have custody."

Making household finances work will mean that couples must pay attention to details and diligently handle legal and financial matters. But in order to truly secure their family's future, each spouse must embrace the planning process as a joint venture.

---

# UNIT 5

# Families, Now and Into the Future

## Unit Selections



## Key Points to Consider

- After having charted your family's lifestyle and relationship history, what type of future do you see for yourself? What changes do you see yourself making in your life? How would you go about gathering the information you need to make these decisions?
- Are you "happy"? Why or why not? What factors in your life have contributed to your present feelings?
- What is the state of rituals in your family? What rituals might you build in your family? Why? How might you use family gatherings and other traditions to build family integration?

**Links: www.dushkin.com/online/**
These sites are annotated in the World Wide Web pages.

**National Institute on Aging**
*http://www.nih.gov/nia/*

**The North-South Institute**
*http://www.nsi-ins.ca/ensi/about_nsi/research.html*

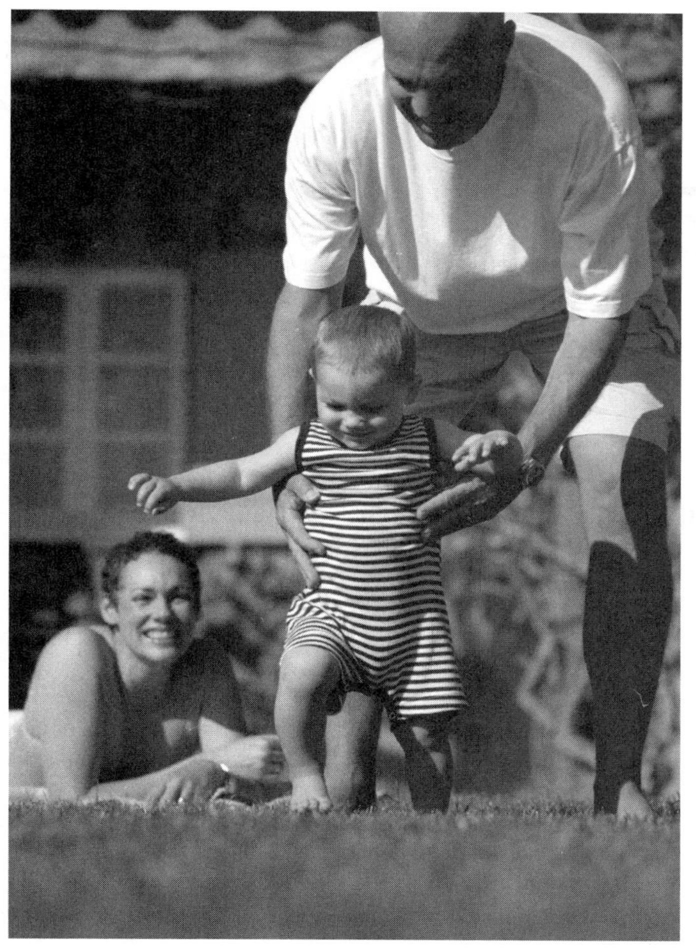

What is the future of the family? Does the family even have a future? These questions and others like them are being asked. Many people fear for the future of the family. As previous units of this volume have shown, the family is a continually evolving institution that will continue to change throughout time. Still, certain elements of family appear to be constant. The family is and will remain a powerful influence in the lives of its members. This is because we all begin life in some type of family, and this early exposure carries a great deal of weight in forming our social selves—who we are and how we relate to others. From our families, we take our basic genetic makeup, while we also learn and are reinforced in health behaviors. In families, we are given our first exposure to values and it is through families that we most actively influence others. Our sense of commitment and obligation begins within the family as well as our sense of what we can expect of others.

Much writing about families has been less than hopeful and has focused on ways of avoiding or correcting errors. The six articles in this unit take a positive view of family and how it influences its members. The emphasis is on health rather than dysfunction.

Knowledge is the basic building block of intelligent decisions regarding family. In "Breaking Free of the Family Tree," Jennifer Matlack describes the genogram, a useful technique for mapping out your family history so that you can anticipate, plan, and possibly change the choices you make in relationships and lifestyle. Information is important in planning for our family's future. One way to gather this information is through interviews, the article "Getting the Word" explains just how this can be done. In "Happiness Explained," Holly Morris examines the science of contentment, happiness, and optimism. One key aspect of happiness is the quality of family life, various techniques can be used to build a strong sense of family and family health. Family rituals can be a powerful force for family cohesion and change and the nature of family rituals is described in "Examining Family Rituals." Concluding this volume, "Reconnect With Your Family," by Joyce Brothers, describes the ways in which family gatherings and other rituals can be used to strengthen families.

relationships

# breaking free of the family tree

Save yourself a lot of bark and spilled sap: Branch out from the usual genealogical charts by mapping your family's behavior tics.

BY JENNIFER MATLACK

Take a good look in the mirror.

Along with the color of your eyes and the shape of your face, you might also have your mother's quirky sense of humor and your father's artistic flair. And it doesn't stop there. One parent's debilitating depression or peculiar obsession may be as much a part of you as the nose on your face.

All families carry baggage. And when it comes to piling it on, families can be awfully generous. You may have ended up with emotional loads you don't even know you're carrying that will affect important relationships in your life and steer you off course in ways you can't imagine.

Lucinda and Dan (names have been changed), a professional couple in their 30s, were each reliving familiar family patterns—and didn't realize it. They only knew their marriage was in trouble, so they sought help from San Diego marriage and family therapist Sally LeBoy. To LeBoy, Lucinda complained that her husband would agree to do a household chore, such as lock the doors at night, and then forget to follow through. Moreover, he didn't seem to care, and his passivity made Lucinda feel as if she didn't have a partner. Dan, on the other hand, told LeBoy that he thought of his wife as a maddening little Miss Wiz—always taking control and getting things done. He was unhappy because it seemed as if Lucinda was constantly nagging him. "They weren't discussing divorce," says LeBoy, "but they knew they had to work out the problem before it got worse."

LeBoy began, as many therapists do, by exploring the family dynamics in the couple's background. Then she created a family diagram, or genogram, which charts patterns of behavior through several generations of a family. Along with normal behavior, distant or hostile relationships and serious mental or physical problems are diagrammed in symbols that appear on a chart. It becomes immediately clear if history is repeating itself. "We claim that we will never be like our parents and have the same relationships they had," says LeBoy. "But how we define ourselves in an intimate relationship comes from what we have learned in our families."

**your family inheritance may be more than you bargained for. The emotional patterns of families can be handed down in the genes along with physical traits.**

Genograms have more details than ancestral trees. They include not only three generations of a family but also live-in partners and other important nonfamily members. In addition to marriages, births, and deaths, genograms record extramarital affairs, miscarriages, abortions, financial problems, serious illnesses, and other major stressful events. The charts also note the personality traits of family members, such as whether someone is emotionally inaccessible, controlling, or passive.

"Think of it as if you're painting a picture of your family," says LeBoy. "The more detail, the better."

Genograms were created by the late psychiatrist Murray Bowen, M.D., developer of the family systems theory in the early 1950s. Bowen's work with schizophrenic patients and their families at the Menninger Clinic in Topeka, Kansas, and later at the National Institute of Mental Health near Washington, D.C., led him to radically depart from previous theories of human emotional functioning. Bowen saw the family as one emotional unit and the individual as part of that unit rather than as an autonomous psychological entity. Through his research, he discovered that an order and predictability in family relationships existed. The recent resurgence of genograms is due in part to New Jersey therapist Monica McGoldrick's use of the charts in family life cycle development and the popularity of her 1999 book, *Genograms: Assessment and Intervention* (W.W. Norton).

## Genograms include details not found on the traditional family tree, such as extramarital affairs, abortions, and financial problems.

Behavioral patterns are passed down from generation to generation by parents, who teach their children how to relate to other people. Therapists also believe that learning interpersonal skills occurs on a subconscious level in children, and recent genetics research suggests that some character traits and behaviors, such as shyness and depression, are actually encoded on genes and thus physically transmitted to the next generation.

In Lucinda and Dan's case, the genogram study showed that their behavior toward one another was directly related to how they functioned subconsciously in their respective families. Lucinda came from a line of strong, reliable women and marginally functioning men. In her immediate family, her father was alcoholic and her mother, perhaps to compensate, was extremely reliable. Dan's family was dominated by his rigid, controlling father, who was determined that all his children should be successful. LeBoy also discovered that Dan left his parents' home at age 18 to attend college on the other side of the country, about as far away from home as he could get.

"For people who grow up in a situation where someone in the family didn't pull their weight, the tendency to overfunction is huge," says LeBoy. Clearly, that's what Lucinda was doing in her marriage.

Dan, on the other hand, according to LeBoy, learned to distance himself physically and psychologically from his overachieving, overbearing family. Thus, the more Lucinda demanded of Dan—as her mother had tried to do with her father—the more Dan withdrew, the same way he had always withdrawn from his own demanding father. Both were extremely ingrained in their particular "learned behaviors," that is, how they react in familiar situations.

LeBoy tried to help Lucinda and Dan unlearn some of their programmed behavior. For Lucinda, this meant dropping her mother's overfunctioning style. Dan's job was first to try to change the relationship with his father by relating to him as a responsible adult, rather than a rebellious child. Once Dan "grew up" and began to feel more autonomous, LeBoy believed he would be able to drop his defensive, passive-aggressive style with his wife, and when Lucinda demanded something of him, Dan would be more willing to cooperate. Becoming aware of the origin of their behavior enabled the couple to set their marriage on a steadier course.

Genograms help people see the big picture, which at times can be scary, and interpreting a baggage-laden lineage is not always easy. Professional guidance is recommended.

"If you do a genogram and discover patterns that you find are negative or disturbing, take this information and work with a therapist," says Ann Kramer, a family counselor in Tampa, Florida. "A professional will help you clarify what you're seeing and perhaps give you some insight you can't see on your own."

Certain key relationship patterns tend to surface repeatedly. One is called "emotional fusion," which occurs when family members fail to establish healthy differences between one another, and function in exclusively codependent ways. "Triangling" is another. It occurs when two people draw in a third person in an attempt to defuse stress and anxiety between one another. A "cutoff" is perhaps the most serious difficulty, which occurs when someone severs ties with his or her family completely. Another important factor to consider in genograms is birth order. Siblings' emotional places in the family are often duplicated in their subsequent intimate relationships. Firstborns, for example, tend to be responsible and serious adults, whereas the babies are more carefree and rebellious.

## Sorting through past family relationships can be an emotional strain, but the rewards of such a cleansing are great.

As difficult as it is to sort through family dynamics and relationships, the rewards are great indeed. But before you can change a problem, you first must realize one exists. Too often, families live in cycles of despair and anger, feeling that there is no way out, and not realizing the door they seek may be the back door of their past.

---

Jennifer Matlack is a writer based in Wilton, Connecticut.

# GETTING the Word

*Oral-history interviewing can enrich your family history and unlock your relatives' memories—if you go easy on the* **who, where** *and* **when** *and focus instead on* **why, how** *and* **what.**

*By Sharon DeBartolo Carmack*

When I started to research my family history, I dutifully interviewed my grandmother, asking her questions like when and where she was born, the names of her parents, when and where they were born, the names and birth dates of her siblings, the names of her grandparents and when and where they were born and died. Then, as all the genealogy how-to books advised, I verified everything she told me in one record or another.

I hated doing oral history interviews. My grandmother hated being interviewed.

It was a long, long time before I tried again. By then, Grandma was gone, so I interviewed her cousin Isabel. I followed the same procedure, asking about names, dates and places. Finally Isabel had enough of my pestering for facts: "Please don't ask me any more questions," she said. "I've told you everything I know." She stopped answering my letters, and when I called she pretended I had the wrong number.

So much for quizzing relatives for genealogical data. Besides, why bother asking questions I could find the answers to in a record somewhere? What was the point?

***"I learned to unlock my relatives' memories and to tap the family history that's not in the record books—people's thoughts, feelings and motivations."***

Then I met a social historian who taught me a better way of doing oral history interviewing—the oral historian's way. Instead of asking *who, where* and *when*, I should have been asking *why, how* and *what*. I learned to unlock my relatives' memories and to tap the family history that's not in the record books—people's thoughts, feelings and motivations. Trust me, the census record enumerating Great-uncle Mortimer's family will still be around long after we're all dead and gone. But the sense of what life was like in the past, the memories that make a person unique, will go to the grave with that person—unless you ask the right questions.

The right questions to ask in an oral history interview go beyond "just the facts, ma'am":

- What were some of your grandfather's positive qualities?
- What about negative qualities?
- How did your grandparents meet?
- What kind of work did your grandfather do?
- What's your fondest memory of your grandfather?
- What do you think he would have wanted to be remembered for? Why?
- As you think of your grandfather, how do you remember him looking?
- How old was he then?
- What did you call him?
- What did his wife and friends call him?
- Tell me a story about your grandfather that shows what kind of a man he was.

Notice that none of these questions can be answered with a simple "yes" or "no." These questions require the person to think about the answers and will give you information that's more interesting than dry names and dates.

## From who to why

When I interviewed my grandmother and poor Isabel, I was laboring under another misconception: that the right time to interview your relatives is when you're just beginning to research your family history. Actually, you should talk to relatives at least twice: once when you first begin, then again after you have gathered quite a bit of research.

The first interview should be short. Your goal is to gather the facts—names, approximate dates, places, and stories about the origins of the family—so you can begin researching in records. But don't belabor this interview, and let your relative know your limited goal. You'll be back again for more after you've done some research and found some records.

Focus the second interview on augmenting information in the records and getting historical content based on that person's life. Anything Great-aunt Esmeralda tells you about ancestors beyond her lifetime is just hearsay anyway. Concentrate on getting stories based on her own lifetime and what she remembers about the oldest people in her life.

You should prepare for this interview by thinking of questions you'll ask on events, emotions and what you found in the records, asking why did this happen, how did you feel about it, and what was it like? My favorite book for helping me to prepare questions is William Fletcher's *Recording Your Family History* (Ten Speed Press, out of print). He subdivides questions into these categories:

- family history
- childhood
- youth
- middle age
- old age
- narrator as parent
- grandchildren
- historical events
- general questions, unusual life experiences and personal philosophy and values
- questions for interviewing Jewish, black and Hispanic relatives

I use the questions Fletcher provides as a starting point, then tailor the questions to the individual I'm interviewing based on my prior or research knowledge. I write these questions out in advance, but I'm prepared to deviate if the person gives me details about a topic I hadn't considered. For example, a general question might be "Where did your father go to college?" Since I knew my subject's father went to Princeton, instead I asked her, "Did you father ever tell you stories about his Princeton years?" Even though I knew what her father did for a living, I still asked, "What kind of work did your father do?" to get her interpretation.

## Getting them to talk

Before I actually begin interviews, I explain to my subjects that not all the material will be used in the family history I write and that they'll have a chance to see and approve what I write before it's published or distributed to other family members. You can't own another person's memories. Get written permission to use the material if you plan to publish or distribute parts of the interview.

### interviewing toolkit

#### PACKING FOR AN INTERVIEW

Before making a trip to visit and interview family members, stock a tote bag with these oral history essentials:

- Cassette tape recorder (microphone if not built in)
- Power cord
- Extension cord
- Cassette tapes and labels
- Extra batteries
- Note pad and pens
- List of questions or a book on oral history interviewing that has simple questions
- An address book to note names and addresses of relatives the person you are interviewing may give you
- Your research notebook with pedigree charts and family group sheets (you can download these from www.familytreemagazine.com/forms/download.html)
- A watch to make sure you're not overstaying your welcome
- Photocopies of any documents you've gathered to show the relative or photographs you need to identify
- Magnifying glass in case the relative needs it to view the photocopies
- Camera to photograph any documents or photographs you relative won't let you take out of the house to copy (you may also consider bringing a laptop computer and handheld scanner)

Label each tape and its storage case with identifying information:

- The person being interviewed
- The date
- The place

After the interview, immediately punch out the tab, making it impossible for someone to accidentally erase the tape or record over it.

I also try to put my interview "victims" at ease by telling them that they don't have to answer all the questions I ask. If it's too personal, just tell me. And if they later regret telling me something, they can contact me and I won't include it. This happened after an interview I did with a lady who commissioned me to write her family history. During the interview, she told me how she and her daughter didn't get along. Afterward, she had second thoughts about seeing that in print, so I left it out. Remember, you're a family historian, not someone out to write an exposé.

You can also put your subject at ease by beginning with a fun, easy question. If I know the person is also interested in genealogy, I ask how he became curious about his ancestry. Typically, fellow genealogy buffs make enthusiastic interview subjects. If I have a reluctant interviewee, however, who can't imagine why I'd want to interview him, I might begin by asking what he does for a living or about one of his hobbies or the family pet.

My aunt was one of those reluctant interviewees. She dreaded coming for a visit because she knew I wanted to interview her. By the second day, however, she informed her daughter who had come along, "You'll have to find something to do to entertain yourself. Sharon and I are going to do more interviewing because this is important, and we have to get this done." Usually, once the reluctant subject sees that I'm not asking for facts—especially about people long dead and buried—but instead for stories about her life and her memories of her parents and grandparents, the "victim" relaxes and thoroughly enjoys the attention.

An interview shouldn't last longer than an hour or two at a stretch. It's tiring for you and the person being interviewed. If you're with the relative only for a day or so, take frequent breaks during the interview, since an intensive interview like this can total six to eight hours. You may want to break up the interview with a visit to the cemetery or a walk around the old neighborhood to get more stories.

Try to interview only one person at a time, alone. People tend to talk over one another and finish each other's sentences—especially couples who've been married a lifetime—making it hard for you to keep up. If you're taping the interview, it's more difficult to transcribe or take notes from the tape with several people talking.

Ask a question, then wait and really listen to the response. Resist the urge to interrupt, to clarify a point or ask another question. Make a note and come back to it. Don't correct your subject. Even though you may have a contrary document, let your relative tell you the way he or she remembers the event and make a note of the discrepancy. Show interest in what your subject is saying by nodding, using appropriate facial expressions or occasionally saying "uh-huh."

## Taping and notetaking

If the interviewee doesn't mind, it's always a good idea to tape the interview, but you should also take notes. Don't rely solely on the tape recorder. I've had recorders malfunction and lost portions of an interview because I wasn't taking notes. Recently I purchased a new tape recorder and was happily interviewing; then it dawned on me that we'd been going longer than the half hour for that side of the tape. The machine had come to the end of the tape, but it didn't click off. My subject and I had to reconstruct about 20 minutes of the interview. If I'd been taking notes, that wouldn't have been necessary.

### Videocameras: Recording Words and Pictures

If you're recording an oral history interview with a videocamera, here are some secrets for success.

- Use a tripod for the videocamera and make sure it's placed in the least distracting spot you can find.
- If your videocamera has a light that flashes when it's recording, place a piece of black electrical tape over it. This light can be distracting to your subject and is a constant reminder that the camera is rolling.
- Pick a room that's brightly lit, or use lots of lights to ensure the best quality picture. But don't have the subject sit in front of a window, which will cause everything in front of it to photograph too dark. Do a "screen test" with the subject to make sure the lighting and sound are acceptable.
- Have visual materials ready (photographs, artifacts, historical documents) so you can get these items on the video when the narrator begins talking about them.
- Punch the tab on the tape as soon as you take it out of the camera, so it can't be accidentally recorded over with next week's "E.R."
- Make a copy of the tape and store in a cool, dry place.

Make a double-space printout of the questions you're planning to ask, then jot down answers and notes next to the questions. You'll want to verify spellings of names, places or unusual or archaic words, but do this at the end of the interview or at the end of a story—don't interrupt the speaker's flow.

Include in your notes a description of where you're conducting the interview. Detail what your subject is wearing, how she looks, whether she smiles over one question and frowns at another, how she fidgets. All these traits show personality, and unless you're videotaping, you won't get these recorded.

Audio taping, rather than videotaping, is the least intrusive to the interview. While videotaping (see box "Videocameras: Recording Words and Pictures") can capture a person's look, facial expressions and personality, some people are more intimidated by a camera than a tape recorder and behave unnaturally.

Always begin each tape with your name, the name of the person being interviewed, how you're related, the date of the interview, whether this is tape number 1 or 21, and where the interview is taking place. Also record this information on the tape or cassette case.

## Getting personal

Some of the best questions to ask are personal—questions that may be slightly embarrassing or make the subject laugh or cry.

These are the questions no one has had the nerve to ask, the answers to which you won't find recorded anywhere, except maybe in a diary. Obviously, you don't want to start the interview with a question like, "So tell me what you and your husband used for birth control in the 1940s." Or, "Tell me about the automobile accident your son died in last year." Interviewing requires sensitivity and a sixth sense of what you can ask and when.

## on the **bookshelf**

READING ABOUT ORAL HISTORY

- *Family Tales, Family Wisdom: How to Gather the Stories of a Lifetime and Share Them With Your Family* by Robert U. Akeret (Henry Holt, out of print)
- *Transcribing and Editing Oral History* by Willa Baum (Altamira Press, $15.95)
- "Searching at Home and Talking With Relatives," in *The Genealogy Sourcebook* by Sharon DeBartolo Carmack (Lowell House, $16)
- *Oral History: From Tape to Type* by Cullom Davis, Kathryn Back and Kay MacLean (American Library Association, $46)
- *Record and Remember: Tracing your Roots through Oral History* by Ellen Epstein and Jane Lewit Lanham (Scarborough House, $10.95)
- *Recording Your Family History: A Guide to Preserving Oral History Using Audio and Video Tape* by William Fletcher (Ten Speed Press, out of print)
- *Nearby History: Exploring the Past Around You* by David E. Kyvig and Myron A. Marty (Altamira Press, $24.95)
- *Video Family History* by Duane and Pat Strum (Ancestry, out of print)
- *How to tape Instant Oral Biographies* by Bill Zimmerman (Betterway Books, $12.99, in bookstores or order direct from www.familytreemagazine.com/store)

Most out-of-print books can be obtained through bookselling Web sites such as www.amazon.com, www.bn.com or www.borders.com.

Often I'll phrase potentially embarrassing questions so they sound general, not personal: "Were many teenage girls in your day having premarital sex?" You may be shocked by the bluntness of the answer, though. One elderly lady responded to this question with, "Oh, sure, my boyfriend and I did it." Another lady told me much more about her sex life than I really wanted to know—but only after I turned off the tape recorder.

And move over, Barbara Walters—I can make the person I'm interviewing cry, too, though that's never my intention. You just never know what question may trigger an emotional response. In one interview, the question that triggered the tears was, "Tell me how you heard World War II had begun." The tears took us both by surprise, but I just let her cry and waited while she composed herself. Uncomfortable? You bet. Hard to wait out the tears? Incredibly. Now I know how my therapist feels.

## Photographs and memories

An oral history interview is the perfect time to bring along old photographs or ask your subject if he or she has any. Ask your interviewee to tell you about the people in the photograph and where and when it was taken. If your subject is also in the photo, ask if she remembers the events that led to the photograph being taken. Was it a special occasion? Did some people not want to be in the photograph? If so, who else was there? Who suggested the pose? What was the conversation before and after the photograph? Yes, these are tough questions, and it will be the rare person who can remember all these details. But it's always worth asking.

Also ask about family artifacts. My grandmother's cousin, Isabel, has the tea set my great-grandmother brought with her from Italy in 1910. I wanted to know whether it had been a wedding present or held some other special meaning and how often the set was used—on special occasions or every day. Perhaps there are interesting stories surrounding an item in your family.

Bring out photocopies of the documents you've been gathering and show them to your relatives. Isabel had never seen her name on the passenger arrival list when she came to this country. She got teary-eyed when I showed it to her, and even more excited when I gave her her own copy.

## Using oral history

So what do you do with your interview materials after you leave your relative's house? First, you'll either need to transcribe your tapes or, if you didn't take notes during the interview, you should make notes from the tapes. Keeping the interview only on tape limits its usefulness to you and your descendants. Technology changes too fast, and the shelf life of an audio- or videotape is only about 10 years before it begins to deteriorate. The printed word is still the most widely used—and reliable—form of preserving history.

Transcribing entire tapes is incredibly time-consuming. To transcribe, edit and proof the transcript against the tape and make a final copy, plan to spend about 22–25 hours for every hour of an interview. I've never transcribed an oral history tape; instead, I take notes from the tape and pull particularly interesting quotes.

Once you have your notes or a transcript, you can combine information from the interview with the records you have researched and the general, relevant historical context to write a narrative account as part of the family history. Here's an example using oral history, a death certificate and historical information on tuberculosis:

*Mary remembers visiting her cousin Ralph who had tuberculosis. "We used to visit him in the sanatorium. It was like a hospital, and because we were too young and it was a contagious disease, we weren't allowed to go up and see him. But he used to wave to us from the window as we played on the grounds." Tuberculosis was the leading cause of death in the 19th century and into the 20th century, when Ralph died from the disease in 1946. Not until 1882 was the tubercle bacillus identified, and doctors realized that the disease was infectious. Confining tuberculin patients in sanatoriums became popular in the late 1890s.*[1]

Using footnotes or endnotes, make sure your readers and descendants know where all the information came from. For example:

[1]*Oral history interview with Mary Bart, October 31, 1997, Simla, Colo.; death certificate, Register of Deaths, Harrison, N.Y.; Sheila M. Rothman,* Living in the Shadow of Death: Tuberculosis and the Social Experience of Illness in American History (Baltimore: Johns Hopkins University Press, 1994),2, 43, 6, 179.

No source you consult while doing your genealogy is 100 percent accurate. Any record, from a birth certificate to even a tombstone, can be wrong. Oral history is no more or less reliable. Yes, memories are prone to lapses, distortions and mistakes. But it depends on the type of information you're seeking: If you're asking Great-uncle Mortimer the dates when all 12 of his brothers and sisters were born, or when they all got married, then you're also asking for trouble. If you're asking him to recount memories of the first car he owned—how did it smell? What did it feel like to get behind the wheel? What color and make was it? where did you first drive it to?—then you're on pretty safe ground.

You'll also find that talking to Great-uncle Mortimer about his memories can be personally rewarding—both for you and for your interview subject. Despite my rocky start as an oral history interviewer, I've come to really enjoy it. I now think of myself more as an oral history therapist, because it's so therapeutic for people to have my full attention for the length of the interview and to reflect on their lives and the lives of their parents and grandparents. One person I interviewed said I asked tough questions—"tough" because I made him think about his relationships, attitudes and feelings. Even though we both walked away from the interview feeling mentally drained, we felt good and knew we'd captured something that would have been lost otherwise.

As you prepare for an oral history interview, think of this African proverb: "When an old person dies, a whole library disappears." Don't let these libraries of memories disappear. With oral history interviewing, you can ensure that the why, how and what of your family's past will be remembered forever.

---

SHARON DEBARTOLO CARMACK is a Certified Genealogist who specializes in writing family history narrative. She is the author of *Organizing Your Family History Search (Betterway), A Genealogist's Guide to Discovering Your Female Ancestors* (Betterway) and *The Genealogy Sourcebook* (Lowell House).

NEWS YOU CAN USE

# Happiness Explained

*New science shows how to inject real joy into your life*

BY HOLLY J. MORRIS

There's an ancient tale of happiness that appears in many cultures, and it goes something like this: Once there was a prince who was terribly unhappy. The king dispatched messengers to find the shirt of a happy man, as his advisers told him that was the only cure. They finally encountered a poor farmer who was supremely content. Alas, the happy man owned no shirt.

Ahhh, happiness. Ineffable, elusive, and seemingly just out of reach. For most of the 20th century, happiness was largely viewed as denial or delusion. Psychologists were busy healing sick minds, not bettering healthy ones. Today, however, a growing body of psychologists is taking the mystery out of happiness and the search for the good life. Three years ago, psychologist Martin Seligman, then president of the American Psychological Association, rallied colleagues to what he dubbed "positive psychology." The movement focuses on humanity's strengths, rather than its weaknesses, and seeks to help people move up in the continuum of happiness and fulfillment. Now, with millions of dollars in funding and over 60 scientists involved, the movement is showing real results. Far from being the sole product of genes, luck, delusions, or ignorance, happiness can be learned and cultivated, researchers are finding.

## CONTENTMENT

**WHAT IT IS:** Feeling safe and calm.

**WAYS TO GET IT:** A friendly, nonthreatening environment is key. If you're not so lucky, relaxation exercises may mimic the body's response to contentment. **Rebecca Shaw** finds it in marriage to Ray Shaw, and in her two children, Christian, 3, and Sierra, 2—and by not putting up with mean people.

Decades of studying depression have helped millions become less sad, but not necessarily more happy—a crucial distinction. When you alleviate depression (no mean task), "the best you can ever get to is zero," says Seligman, a professor at the University of Pennsylvania. But "when you've got a nation in surplus and at peace and not in social turmoil," he explains, "I think the body politic lies awake at night thinking about 'How do I go from plus 2 to plus 8 in my life?'"

Indeed, people in peaceful, prosperous nations aren't necessarily getting any happier. Though census data show that many measures of quality of life have risen since World War II, the number of people who consider themselves happy remains flat. And people are 10 times as likely to suffer depression as those born two generations ago. Researchers have scads of information on what isn't making people happy. For example, once income provides basic needs, it doesn't correlate to happiness. Nor does intelligence, prestige, or sunny weather. People grow used to new climates, higher salaries, and better cars. Not only does the novelty fade but such changes do nothing to alleviate real problems—like that niggling fear that nobody likes you.

**Happiness helpers.** Scientists also know what works. Strong marriages, family ties, and friendships predict happiness, as do spirituality and self-esteem. Hope is crucial, as is the feeling that life has meaning. Yes, happy people may be more likely to have all these things at the start. But causality, researchers find, goes both ways. Helping people be a little happier can jump-start a process that will lead to stronger relationships, renewed hope, and a general upward spiraling of happiness.

The average person has a head start. Decades of international survey research suggest that most people in developed nations are basically happy. This tendency toward mild cheerfulness may have evolved to keep peo-

## CHANGE

**WHAT IT IS:** What you need when your goals aren't satisfying you.

**WAYS TO GET IT:** Figure out why what you're doing isn't working. **Allison Waxberg**, a scientist in the cosmetics industry, wanted more creativity in her life. She took art classes, realized she had talent, and now attends Brooklyn's Pratt Institute.

ple moving—glum ancestors would have moped, not mobilized.

Some have more of a head start than others. University studies of twins suggest that about half of one's potential for happiness is inherited. Researchers think happiness is influenced not by a single "happy gene," but by inborn predispositions toward qualities that help or hinder happiness, such as optimism or shyness. And personality doesn't fluctuate that much over an average life span. People seem to have "happiness set points"—base lines that mood drifts back to after good and bad events.

There's a lot of wiggle room on either side of that base line, though. Most positive psychologists refer to a set range. "If you're a more gloomy, pessimistic person, you're probably never going to be really deliriously happy, but you can get into the high end of your possible range and stay there," says psychologist Ken Sheldon of the University of Missouri.

Michael Lee, too, believes happiness can be learned. "You practice it day in and day out," says the 28-year-old marketing director from San Jose, Calif. He has always been pretty happy but has seen his joy grow. A Catholic, he started a faith-sharing group with childhood friends. Under guidance from Jesuit priests, they learned to take time each night to reflect on the positive in their everyday lives—"subtle things like meeting a new person... or kids sitting out in the yard playing." In cultivating his appreciation of the routine, and surrounding himself with other happy people, Lee grew happier. Boosting your happiness isn't always easy, though: Moving up within your range can mean working against your inborn personality traits, learned thinking habits, environment, or all three. But the latter two can change. "If you want to keep your happiness at the higher end of the set range," says Sonja Lyubomirsky, a psychologist at the University of California-Riverside, "you have to commit yourself every day to doing things to make you happy."

One way is to find the right goals and pursue them. Sheldon's research suggests that goals reflecting your interests and values can help you attain and maintain new levels of happiness, rather than returning to base line. By setting and achieving a progression of goals, you can boost your well-being. Even when you fail, you can better maintain that higher level next time you reach it, though you'll probably top out at the high end of your range.

MOOD MEASUREMENT

## How happy are you? Find out

One way scientists measure happiness is by simply asking people to evaluate their overall satisfaction with their lives. This scale of life satisfaction was developed by psychologist Ed Diener of the University of Illinois-Urbana-Champaign and is used worldwide to gather data on happiness. The scoring at the bottom shows how you compare with other Americans.

### Taking the test

For each of the five items below (A-E), select an answer from the O-to-6 response scale. Place a number on the line next to each statement, indicating your agreement or disagreement with that statement.

**6:** Strongly agree
**5:** Agree
**4:** Slightly agree
**3:** Neither agree or disagree
**2:** Slightly disagree
**1:** Disagree
**0:** Strongly disagree

**A** _____Your life is very close to your ideal.
**B** _____The conditions of your life are excellent.
**C** _____You are completely satisfied with your life.
**D** _____So far you have obtained the important things you want in your life.
**E** _____If you could live your life over, you would change nothing.
_______**TOTAL**

**26 to 30:** Extremely satisfied, much above average
**21 to 25:** Very satisfied, above average
**15 to 20:** Somewhat satisfied, average for Americans
**11 to 14:** Slightly dissatisfied, a bit below average
**6 to 10:** Dissatisfied, clearly below average
**0 to 5:** Very dissatisfied, much below average

Allison Waxberg, 30, wasn't miserable and wasn't depressed—but she wasn't especially happy, either. After six years as a skin scientist in the cosmetics industry, she longed for more-creative work. "I grew up drawing, but I always felt like I had to do something like be a doctor or a lawyer or something professional," she says. When people feel they have no choice in the goals they pursue, they're not going to be satisfied. Goals that derive from

GAGGLE OF GIGGLES

## Laughter as its own punch line

Peals of laughter cut through the persistent early-morning drizzle at Seattle's Green Lake Park. As passers-by gape—and then grin—four men and women titter, giggle, chortle, and guffaw, in what looks like a yoga class gone goofy. Led by energetic Stephanie Roche, they alternate rhythmic chanting and clapping with penguinlike waddling and pretend sneezing—all while howling with laughter. There's no punch line; there's not even a joke. This is a laughing club, one of at least 20 begun in the United States this year. They are held in parks, churches, and often in nursing homes, where the gentle cheer is especially welcome.

Laughing clubs are an export from India, where they're familiar sights in hundreds of neighborhoods. Invented by physician Madan Kataria in 1995, the clubs don't rely on humor or jokes. Rather, they focus on the act of laughing, which releases stress and promotes deep, healthy breathing. At first, the ha-has and hee-hees can be forced. Eye contact is required, which helps break the ice. But few can resist breaking into spontaneous laughter during the "lion laugh"—stick out your tongue, google your eyes, and use your hands as paws. "Sometimes people have to fake it," says psychologist Steve Wilson, 60, of Columbus, Ohio, whose World Laughter Tour trains laughter-club leaders. "And then it flips and it just becomes hysterical."

Roche's laughing club started a mere two weeks ago. After she saw a documentary, *The Laughing Club of India*, at a Seattle film festival (it airs August 28 on Cinemax), she became a "certified laughter leader" at one of Wilson's workshops. She patterned her club after the Indian versions, holding it in a neighborhood park three days a week at 7 a.m. Clubs are encouraged to create their own laughs: Wilson can reel off a long list of obscure ones, such as the "airline safety instruction laugh," in which you gesture at exits and don an imaginary oxygen mask. The Seattle group is already customizing. Karen Schneider-Chen, a 49-year-old jail outreach worker, mimics raindrops with fluttering fingers. "We're working on a Seattle rain laugh," she says.

—*H.J.M., with Bellamy Pailthorp in Seattle*

## FLOW

**WHAT IT IS:** The state of intense concentration that occurs during challenging, goal-directed activities.

**WAYS TO GET IT:** Flow can arise from pastimes, like playing sports or music, but also from reading and good conversation. College sophomore **Jason Vincens** finds flow in competitive wrestling.

fear, guilt, or social pressure probably won't make you happier, even if you attain them. "Ask yourself, 'Is this intrinsically interesting and enjoyable?' If it isn't, do I at least believe in it strongly?" says Sheldon. "If I don't, why the hell am I doing it?"

Waxberg tried a series of jobs, including making prosthetic limbs, but had yet to combine her technical and creative sides. Finally, she took some art classes and proved to herself that she had talent. She's now earning an industrial design master's from Brooklyn's Pratt Institute, where she has won acclaim for her ceramics, and is doing her thesis on skin. She hopes to start a new career as a design consultant this year.

For Waxberg, finding the right goal was key—but first she had to figure out why the old ones weren't working. The trick is to know what kind of goals you have. Diffuse goals, such as "be someone," are next to impossible to achieve. More-concrete goals ("get a job") that relate back to the abstract goal ("be a success") are more satisfying. That also goes for the goal of "being happy." "You'll be happier if you can get involved in things and do well at them, but don't be thinking too much about trying to get happier by doing them," says Sheldon. "It's really kind of Zen in a way."

**Out with the bad.** Another path to greater happiness is cultivating positive emotions. They're good for more than warm fuzzies: Good feelings broaden thinking and banish negative emotions, says Barbara Fredrickson, a psychologist at the University of Michigan. Negative emotions narrow thought, by necessity. Ancestors didn't have time to sift through creative escape options when fears loomed. But positive emotions open new routes for thinking. When researchers induce positive emotions, thinking becomes more expansive and resourceful.

Most people can't feel positive emotions at will. But you can approach events in a way that gets them going, then let momentum take over. Jay Van Houten made a decision to see the positive when faced with a potentially fatal brain tumor. The 54-year-old business manager from Boise, Idaho, listed the benefits, such as "a built-in excuse for not hearing things like 'Please take out the trash,' " as the surgery left him deaf in one ear.

Though laughing at yourself is fleeting, Fredrickson believes such moments have lasting consequences. "Pos-

HIGHS AND LOWS

## Taking one's happy temp

Scientists also measure happiness with "experience sampling," in which mood is assessed on multiple occasions over time. With Palm devices that beeped at random intervals, two *U.S. News* writers answered questions such as "How pleasant are you feeling?" several times a day for a week. Researcher Christie Scollon of the University of Illinois analyzed the data. The red and orange lines combine positive and negative emotions to show overall mood. Person A is happier than the average American—she feels more positive than negative emotions. Person B is unhappier than most—and she's moody. She feels a log of bad along with the good. This illustrates an important notion: Feeling good is more than just not feeling bad.—*H.J.M.*

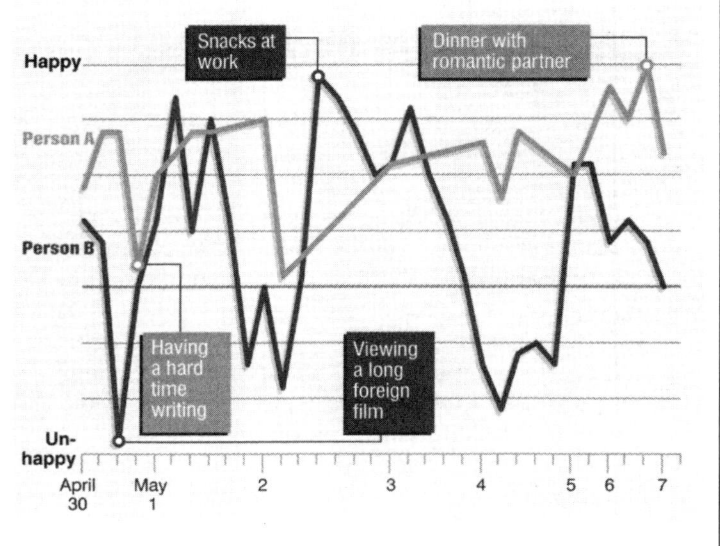


## PERSPECTIVE

**WHY GET IT:** It helps peolple see the good in their lives when things are going badly.

**WAYS TO GET IT:** Comparing one's situation with a worst-case scenario really can make people feel better. After a potentially fatal brain tumor, not much fazes **Jay Van Houten** these days. ...he volunteers with the mentally and physically disabled.

itive emotions and broadened thinking are mutually building on one another, making people even more creative problem-solvers over time, and even better off emotionally," she says. Coping with one problem well—as Van Houten did with humor—may make people more resilient next time trouble comes along. Van Houten says he's much happier now, especially as nothing seems as bad as a potentially fatal brain tumor. After his surgery, he had to relearn balance. "I still drill into the ground if I turn too fast," he says. "You've got to approach it with a certain amount of humor to get you through the day."

Using humor to feel better works because thinking can't be both narrow and broad. To test this idea, Fredrickson had subjects prepare a speech, then let them off the hook. As they calmed, she showed them video clips that sparked various emotions: a puppy playing with a flower (joy), ocean waves (contentment), a scene from the 1979 tear-jerker *The Champ* (sadness), and a computer screen-saver (neutral). Those who felt joy and contentment calmed down faster. This doesn't mean you should think about puppies when you're down (though if it helps, go for it), but that when you've done all you can about a problem, a positive distraction can banish lingering bad feelings.

One of the worst enemies of positive emotions is feeling threatened, says Fredrickson. A safe environment is key. Rebecca Shaw found that happiness just needed a chance to flourish. "The day I met my husband was the day my boyfriend broke up with me, and I was pregnant," says the 32-year-old of Ridge, Md. Miserable, lonely, and despairing, she had just moved back in with her parents to get her bearings. Then she ran into an old friend, Ray Shaw. As they spent time together in the following weeks, happiness "stole up" on her. "Suddenly I was just smiling and didn't even realize it—it was just such a subtle turn," she says. Now, four years after their marriage, the defense contractor, inventor, and stay-at-home mom doubts she could be happier. "My husband didn't replace any of the things that were missing," she says. "He just kind of gave me the sanctuary to go and find them myself."

Part of seeking positive emotions is being open to them in everyday life. Mindfully approaching sources of good feelings can be more lasting than seeking instant gratification. Distinctions can disappear. "Overeating ice cream and shopping get lumped in with spending time with your family or pursuing an interesting activity," says Fredrickson. People may choose shortcuts with little meaning over activities with positive consequences. A more nuanced appreciation of good feelings—"experiential wisdom," Fredrickson calls it—may help people benefit more from positive emotions. So think: Is ice cream really going to make me feel better for longer than the time it takes to eat it?

Some emotions simply aren't that hard to feel, if you take the time. Take gratitude. Robert Emmons of the University of California-Davis found that people who wrote down five things for which they were grateful in weekly or daily journals were not only more joyful; they were healthier, less stressed, more optimistic, and more likely to help others. You don't have to write things down to be grateful for them, of course, though it helps to make them concrete. During difficult times, "I just tend to focus on the things I'm grateful for and the parts of life that are good," says Sean David Griffiths, 38, a project officer at the Centers for Disease Control and Prevention in Atlanta. And gratitude could help ward off mindless materialism, says Emmons. "When you don't appreciate stuff is when you get rid of it and get something else."

Researchers are also finding more positive emotions than once were thought to exist. Anyone who has witnessed a touching good deed will recognize the heartwarming tingling in the chest that follows. Psychologist Jonathan Haidt of the University of Virginia dubbed this uplifting emotion "elevation," and finds that it makes people want to be kind. Such emotions break down mental barriers and help people see the world in new ways. Even mild feelings of elevation can change minds. Haidt found that students who watched a documentary about Mother Teresa were more interested in activities like volunteer work. (In contrast, the subjects who watched clips of *America's Funniest Home Videos* were interested in self-focused activities like watching TV and eating.)

The feeling of hope is one reason spirituality may correlate with well-being. Hope fosters optimism, and faith is, by definition, hope for the future. And the churchgoing form of faith can be a built-in social support network. This is not to say that atheists can't be happy, but it helps explain why so many do find happiness in faith, and why researchers continue to find connections between faith, optimism, and physical health.

**Teaching positive.** Nurturing optimism is a key way to help hope and happiness flourish. Optimism predisposes people toward positive emotions, whereas pessimism is a petri dish for depression. Over 20 years ago, Seligman and his colleagues developed a method to teach optimism by helping people recognize and dispute inaccurate thoughts. Called "learned optimism" (and outlined in the book of the same name), they found it could inoculate against depression as well. Teaching optimistic thinking styles to middle schoolers lowered the occurrence of depression as the children aged. Even optimistic children grew happier. "These are sticky skills," says Karen Reivich, codirector of the Penn Resiliency Project. "Once you start using them, you feel better, and you keep using them."

The skills of learned optimism are based on findings that pessimists blame themselves for problems, figure they will last forever, and let them invade every corner of their lives. Good events are freak occurrences. Optimists look for outside causes of bad events and assume they will be fleeting—but take credit for good events and bet they'll keep happening. (Because optimism tends to act as a self-fulfilling prophecy, they often do.) By learning new ways to explain events, pessimists can become more optimistic and more resilient, leaving them better equipped to appreciate the good and cope with the bad. Today, these skills are taught in Pennsylvania schools by teachers trained through Adaptiv Learning Systems, which also offers a more grown-up version to the corporate world.

One of the most positive states of all is easy enough to come by—if you're willing to concentrate. Dubbed "flow" by psychologist Mihaly Csikszentmihalyi, director of the Quality of Life Research Center in Claremont, Calif., it's the single-minded focus of athletes and artists, scientists and writers, or anyone doing anything that poses a challenge and demands full attention. People in flow are too busy to think about happiness, but afterward they think of the experience as incredibly positive. And it's followed by well-earned contentment.

People find flow in myriad ways—any hobbyist or athlete can tell you that. "The secret to my happiness isn't a secret at all," says 19-year-old Jason Vincens, a sophomore at the University of Illinois. "I found something I love and I'm doing it." He has been wrestling competitively since sixth grade. When he wrestles, he doesn't worry about anything else. Afterward, he doesn't have the energy. But you don't have to take up tennis or the violin to find flow: A discussion with good friends can do the trick.

The paradox of flow is that many people have it, but don't appreciate it. Csikszentmihalyi is endlessly puzzled that adults and teenagers feel more creative and excited while working but would rather be doing something else. "I think it's basically a set of assumptions for many people, that work is something that we do simply for our paycheck," he says. So rather than enjoy it, people tend to rush home and watch TV, which rarely provides much pleasure. It's the same principle that causes people to put off activities they enjoy, but which require effort, such as swimming laps.

**With age, serenity.** Wait around if you must, as some research suggests that people grow happier with age. You don't have the high highs of youth, but neither do you have the low lows. Older people often pursue goals less out of guilt or social pressure and more for their own satisfaction. Also, age often brings wisdom, which adds depth to happiness. You could think of happiness growing out, rather than up.

And yet the stereotype that happy people are shallow persists. "Me being a chronically happy person doesn't mean that I haven't had some real down spells," says Lars Thorn, 24, who works in marketing in Manchester, Vt. During a difficult breakup, he told a friend he was feeling terrible. "And she said, 'Oh, no you're not—you're Lars!'" he recalls. "I was perceived as being a cardboard cutout of a person with no real emotion." But new research suggests happy people may be more realistic than unhappy folks. Psychologist Lisa Aspinwall of the University of Utah finds that optimists are more open to negative information about themselves than pessimists.

Positive mood gives them the resources to process bad news. Optimists are also more likely to accept what they cannot change and move on, says Aspinwall. Indeed, she says, they have an intuitive grasp of the Serenity Prayer, which asks for the wisdom to know the difference between what one can and cannot change.

There's no disputing that positive psychology's findings echo the exhortations of ancient wisdom, and let's face it—Oprah. Be grateful and kind and true to yourself. Find meaning in life. Seek silver linings. But then, what did you expect—be mean to children and animals?

So are people just not listening to their grandmothers and gurus? Psychologist Laura King of the University of Missouri has found that people at least say they know these things and consistently rate meaning and happiness above money. But in a study with colleague Christie Scollon, she found that people were all for meaning, yet most said they didn't want to work for it. Other evidence echoes her findings: People *say* one thing but do another. "One of the problems," says King, "might be that people don't understand that lives of happiness and meaning probably involve some hard work."

Will people work to learn happiness? Positive psychologists think that if they can tease out the best in people, happiness will follow. To Seligman, happiness is "the emotion that arises when we do something that stems from our strengths and virtues." And those, anyone can cultivate. "There's no set point for honesty," he says. The idea that happiness is the sum of what's best in people may sound suspiciously simple, but it's a whole lot easier than finding that happy man's shirt.

## SPIRITUALITY

**WHAT IT DOES:** People with some form of spirtual belief (not just religion) are often happier and more optimistic.
**WHY IT WORKS:** Possibly because it can promote hope and social support. **Michael Lee** started Lighthouse, a faith-sharing group. ...he prays with his wife, **Agatha Chung**, at a meeting.

# Examining Family Rituals

**Grace M. Viere**
*James Madison University*

*In this column, the notion of rituals from a historical perspective is provided. The definitions and classifications of family rituals as well as empirical studies are examined.*

Family rituals, originating as a belief in mystical powers, have evolved into a vital component of family life that transcends race, culture, and socioeconomic levels. Researchers and practitioners have begun to incorporate family rituals into a variety of studies and therapeutic practices. This article reviews the definition and meaning of rituals and implications of family rituals for the health and well-being of families.

## Rituals Defined

Anthropologist Victor Turner (1967) originally defined *ritual* as a "prescribed formal behavior for occasions not given over to technological routine, having reference to beliefs in mystical beings or powers" (p. 19). Turner's definition emphasizes symbols as the building blocks of rituals. The significance of symbols is explained in the following three areas: the ability to carry multiple meanings and thus contribute to the open parts of rituals, the ways symbols can link several disparate phenomena that could not be joined as complexly through words, and the ability of symbols to work with both the sensory and cognitive poles of meaning simultaneously.

Moore and Myerhoff (1977) suggested that the anthropological study of ritual has often been limited to religious and magical aspects of a culture partly because anthropologists have often worked in societies "in which everything has a religious significance" (p. 3). As societies become more secular, they continue to carry within them beliefs that have a similar role in society as religion. Moore and Myerhoff stressed the importance of recognizing the sacredness of these beliefs and the rituals carried out around them. Their definition of *sacred* reaches beyond the traditional religious definition to focus on "specialness" or "something colored with meaning beyond the ordinary."

Rappaport (1971) also suggested that the term *ritual* is not limited to religious practices. He described the following six key aspects to ritual of which family rituals are a part:

1. repetition: not necessarily just in action but also of content and form,
2. acting: not just saying or thinking something but also doing something,
3. special behavior or stylization: where behaviors and symbols are set apart from their usual common uses,
4. order: some beginning and end and containment for spontaneity.
5. evocative presentational style: where through staging and focus an "attentive state of mind" is created,
6. collective dimension: where there is social meaning.

Van Gennep (1960) developed three stages of rituals. In the first stage, separation, special preparations are made and new knowledge is passed on as the frame is set for marking a particular event. This time of preparing for the ritual is as important a part of the ritual process as the actual event itself. The second stage is transitional, in which people actually partake of the ritual and experience themselves in new ways and take on new roles. The third stage is reintegration, in which people are reconnected to their community with their new status. Ritual is not just the ceremony or actual performance but the whole process of preparing for it, experiencing it, and reintegration back into everyday life.

## RITUALS IN FAMILIES

Wolin and Bennett (1984) viewed family ritual as a "a symbolic form of communication that, owing to the satisfaction that family members experience through its repetition, is acted out in a systematic fashion over time". They identified six typologies of ritual use in families. First is underritualized, in which families neither celebrate nor mark family changes nor join much in larger societal rituals. This underutilization leaves the family with little access to some of the benefits of ritual such as group cohesion, support for role shifts, and the ability to hold two dualities in place at the same time. Second is rigidly ritualized, in which there are very prescribed behaviors, a sense of "we must always do these things together in this way at this time." There are few open parts in the rituals, and rituals tend to stay the same over time rather than evolving. Third is skewed ritualization, in which one particular ethnic tradition in the family, or religious tradition, or even one particular side of the family has been emphasized at the expense of other aspects of the family. Fourth is hollow ritual as event, not process. This takes place when people celebrate events out of a sense of obligation, with little meaning found in either the process or the event. This may happen because rituals have become too closed or end up creating undue stress for family members. Fifth is ritual process interrupted or unable to be openly experienced. This occurs after sudden changes (e.g., death, moving, and illness) or traumatic events in the family or larger culture (e.g., war oppression and migration). Families may be unable to fully experience the whole ritual process. And finally, flexibility to adapt to rituals is the ability to change rituals over the life cycle, keeping the rituals meaningful for families and reworking roles, rules, and relationships.

Despite differences among families in terms of factors such as socioeconomic status, ethnic background, and religious orientation, the following four types of rituals are universal to nearly all families: family celebrations, family traditions, family life cycle rituals, and day-to-day life events that have become ritualized (Wolin & Bennett, 1984).

Family celebrations are defined as rituals that are widely practiced around events that are celebrated in the larger culture. Through larger cultural expectations, the society to some extent organizes the time, space, and symbols of these rituals. Examples include Passover and Christmas. Family traditions are less anchored in the culture and are more idiosyncratic to the family, based on what might be called an inside instead of an outside calendar. Anniversaries, birthdays, family reunions, vacations, and so on all fall into this category. Although the practice of traditions is influenced to some extent by the culture, the individual family determines which occasions it will adopt as traditions and how these activities will be enacted. Family life cycle rituals include weddings, showers, christenings, graduations, and retirement parties. These are events that mark the progression of the family through the life cycle. Rituals of daily family life, such as dinnertime, bedtime, and recreation, are those events that are infused with meaning as the family creates its roles, rules, and norms. Day-to-day rituals are the least deliberate and consciously planned of the family rituals as well as the least standardized across families, the most variable over time, and the most frequently enacted.

Family rituals provide the family and individual members with a sense of identity by creating feelings of belonging (Bennett, Wolin, & McAvity, 1988; Fiese, 1992). Rituals are the occasions during which family members transmit family values and beliefs (Steinglass, Bennett, Wolin, & Reiss, 1987), reinforce the family's heritage (Troll, 1988), and recognize change in the family (Wolin & Bennett, 1984).

All families experience crisis or stress, and rituals have the capacity to provide families stability during these time (Cheal, 1988). For example, with a funeral wake or sitting Shiva, there are certain prescribed times for mourning. Groups of people meet to support and comfort each other in their sorrow, foods are shared, specific clothes may be worn, and certain words are said. Families draw comfort from knowing they can experience strong feelings of grief with some circumscribed limits and group support (Scheff, 1979).

Rituals can hold both sides of a contradiction at the same time. All individuals live with the ultimate paradoxes of life/death, connection/distance, ideal/real, and good/evil, and rituals can incorporate both sides of contradictions so that they can be managed simultaneously. For example, a wedding ceremony has included within it both loss and mourning and happiness and celebration. Parents give their child away at the same time they welcome another member into their extended family.

## Ritual Versus Routine

Steinglass et al. (1987) described the following five types of family rituals that clearly distinguish between family rituals and daily routines: (a) bounded rituals, which are prepared with anticipation and have a clear beginning, middle, and end; (b) identifiable rituals, in which families are aware of their rituals and can clearly describe the organization and patterning of these behaviors; (c) compelling rituals, which families make rigorous efforts to maintain; (d) symbolic rituals, which are associated with meanings and strong emotions; and (e) organizing rituals, which are major regulators of stability for family life.

Although routines are observable and repetitious family behaviors that are important in structuring family life, they lack the symbolic content and the compelling, anticipatory nature that rituals possess (Keltner, Keltner, & Farren, 1990). Routines are activities that family members have to do rather than want to do. Routines have the potential to acquire ritual status if they exceed their functional purpose and become filled with psychological intensity and symbolic meaning (Boyce, Jensen, James, & Peacock, 1983). Conversely, rituals that lose meaning or become mundane may take on routine status for families. Sometimes family members simply outgrow a ritual. Another distinction that can be made between ritual and routine is the capacity of rituals to serve several distinct functions for the family that are symbolically important for the psychological well-being of the family system. Rituals are powerful organizers of behavior within the family system that provide the family with a sense of stability, a unique identity, and a means for socializing children within their cultural context.

## Empirical Studies on Family Rituals

Systematic research on family rituals has focused on family risk conditions such as alcoholism and points of family transition such as becoming parents. Beginning in the 1970s, Wolin and Bennett began a series of studies examining the relationship between family rituals and alcoholism. In the first study, the relationship between ritual disruption and alcohol transmission was examined. The researchers hypothesized that families with more intact rituals would be less likely to transmit alcoholism in the next generation. Ritual disruption was assessed using the family ritual interview, focusing on the effect of the alcoholic parent's drinking behavior on family rituals. *Subsumptive* families, in which alcohol use had overridden and effectively controlled the practice of family rituals, were identified, as were *distinctive* families, in which the practice of family rituals remained distinct from alcohol use. The families in which alcohol had subsumed family ritual practice were more likely to have children who developed problematic drinking or married individuals with alcohol problems (Wolin, Bennett, Noonan, &

Teitelbaum, 1987). Furthermore, protective factors were identified in the study of individuals raised in alcoholic households. When children of alcoholics chose spouses with highly developed nonalcoholic family rituals, there was less likelihood of developing an alcoholic family identity. The second protective factor was a distinctive dinner ritual in which children from alcoholic families whose parents preserved the dinner ritual had a higher likelihood of a nonalcoholic outcome (Bennett, Wolin, Reiss, & Teitelbaum, 1987).

Fiese (1992) found similar evidence for the role of family rituals in protecting children from the effects of family alcoholism. Using the Family Ritual Questionnaire and self-report measures of problematic drinking and health symptomatology, it was noted that the adolescents who reported meaningful family rituals in addition to parental problematic drinking were less likely to develop anxiety-related health symptoms than adolescents reporting parental problematic drinking and relatively hollow family rituals. The results from these studies suggest that under potentially stressful child-rearing conditions, such as parental alcoholism, family rituals may serve a protective function. In setting aside family gatherings as distinct from alcoholic behavior and in imbuing meaning and deliberateness in the practice of patterned family interactions such as dinnertime, the child may develop an identity of the family that is separate from the disruptions associated with alcoholism.

Family rituals may also serve a protective function during periods of normative family transitions. The transition to parenthood has been identified as a potentially stressful period for couples. A study of 115 married couples found that couples with preschoolers who were able to practice meaningful family rituals reported more marital satisfaction than those who reported relatively hollow family rituals (Fiese, Hooker, Kotrary, & Schwagler, 1993).

Two empirical studies investigated family rituals in families of children with disabilities. Gruszka (1988) examined families of children with mental retardation. She found that mothers of these children perceive that their families engage in fewer family celebrations than mothers of children who did not have any disabilities. Another study (Bucy, 1995) investigated rituals and parenting stress and their relationship to the disability characteristics of preschool children. Bucy (1995) found parents of preschool children with social skill deficits or motor impairments practice more religious and cultural family rituals than families of preschool children with cognitive delays. Furthermore, mothers of preschool children with disabilities that maintained meaningful participation in family rituals evidenced better abilities to cope with parenting stress than did mothers with less ritual participation.

## SUMMARY

Rituals both reflect and shape the way people think about themselves and their world. Papp (1983) suggested rituals have a unique ability to "address themselves to the most primitive and profound level of experience" (p. vii)—the level where resistance lies and where real change often begins.

Family rituals provide the family and individual members with a sense of identity by creating feelings of belonging. Rituals are the occasions that serve to facilitate social interaction among family members so that families can transmit cultural and normative information as well as beliefs and values across generations. All families experience crisis or stress, and rituals have the capacity to provide families stability during these times. Rituals may provide a way for people to find support and containment for strong emotions. Families may be encouraged to examine their family rituals and continue those rituals that are working for them as well as to develop new rituals and adapt those that are no longer valued.

## References


Bennett, L. A., Wolin, S. J., & McAvity, K. J. (1988). Family identity, ritual and myth: A cultural perspective on life cycle transition. In C. J. Falicov (Ed.), *Family transitions* (pp. 211–234). New York: Guilford.

Bennett, L. A., Wolin, S. J., Reiss, D., & Teitelbaum, M. A. (1987). Couples at risk for transmission of alcoholism: Protective influences. *Family Process, 26,* 111–129.

Boyce, W., Jensen, E., James, S., & Peacock, J. (1983). The family routines inventory: Theoretical origins. *Social Science Medicine, 17,* 193–200.

Bucy, J. E. (1995). An exploratory study of family rituals, parenting stress, and developmental delay in early childhood. *Dissertation Abstracts International, 57*(2A), 575.

Cheal, D. (1988). The ritualization of family ties. *American Behavioral Scientist, 31,* 632–643.

Fiese, B. H. (1992). Dimensions of family rituals across two generations: Relations to adolescent identity. *Family Process, 31,* 151–162.

Fiese, B. H., Hooker, K. A., Kotrary, L., & Schwagler, J. (1993). Family rituals in the early stages of parenthood. *Journal of Marriage and Family, 55,* 633–642.

Gruszka, M. A. (1988). Family functioning and sibling adjustment in families with a handicapped child. *Dissertation Abstracts International, 50*(OB), 748.

Keltner, B., Keltner, N. L., & Farren, E. (1990). Family routines and conduct disorders in adolescent girls. *Western Journal of Nursing Research, 12,* 161–174.

Moore, S. F., & Myerhoff, B. G. (1977). (Eds.). *Secular ritual.* Amsterdam: Van Gorcum.

Papp, P. (1983). Preface. In O. Van der Hart (Ed.), *Rituals in psychotherapy: Transition and continuity* (pp. v–ix). New York: Irvington Publications.

Rappaport, R. A. (1971). Ritual sanctity and cybernetics. *American Anthropologist, 73,* 59–76.

Scheff, T. J. (1979). *Catharsis in healing, ritual, and drama.* Los Angeles: University of California Press.

Steinglass, P., Bennett, L. A., Wolin, S. J., & Reiss, D. (1987). *The alcoholic family.* New York: Basic Books.

Troll, L. E. (1988). Rituals and reunions. *American Behavioral Scientist, 31,* 621–631.

Turner, V. (1967). *The forest of symbols: Aspects of Ndembu ritual.* Ithaca, NY: Cornell University Press.

Van Gennep, A. (1960). *The rites of passage.* Chicago: University of Chicago Press.

Wolin, S. J., & Bennett, L. A. (1984). Family rituals. *Family Process, 23,* 401–420.

Wolin, S. J., Bennett, L. A., Noonan, D. L., & Teitelbaum, M. (1987). Disrupted family rituals: A factor in the intergenerational transmission of alcoholism. *Journal of Studies of Alcoholism, 41,* 199–214.


***Grace Viere**, Ph.D., is an assistant professor of counselor education at James Madison University in Harrisonburg, VA. Her current research interests include the examination of the relationship between family rituals and attachments and the use of family rituals by families with children who are adopted.*

From *The Family Journal: Counseling and Therapy for Couples and Families*, July 2001, pp. 285-288. 

*Our earliest relationships are irreplaceable, and we pay a steep price for severed ties. But if you value a person and the memories you share, says the author, you can…*

# RECONNECT WITH YOUR FAMILY

## *Resolve to change the patterns of personal hurt that lie at the heart of too many family gatherings.*

BY DR. JOYCE BROTHERS

THANKSGIVING IS almost here, and Christmas and Chanukah are waiting in the wings. What could be better than planning to celebrate with our families?

But while the turkey may be perfect, your family's behavior may not be: Siblings snipe at one another, grandparents lose their patience, cousins drift off to watch TV, feuding relatives pout, and every single trait that ever annoyed you about a particular family member makes an appearance.

Even if you've had this experience, you may well be trying again this year, because hope springs eternal when it comes to holidays and families. You can be more effective if you understand why things sometimes go awry at holiday time and what you can do about it.

### THE DEEPEST TIES

After the recent attacks on our country, all of us have been left with a heightened awareness of the preciousness of family ties: In its aftermath, fathers, mothers, sisters, brothers, uncles and aunts felt compelled to check on the well-being of relatives wherever they were and to reaffirm their love.

**Thanksgiving dinner can be a time to cement relationships and foster warmth among young and old.**

Indeed, even if families fail us in some ways, they're still the greatest influence on our lives. A decade ago, some therapists advised breaking away from families that were "toxic." Today, it's believed that it's best to stay connected, unless a family is very dysfunctional or abusive. There's a high emotional price for maintaining a "non-relationship," says family therapist Monica McGoldrick, author of *You Can Go Home Again.* Severed family ties cannot be replaced by lovers, children, friends or work, she maintains. A part of your spirit remains buried.

If you want to reconnect as a family, you first need to think about why problems arise.

## GHOSTS AT THE HOLIDAY TABLE

Family get-togethers are crowded with ghosts—memories, relatives who are no longer alive and, particularly, old patterns of behavior. All strike at the way people relate to one another. Here are some unwelcome "guests" that can show up:

• *Sibling warfare.* There's no age limit on sibling rivalry. I was once at a Thanksgiving dinner where two elderly sisters were among the guests. The older sister passed around photos of her new grandchild. When they reached the younger sister, who had no grandchildren, some soup just happened to spill on them. Since childhood, the sisters had had a close but competitive relationship. The older sister thought her parents favored the younger one. The younger sister resented her sister's tendency to show off. Did the younger sister brush her hand against the soup plate? Who knows?

• *Childhood revisited.* "It doesn't matter how old I get," a friend said. "When I walk through my parents' door on Christmas Eve, I feel like a little girl again." She experiences the old anxiety of needing to please her parents. She becomes anxious and hypersensitive, interpreting a remark like "you've done something to your hair" as criticism.

• *Parental discontent.* A family gathering can provide the perfect opportunity for subtle propaganda from parents who haven't lost hope of getting an adult child to live up to their expectations. Any single daughter who's had to smile sweetly while a parent asks, "Are you dating anyone special?" knows what I mean.

• *Hidden hurt.* Years ago, Cousin Bob invited the family to a barbecue but neglected to invite Uncle Fred, whom he thought was out of town. Fred didn't ask the reason for the slight but, to this day, has carried a grievance against Bob. At some level, Fred enjoys nursing the grudge. He doesn't realize that his feelings put a damper on all family relationships.

• *Outsider syndrome.* Families don't always alter their traditions to accommodate newcomers. There may be family jokes that never get explained or a favorite dish that's always served. Even timing can be an issue. I know a family that enjoys a slow-paced Thanksgiving, but the daughter-in-law, who's used to a much faster celebration, feels impatient and left out.

## MAKE A COMMITMENT TO RECONNECT

Personal hurt is at the heart of every family holiday gone wrong. But you can make things better. Here's how:

• *Ask, "Is it worth it?"* Think hard. If you value the individual with whom you're having difficulties, if there are happy mem-

## TEN WAYS TO HEAL A FAMILY FEUD

*A good mediator for family disputes can be a counselor, a spiritual advisor or a respected family member, such as yourself. If you're acting as a go-between, here are some steps you can take:*

**1** DON'T WAIT. If your family feud is like most, enough time has gone by.

**2** MEET IN A NEUTRAL BUT COZY PLACE, such as your home. A restaurant or other public place is not a good idea.

**3** MAKE IT CLEAR THAT YOU WON'T PLAY FAVORITES. Neither side should question your neutrality.

**4** ESTABLISH A COMFORT LEVEL. Chat about the weather or a movie—anything to get the participants relaxed.

**5** ASK HOW THE CONFLICT BEGAN. You'll often find that people don't remember, which means the issue has dissipated in some way. If so, you can say: "Well, I guess we can go on from here then."

**6** REPHRASE THE QUARREL. If a feud no longer makes sense, rephrasing can drive home the point. For example, "Are you saying that at Thanksgiving 10 years ago she said you weren't entitled to Grandma's jewelry, and you've been angry ever since?"

**7** ASK EACH TO SEE THE OTHER'S VIEWPOINT. Once the quarrel seems less serious, it's easier for the participants to do this.

**8** SHARE HAPPY MEMORIES from a time when the relationship was positive. Ask each person to state at least one good quality about the other.

**9** LOOK TO THE FUTURE. Point out that the clock is running. Why be alone at age 80? Time is short for all of us.

**10** SETTLE FOR SATISFACTORY. Recognize that you won't attain a perfect level of reconciliation. Accept cordiality for starters. If the parties agree to talk to one another and attend the same family events, you've accomplished a lot.

ories and positive ties, it's probably worth working on the situation.

• *Analyze the problem* so that it does not sneak up and surprise you at the family gathering. Let's say you have a sister whose "helpful" advice somehow makes you feel terrible. She may suggest that you take the turkey out of the oven sooner than planned, so it doesn't get overdone the way it did last year. She might point out the lint on your jacket so you can brush it off. Ask yourself, "Why does she have the ability to push my buttons?" You may find that her ability to annoy is fueled by your own insecurities.

• *Evaluate whether it's possible for the person to change.* If so, take the initiative, particularly if you've been on the outs. Send a note, or phone and make an appointment to meet.

• *Sit down and talk.* The fundamental rule, says Monica McGoldrick, is: Don't attack and don't defend. Also, don't be judgmental. Instead, describe the situation from your perspective. For example, "I know you want to be helpful, but I feel hurt when you keep pointing out what I'm doing wrong." Limit your remarks to a few minutes and give the other person equal time to respond. Then try to recap what was said: "Are you saying that you'll try to give me less advice this year?" If the person is a sibling, you can point out that you don't have to compete for your parents' love anymore. And add an expression of affection: "We may have had our difficulties, but I'm so glad you're my sister. Let's keep on talking."

***Get everyone involved in sharing old traditions and creating new ones.***

## TRANSFORM THE RELATIONSHIP

Reaching out is vital, but so is looking within. Altering your own point of view can free both of you from harmful patterns of behavior. Try to:

• *Change the interaction.* You can neutralize a problem simply by changing your response. Rather than becoming annoyed at an overbearing sister, for example, thank her for the advice but state firmly that you are in control of what needs to be done. Then move on to another subject. Before a family gathering, visualize the new interaction. Practice letting annoyances float away.

• *Walk in the other person's shoes.* It helps to see the situation as complex and not only aimed at you. Generally, troublesome family members don't feel too good about themselves. If you think about the factors contributing to their behavior, you may be able to develop a sense of empathy. Empathy not only lowers your blood pressure, it also drains away anger.

• *Lower expectations.* Because feelings run so strong, we tend to be harder on family members than on others. Pretend that your family is a group of people you've never met before. You might find that you're less critical.

• *Value the payoffs.* Siblings grow closer through the years, no matter what their early relationship, according to Dr. Victor Cicirelli of Purdue University, who studied the sibling relationships of 300 older men and women.

• *Forgive, forgive, forgive.* Nothing brings families together faster than forgiveness. That should make it Step No. 1, but most of us find forgiving hard. We associate it with weakness and losing when, actually, the reverse is true. When you forgive, you gain strength and come out a winner. You break free of control by the other person's actions. You also free your body of the great stress that anger inflicts.

## MAKE A FEAST OF RECONNECTION

Let's say you've resolved the differences between you and a family member. Now make your gathering a true feast of reconnection for the entire family.

*If you're the host, you can ask for suggestions to make your time together easier and more fun.* If you're talking to a family newcomer—a daughter-in-law, for example—you can say, "We have our ways of doing things, but I know you must have family traditions too. Is there something you'd like us to include?" Just posing the question creates a welcoming attitude.

*Write down the ideas you receive.* A common suggestion is that everyone shares in bringing food or cleaning up.

You may be surprised at the extent of the interest in the family's past. One friend of mine asked family members to bring along their favorite family pictures. After the Thanksgiving meal, the family had a grand time looking at previous celebrations, some dating back 30 years. Photos remind the family that they are, and always will be, connected.

*Ask your family genealogists to distribute copies of the family tree and recount the family history.* Or ask everyone to bring along items of family memorabilia—a great-grandparent's citizenship papers, for example. Even prosaic objects can testify to family history. I know a woman who always puts her grandmother's grater on the family Chanukah table, even though the grater has long since been replaced by a food processor for making potato pancakes. And remember, special crafts made by a child, such as a crepe-paper turkey centerpiece, are the makings of new "memorabilia."

*Always emphasize the transition from the old to the new.* The older generation can tell family stories as the young generation writes them down or records them with a tape recorder. By linking the two generations, you stress family continuity.

*Welcome ideas for new rituals.* They can be as simple as recounting the stories behind the ornaments on the Christmas tree, deciding to plant a flower each time a family member achieves something important or reading something inspirational at the holiday table.

*Talk about ways to keep the family together after the holiday*—even beyond telephone calls, e-mail and videotapes. A family newsletter, created with a computer-publishing program, can include photos, birth announcements and family history. Be sure to divide the cost of printing and mailing among family members, so that no one feels overly burdened and there are no hurt feelings.

Or create a family Web page at sites such as *www.myfamily.com* or *www.familybuzz.com.* They allow you to share photos, post news, chat online, exchange e-mail and even store the family tree.

Technology has made it easy for families to keep in touch, but the real connection begins in the heart. Joyful families send out vibrations that touch friends and neighbors and even reach across the globe. Pope John Paul II said it best: "As the family goes, so goes the nation and so goes the whole world in which we live." Happy holidays.

# Test Your Knowledge Form

We encourage you to photocopy and use this page as a tool to assess how the articles in *Annual Editions* expand on the information in your textbook. By reflecting on the articles you will gain enhanced text information. You can also access this useful form on a product's book support Web site at *http://www.dushkin.com/online/*.

NAME: DATE:

TITLE AND NUMBER OF ARTICLE:

BRIEFLY STATE THE MAIN IDEA OF THIS ARTICLE:

LIST THREE IMPORTANT FACTS THAT THE AUTHOR USES TO SUPPORT THE MAIN IDEA:

WHAT INFORMATION OR IDEAS DISCUSSED IN THIS ARTICLE ARE ALSO DISCUSSED IN YOUR TEXTBOOK OR OTHER READINGS THAT YOU HAVE DONE? LIST THE TEXTBOOK CHAPTERS AND PAGE NUMBERS:

LIST ANY EXAMPLES OF BIAS OR FAULTY REASONING THAT YOU FOUND IN THE ARTICLE:

LIST ANY NEW TERMS/CONCEPTS THAT WERE DISCUSSED IN THE ARTICLE, AND WRITE A SHORT DEFINITION:

# We Want Your Advice

ANNUAL EDITIONS revisions depend on two major opinion sources: one is our Advisory Board, listed in the front of this volume, which works with us in scanning the thousands of articles published in the public press each year; the other is you—the person actually using the book. Please help us and the users of the next edition by completing the prepaid article rating form on this page and returning it to us. Thank you for your help!

**ANNUAL EDITIONS: The Family 05/06**

## ARTICLE RATING FORM

Here is an opportunity for you to have direct input into the next revision of this volume.
We would like you to rate each of the articles listed below, using the following scale:

1. **Excellent: should definitely be retained**
2. **Above average: should probably be retained**
3. **Below average: should probably be deleted**
4. **Poor: should definitely be deleted**

Your ratings will play a vital part in the next revision.
Please mail this prepaid form to us as soon as possible.
Thanks for your help!

| RATING | ARTICLE |
|---|---|
| ______ | 1. The American Family |
| ______ | 2. American Families Are Drifting Apart |
| ______ | 3. Are Boys the Weaker Sex? |
| ______ | 4. Sexual Stereotypes |
| ______ | 5. In Praise of Nurturing Men |
| ______ | 6. Can Men and Women Be Friends? |
| ______ | 7. Love Is *Not* All You Need |
| ______ | 8. Go Ahead, Kiss Your Cousin: Heck, Marry Her if You Want To |
| ______ | 9. Interracial Intimacy |
| ______ | 10. Sexual Satisfaction in Premarital Relationships: Associations With Satisfaction, Love, Commitment, and Stability |
| ______ | 11. Sex for Grown-Ups |
| ______ | 12. What Turns You On? (Hint: It's Not Work!) |
| ______ | 13. The Abortion Wars: 30 Years After Roe v. Wade |
| ______ | 14. Brave New Babies |
| ______ | 15. Making Time for a Baby |
| ______ | 16. Barren |
| ______ | 17. Inside the Womb |
| ______ | 18. Who's Raising Baby? |
| ______ | 19. No Wedding? No Ring? No Problem |
| ______ | 20. Marriage at First Sight |
| ______ | 21. The War Over Gay Marriage |
| ______ | 22. New Evidence for the Benefits of Never Spanking |
| ______ | 23. Father Nature: The Making of a Modern Dad |
| ______ | 24. What About Black Fathers? |
| ______ | 25. Adoption by Lesbian Couples |
| ______ | 26. Are Married Parents Really Better for Children? |
| ______ | 27. The Perma Parent Trap |
| ______ | 28. Oldest, Youngest, or In Between |
| ______ | 29. Why We Break Up With Our Siblings |
| ______ | 30. The Grandparent as Parent |
| ______ | 31. Hitting Home |
| ______ | 32. The Myths and Truths of Family Abduction |
| ______ | 33. Is Your Dog (Cat, Bird, Fish) More Faithful Than Your Spouse? |
| ______ | 34. What Kids (Really) Need |
| ______ | 35. For Better or Worse: Couples Confront Unemployment |
| ______ | 36. The Binds That Tie—and Heal: How Families Cope With Mental Illness |
| ______ | 37. Tough Medical Tasks Fall to Families |
| ______ | 38. Home Alone |
| ______ | 39. Terrorism, Trauma, and Children: What Can We Do? |
| ______ | 40. Marriage and Divorce American Style |
| ______ | 41. Dating After Divorce |
| ______ | 42. Divorced? Don't Even Think of Remarrying Until You Read This |
| ______ | 43. Managing a Blended Family |
| ______ | 44. Breaking Free of the Family Tree |
| ______ | 45. Getting the Word |
| ______ | 46. Happiness Explained |
| ______ | 47. Examining Family Rituals |
| ______ | 48. Reconnect With Your Family |

*(Continued on next page)*

NO POSTAGE NECESSARY IF MAILED IN THE UNITED STATES

**BUSINESS REPLY MAIL**
FIRST CLASS MAIL PERMIT NO. 551 DUBUQUE IA

POSTAGE WILL BE PAID BY ADDRESEE

McGraw-Hill/Dushkin
2460 KERPER BLVD
DUBUQUE, IA 52001-9902

## ABOUT YOU

Name ______________________________ Date ______________

Are you a teacher? ❒ A student? ❒
Your school's name ______________________________

Department ______________________________

Address ______________ City ______________ State ______ Zip ______

School telephone # ______________________________

## YOUR COMMENTS ARE IMPORTANT TO US!

Please fill in the following information:
For which course did you use this book?

Did you use a text with this ANNUAL EDITION? ❒ yes ❒ no
What was the title of the text?

What are your general reactions to the *Annual Editions* concept?

Have you read any pertinent articles recently that you think should be included in the next edition? Explain.

Are there any articles that you feel should be replaced in the next edition? Why?

Are there any World Wide Web sites that you feel should be included in the next edition? Please annotate.

May we contact you for editorial input? ❒ yes ❒ no
May we quote your comments? ❒ yes ❒ no